DEPRESSION TO COLD WAR

DEPRESSION TO COLD WAR

A HISTORY OF AMERICA FROM HERBERT HOOVER TO RONALD REAGAN

Joseph M. Siracusa and David G. Coleman

Perspectives on the Twentieth Century
Edward Beauchamp, *Series Adviser*

Westport, Connecticut
London

Library of Congress Cataloging-in-Publication Data

Siracusa, Joseph M.
   Depression to Cold War: a history of America from Herbert Hoover to
Ronald Reagan / Joseph M. Siracusa and David G. Coleman.
       p.   cm.—(Perspectives on the twentieth century, ISSN 1538–9626)
   Includes bibliographical references and index.
   ISBN 0–275–97555–X (alk. paper)
   1. United States—History—20th century.   2. United States—Politics and
government—20th century.   3. United States—Foreign relations—20th century.
4. Presidents—United States—History—20th century.   I. Coleman, David G.
II. Title.   III. Series.
   E741.S525   2002
   973.91—dc21   2002022433

British Library Cataloguing in Publication Data is available.

Copyright © 2002 by Joseph M. Siracusa and David G. Coleman

Library of Congress Catalog Card Number: 2002022433
ISBN: 0–275–97555–X
ISSN: 1538–9626

First published in 2002

Praeger Publishers, 88 Post Road West, Westport, CT 06881
An imprint of Greenwood Publishing Group, Inc.
www.praeger.com

Printed in the United States of America

The paper used in this book complies with the
Permanent Paper Standard issued by the National
Information Standards Organization (Z39.48–1984).

10 9 8 7 6 5 4 3 2 1

Contents

Photo Essay follows page 136.

Series Foreword

Whoever first coined the phrase, "When the siécle hit the fin," described the twentieth century perfectly! The past century was arguably a century of intellectual, physical, and emotional violence unparalleled in world history. As Haynes Johnson of the *Washington Post* has pointed out in his *The Best of times: The Clinton Years* (2001), "since the first century, 140 million people have died in major wars; 111 million of those deaths occurred in the twentieth century. War deaths per population soared from 3.2 deaths per 1,000 in the sixteenth century to 44.4 per 1,000 in the twentieth."[1] Giving parameters to the twentieth century, however, is not an easy task. Did it begin in 1900 or 1901? Was it, as in historian Eric Hobsbawm's words, a "Short twentieth century" that did not begin until 1917 and end in 1991?[2] Or was it more accurately the "long twentieth century," as Giovanni Arrighi argued in *The Long Twentieth Century: Money, Power, and the Origins of Our Times*?[3] Strong cases can be made for all of these constructs and it is each reader's prerogative to come to his or her own conclusion.

Whatever the conclusion, however, there is a short list of people, events, and intellectual currents found in the period between the nineteenth and twenty-first centuries that is, indeed, impressive in scope. There is little doubt that the hopes represented by the Paris Exhibition of 1900 represented the mood of the time—a time of optimism, even utopian expectations, in much of the so-called civilized world (which was the only world that counted in those days). Many saw the fruits of the Industrial Revolution, the application of science and technology to everyday life, as having the potential to greatly enhance life, at least in the West.

In addition to the theme of progress, the power of nationalism in conflicts of the early 1900s to the "Great" War of 1914–1918 that resulted in unprecedented conflict over the remainder of the century.

Every century has its "great" as well as "infamous" individuals, most often men, although that too would begin to change as the century drew to a close. Great political figures such as Lenin, Trotsky, Stalin, Hitler, Mussolini, Churchill, the two Roosevelts, de Gaulle, Adenauer, Mahatma Gandhi, Mao Tse-Tung, Ho Chi Minh, and others were joined in the last part of the century by tough competent women like Golda Meir, Indira Gandhi, Margaret Thatcher, and scores of others who took the reigns of power for the first time.

A quick listing of some major events of the century includes World War I, the Russian Revolution, the Rise of Fascism, the Great Depression of the 1930s, the abdication of Edward VIII, Pearl Harbor and World War II, the unleashing of atomic bombs on Hiroshima and Nagasaki, the long Indochina War, the Cold War, the rise of nationalism (with an increase in nation states from about fifty to almost two hundred), the establishments of Israel, the triumph of the free market, an increasingly strident battle between religious fanaticism and secular preferences, and on and on. At the same time that these events occurred, there was a great creative flourishing of mass entertainment (especially television and the Internet), not to mention important literary, dramatic, cinematic, and musical contributions of all kinds.

These elements incorporate some of the subject matter of this new series focusing on "Perspectives on the Twentieth Century," which strives to illuminate the last century. The editor actively seeks out manuscripts that deal with virtually any subject and with any part of our planet, bringing a better understanding of the twentieth century to readers. He is especially interested in subjects on "small" as well as "large" events and trends, including the role of sports in various societies, the impact of popular music on the social fabric, the contribution of film studies to our understanding of the twentieth century, and so on. The success of this series is largely dependent on the creativity and imagination of its authors.

Edward Beauchamp

NOTES

1. Haynes Johnson, *The Best of Times: America in the Clinton Years* (New York: A James H. Silberman book, Harcourt, Inc., 2001), p. 3.

2. Eric Hobsbawm, *The Age of Extremes: A History of the World, 1917–1991* (New York: Pantheon, 1994).

3. Giovanni Arrighi, *The Long Twentieth Century: Money, Power, and the Origins of Our Times* (London: Verso, 1994).

Preface

We have sought in the following pages to write a concise history of the United States between 1929 and 1989, that is, the period between Herbert Hoover and Ronald Reagan. Organizing our chapters around the various presidencies—"the ultimate source of action" in John F. Kennedy's felicitous expression[1]—we have attempted to focus on American behavior at home and abroad. Within this context two major interrelated themes emerge. Domestically, American society continued the process of industrialization and urbanization that had begun in the late nineteenth century. Industry, and agriculture to a lesser degree, increasingly developed into big business absorbing vast amounts of capital and controlled by a corporate elite only theoretically answerable to stockholders. "Organizational" or corporate capitalism thereby nationalized American industry and finance. Urban growth accompanied industrialism and, as more and more Americans lived in the cities, posed vast new social problems of employment, housing, education, health, and recreation. Rural habits, values, and traditions gradually gave way to social modes and thought more suitable to urban life, though the transition often was disturbing and painful.

Government also had to adjust and expand its functions beyond its traditional scope. In 1929, the federal government was still comparatively a small enterprise; challenges of the next six decades transformed it almost beyond belief, touching in one way or another almost every facet of American life. Before the New Deal, the majority of Americans did not expect government to do anything for them; in fact, they did not think that government could or should do anything for them. By the end of World War II, and against the great weight of tradition, Americans had finally become persuaded to look to Washington for help. It is in this sense, then, that the New Deal was a political revolution. Every president since then, including Ronald Reagan, has had to cope with its implications.

The second theme to emerge from our text relates to foreign affairs. Because of its industrial growth and vast wealth, and consequent interest in foreign markets, the United States naturally became one of the foremost great world powers whose very existence necessarily affected the global balance of power. American actions as a nation, whether as positive attempts to mold events abroad or as negative efforts to enjoy material abundance in relative political isolation, could not help affecting the course of world history. But that mantle was not always worn easily; here, too, Americans found it difficult to adjust to changing conditions. Despite involvement in World War I, which should have made it obvious that the United States could not insulate itself from world distress and conflict, many Americans clung to traditional foreign policy attitudes and refused to allow the nation to play the kind of constructive political role that its own enlightened interests demanded. Or as Ernest R. May put it, the government of this indisputable great power had continued until the 1930s to be little more than that of a provincial confederation concerned more with delivering the mail, collecting customs, and regulating immigration than with dealing with external threats posed by the emergence of the totalitarianism.[2] Yet economic and educational forces, and the sheer exigency of events, culminating in the nation's participation in World War II, gradually broke down the isolationist psychology and prepared most Americans for belated acceptance of the fact and responsibilities of a great power. This theme runs like a straight line through the cold war to the collapse of the Soviet Union and beyond.

By the end of the Reagan years in the late 1980s, as was the case in the late 1930s, the United States once again sought a redefinition of its proper relationship with the outside world, a reaction in large measure to the so-called triumph of liberal internationalism. The "American Century" that Henry Luce anticipated in 1941—a nation that would be "the powerhouse from which the ideals spread throughout the world and do their mysterious work of lifting the life of mankind from the level of beasts to what the Psalmist called 'a little lower than the angels' "[3]—had apparently matured. Whether the United States was on the verge of another "American Century" remained to be seen.

NOTES

1. Cassette K, Presidential Recordings Collection, President's Office Files, John F. Kennedy Library, Boston, Massachusetts.

2. Ernest R. May, "The Impact of Nuclear Weapons on European Security, 1945–1957," in *The Quest for Stability: Problems of West European Security, 1918–1957,* edited by R. Ahmann et al. (London: Oxford University Press, 1993), p. 515.

3. Henry Luce, "The American Century," *Life*, 17 February 1941.

Acknowledgments

In addition to the scholars on whose shoulders I have stood for the past thirty years and who are recognized in the text, footnotes, and bibliography, I should like to thank the many archivists and librarians in the United States, Australia, and the United Kingdom whom I have all too often taken for granted. At the more personal level, this book owes much to my first cousin, Andrew Cuccio, in Chicago, who provided more support than he could have imagined; to my children—Hanna, Tina, and Joseph—who will inherit the world that the twentieth century left them; and to Candice for her unstinting support at every stage in the preparation of this manuscript.
—Joseph M. Siracusa

I am grateful to my co-author and friend, Joe Siracusa, for the opportunity to collaborate on this book. It has been, every step of the way, a privilege and a pleasure. The University of Virginia's Miller Center of Public Affairs has been a wonderful place to study and teach history and politics, and I thank my colleagues for making it that way.

We should both like to thank the series editor, Ed Beauchamp, and our editor, Heather Staines, for their patience and professionalism. Finally, Larissa has been a constant source of encouragement and support for me once again.
—David G. Coleman

DEPRESSION TO COLD WAR

CHAPTER 1

The Turn of the American Century

The Great Depression was a rude, jolting awakening from the so-called Roaring Twenties. To most Americans of the 1920s, the era appeared to provide material proof that their nation's destiny lay in perpetual prosperity. Rarely have hopes been higher or so speedily and cruelly disappointed. By the end of 1929, the disastrous stock market crash raised questions about the soundness of the very foundations of the capitalist system—and years of bleak, grinding economic depression faced the American people. Revered prophets of the twenties—businessmen, economic soothsayers, and politicians—overnight became figures of scorn and ridicule. Cherished values and traditions of free enterprise and economic opportunity suddenly acquired a hollow, cynical ring, as people frantically sought panaceas for their stunning economic blight. More than ever before in American history, the multitudes trapped in an apparently inexplicable economic debacle looked to Washington for rescue. Government, reluctantly during the presidency of Herbert Hoover and more readily during the era of Franklin D. Roosevelt's New Deal, felt compelled to prod, regulate, and tinker with the economy in desperate attempts to halt the downward spiral and to stimulate recovery. The interventionist welfare state emerged, as so-called laissez-faire policies of the past were abandoned for those of at least a partly planned and managed society. Thus dawned the American Century, neither with triumph nor accomplishment, but rather in a painful struggle to rebuild.

BOOM AND BUST

Prosperity seemed a fact of life to many Americans by 1929. Only a decade after the post–World War I reconstruction began, the stock market soared on the wings of a new taste for consumerism. Four years earlier, President Calvin Coolidge had proudly declared that "[t]he chief business of the American people is business" and by the time Herbert Hoover, the great engineer of the new business era of the Roaring Twenties, prepared to enter the White House, this sentiment permeated all aspects of public life. The clamor for material wealth drowned out those voices—even that of Coolidge—calling for Americans to remember that "[p]rosperity is only an instrument to be used, not a deity to be worshipped." Coolidge observed in his final State of the Union address, albeit with some private qualms, that few presidents had the pleasure of observing such high prospects for the nation. With tranquility and contentment in the domestic field, and the highest record of years of prosperity, Coolidge observed that the American people could "regard the present with satisfaction and anticipate the future with optimism."

This positive outlook showed no signs of waning when Herbert Hoover entered the White House in March 1929. "The future is bright with hope," observed Hoover in his inaugural address, and indeed, few men have entered the presidency with brighter prospects than Hoover; few, though, would leave the presidency so burned by public opinion. In the context of the late 1920s, Hoover seemed to embody all that a modern public leader should. He was a self-made man in every sense. Born the son of a Quaker blacksmith in West Branch, Iowa, Hoover was orphaned by the age of nine, a millionaire by the age of forty, and president at age fifty-five. From his rapid rise he learned a fierce self-reliance and a devotion to the ideology of American capitalism. After graduating from Stanford, he soon found himself in outback Australia prospecting for gold on behalf of a London firm. Quickly establishing for himself a reputation of providing his employers with handsome returns, he traveled widely through Asia as a kind of rescuer of struggling mining operations, accruing a reputation and a personal fortune in the process.[1] During World War I, he put his talent for organization to use heading the relief effort for besieged Belgium. Pleased with Hoover's performance in that capacity, President Woodrow Wilson asked Hoover at the end of the war to head the new U.S. Food Administration. As secretary of commerce from 1921 to 1928, he had been an active member of the Harding and Coolidge cabinets. From this position he had been a leading figure in the government's efforts at post–World War I national reconstruction and had proven himself a trusted friend and ally to business. He was an able, even talented, administrator with an impressive record of public service; and yet once elected, he persistently demonstrated remarkable lapses in political judgment.[2]

While Hoover's personal philosophy helped his rise, the rigidity of his adherence to it and his inability to move with the tides of the national mood proved his undoing. Hoover assumed the presidency without pretense of leading America into a new era. Rather, he viewed the president's role more as a facilitator than leader. Proud of his own experience of becoming a self-styled success story, Hoover placed overwhelming faith in an "American system" based on individualism, economic opportunity, and private enterprise, with the government's role restricted to that of an umpire to regulate and encourage private initiative and responsible self-government. As he said during the 1928 campaign: "It is as if we set a race. We, through free and universal education, provide the training of the runners; we give to them an equal start; we provide in the government the umpire of fairness in the race. The winner is he who shows the most conscientious training, the greatest ability, and the greatest character."

Hoover's view of a government reluctant to interfere in America's business seemed perfect for the times. Indeed, the administration's early legislative reforms, particularly in the areas of civil rights, conservation, and Native American affairs, seemed to promise progressive legislative gains ahead.[3] For the first months of Hoover's administration, America's progress seemed as assured as its prosperity. An increasingly urbanized population reaped the benefits of commercially funded scientific and technological breakthroughs, especially in the area of communications, along with improving working conditions, leading in turn to a transformation in popular lifestyles. Charlie Chaplin and Rudolph Valentino commanded the screen in silent movies, and by the end of the decade, Al Olson could be heard on film proclaiming that "you ain't heard nothin' yet!" as Hollywood's box offices gladly obliged the nation's insatiable appetite for the new innovation of "talkies." Charles Lindbergh and Amelia Earhardt's record-shattering solo flights pioneered new innovations in long distance travel. Penicillin and insulin revolutionized the practice of medicine, while the use of insecticides ensured farmers a more reliable crop. And the newly built Yankee Stadium erupted in delight to the all-conquering Babe Ruth.

It was the national economy that defined the era. The urge to get rich quick was a logical, if distorted, reflection of the mood of the twenties. Hopes of obtaining wealth without effort and without serious risks seemed almost universal, as the frenzied booms in real estate and the stock market revealed. The economic environment certainly invited such hopes. While the system was not laissez-faire in the purest sense—government regulated several key aspects such as banking and public utilities—it was nevertheless remarkably fluid and responsive to its own forces. During boom times, this was an advantage. In time, however, the absence of government control became a liability.

Prior to 1924, stock market trading had been comparatively cautious and the dividends most stocks paid corresponded reasonably to their market prices. It was not until the later part of that year when the prices truly became inflated, as the so-called bull market took hold. The average of the *New York Times* index of selected industrial stocks rose from 106 at the beginning of 1924 to 245 by the end of 1927. This did not indicate speculation, defenders of the market claimed, but only a delayed catching up of stock prices to increased corporate earnings. In 1928 the rise in stock prices became even steeper, with prices advancing as much as 20 points a day. The *New York Times* index reached 331 or a gain of 86 points during the year. Some stocks that had never paid a dividend rose even more spectacularly. In this sense, the majority of the stock market transactions reflected short-term gambling rather than long-term investments. Other fortunes were made in a rapid increase in buying on margin, a practice whereby a purchaser pays only part of the cost of the stock and a broker lends the remainder. Banks and insurance companies, attracted by the high interest rates for "call money" used in margin transactions, diverted funds from capital investments and construction to the stock market. Such funds jumped from about $1 billion in 1924 to nearly $8.5 billion prior to the crash in 1929. The high returns of the American market were also lucrative to overseas investors and foreign money poured in. Prices advanced to new highs in 1929, with little if any relationship to the actual earning power or worth of the stocks. Investment trusts multiplied, offering portfolios of stocks to those too inexperienced or cautious to invest directly. Local stock exchanges flourished across the country, and many banks set up special facilities for investors. By the summer of the first year of the Hoover administration, the *New York Times* index recorded a high of 449, up a record 110 points in three months.

Yet to some people at the time—and certainly in retrospect—there were signs of trouble. A few voices warned of the dangers of such wild gambling, but most spokesmen continued optimistically to predict even greater gains. The Federal Reserve Board, acting cautiously to avoid precipitating a crash, cautioned member banks in 1929 not to lend money for speculation and raised the discount rate to 6 percent, but without a noticeable effect. There were other signs. Residential construction had fallen a billion dollars below the 1928 rate. Consumer spending slowed, unsold business inventories rose sharply, and industrial production fell off with an increase in unemployment. Businessmen and consumers found credit tight and costly, and the rate of industrial plan growth declined. In addition, agriculture and certain other industries had never experienced prosperity throughout the decade. But these signs of imminent recession were regarded by most as anomalies easily ignored.

When the crash came, it came with stunning force. In September and early October 1929, the market began to fluctuate uneasily. On October 23, thousands of speculators suddenly lost confidence and tried to dispose of their holdings. Panic struck the next day, "Black Thursday," when brokers sold nearly thirteen million shares of stocks forcing prices to plummet disastrously. Crowds gathered on Wall Street outside the New York Stock Exchange, attracted by rumors that eleven speculators had jumped to their deaths in despair. Inside the exchange, many frantic sellers found it impossible to find buyers for their holdings. Brokers, facing ruin, sold out margin buyers with heavy losses.

At noon on October 24, a group of bankers representing J. P. Morgan and Company and several major New York banks met to try to stem the flow. They pledged a pool of investment money, estimated to have been as much as $240 million, to halt the decline. Widely hailed as saviors, the financiers were motivated to a large degree by self-preservation; only by stabilizing the market could they gain the time to get out without sustaining heavy losses themselves. Richard Whitney, the agent of these "Lords of Creation," entered the New York Stock Exchange and dramatically placed large purchase orders for major stocks at above the current bidding price. But the gesture, executed with such confidence, had only a temporary effect. All across the nation thousands of stockholders continued to dump their holdings frantically. The bottom fell out on Tuesday, October 29, the worst single day in the history of the market. Brokers sold nearly sixteen and a half million shares and the tickertape ran hopelessly behind as more sellers than buyers appeared. Prices continued to decline, within a few weeks wiping out paper values of nearly $30 billion. Despite optimistic statements by President Hoover and Secretary of the Treasury Andrew Mellon, and industrialists such as John D. Rockefeller, the collapse continued. By the end of the year, the *New York Times* average had plummeted to 224 from the previous high of 452. Investment trust stocks became nearly worthless, and even the value of such blue-chip companies as American Telephone & Telegraph fell by 40 percent or more. The downward spiral continued throughout the next two years, until the *New York Times* index stood at an all time low in mid-1932 of 58 points, almost half of what it had been at the beginning of 1924 and one-eighth of what it had been at its peak. An estimated $74 billion in stock values had simply disappeared.

As businesses and industries responded to the disaster, the trail of ruin radiated out from Wall Street to the wider community. Production dropped as factories responded to reduced consumption by laying off employees and curtailing operations, creating still lower consumer demand and more layoffs in an ever-worsening spiral. By 1932, industrial production had fallen to less than half the pre-crash level, and the annual national income had dropped from $82 billion in 1928 to $40 billion. Bankers found themselves hard hit as debtors defaulted, real estate loans lost value, and speculative ventures collapsed. Loss of public trust and unsound practices resulted in numerous bank failures, especially among the smaller state banks unaffiliated with the Federal Reserve System.

As fortunes dwindled, unemployment grew sharply. From an average of about two million in the Coolidge era, unemployment rose to three million in the spring of 1930, nearly four million by the end of that year, and almost seven million in late 1931. By 1932 between twelve and fifteen million Americans lacked jobs. Even those still employed often experienced sharp reductions in wages or were on part-time work. Farm prices, already depressingly low, fell 64 percent below the 1929 level. Some farmers resorted to burning corn for fuel, since they had unsold supplies and coal was relatively expensive. Farm income dropped proportionately, with the inevitable results of widespread debt, mortgage foreclosures which would ultimately result in a quarter of all farmers losing their farms, farm tenancy, and grinding poverty. Professional groups also felt the squeeze in lowered income and mounting debts.

Local relief and philanthropy proved hopelessly incapable of meeting the staggering burden of unemployment. Philadelphia had 300,000 people out of work by 1932, in contrast to the normal figure of 40,000; 55,000 families were on relief, receiving $4.23 a week which it was estimated provided only two-thirds of a minimum healthy diet. New York City found it necessary, because of lack of revenue, to reduce the weekly relief allowance to $2.39 a family and even then could provide for only half of the needy. The Toledo, Ohio, commissary could spend only slightly above two cents per meal for those in want. In the larger cities, groups of ragged men, women, and children scavenged garbage dumps for scraps of food or clothing. In Chicago, according to one reporter, around a truck that was unloading garbage and other refuse were about thirty-five men, women, and children. As soon as the truck pulled away from the pile, all of them started digging with sticks, some with their hands, grabbing bits of food and vegetables. So-called Hoovervilles or makeshift settlements, festered around the larger cities, where homeless families dwelt in worn-out cars, tin shacks, or caves. Hundreds of single men and women slept in the parks even during inclement weather, while others sought warmth and food in the jails. New "industries" sprang up, such as apple selling on the streets or shoeshine "boys" of all ages and backgrounds. Illustrating the desperate mood of the American unemployed, the Soviet Union advertised in 1931 for 6,000 skilled workers to go to the U.S.S.R. and was flooded with over 100,000 applications.

As always, youth was especially hard hit. A survey in New York City in 1932 revealed that 20 percent of the children suffered from malnutrition as the "American Dream" suffered the ignominy of starvation in the land of supposed plenty. Teachers in Chicago fed 11,000 hungry school children from their own meager resources. Teachers received sharp salary cuts, with payment often in arrears. Chicago, whose teachers went unpaid for six months, issued promissory notes, or scrip, as tax revenues fell off. A number of schools closed their doors, particularly in rural areas and in the South. Georgia, for example, closed 1,318 schools with a total enrollment of over 170,000 pupils. With schools closing and no prospects of regular paid employment, hundreds of thousands of jobless youth took to the road and drifted aimlessly across the country in search of opportunity, hitchhiking or riding the rails on freight trains. Whole families packed their belongings and set off in ramshackle cars, attracted by rumors of jobs in California or elsewhere. No longer, it seemed, would thrift, hard work, and diligence inevitably be rewarded with prosperity. The diligent and the improvident alike experienced the same fate. Relief and charity weakened habits of self-reliance, and prolonged joblessness caused despair and fear. Security, rather than advancement or daring enterprise, seemed to have become the new universal goal.

The causes and cure of the Great Depression were endlessly debated. Economist William T. Foster attributed the collapse to oversavings, reducing ability to consume goods. He contended that recovery would come only from heavier private and especially governmental spending. John Maynard Keynes, the brilliant British economist, agreed in his *Treatise on Money* (1930) that the depression was "a crisis of abundance" resulting from underconsumption. In this and subsequent writings, especially *The General Theory of Employment, Interest, and Money* (1936), Keynes advocated massive government spending via public works and other projects to create purchasing power and to revive the economy. In reality, Keynesianism always meant more than mere deficit spending; it called for nothing less than for government to plan for full employment and consumption. A Utah banker, Marriner Eccles, reached similar conclusions about the need for federal spending. Gardiner C. Means and Adolf A. Berle, Jr., authors of *The Modern Corporation* (1933), and Rexford Guy Tugwell concluded that the vast growth of corporate power and *de facto* price fixing made meaningless older assumptions about a free market and required a large measure of public planning of the economy and government spending to balance production with consumption.

In the words of the *New Republic*, many critics saw the depression as a great opportunity for the "democratization of industry." The experiences of World War I seemed particularly appropriate, for then, as philosopher John Dewey pointed out, all the belligerent countries had emphasized production for need and use rather than merely for profit. Gerard Swope of the General Electric Company proposed a World War I-type of Liberty Bond drive to raise money for large-scale governmental spending; subsequently, he advocated the "Swope Plan" for a national economic council to supervise a network of private trade associations that would stabilize production, employment, and prices. William G. McAdoo, formerly secretary of the treasury in the Wilson administration, called for a Peace Industries Board, resembling the old War Industries Board, to mobilize the economy in the new crisis. Whether advocating more business self-government, federal planning, or heavy pump-priming spending by Washington, all these voices agreed upon the necessity for greater governmental effort. Startling though these proposals seemed to many, they actually were only logical extensions of the tendency toward greater nationalization and organization of the economy that had been underway since the turn of the century.

It has since become generally agreed that the stock market crash, largely the result of gambling and speculative mania, contributed to the Great Depression. If the basic economy had been healthier, economist John Kenneth Galbraith pointed out, the collapse of the boom in stocks probably would have been less acutely felt. Since the reverse was true, the Wall Street debacle triggered a spiral of other collapses in the economy. When examining these underlying factors, it must be borne in mind that much of the prosperity of the 1920s had been founded on consumer industries rather than on heavy industry. Production of basic necessities such as food tended to be surpassed in importance by the production of durable or semidurable goods, formerly considered luxuries, and by the growth of distributive and service industries. By their very nature, consumption of such goods and services could be sharply curtailed in times of economic distress, whether individual or national. Consequently, the misdistribution of income in the decade, when industry retained too much of the gains of increased productivity as profits and passed on a disproportionately small share in the form of higher wages and lower prices, meant a sharp limitation in the ability of the average American to consume an ever-growing flood of goods and services. It has been estimated that 60 percent of American families received less than the $2,000 annual income necessary to buy the minimum essentials. Industry simply produced far more than consumers easily could buy under prevailing wages and prices, even when aided by the new system of installment or credit purchasing. Production outstripped consumption, with the inevitable results of gluts of unsold goods, factory cutbacks, unemployment, and a further reduction of consumer purchasing power that touched off more rounds of retrenchment.

Other contributing factors involved a precarious corporate structure of holding companies piled on top of holding companies; a weak banking system marked by unsound credit practices and speculative loans and inadequate state or federal regulation; technological unemployment and the absence of unemployment compensation; and the diversion of profits and dividends from plant expansion or construction to stock market speculation. A series of business-oriented administrations had failed to deal with a depressed agriculture or to enforce existing regulatory laws and had encouraged inflation and cheap money during most of the decade. World conditions undoubtedly contributed, though the depression came first to America and was felt more severely there. Foreign trade was unhealthy, and a vast burden of intergovernmental and private international debts existed, made worse by the high tariff and war debt policies of the American government.

HOOVER AND THE GREAT DEPRESSION

Contrary to a widely held opinion, Hoover recognized early that a severe depression had hit America, even if, like some others, he failed to perceive just how grave and prolonged it would be.[4] In past economic crises, recovery had set in by the operation of so-called natural laws. Decreased production had permitted surpluses to be absorbed, and declining costs in labor and raw materials had allowed the prices of goods to fall also with a consequent revival of economic activity, aided by foreign markets and a growing population. These processes, owing to a fairly stable population in the 1930s and to a worldwide depression, operated poorly if at all in the current crisis. Despite his strong preference for letting market forces and private enterprise drive the economy, Hoover nevertheless recognized that sometimes government must be more active in trying to quicken the economy. Unlike the hands-off attitude of his predecessors during past slumps, Hoover involved the federal government as never before in antidepression measures such as initiating public works to stimulate employment.[5] Especially in the last two years of his administration, he clearly foreshadowed some of the approaches of Roosevelt's New Deal, yet he changed too slowly when the times demanded rapid and even desperate measures. Above all, he clung stubbornly to his belief that while the national government must help the people to recover, the public would have to bear the major burden and should not expect miracles. A prisoner of his earlier experiences and of Republican policies, he relied too much upon voluntary effort, cooperation, and persuasion. He viewed direct federal aid as dangerous, for it might weaken private initiative and responsibility and lead to federal control of the economy. America had been built on the principle of individual self-help and local responsibility, he firmly believed, and to weaken that by federal actions would endanger the very qualities that had made the nation great.

Hoover called a special session of Congress, prior to the 1929 crash, to cope with the farm problem and the tariff. Congress authorized the creation of a Federal Farm Board with a revolving fund of one-half billion dollars to encourage farmers to plan production and marketing, especially through the formation of nationally organized cooperatives. According to this self-help theory, farmers could be educated voluntarily to restrain production in order to raise market prices. With the encouragement of the farm board, farmers formed national cooperative associations or corporations for those producing grain, wool, cotton, livestock, fruits and vegetables, and other commodities. Using pool selling, loans on products stored for later sale, and other devices, the farm board hoped to provide for more orderly marketing and improving prices. As a temporary device to remove surpluses and generate a price rise, the cotton and grain stabilization corporations lent funds and then purchased those crops on the open market. At Hoover's insistence, the farm board could not impose production controls; consequently, farmers continued overproduction of cotton and wheat, despite farm board recommendations for restraint and the plowing under of cotton. The stabilization corporations accumulated huge unsaleable stocks before admitting failure and abandoning their efforts in 1931 to prop up prices. As the depression deepened, wheat prices skidded to fifty-seven cents a bushel in 1931 and cotton sold for five cents a pound by 1932.

After the Wall Street debacle, Hoover appreciated that the country faced more than a mere financial panic. Publicly, he exuded confidence. In October, he stated that "the fundamental business of the country . . . is on a sound and prosperous basis," and in November he declared that "any lack of confidence in the economy future or the basic strength of business, is foolish." Privately, however, the president decided not to follow Treasury Secretary Mellon's classic formula of letting the depression run what he described as its natural course until a bottom was reached and recovery began. Instead the president hoped to use governmental persuasion to cushion the shock and generate a more rapid revival of the economy. Using the organizational and administrative power of the federal government, Hoover hoped that the government could act as a powerful institutional ally to individual initiative without becoming a hindrance and burden. To that end, he called a series of conferences in Washington of businessmen, industrialists, agricultural spokesmen, and labor leaders and obtained promises to maintain wage rates and to continue capital investments. The conferences and optimistic statements illustrated Hoover's faith in encouraging cooperation between various groups in the private economy.[6] Unfortunately, as the depression deepened, the promises he obtained from business leaders could not be or were not kept. The Federal Reserve Board relaxed credit and the farm board tried to raise agricultural prices. Hoover proposed to expand federal public works and urged the states to adopt similar programs. The Hawley-Smoot Tariff of 1930 increased duties on agricultural and industrial imports but proved to be a false hope as a weapon against the depression. Congress also enacted a tax cut in 1929 to stimulate the economy. But since taxes already had been very low, the reduction had negligible results.

At Hoover's suggestion, Julius H. Barnes of the United States Chamber of Commerce invited important businessmen in a National Business Survey Conference to discover and remove the key barriers in the economy in order to restore prosperity. The organization faded away by 1931, obviously a failure. The simple fact, to be repeatedly demonstrated during the depression, was that businessmen and farmers were too individualistic to voluntarily take collective measures to raise wages and to regulate production. When the pinch became tighter, most businessmen forgot about cooperation and adopted measures to protect themselves—wage slashes, layoffs, and production reductions—ensuring further declines in the economy. For example, a National Credit Corporation formed by bankers in response to administration suggestions to enable stronger banks to strengthen essentially sound but temporarily endangered banks failed because the larger banks were unwilling to take the risk. At no time did President Hoover recommend any fundamental reform of the nation's economic machinery, though reform seemed necessary to most critics in the areas of stock market operations, banking, and the corporate structure.

To generate confidence and to minimize the hoarding of money, Hoover and his administration issued an unending stream of optimistic statements. Unfortunately, the president fell victim to his own optimism. Repeatedly he misinterpreted slight upward fluctuations in a generally downward economic spiral to reassure the country. Thus on May 1, 1930, Hoover proclaimed to the U.S. Chamber of Commerce, "we have now passed the worse and with continued unity of effort we shall rapidly recover." The spring upsurge, however, quickly passed and the depression continued. Had the economy been sounder, his methods might have succeeded as similar ones had in the 1921 slump. Unfortunately he let pass a crucial period when a relatively small increase in federal spending might have restored a balance.

Hoover refused to admit the failure of his indirect methods, despite further declines in the economy and growing popular criticism. The 1930 mid-term elections, though not a Democratic sweep, registered large gains for the opposition party. The Democratic National Committee was largely successful in fixing the responsibility for the depression on Hoover. The results of the election gave the Democrats a narrow control in the House of Representatives and a forty-seven to forty-eight balance in the Senate. Because of growing insurgency among western Republicans, Hoover faced an increasingly hostile Congress during the last two years of his term. Yet he resisted pressures for massive federal spending and stubbornly maintained that his recovery measures met the needs of the country.

A new, disturbing danger also presented itself to the president. Declining federal revenues threatened to result in a huge public debt and possible abandonment of the gold standard. Falling revenues and the amount of deficit spending that Hoover reluctantly accepted increased the national debt from slightly over $16 billion in 1930 to $19.5 billion in 1932. The deficit for 1931 alone neared $1 billion. To counter the deficit, Hoover slashed outlays for public works in order to avoid throwing the budget further out of balance. As the depression grew worse, Hoover blamed everything but the American economic system. Earlier he had condemned domestic overspeculation as the cause of the crash, but now he pointed to world conditions as the culprit. When the Creditanstalt Bank in Vienna collapsed, triggering similar financial debacles across much of the continent, Europeans dumped American securities, resulting in a heavy flow of gold from America to Europe. To stem the tide, the Federal Reserve Board raised the rediscount rate from 1.5 percent to 3.5 percent, saving the gold reserve but making credit tighter for businessmen. In still another attempt to cope with the world depression, Hoover in 1931 proclaimed a moratorium on inter-governmental debt payments in the vain hope of stemming the collapse abroad.

Although state, local, and private relief agencies proved obviously inadequate, Hoover stubbornly clung to the conviction that they could meet the problem of unemployment. Even years later he was reluctant to admit the magnitude of unemployment. In his memoirs, he explained the large-scale phenomenon of apple-selling on the streets as a shrewd scheme by the apple growers: "Many persons left their jobs for the more profitable one of selling apples." He did appoint an Emergency Committee for Employment, subsequently reconstituted as the President's Organization on Unemployment Relief, to stimulate voluntary and local charity. The first director, Colonel Arthur Woods, concluded that more was required on the part of the federal government and soon resigned. His replacement, Walter S. Gifford of American Telephone and Telegraph, fully concurred with the president's views. With much ballyhoo, Gifford launched "a great spiritual experience" to remedy joblessness by persuading more people to employ one another. Testifying before Congress, Gifford insisted upon the soundness of the administration's policy, and he condemned all proposals for federal relief. Business leaders claimed there would be recovery if government did not interfere by direct relief. They proposed (courtesy of J. P. Morgan) a "block system" whereby residents in an area would pledge weekly contributions for relief and another plan for the collection of restaurant leftover food to be distributed to the poor.

In Hoover's mind, direct federal relief would destroy individual initiative and self-respect, weaken local government and voluntary charity, and result in a dangerous federal paternalism. Brushing aside unpleasant facts, Hoover repeatedly declared that all the needy were being taken care of. Far from there being any starvation, he assured the nation, the national health standards in fact had improved. Yet agonized appeals continued to flood into Washington for measures to prevent misery and suffering. When one group called on him at the White House in mid-1931 to urge direct federal action, Hoover confidently declared that the depression was over: "Gentlemen, you have come six weeks too late."

Hoover did consent to federal loans to buy seeds and tools for farmers stricken by the great drought in the Southwest's Dust Bowl in 1931, but he baulked at a proposal to feed the farmers and their families or to extend direct relief to the unemployed. In the Senate, Robert F. Wagner of New York, who sympathized with the lowly and the unfortunate perhaps because he had been poor, led the fight for more accurate statistics on joblessness, proposed the expansion of public works, and backed other relief measures. The president, however, adamantly opposed such proposals. "Never before," he declared on vetoing a relief bill, "has so dangerous a suggestion been seriously made in this country." The president reluctantly signed into law in 1932 the Norris-La Guardia Anti-Injunction Act, sought by organized labor to curb antistrike court injunctions, but he vetoed a bill to strengthen the Federal Employment Service established in 1907.

The administration did act more boldly in two areas, if only in accordance with Hoover's philosophy. A federal Home Loan Act was passed in 1932 to strengthen building and loan associations. Unfortunately thousands of home owners had already lost their homes—273,000 in 1932 alone. The Reconstruction Finance Corporation (RFC), established in early 1932 and based on the War Finance Corporation of World War I, represented a more imaginative measure. Congress authorized the RFC to lend money to banks, insurance companies, railroads, and agricultural credit associations. Although one critic derisively dismissed the RFC as a "millionaire's dole," Hoover intended it to restore confidence in the nation's financial structure. He hoped in fact that its mere creation would be enough so that actual lending could be kept to a minimum. Unfortunately, RFC's first director, Charles G. Dawes, stirred up a tirade of denunciations when it became known that shortly after he had resigned from the RFC that agency had loaned Dawes's own bank, the Central Republic Bank and Trust Company in Chicago, $90 million in a vain effort to shore it up. Hoover correctly defended the loan as proper, but it seemed to many to demonstrate the willingness of the administration to help only big business. Yet despite such criticisms, the RFC strengthened otherwise sound institutions and was a direct precursor to the New Deal's lending policy. Hoover reluctantly accepted subsequent legislation for the RFC to lend up to $300 million to the states for relief purposes. The nearly bankrupt states, however, responded unenthusiastically because they preferred gifts. The RFC and the states used loans so sparingly that only a few million dollars were actually advanced. The New Deal was to expand vastly the scope of the RFC.[7]

DEPRESSION POLITICS

Not surprisingly, Hoover's political fortunes had all but eroded by the presidential election campaign of 1932. The American public, yearning for strong leadership, were unlikely to find it in someone distrustful of such a concept. Therefore, the voters looked elsewhere, swelling the ranks and power of Hoover's political opposition. Workers, hit particularly hard by economic hardship, became targets of political opportunism. The Communist Party gleefully hailed the depression as proof of the bankruptcy of the capitalist system and eagerly anticipated revolution. It sent organizers to various cities to win over the jobless, organized protest meetings and marches, and in 1931 called for a National Hunger March on Washington. Intellectuals, disillusioned by the crassness of the 1920s and the economic debacle of the 1930s, seemed more attracted to the cause than workers. Michael Gold edited the *New Masses*, a Communist revival in 1927 of the old radical *Masses* of the Progressive era, and printed much crude "proletarian" literature. A number of able writers either joined the Communist Party or contributed to the *New Masses*—John Dos Passes, Granville Hicks, Theodore Dreiser, Erskine Caldwell, and others. The aging muckraker and radical, Lincoln Steffens, in his *Autobiography* (1931) reiterated his earlier conviction that progressive reforms had not been enough; the capitalist system must be replaced and business nationalized as the Communists had done in the Soviet Union. He commented that "all roads in our day lead to Moscow." John Chamberlain's *Farewell to Reform* (1932) agreed that time had revealed the futility of progressivism and liberalism. Yet, despite the despair of the times presenting an unparalleled opportunity to Communist Party recruiters, the party garnered only a small number of converts; by 1932 the Communist Party only had about 12,000 American members. Most Americans felt alienated by the revolutionary jargon of the Communists and still clung to faith in law and order and the private property system. Even the small number of intellectuals won over tended to become speedily disillusioned by the dogmatism of the party and the brutal fanaticism of Joseph Stalin's dictatorship in the U.S.S.R.

Nevertheless, with the combination of an increasingly organized and visible Communist Party leadership and a growing—even eager—audience, it seemed to many observers in the early 1930s that the United States faced imminent revolution. Even desperate farmers sometimes resorted to violence to prevent or interfere with mortgage foreclosure sales. In the Midwest, an aggressive movement known as the Farmers' Holiday Association (FHA) emerged. Like previous expressions of agrarian radicalism, the FHA arose in a period of severe economic hardship; but, unlike earlier protests when wheat farmers assumed leadership, the depression farmers' protest of the late twenties and early thirties was led by corn, hog, and dairy farmers. But the most volatile clashes occurred in the cities. Hunger riots occurred in several cities, mobs smashing and pilfering stores and warehouses in search of food and clothing. Violence erupted when large-scale protests—some inspired by Communist agitators and some that were not—were met by government police forces and army troops armed with tanks, bayonets, and tear gas. In New York City, 35,000 people tried to march on the city hall. Detroit, the automotive capital, had such vast unemployment that William Z. Foster and the Communist Party picked it as the target for a major effort at unionization and increased party influence. Three thousand unemployed advanced from the city in an orderly procession on Henry Ford's River Rouge plant at Dearborn to deliver a petition, only to be turned back by police fire that killed four and wounded several. A funeral procession for the martyrs carried banners proclaiming that "Ford Gives Bullets for Bread." In one particularly notorious confrontation in the summer of 1932, a group of 20,000 war veterans nicknamed the "Bonus Expeditionary Force" or "Bonus Army" because they sought cash advances on their "bonus" due to mature in 1945, descended on Washington, D.C. Even after Hoover and Congress made it clear that their protests were in vain, many protesters refused to disperse. When the District of Columbia police proved unable to control the situation—and in fact had made it worse by killing two of the protesters—Hoover, mistakenly believing that Communist subversion was responsible for the turmoil, ordered the U.S. Army to settle the matter, creating the spectacle of a "war" of sorts on Pennsylvania Avenue as army troops under the command of General Douglas MacArthur, along with majors Dwight D. Eisenhower and George S. Patton, confronted 10,000 angry veterans. Hoover expressly forbade MacArthur from crossing the Anacostia River and entering Hooverville where most of the protesters had set up makeshift homes. In a move that exemplified the type of "initiative" that characterized his career, MacArthur defiantly crossed the line drawn by his president, ordering his troops to torch the encampment for good measure. Hoover was left to pay the political price for MacArthur's "initiative" and pay he did. Newspapers, which prior to July 28 had been largely supportive of the government in its battle with the Bonus Marchers, now turned on the administration, gracing their front pages with dramatic images of burning encampments in the shadow of the Capitol's rotunda.[8] It was clear that Hoover had for all intents and purposes lost control.

Although tired of coping with the depression, Hoover sought vindication of his policies by running for re-election in 1932, and he won renomination, though without any great enthusiasm on the part of the Republican Party. Many progressive-minded Republicans either responded apathetically or deserted to the Democrats. Increasingly, the rigid and self-righteous president became the target of widespread criticism and abuse. Cruel jokes circulated that he was indeed the world's greatest engineer, having "drained, ditched and damned" the entire country within the span of a few years. One popular joke had Hoover asking Andrew Mellon for a nickel to telephone a friend, and the latter replied, "Here's a dime; call all your friends." Hoover's very name became an epithet, a symbol for despair and misery: "Hoover wagons" were old broken-down cars, "Hoover blankets" referred to newspapers that covered forlorn men sleeping in the parks, and lean jackrabbits were re-christened "Hoover hogs." Opening his campaign in Iowa, Hoover encountered protest picketers carrying placards. One sign read "In Hoover We Trusted; Now We Are Busted." People booed him in Philadelphia and Salt Lake City, and he was jeered at in Detroit by several thousand veterans, unemployed, and some Communists who surrounded his train, throwing eggs and tomatoes. The hapless president reassured the nation that no "deserving American fireside" would experience cold or hunger that winter, small comfort to the millions of presumably "undeserving" who did.

Hoover's main challenger for the White House was Franklin D. Roosevelt, one of the most charismatic figures in American political history, who held the front-runner position among Democrats in 1932. Born in 1882 into the aristocratic Roosevelt family at Hyde Park, New York, Franklin grew up imbued with a sense of duty and service to family and the community. After education at Groton and Harvard, where his grades were gentlemanly but not outstanding, Franklin briefly went into law before he decided to emulate his famous cousin, Theodore Roosevelt, by entering politics. He married Eleanor Roosevelt, Theodore's niece, in 1905. A sensitive woman with an unhappy childhood, and deeply sympathetic with the less fortunate of this world, Eleanor had an incalculable influence in the development of her husband's social conscience and his interest in reform. Roosevelt received an excellent political education while serving in the New York State Senate. For the first time aware of the plight of the lower classes, he began to reveal attitudes and convictions regarding labor and agriculture that subsequently shaped the New Deal. He also learned invaluable political lessons about party regularity, and he perceived firsthand that machine politicians, such as Al Smith, could also be men of honesty dedicated to public service. During the Wilson administration, he served ably as assistant secretary of the navy under Josephus Daniels. In 1920 Roosevelt received the vice-presidential nomination on the ticket with Governor Cox of Ohio and campaigned energetically in a lost cause for the Democrats.

Stricken with polio in 1921, when he was thirty-nine years old, Roosevelt spent years in confinement struggling to regain the use of his legs, a struggle he never won. Remaining actively interested in politics despite his illness, Roosevelt formed a political alliance with New York's Al Smith—although their personal relations remained cool at best—and supported him in his bids for the presidency in 1924 and 1928. At the 1924 convention, Roosevelt on crutches hailed Al Smith as the "Happy Warrior" of politics and made a moving impression on the delegates. Roosevelt returned to active political life in 1928, when he won the governorship of New York after Smith obtained the nomination. Despite the defeat of the national ticket, Roosevelt battled for regional planning to help both the farmer and the state in general. He got a constitutional authorization in 1931 for state acquisition of abandoned farms for reforestation and backed other conservation measures. Roosevelt also continued Smith's program for public power development on the St. Lawrence River.

When the depression came, Roosevelt operated "a little left of center" in his efforts to cope with state problems of unemployment and relief. He established a Commission on the Stabilization of Employment within the state and approved the concept of unemployment insurance. He created a state emergency relief administration, under the direction of Harry Hopkins. But even Roosevelt, probably the most progressive state governor then on the national scene, at first showed a marked lack of enthusiasm for expanding public works, and he tried to finance relief by raising taxes until compelled to accept larger deficits. He had not yet fully envisioned the positive role government intervention could play in the economy, still sharing the conservative belief in an unhampered free enterprise system. Nevertheless, he managed to create an image of himself as a dynamic political leader fighting the depression, which stood in stark contrast to the widely held perception of Hoover's do-nothing approach. Aided by able political advisers such as James Parley, his private secretary Louis M. Howe, and speechwriter Samuel J. Rosenman, Roosevelt won re-election as governor in 1930 by a heavy margin. Thereafter, his national political star was on the rise, and he became a serious challenger to Republican dominance. In several addresses early in 1932, Roosevelt sharpened his attack on the Hoover policies. The emergency was worse than 1917, he declared, and it required similar planned effort to "build from the bottom up" and not to neglect the "forgotten man," a message that received a warm and widespread reception. Roosevelt thus was in a good position to win the Democratic presidential nomination in 1932, though he first had to brush aside Smith, who had moved increasingly toward the conservative wing of the party. Having sacrificed himself in the Republican year of 1928, Smith thought he deserved another chance. Despite primary election setbacks in Massachusetts and California (Smith won both handily), the Roosevelt forces beat back Smith and such rivals as Governor "Alfalfa Bill" Murray of Oklahoma. Roosevelt won the nomination on the fourth ballot at the Democratic convention in Chicago. John N. Garner of Texas got the second place on the ticket.

Roosevelt set the tone of the campaign in his precedent-shattering appearance before the convention to accept the nomination. Dramatically flying to Chicago, he proclaimed to the assembled delegates and the nation, "Ours must be a party of liberal thought, of planned actions, of enlightened international outlook, and of the greatest good to the greatest number of our citizens." He then spoke in general terms of the necessity for government aid and encouragement for agriculture, business, and the unemployed. "I pledge you [the delegates at the convention], I pledge myself, to a new deal for the American people . . . this is more than a political campaign; it is a call to arms. Give me your help, not to win votes alone, but to win in this crusade to restore America to its own people." His stirring promise of a New Deal captured the public's imagination and furnished a convenient and apt label for his subsequent administration.

Roosevelt sought to win an election and naturally wanted to alienate as few voters as possible. In the process he earned criticism for delivering vague speeches that, for all his condemnation of Hoover's policies, failed to spell out a plan of action of his own. The *New Republic*, for example, evaluated Roosevelt as a man of good intentions but without great intellectual or moral force. Commentator Walter Lippmann dismissed him as "a pleasant man who, without any important qualifications for the office, would like to be President." Yet he was not an opportunist in the crass sense, for he believed in certain principles of responsible democratic government and its obligations to promote the welfare of all its citizens. Roosevelt in office revealed a pragmatic and experimental approach, willing to borrow ideas and programs from diverse sources in the desperate battle to relieve suffering and restore national prosperity. More importantly, he promised leadership, drawing a sharp distinction between his own view of the presidency and that of the incumbent, declaring that, "The presidency is not merely an administrative office. That's the least of it. It is more than an engineering job, efficient or inefficient. It is preeminently a place of moral leadership." [9]

Although short on specifics, Roosevelt did indicate in a general way the course his administration subsequently followed. Aided by his "brains trust"—Felix Frankfurter of Harvard, and Raymond Moley, Adolf Berle, and Rexford Tugwell of Columbia—he outlined some of the essentials of the subsequent New Deal program in a series of major speeches. In Topeka, Kansas, Roosevelt indicated the need for a federal crop-control program to rescue the farmers. He talked of regulation and aid for the bankrupt railroads in Salt Lake City, the dangers of a high tariff in Seattle, Washington, and in Portland, Oregon, he called for federal dam and power projects. He made his most radical proposals before the Commonwealth Club in San Francisco. There the Democratic candidate spoke of the need for an economic bill of rights including a decent minimum living standard, economic order, and government planning. When Hoover attacked him for advocating collectivism, charging that the New Deal would enslave America, Roosevelt toned down his speeches and began to criticize the Republicans for an unbalanced budget and a growing national debt. Hoover's $2.75 billion deficit, he declared, represented "the most reckless and extravagant [one] . . . that I have been able to discover in the statistical record of any peacetime Government anywhere, anytime." While pledging himself to greater economy in government and a balanced budget, in which he sincerely believed, Roosevelt left a loophole that more federal funds would be expended if necessary to relieve dire need and avert starvation. An experimental approach, more governmental regulation and intervention in the economy, some economic and social planning—the welfare, interventionist state—came to epitomize the New Deal.

When the polls closed on Election Day 1932, it was clear that the voters had created a Democratic landslide. Having claimed credit for the prosperity of the 1920s, the Republicans had now been caught by the depression in a trap of their own making. Most voters remained impervious to Hoover's warning issued a few days before the balloting that if Roosevelt won "the grass will grow in the streets of a hundred cities, a thousand towns; the weeds will overrun the fields of millions of farmers. . . . Their churches and school houses will decay." Roosevelt won the votes of 22.8 million Americans, or 57.3 percent, to Hoover's 15.8 million votes and 39.6 percent of the popular total. Despite the widespread hardship and the obvious breakdown of the capitalist system, candidates on the far left faired poorly: Socialist Norman Thomas only polled 2 percent, less than in 1912, and the Communist Party candidate, William Z. Foster, only managed to attract less than 0.3 percent. Hoover carried only six states and was as badly defeated as Smith had been in 1928. As Hoover later wryly commented, "Democracy is not a polite employer. The only way out of elective office is to get sick or die or get kicked out." The Congress became overwhelmingly Democratic, as the party not only capitalized on the urban minorities of the great cities but even broke into traditional Republican strongholds in the agricultural Midwest. The political revolution symbolized by Al Smith in 1928, when the Democratic Party first significantly benefited from the growing political consciousness of urban ethnic and religious minorities and organized labor, now approached fulfillment, much to Roosevelt's benefit.

Between November 1932 and inaugural day in March 1933, Hoover found himself a lame duck president as all eyes focused on the president-elect. The two met in the White House in late November 1932, and their representatives held several conferences. Pleading the need to bolster business confidence, Hoover tried to persuade Roosevelt to continue Republican policies and not to embark upon the experimental tack indicated in the recent campaign. Specifically, he urged pledges not to tamper with the dollar nor to unbalance the budget—which, incidentally, Hoover already had unbalanced. When Roosevelt warily declined to assume responsibility or to commit himself prior to taking office, the embittered Hoover blamed him for the further deterioration of the economy and the banking panic that became acute in the early months of 1933. Hoover left office persuaded that his methods had put the economy on the way to recovery until Roosevelt's election had shattered business confidence by the threat of federal tinkering with an otherwise sound economic system. Few, however, have subscribed to Hoover's diagnosis.[10]

NOTES

1. Geoffrey Blainey, "Herbert Hoover's Forgotten Years," *Business Archives and History* 3 (1963): 53–70.

2. Robert Dallek, *Hail to the Chief: The Making and Unmaking of American Presidents* (New York: Hyperion, 1996), p. 103.

3. See particularly David Burner's essay in *The Hoover Presidency: A Reappraisal*, edited by Martin L. Fausold and George T. Mazuzan (Albany: State University of New York Press, 1974).

4. Arthur Schlesinger, Jr., "Hoover Makes a Comeback," *New York Review of Books* (8 March 1979): 10.

5. Udo Sautter, "Government and Unemployment: The Use of Public Works before the New Deal," *Journal of American History* 73 (1986): 59–86.

6. Joan Hoff-Wilson, *Herbert Hoover: Forgotten Progressive* (Boston: Little, Brown, 1975); and David Burner, *Herbert Hoover: A Public Life* (New York: Knopf, 1979).

7. James S. Olson, *Herbert Hoover and the Reconstruction Finance Corporation, 1931–1933* (Ames: Iowa State University Press, 1977).

8. See particularly Arthur Schlesinger M., Jr., *The Crisis of the Old Order, 1919–1933* (Boston: Houghton Mifflin, 1957), pp. 256–65; and Louis Liebovich, "Press Reaction to the Bonus March of 1932: A Re-evaluation of the Impact of an American Tragedy," *Journalism Monographs* 122 (August 1990).

9. *The New York Times Magazine*, 11 September 1932.

10. Works published since the mid-1960s, when portions of Hoover's papers first became available at the Herbert Hoover Presidential Library, have often regarded Hoover more favorably than did his contemporaries. For discussions of the historiography of the Hoover period, see particularly Mark M. Dodge, ed, *Herbert Hoover and the Historians* (West Branch, IA: Herbert Hoover Presidential Library Association, 1989); and Arthur M. Schlesinger, Jr., *The Cycles of American History* (Boston: Houghton Mifflin, 1986), pp. 374–87.

CHAPTER 2

A New Deal for the American People

Having been swept into office on a wave of public dissatisfaction with Herbert Hoover's handling of the Great Depression, Franklin Delano Roosevelt recognized that America's economic blight could not be cured with conventional palliatives; it would require nothing less than a political revolution. Committing the federal government to leading America's way to recovery, Roosevelt instituted an innovative program of public works on a massive scale and devised legislation to spend America into the black. Often missing the mark, the New Deal was not a magic cure; but neither was it a sugar pill. Although primarily an economic program, perhaps the most profound impact of the New Deal was in revolutionizing the relationship between the government and the people. Americans, who had generally never held the government directly accountable for the quality of their lives, now looked to Washington for help. The American political experience has never been the same since.

THE FIRST NEW DEAL

Inaugural Day 1933, dawned cold and overcast in Washington. The prevailing mood across the nation, however, was one of expectancy. As the *New York Times* summed up: "No President . . . ever came to greater opportunities amid so great an outpouring of popular trust and hope." The economy was continuing its sickening and bewildering downward lurch amidst misery and ruin. The very existence of the republic seemed imperiled, and the people looked to the new chief executive for leadership.

Franklin D. Roosevelt radiated confidence and determination. His inaugural address, vague on specific proposals but exuding hope and the promise of energetic action, galvanized the American people and renewed their spirit: "This great Nation will endure as it has endured, will revive and prosper. So, first of all, let me assert my firm belief that the only thing we have to fear is fear itself—nameless, unreasoning, unjustified terror which paralyzes needed efforts to convert retreat into advance." Although the outgoing Hoover visibly shuddered at what he regarded as the demagoguery of Roosevelt's inaugural remarks, the people were impressed.

During his first two weeks in office, Roosevelt moved quickly to dispel the national mood of despair. Rising early on his first full day in the White House, Roosevelt was wheeled by his aides into his still bare study and dealt the first hand of his program for American recovery. It was not so much what he did—at this stage his acts were rather conservative and orthodox—but that, in contrast to Hoover, Roosevelt seemed to be grappling decisively with the depression; Roosevelt quickly demonstrated that he expected the White House to lead, not act as umpire.

The new chief executive faced an immediate crisis in banking. The annual number of bank failures had increased from 167 in 1920 to 2,294 in 1931, and to an incredible 4,004 in 1933. Loss of confidence among depositors led to runs on many otherwise sound banks and to the hoarding of gold. By Inaugural Day, thirty-eight states had been forced either to close all banks or to permit only limited operations. Responding to desperate pleas from the financial world and anxious to protect hundreds of thousands of large and small depositors, Roosevelt, on March 5, proclaimed a national bank holiday. All banks would be closed, to gain time to reopen sound institutions and liquidate others with minimum losses. Called into special session, Congress quickly passed the Emergency Banking Act. The House of Representatives voted by acclamation, without seeing a copy of the bill that authorized issuance of new federal currency, and gave the president full authority over gold transactions. In this first week, Roosevelt met the governors of the states in conference and assured them of federal help. Two days later, he held his first press conference, where he abolished Hoover's requirement that all questions from reporters be submitted in written form. Then in his first "fireside chat," an informal radio report to the nation that he was to use repeatedly and effectively, Roosevelt announced the reopening of the sound banks and urged the return of withdrawn funds. In an impressive demonstration of confidence in the president, on the following day long lines formed across the country as recently frightened depositors returned their money to the banks.

Roosevelt's handling of the banking crisis revealed the essentially conservative nature of the early New Deal. In view of the public's loss of faith in the banking system and hatred of bankers, Roosevelt probably could have obtained congressional approval for truly drastic measures, even nationalization of the system. Instead he remained content with legislation to restore confidence and improve the banks by closer federal regulation, while still leaving them under private ownership and management. The Glass-Steagall Act of 1933 separated commercial from investment banking, increased the powers of the Federal Reserve Board to curb speculation by banks, and established the Federal Deposit Insurance Corporation to insure all deposits in Federal Reserve banks up to $2,500. Another measure two years later reorganized the Board of Governors of the Federal Reserve System and further increased its regulatory authority over bank credits and reserves. These measures helped to reduce drastically the rate of bank failures, whereas even before the depression that rate was in the hundreds per year; after the measures were implemented it was reduced to fewer than ten.[1]

At the president's request, Congress passed the Beer Act, legalizing the sale of light wines and beer. Repeal of Prohibition by the Twenty-first Amendment to the Constitution followed soon thereafter. Keeping his campaign promises to reduce federal expenditures and balance the budget, Roosevelt persuaded a rather reluctant Congress to approve the Economy Act. That act slashed about $500 million from veterans' benefits and the salaries of federal employees. These and other planned actions caused thousands of congratulatory telegrams to flood into the capital, while newspaper columnists and editors lavished praise on the new administration. Congress reflected the national mood of urgency by passing legislation hastily and almost without debate. The temper of Congress in fact seemed to favor even more drastic and sweeping action than the executive proposed. In the remainder of his first hundred days in office, Roosevelt obtained congressional approval for measure after measure with minimal debate and controversy. Congress enacted fifteen major bills and numerous lesser acts, a legislative record unsurpassed in American history.

Conventionally, Roosevelt's administration has been seen as falling into two rather clear divisions or periods. The so-called First New Deal, from 1933 to1935, presumably concentrated on relief and recovery activities; the Second New Deal, from 1935 to 1938, emphasized broad social and economic reform intended to preclude future economic catastrophes and to promote a larger degree of social justice for all citizens.[2] Historian Arthur M. Schlesinger, Jr., prefers a different set of interpretative labels: the "New Nationalism" for the first period, characterized by greater emphasis on government planning, integration, and regulation of the economy; versus the return to "New Freedom" approaches in 1935, when the administration manifested greater suspicion toward big business and placed more reliance upon trust-busting and punitive measures to cope with abuses in business and finance.[3] Both interpretations have much validity and are useful tools in understanding the thrust and nature of the New Deal. They should not be taken too rigidly, however, for concern with issues of relief, recovery, and reform remained a constant preoccupation of the administration until the outbreak of the Second World War. Moreover, President Roosevelt manifested a nontheoretical and dogmatic approach to politics and government. Far from being radically inclined, the president leaned toward economic orthodoxy and conservatism. The depression compelled him to experiment and improvise, to borrow ideas and programs from a variety of sources, but underlying all this was a commitment to lead the government to a balanced budget as soon as possible. In short, Roosevelt hoped to reform capitalism as a bulwark of American democracy.

Columnist Walter Lippmann once commented that the major difference between the Hoover and the Roosevelt administrations seemed to be the willingness of the New Deal to spend larger sums with less regret. That interpretation had validity for early New Deal relief activities, but not later when the administration placed greater emphasis upon conserving human skills and dignity while providing relief. Hoover also had run deficits in fighting the depression, but he had refused to involve the federal government in direct relief to the needy and unemployed. Critics had condemned his approach as too timid, and many argued that conditions required direct pump-priming expenditures to revive mass consumer purchasing power. The existing system of private, local, and state relief by 1933 obviously proved incapable of coping with the problem. Although Roosevelt preferred a balanced budget (he made a distinction between the ordinary budget that would be balanced and the emergency one that required compensatory expenditures), he plunged into direct federal relief. The president continued to anticipate an early end to such outlays and a return to fiscal solvency and a reduction of the national debt. He never accepted the Keynesian argument for protracted and massive federal spending and did not venture beyond comparatively modest emergency measures. While he managed to relieve acute suffering, he failed to eradicate unemployment and restore full prosperity. These goals remained unachieved until World War II at last mobilized the national wealth and energies and increased the national debt by truly astronomical sums.

The New Deal contributed to the language a new glossary of alphabetical agencies, many of them created to cope with relief. Harry Hopkins, a highly controversial figure and a New York state relief director under Roosevelt, assumed the primary responsibility in this area. One observer once described the outwardly cynical and often profane Hopkins as having "the purity of St. Francis . . . combined with the sharp shrewdness of a race track lout." Hopkins viewed the essential challenge as how to administer relief not only to feed people but to preserve their skills and self-respect. While he accepted the immediate necessity for direct handouts, he sought, with the president's approval, to supplant the dole with work-relief as soon as possible. In May 1933, Congress appropriated $500 million for relief through the states and local agencies, largely handled through Hopkins's Federal

Emergency Relief Administration (FERA). Hopkins insisted that relief hand-outs be given to the needy in cash rather than script redeemable in food, and that relief include not only food but housing, clothing, and medical needs. The administration established the Civil Works Administration (CWA), a subsidiary of the FERA, in late 1933 as a makeshift effort to give emergency jobs to the unemployed during the winter of 1933–34 at a minimum wage eventually fixed at thirty cents an hour. By early 1934, Hopkins had expended close to $1 billion through the CWA and provided temporary employment to over four million people. Convinced that such heavy expenditures had achieved little beyond emergency relief, Roosevelt terminated the CWA in the spring of 1934. Other forms of aid continued, however, and over $2 billion had been spent for relief by the end of the year.

The administration launched a second major attack on relief in 1935. Roosevelt asked for nearly $5 billion for a massive program of federal emergency employment, the largest single appropriation to that date in world history. Conservative critics preferred the less expensive dole and opposed the bill as an unwise extension of executive powers. Republican Senator Arthur H. Vandenburg of Michigan reflected the view of the minority in Congress: "This measure requires Congress to abdicate; it requires the country to lean on a dubious dream; it requires posterity to pay the bills." Many supporters, however, feared that not enough funds had been requested. Congress passed the measure after much debate. Roosevelt divided the funds between Hopkins's newly created Works Progress Administration (WPA) and Harold Ickes's Public Works Administration (PWA). Hopkins and Ickes were in a sharp rivalry for funds, and because Ickes's PWA necessarily expended money more slowly on carefully planned public projects, to his great distress his funds tended to be diverted to the freer spending WPA. Nevertheless, and as an indication of the scale of federal government spending, between 1933 and 1939, Ickes's PWA built nearly two-thirds of the nation's new school buildings, county courthouses, and city facilities; one-third of the hospitals and public health service buildings; and a number of warships for the navy, including the aircraft carriers *Yorktown* and *Enterprise*.

Charges of worthless make-work projects and of "boondoggling" to the contrary, WPA represented a notable attempt not only to conserve skills and relieve unemployment but also to perform socially useful work. It paid "security wages" that were higher than the dole but sufficiently below private wages to provide incentive to seek regular employment. Normally in a private profit economy such as that in the United States genius and money are lavished on the private sector of the economy while the public sector is sadly neglected. Now during a national emergency, the WPA and other New Deal agencies could perform invaluable work. By 1941, the WPA had expended nearly $11 billion, employed a grand total of about 8 million people, and completed 250,000 projects. Some waste inevitably occurred, but the gigantic effort remained remarkably free from overt politicking, while performing much useful labor that normally would not have been undertaken. Relief agencies built around 600 aircraft landing fields; constructed 500,000 miles of roads; completed over 100,000 bridges or viaducts; built or repaired 110,000 public libraries, schools, auditoriums, and hospitals; and served 600 million school lunches. These deeds represented remarkable achievements in view of the fact that WPA had to choose projects that could be completed quickly and that would not compete with private industry or regular and more substantial public works.

To utilize and improve existing skills, Hopkins established under his agency a Federal Theater Project that employed 13,000 people and staged plays for thirty million people, while the Music Project in its first fifteen months presented live concerts before audiences totaling fifty million. The Federal Writers Project produced numerous publications from historical projects to state and local guides. The Federal Art Project employed needy artists to beautify public buildings and stage educational art displays. Another agency, the National Youth Administration, provided part-time jobs for 600,000 college students and 1.5 million high school students and aided an even larger number of nonschool youths in acquiring vocational training. A veritable cultural revolution occurred under New Deal auspices, encouraging creativity and making its achievements accessible to the people. Although denounced by conservatives as frivolous and havens for radicals, Hopkins's agencies undoubtedly reduced the appeal of the Communists.

The New Deal created other agencies that combined goals of relief, recovery, and reform. President Roosevelt's personal brainchild, the Civilian Conservation Corps (CCC), organized under civilian direction with army reserve officers in charge, removed thousands of jobless youths from the city streets and gave them useful employment in more healthful rural environments.[4] Thought of as a sort of moral equivalent to war, uniformed CCC youth fought fires, reseeded forests, and engaged in flood prevention work. In 1932, when some 273,000 home owners lost their homes through mortgage foreclosures, Hoover had approved a system of Federal Home Loan Banks to bolster building and loan associations. Since that offered little direct help, Congress approved a Home Owners' Loan Corporation (HOLC) in 1933 to lend money to refinance home mortgages and repairs. By 1935, HOLC had loaned over $3 billion and held one-sixth of the national home mortgage indebtedness. The administration obtained a Federal Housing Agency in 1934 to encourage new home building, followed by a U.S. Housing Authority in 1937 that advanced money for slum clearance and low cost housing projects. A modest success, about one-third of the housing projects benefited low-income African-American families.

The Farm Credit Administration provided similar relief to threatened farmers. The Resettlement Administration under Rexford Tugwell established three "greenbelt towns" of 500 to 800 families each near Washington, Cincinnati, and Milwaukee, and tried to help rural people move from worn out farms to better land. Faced with conservative southern opposition, the Resettlement Administration never could obtain sufficient funds to reduce sharply farm tenancy. After two years, it had only purchased five million acres of land and resettled 4,441 families. A southern Tenant Farmers' Union tried to organize sharecroppers and complained that most of the federal rural aid went to the larger landowners. The Farm Security Administration replaced the Resettlement Administration in 1937 to lend money to tenants to buy farms and to improve the lot of migrant farm laborers. The Rural Electrification Administration advanced funds to cooperatives to build electric power transmission facilities, so that where only 580,000 farms had been electrified in 1929 the number increased to about 2 million by 1941. Among other effects, rural electrification created a whole new market for electrical equipment and appliances, a good example of how apparently competitive government programs often benefit the private economy.

The Tennessee Valley witnessed one of the boldest and most controversial experiments in planned recovery and reform. In 1933, Congress authorized creation of the Tennessee Valley Authority (TVA) to operate the existing Wilson Dam at Muscle Shoals and to construct new dams to prevent floods, to manufacture fertilizer and explosives, and to generate and distribute electrical power in the area. The activities of the TVA helped transform the lives of the people in seven southern states, freeing them from floods, supplying cheap power, and encouraging development of diversified agriculture and industry. By 1940, per capita income in the valley had risen 73 percent over 1933. Despite criticism of this type of governmental regional planning as socialistic, the vast experiment aroused worldwide interest and created industrial facilities that proved of enormous national value during World War II. Opponents, however, prevented other power projects, such as Bonneville Dam on the Columbia River and Grand Coulee in Washington state, from undertaking a similar experimental approach.[5]

The New Deal turned Hoover's Reconstruction Finance Corporation (RFC) into one of the most successful ventures in the struggle for recovery from the depression. Under the direction of Jesse Jones of Texas, the RFC loaned funds not only to the larger financial institutions, as under Hoover, but to needy railroads, medium and small businesses, farmer cooperatives, and rural electrification projects. By 1938, the RFC had loaned $10 billion and had become the largest single source of credit and investment funds in the nation. Nearly all of the loans eventually were repaid in full.

Roosevelt pinned his main hopes for quick knockout victory over the depression on the National Industrial Recovery Act (NIRA), passed by Congress in June 1933. The idea, another example of the influence of the Progressive era on the New Deal, derived from the War Industries Board of World War I that had been remarkably successful in obtaining business and governmental cooperation during that great emergency. Now a new and equally great emergency seemed to require a similar mobilization. The National Recovery Administration (NRA), directed by the flamboyant General Hugh Johnson, undoubtedly constituted a departure from the *laissez-faire* attitudes of the past. Yet it was not a radical one, for apart from World War I experiences, the NRA had a precedent in the trade associations that had flourished during the twenties. It went a step beyond, however, by placing federal authority behind attempts to regulate production and prices. NRA encouraged various industries to frame codes of fair competition, exempt from the antitrust laws but subject to governmental approval. Business in effect agreed in these codes on minimum wages and maximum hours in exchange for federal help in stabilizing production and prices. Section 7(a) of the NIRA recognized the right of workers to organize and bargain collectively with employers and prohibited compulsory company unions (employer unions established to offset independent national unions). Consumers theoretically had representation in the NRA but never effectively.

NRA initially had the support of most businesspeople. The administration hoped it would promote friendly cooperation between business and labor by eliminating wasteful competition and stabilizing prices and wages. Despite the objections of a few industrialists such as Henry Ford, who charged a plot by his competitors and what he called the "bankers' international," Johnson obtained codes for the major industries. He also launched a nationwide campaign with parades and flashy appeals to sign up over two and a quarter million employers under the NRA Blue Eagles (the Blue Eagle symbol was patterned after the Navajo thunderbird emblem). NRA in fact drew up far too many codes, many for unimportant "industries"; the 800 codes even included the dog food industry, mop stick manufacturers, and the burlesque theater. Johnson relied upon persuasion and appeals to patriotism, rather than legal action, to enforce the codes against violators and chiselers. After the first flush of enthusiasm, it proved to be a losing struggle. Complaints swiftly multiplied. Businessmen objected to organized labor's aggressive use of Section 7(a) to unionize workers.[6] Small businessmen and liberals complained that the codes were fascistic and facilitated the growth of big business and monopoly, while consumers reacted unhappily to production curbs and increases in prices. An investigation by a review board under Clarence Darrow confirmed many of the charges and caused the president to restrict price fixing and the proliferation of codes for small industries. The administration soon eased out the quick-tempered and often rash Johnson, noted for heavy drinking and "shooting from the hip." Although many observers viewed NRA as a failure, President Roosevelt thought otherwise and was displeased when it was invalidated by the Supreme Court in 1935. NRA had tended to reduce production and raise prices and costs, but it could take credit for increasing employment by an estimated two million, reducing child labor, and improving working conditions across the nation. Above all, NRA helped restore the nation's confidence during the darkest days of the depression.

The first Agricultural Adjustment Act (AAA) adopted in May 1933, constituted another long step toward the interventionist state and a planned economy. The desperate plight of farmers, resulting from overproduction and declining prices and worsened by the depression, seemed to require a new remedy. Henry A. Wallace, the secretary of agriculture, can perhaps be called a mystic and faddist—he once tried to live on a diet of corn meal and milk after the example of Caesar's troops in Gaul—but he had a profound knowledge of agriculture. Wallace saw his task as leveling off farm production to avoid overproduction and to achieve "parity" in farm income comparable to other groups in the economy. The AAA went beyond the Hoover farm program to include not only price supports but curtailment of production. It levied a special tax on food processors to finance government purchases of surpluses and set acreage and production limitation on cotton, wheat, corn, and hogs. The first year the AAA slaughtered six million young pigs and 200,000 sows (salvageable meat was used to feed the needy) and ploughed under ten million acres of cotton. Aided by a drought in 1934, the program sharply reduced production, and farm income had risen by 50 percent at the end of Roosevelt's first term. Like the NRA, however, the AAA and its successors benefited the large producers, who could control the local agencies, more than small farmers, tenants, or sharecroppers.[7]

Searching for still other ways to speed recovery, and under great pressure from inflationists, Roosevelt, with Congress's authorization, turned to money manipulation. The theories of Cornell University's George F. Warren and others that the price of gold controlled the general commodity price level persuaded Roosevelt to experiment with the gold content of the dollar. Roosevelt incurred the wrath of the orthodox by taking the country off the gold standard and then by buying gold at rates above the current world market price, hoping to encourage foreign trade and raise domestic price levels. Al Smith echoed the sentiments of the traditionalists when he sneered at the new "baloney dollar." The president finally abandoned the experiment and under the Gold Reserve Act of 1934 fixed the reserve gold content of the dollar at 60 percent of the 1933 rate of $35 per ounce. In 1936, an agreement with Britain and France achieved stabilization of currency exchanges. To satisfy the silver interests and inflationists, the Treasury purchased silver at well above the world market price. The only appreciable effect of this action, besides bringing prosperity to silver miners, was the endangerment of the silver-based currencies of China, Mexico, and Peru. Conservatives were horrified; one professed to fear that the monetary experiments threatened the end of civilization.

ATTACKS FROM THE RIGHT AND THE LEFT

Up to 1934, Roosevelt had followed the "politics of consensus," asking and getting support from all groups including business. As the midterm elections loomed, his coalition began to break down under assaults from the right and the left of the political spectrum. However, he retained the support of the farmers, labor, the unemployed, and the underprivileged, and the Democratic Party in the 1934 elections substantially increased its control of Congress. By 1934, a number of conservatives and businessmen had become highly disenchanted with the New Deal. The NRA had proved a disappointment, the national debt had mushroomed, and new agencies such as the Securities and Exchange Commission and the Federal Communications Commission, supervising the radio, telephone, and telegraphic systems, seemed to presage even greater federal control. In August, a group of alarmed conservatives founded the American Liberty League to battle the New Deal and expose its allegedly dangerous drift toward socialism. Led by such bitter anti–New Dealers as Al Smith, John W. Davis, and some top industrialists from DuPont and General Motors, the Liberty League crusaded to preserve the free enterprise system. Its adherents believed firmly in the Social Darwinist *laissez-faire* world expounded in the late nineteenth century by William Graham Sumner. Natural economic law governed the world and, left unmolested, would bring recovery as surely as it had brought the depression. They viewed the New Deal as trying to replace these economic laws with a planned socialist society.

Many conservatives were outraged at the large number of academicians and experts used by the New Deal, the so-called Brains Trust. The *Chicago Tribune* repeatedly printed a cartoon caricaturing a college teacher in academic gown offering ridiculous advice to people wiser than he. The Hearst and Scripps-Howard newspapers, among others, joined the outcry. The *Saturday Evening Post* shrilly declared, "It is our country and not a laboratory for a small group of professors to try out experiments." One New Deal intellectual, Rexford Tugwell, has wryly retorted that such criticisms of brains caused him to wonder by what other part of the human anatomy government should be guided. In fact the Brains Trusters differed greatly among themselves, from the orthodox Raymond Moley to the liberal Harry Hopkins. In any case, they did not dominate Roosevelt, for he used them as he saw fit.

The true explanation of conservative discontent, of course, went deeper than this. The depression had toppled the high priests of finance and industry from their exalted position and, stunned by their loss of prestige, embittered businessmen sought a scapegoat and vented their spleen on the essentially conservative Roosevelt. The president viewed his administration as remarkably moderate in its efforts to avert national collapse, and he reacted with hurt and anger to conservative attacks. He thought of himself as the savior, not the destroyer, of the capitalistic system. Roosevelt's "swing to the left" in 1935 in large part reflected a reaction to what he regarded as uncomprehending and unfair criticism.[8]

Attacks came from the left as well. Soothsayers peddled easy panaceas to exploit social ills and grievances. In Louisiana, Senator Huey P. Long, called the "Kingfish" after a character in the popular Amos 'n Andy radio comedy act, seriously worried Roosevelt with his "share our wealth" program. Roosevelt once referred to Long as "one of the two most dangerous men in the country," comparing him to Germany's Adolf Hitler; the other man, in his view, was General Douglas MacArthur, whom he thought an ideal leader for those citizens willing to discard democracy for strong-man rule.[9] The seventh of nine children, Long had been born in a log cabin in the uplands of Louisiana. After education at Tulane University, he practiced law and entered politics as the defender of the popular interests against the entrenched railroad, oil, and utility interests that dominated Louisiana and gave it the reputation as one of the worst governed states in the union. An intelligent man despite his hillbilly attitude and his intentionally crude and offensive manners and flashy clothes, Long won the governorship in 1928, appealing to the poor "red-necked" farmers. He pushed through reforms in Louisiana and by ruthless methods built a powerful state machine. Long obtained from the legislature measures to build roads, schools, and hospitals; taxed the privileged industries; and smashed the former ruling oligarchy. Not a die-hard racist, Long conferred benefits on both poor whites and blacks through free schools and other programs. On the other hand, Long did little to raise wages or aid the unemployed or needy through welfare legislation.[10]

After Long was elected to the U.S. Senate in 1930, he first supported Roosevelt, but he soon broke with the New Deal and tried to attract a national following of his own. He confidently predicted that he would win the White House in 1936. Aided by a fundamentalist revivalist minister, Gerald L.K. Smith, Long called for confiscating all large fortunes and redistributing the wealth. Each family should be guaranteed a minimum living wage, pensions for the elderly, and free college education for all who wanted it. By early 1935, Long claimed 27,000 Share-out-Wealth Clubs with a mailing list of 7.5 million people. Meanwhile, he made himself virtual dictator in Louisiana and ruled by force and intimidation, until assassinated in the corridor of the state capital building in September 1935 by the son of one of his opponents whom the Long machine was trying to ruin.

In California, already a mecca for the retired and the elderly, the sixty-seven-year-old Dr. Francis Townsend promoted a scheme to cure the depression by aiding the millions of needy elders. Known as the "Ham and Eggs" movement, Townsend's plan called for payment of $200 a month to each person over age sixty. Since the money would have to be spent in the month it was paid and would be financed by a 2 percent sales tax, the rapid turnover would generate vast purchasing power and restore prosperity.

Although financial experts pronounced the scheme absolutely unworkable, Townsend had established 12,000 clubs by 1934 and enlisted millions of members. Meanwhile, the old socialist warrior, Upton Sinclair, had another cure for the depression. EPIC, or End Poverty in California, advocated state operation of uncultivated farms and idle industry for the benefit of the jobless. Land colonies and workers' villages would produce for their own use rather than for profitable sale, and this socialist-syndicalist system would eventually spread across the nation to transform society and the economy. A strange movement known as Technocracy also emerged in California and elsewhere. Inspired by the writings of the unorthodox economist, Thorstein Veblen, its advocates called for discarding democracy and the capitalist system and allowing the engineers to run the economy on the basis of full production where everybody "produces what he uses and uses what he produces." Father Charles Coughlin, the Roman Catholic radio priest of Detroit, proposed still another cure-all. He had turned against the New Deal in 1934 and founded his National Union for Social Justice. He preached a type of Christian fascism to his radio audience of between thirty and forty-five million listeners, flailing away at evil bankers and advocating nationalization of the banks and inflation of the currency. These groups cooperated very ineffectively in an effort to defeat Roosevelt, forming the Union Party in 1936 and running William Lemke for the presidency.

A rash of strikes began in 1934, triggered in part by long-standing grievances and in part by the more favorable climate of unionization created by the attitude and policies of the Roosevelt administration. Radical leaders directed severe industrial action against such cities as San Francisco, Minneapolis, Toledo, and Milwaukee; the majority of these actions, including the general strike in San Francisco, failed. In the twenties the American Federation of Labor (AFL), with its craft philosophy, had proven unequal to the challenge of unionizing the mass industries. In fact, AFL membership dropped from nearly four million in 1921 to slightly over two million in 1933. Clinging to the traditional emphasis on voluntarism and self-reliant unionism—the hallmark of the movement's foremost spokesman, Samuel Gompers, who died in 1924—some of the leaders of the AFL either opposed or were lukewarm at first to proposals for government support of collective bargaining, as well as federal unemployment insurance and old age pensions. Section 7(a) of the NIRA, however, offered unprecedented opportunities for smashing company incomes and organizing semiskilled and relatively unskilled laborers in the major mass production industries, such as steel, automobiles, and coal. For its part, the majority of the AFL leadership preferred to recruit these workers not into one industrial union but into separate craft unions.

Among others, John L. Lewis, president of the powerful United Mine Workers; Sidney Hillman of the Amalgamated Clothing Workers; and David Dubinsky of the International Ladies/Garment Workers established a

Committee for Industrial Organization for recruitment on an industry-wide basis in 1935. After sharp fights with older craft unions—Lewis, the Iowan-born son of a Welsh miner, actually exchanged blows with one craft leader at the AFL convention in 1935—the rebel faction split off from the AFL in 1936 and set up what became known as the Congress of Industrial Organization (CIO).[11] The AFL, under the direction of the mild-mannered William Green, fought back, mobilizing local opposition to the CIO, as well as collaborating with employers in resisting the unionizing efforts of the new organization. Within a short period, the CIO set out to organize the steel and automobile industries, the latter of which provided the CIO with its first great test of strength. On New Year's Eve 1936, several hundred workers seeking to gain recognition of the newly organized United Auto Workers, seized a number of General Motors plants in Flint, Michigan, staging what was to be the beginning of a spectacular "sit-down strike" in which strikers barricaded themselves inside factories. The strike, which saw violent clashes between the strikers on one side and strikebreakers and police on the other side, lasted forty-four days and involved 150,000 workers—directly and indirectly. Fortunately for the strikers, the Roosevelt administration and the governor of the state of Michigan, Frank Murphy, assumed a tolerant position toward labor and thus ruled out governmental intervention. At the time, the president noted: "It [the strike] is illegal, but shooting it out . . . [is not] the answer." In February 1937, General Motors, which feared the very destruction of its plants, and the United Auto Workers came to terms, giving the CIO its first significant victory. The other automotive manufacturers followed suit. Sit-down strikes, which were ultimately declared illegal by the Supreme Court in *Hague v. CIO* in 1939, quickly spread to other industries, including rubber, textiles, oil refining, shipbuilding, and steel. Within a brief space of time, the CIO achieved a second stunning success, this time in the steel industry. In March 1937, after a bitter strike, U.S. Steel yielded to the demands of the Steel Workers' Organizing Committee, recognizing that body as the bargaining agency of its employees and agreeing to a wage increase of 10 percent and a forty-hour week with time and a half for overtime. Lesser steel companies—known collectively as "Little Steel"—led by Tom Girdler of Republic Steel proved adamant in refusing to follow the lead of U.S. Steel. The issue reached a climax when a group of union demonstrators were fired upon by police at the Republic plant in South Chicago on May 30, 1937. In the so-called Memorial Day Massacre that ensued, ten people were killed and eighty-four were injured by the end of the year. "Little Steel" had defeated unionization. Other industries, however, fell into line, and by 1939, the CIO had become a major rival to the older AFL. Union membership in general had grown prodigiously under the New Deal, reaching a figure of almost nine million by 1938.

Responding to pressures from the left and attacks from the right, Roosevelt's annual message to Congress in January 1935 outlined a bold new approach. "In spite of our efforts and in spite of our talk," Roosevelt declared, "we have not weeded out the overprivileged and we have not effectively lifted up the underprivileged." He called for measures to provide adequate housing, social security, and a decent living standard for all. Flaying obstructionism by big business and the wealthy, the president also advocated a new and more equitable tax policy to shift the burden of public expenditures to those better able to bear it. Two days later, Roosevelt asked Congress for billions of dollars for a massive assault on unemployment, to be waged primarily by Henry Hopkins's WPA.

During the summer of 1935, Roosevelt cracked the whip over Congress and launched the Second New Deal. Advisers, such as Felix Frankfurther and Supreme Court Justice Louis Brandeis, argued that cooperation with big business had failed and that an all-out effort was necessary. If Roosevelt's first hundred days in office had set a new record for legislative action, the agenda for the second hundred days promised to accelerate that pace. The Wagner Labor Relations Act, accepted by Roosevelt as a replacement of Section 7(a) of the NIRA, reaffirmed the right of labor to organize and bargain collectively with employers. Congress approved creation of a National Labor Relations Board (NLRB) to outlaw unfair labor practices and to conduct elections in industry to certify union bargaining agencies. The NLRB understandably enraged business leaders. This measure was supplemented in 1938 by the Fair Labor Standards Act, which banned child labor under sixteen and fixed a national minimum wage, at first at forty cents an hour, a maximum forty-hour work week, and time and a half for overtime work. Although its terms were to go into effect over a period of years and a minimum wage of $16 per week was obviously inadequate, many businessmen and others, especially southerners in the low-wage South, roundly denounced the measure. Other measures launched slum clearance and public housing projects and strengthened the TVA. A furious battle was waged over the Utility Holding Company Act. Drafted by New Dealers Thomas C. Corcoran and Benjamin V. Cohen, the bill provided for federal regulation and coordination of utility companies to obtain greater efficiency and contained a highly controversial "death sentence" clause, allowing the Securities and Exchange Commission to dissolve holding companies that could not demonstrate that they contributed to the efficiency of the actual operating firms they controlled. The utility companies fought back, led by Wendell Willkie of Commonwealth and Southern Corporation, the nation's largest utility holding company. They flooded Congress with lobbyists and letters of protest. Congress finally passed a so-called compromise measure that was still very tough: The government would have to defend the dissolution order to utility holding companies.

Two other measures, the income tax and social security, aroused business and conservative hostility. Roosevelt told Congress and the nation that past tax laws had "done little to prevent an unjust concentration of wealth and economic power," and a new approach was needed that would promote "a wider distribution of wealth." The resultant Wealth Tax Act of 1935 increased the graduated income tax on the upper brackets to a maximum of 75 percent, and imposed higher inheritance, gift, and corporate income levies. Though denounced as a socialistic measure to redistribute wealth, the tax hike was rather moderate by later standards; in any case, such taxes have failed to reduce significantly the share of wealth received by the upper-income groups. Studies in the 1970s revealed that while the overall living standard has advanced greatly since the depression, wealth remains concentrated in a few hands. In 1922, the top 2 percent of all families held 33 percent of the nation's private wealth, versus 32 percent in 1958; the top tenth of income recipients got around a third of the total income in 1910, versus 30 percent in 1960.

The nation was not just in economic flux; during the 1930s, the demographics of America changed considerably, creating new challenges and placing new burdens on the nation's ability to protect the welfare of its citizens. During the decade, the birth rate decreased by over a third of its previous average, and immigration decreased by nearly 90 percent.[12] Another problem was that the population was aging. In 1861, only one of forty Americans was sixty-five years or over, but by 1940, the number had increased to one out of every fifteen and was mounting. Most major industrial countries in Europe had recognized the problem long before and had adopted compulsory old-age insurance programs. The elderly particularly suffered from the depression, as they exhausted savings and private insurance and could not find employment. Washington's response came in the form of the Social Security Act of 1935. Yet conservatives denounced any government plan for aiding these unfortunates as socialistic and destructive of self-reliance. Introduced in Congress by Senator Robert Wagner (D-NY), the Social Security Act, as it was finally tabled, provided a New Deal agency that was politically flexible while remaining faithful to its purpose.[13] It provided old age insurance for those aged sixty-five and over, to be financed by taxes on wages and payrolls. Supporters added a system of federal-state unemployment compensation, plus aid to dependent mothers and children and the physically handicapped. Although the act had defects, especially in failing to provide for the elderly indigent already retired, it represented a notable landmark in catching up with the social problems of the twentieth century. As Roosevelt remarked at its formal signing, the Social Security Act did not remove all the dangers and risks of life, but it gave some measure of protection to the average citizen and extended *de facto* "social rights" for the unemployed and elderly.

THE HIGHS AND LOWS OF THE NEW DEAL

Ignoring Al Smith's disgruntled plea to pick "some genuine Democrat," the Democratic convention in 1936 renominated Roosevelt by acclamation. The platform, which reflected the New Deal's turn against big business, pledged a vigorous enforcement of the antitrust laws. The Republicans chose Governor Alfred M. Landon of Kansas; Frank Knox, owner and editor of the Chicago *Daily News* and a strong opponent of the New Deal, received second place on the ticket. The Republican platform realistically conceded many of the New Deal reforms, merely promising to administer them more efficiently and economically. The colorless Landon, often called a Kansas Coolidge, had moderately liberal views, but he was embarrassed by support of the conservative Liberty League. Al Smith, having long withdrawn his support for Roosevelt, deserted the Democratic Party to support Landon, calling the New Deal a "dismal, dull, dark, and dreary failure."[14] Other dissident Democrats, among them Bainbridge Colby and John W. Davis, declared for Landon. To his great distress, Landon also found himself upstaged in the closing weeks of the campaign by Herbert Hoover's unwanted and increasingly bitter denunciations of the New Deal.

Roosevelt waged a vigorous campaign. In his acceptance speech, he excoriated what he described as the "economic royalists," those special interests that sought to preserve their privileges and to block reform and regulation. In moving phrases, he proclaimed that "this generation of Americans had a rendezvous with destiny." It was good politics, even though critics—whose ranks now included former ally Al Smith—accused him of stirring up class hatreds, threatening public freedoms, and arbitrarily wasting national resources. In subsequent speeches, Roosevelt emphasized the anti-big business orientation of the Second New Deal and the need to increase individual opportunity and freedom. With an efficient political organization directed by Postmaster General James A. Farley, Roosevelt attracted the support of organized labor, farmers, the reliefers, and small businessmen. Most newspaper owners and editors opposed Roosevelt but working reporters overwhelmingly favored him. Attesting to his successful undercutting of the radicals, the Union Party of William Lemke ran poorly, polling only 882,479 votes instead of the 10 million or more predicted by Father Coughlin; the Socialist vote declined to less than 200,000, and the Communists fell to a low of 80,159 out of 45.6 million votes cast.

The black population outside the South had increased rapidly since World War I and comprised an important element in the urban vote. Traditionally Republican since the Civil War, even as late as 1932, northern blacks voted Democratic in 1936 by heavy margins. The New Deal had earned their support not only by nondiscriminatory relief measures but also by appointing some blacks to political office. Eleanor Roosevelt, the president's wife, was known to sympathize with blacks, and Roosevelt often consulted black leaders. No doubt the New Deal gave racial equality only token support, but it seemed a clear improvement over the past. Roosevelt thus carried by huge majorities the larger cities and eastern industrial states.

The final tally in 1936 revealed that Roosevelt had polled 27,476,673 votes, or 60.2 percent of the popular vote, to Landon's 16,679,583 or 36.5 percent. Roosevelt carried every state except Maine and Vermont. As Roosevelt quipped about his tidal wave triumph, it had been a baptism by total immersion in which the other fellow nearly drowned. The Democratic Party had become the new majority party, exploiting an urban political revolution through its appeal to the city masses. Yet ironically 1936 marked the high water mark of the domestic New Deal, for Roosevelt subsequently encountered increasing resistance in his efforts to extend reform.

The federal judiciary during Roosevelt's first term remained heavily Republican and conservative in tone. Only an estimated 28 percent of the 266 federal judges were Democrats. The Supreme Court contained four very conservative justices, George Sutherland, Willis Van Devater, James C. McReynolds, and Pierce Butler; three more liberal justices, Harlan F. Stone, Louis Brandeis, and Benjamin N. Cardozo; while Justice Owen J. Roberts and Chief Justice Charles Evans Hughes apparently sought to preserve a balance between the two groups. The average age of the Justices was nearly seventy-two. The federal judiciary at all levels seemed to be mounting an attack upon New Deal legislation, issuing 1,600 injunctions against the government—in 1935, there were 36 alone. The administration watched anxiously as some of these cases moved up to the Supreme Court. A series of blows fell quickly as the Court ruled adversely on the "hot oil" case (a law banning interstate shipment of oil produced in violation of state quotas) and the Railroad Retirement Act. Then in May 1935, the Court unanimously struck down the NRA in the Schechter Poultry or "sick chicken" case. The Court majority ruled that the selling of poultry did not come under the interstate commerce powers of the federal government and that Congress unconstitutionally had delegated legislative powers to the executive. The Court invalidated the AAA in 1936 by a vote of six to three, on the grounds that the processing tax constituted an improper delegation of legislative functions and an invasion of the reserved powers of the states. The justices also struck down the Guffey-Snyder Bituminous Coal Act in a five to four decision and restricted the powers of the Securities and Exchange Commission in another decision. The Court, in a case directly affecting presidential powers, ruled that the chief executive could not remove members of such quasi-judicial bodies as the Federal Trade Commission. Clearly many of these decisions reflected not so much the requirements of the Constitution as the personal preferences and prejudices of the justices. The deeply disappointed Roosevelt exclaimed to reporters, "We have been relegated to the horse-and-buggy definition" of the Constitution.

Apparently Roosevelt had decided to attack the Supreme Court even prior to his re-election in 1936. Meanwhile, he sought to repair much of the damage done by the adverse decisions by obtaining stop-gap legislation from Congress. As noted earlier, the Wagner Act in 1935 saved the labor provision of the NRA. The Soil Conservation and Domestic Allotment Act of 1936 managed to curtail agricultural production through voluntary and compensated withdrawal of acreage for conservation purposes. In 1938, Congress enacted the second Agricultural Adjustment Act to limit production and achieve parity prices for crops via subsidies on a voluntary basis. Yet the administration feared that the Court might also strike down these and other measures. In his annual message in January 1937, Roosevelt called for legislation to promote opportunity for all citizens as "the deeper purpose of democratic government." Again, in his second inaugural address, the president spoke of "one-third of a Nation ill-housed, ill-clad, ill-nourished," and declared that the goal of his second administration would be to eradicate these ills.

But would the Supreme Court abide by the election returns and accept new sweeping social measures? Or would these too be doomed by hidebound justices? To forestall that possibility, Roosevelt in early 1937 suddenly sprang his "court packing" plan on a stunned Congress and nation. He believed that he had a popular mandate to achieve additional reform, and he resolved not to let the "Nine Old Men" on the Court frustrate the national will. To do otherwise, he feared, would entail the risk that society might break down and collapse into anarchy or fascist reaction.

Roosevelt had committed a serious political blunder, probably the greatest of his career. He failed to consult congressional leaders prior to his decision, and he underestimated the popular reverence for the Supreme Court as a body above politics. Instead of openly advocating a constitutional amendment to restrict the Court's powers, he presented to Congress a scheme that claimed to be a reform to improve the efficiency of the judiciary. For each Supreme Court justice reaching the age of seventy and not retiring, a new justice could be appointed up to a total membership of fifteen; additional judges would also be appointed on the lower levels of the judiciary, and other measures would be adopted to quicken the processes of adjudication. Chief executives since Thomas Jefferson's day had often fumed about the obstructionist role of the Supreme Court and had contemplated attempts to curb its review power. Yet conservatives condemned Roosevelt's plan as destroying the constitutional balance of the national government; bar associations denounced it, and so did a number of liberal supporters of the New Deal, such as Senator Burton K. Wheeler of Montana. Voluntary organizations to "save the Constitution" sprang up across the nation, and several state legislatures adopted resolutions against what Hoover labeled a court-packing scheme.

Too late to repair the damage, Roosevelt in a fireside talk tried frankly to explain his case to the people. His proposal, he declared, sought to "save the Constitution from the Court and the Court from itself." He unwisely refused compromises such as requiring a seven to two majority by the Court to invalidate federal laws or enlarging the Court by the addition of two more justices. Roosevelt was supremely confident after his re-election and determined to curtail the power of the Court. His case received a blow when Chief Justice Charles Evans Hughes publicly denied that the Court lagged in its work. Finally the Court undercut the president by reversing its recent trend. (Apparently the change was not a response to Roosevelt's attacks and had begun to take place before he announced the court scheme.) By a vote of five to four, the high court upheld the Wagern Act in the Jones and Laughlin Steel case and thereby seemed to presage acceptance of other important New Deal laws. Justice Van Debater also resigned under a new law permitting retirement at age seventy with full salary, and Roosevelt had his first opportunity to fill a vacancy. Subsequently the Court also validated the Social Security Act. Yet Roosevelt persisted in the fight, despite an adverse majority report by the Senate Judiciary Committee. Finally, after his loyal floor leader, Senator Joseph T. Robinson of Arkansas, died of apparent overstrain, Roosevelt had no choice but to retreat. Too many important members of his own party in Congress, many conservative southern Democrats but also a number of moderates and liberals, had opposed his plan. Although he took some comfort in the Court's more liberal turn—he had lost the battle but won the war, many said—Roosevelt had experienced his first serious defeat and blow to his myth of political invincibility that opened deep rifts within his own party. Yet, the Court fight at least speeded up the legitimatizing of the New Deal's vast expansion of federal powers and the changed role of government.[15]

THE CONSERVATIVE REACTION

A conservative coalition of Republican and southern Democratic congressmen, largely from rural areas, began to take shape. Members of this loose bloc shared a preference for balanced budgets and states' rights and looked with suspicion on welfare programs and the rise of organized labor. Southern white conservatives especially disliked the egalitarian effect of New Deal legislation on African Americans in the South and feared for the southern way of life. Moreover, as Jeffersonian Democrats, they disliked the burgeoning bureaucracy of the New Deal and its increasing orientation toward the urban masses after the 1936 elections. Many southern Democratic congressmen had given the New Deal only reluctant support in the past— on occasion not even that—and the Court fight emboldened them to move into more open opposition (Roosevelt's appointment of the liberal Senator Hugo Black of Alabama to Van Debater's place added to their displeasure).

The conservative coalition drew support from the public reaction against sit-down strikes and labor unrest during 1937, widely blamed on New Deal radicalism and "coddling" of the unions. Despite the new bloc's informality and lack of cohesion on all issues, it functioned well enough by 1939 to prevent further significant gains in New Deal legislation.

The year 1937 proved a difficult one for Roosevelt. Not only did he experience the Court defeat but Congress refused to endorse his plan for a sweeping reorganization of the executive branch. Roosevelt had proposed combining or subordinating a number of semi-independent executive agencies; the creation of two new cabinet-level departments, Social Welfare and Public Works; and provisions for six presidential administrative assistants. Many thoughtful observers, including a number of political scientists, had long advocated such reforms. Hoover had favored such a reorganization when president. Yet conservatively inclined Republicans and southern Democrats resisted strenuously and charged presidential dictatorial ambitions. They blocked the measure in 1937 and 1938, although it finally obtained approval in 1939 in a much weakened version. Even so, the act marked a major advance in managing a modern complex governmental machine.

A sharp economic slump in 1937 added to Roosevelt's difficulties. The president, influenced by his fiscally more conservative advisers led by Henry Morgenthau, Jr., the secretary of the treasury, and by his own inclinations, had reduced deficit spending and slashed WPA payrolls in 1936 in the mistaken belief that prosperity had returned. A recession promptly set in during the summer of 1937, causing farm prices to decline and unemployment to rise from about five to over nine and half million. Obviously the economy still required heavy federal spending, and Roosevelt by 1938 felt compelled to override conservative opposition to secure approval for increased outlays by the WPA. New Deal measures had not cured the depression but only alleviated it. Probably only really massive federal expenditures, as urged by Keynes and others, would have worked, but Roosevelt was too orthodox to accept that solution.

Despite huge Democratic majorities in Congress, Roosevelt had encountered serious resistance to the program he had presented to Congress in 1937. Resolving to remold his party into a more liberal movement, he attempted in the 1938 primaries to purge certain conservatives. Democratic senators and representatives, mostly southerners, such as senators Walter George of Georgia and "Cotton Ed" Smith of South Carolina. The effort backfired as most of them survived; the new Congress, with a larger Republican minority, thus became even more conservative. The major parties remained as coalitions of divergent interests without clear philosophical and ideological differences. The New Deal virtually came to an end. After 1938, the emphasis shifted to digesting gains already made and to questions of foreign policy that seemed more imperative as the world plunged toward another global conflict.[16]

Probably no chief executive since the days of Andrew Jackson aroused as much impassioned controversy as Roosevelt and his New Deal. Criticism varied from shrilly intemperate charges of dictatorship, socialism, or communism, to more reasonably expressed disapproval of centralization of federal authority at the expense of the states, impairment of self-reliance and initiative through welfare programs, and wasteful deficit spending and a huge public debt. Roosevelt personally became the butt of many ribald and cruel jokes about his health and family life. Some apoplectic critics could only refer to him as "that man." His wife Eleanor especially drew much abuse because of her clearly expressed sympathy for the lowly and oppressed of all races and her endorsement of liberal causes. Of course, Roosevelt also aroused deep affection and dedicated support, as the millions of votes he polled amply attested.

Was the New Deal revolutionary or evolutionary? Or essentially conservative? Oceans of ink have been used in attempts to answer these questions. Most historians now emphasize the continuity of the New Deal with the past. In their desperate battle against the depression, Roosevelt and his advisers drew freely from the ideas and programs of earlier years. The Populist and Progressive eras supplied a number of specific proposals for regulating the worker and less fortunate members of society. The experiences of mobilization in World War I provided another fruitful source of ideas and programs. Even the prosperous years of the twenties and the Hoover administration offered precedents for New Deal experiments and measures. In fact, it is difficult to think of a single New Deal program that in some way had not been suggested or tried in the past. In this sense, Roosevelt and his administration were not highly original. Most of his reforms flowed from existing circumstances and reflected public demands to cope with the deep social needs created or emphasized by the Great Depression.[17] Or to express it differently, the New Deal represented the culmination of a half-century of historical change marking the rise of an organizational type of capitalism and the development of the regulatory interventionist state.

Roosevelt's greatest personal contributions probably lay in his dynamic personality and optimism, his sympathy with the underprivileged and distressed, and his willingness to experiment and use more fully the powers of government in long overdue efforts at relief and reform; in all these, he benefited from comparison with his predecessor. Although a good politician, he was not the master politician often assumed as his defeats in the Court fight and his failure to remold the Democratic Party in the 1938 congressional elections revealed. His administrative tactics also left much to be desired, characterized by dependence on conflicting conservative and liberal advisers and his reluctance to grant clear-cut delegations of power and responsibility. New Deal agencies overlapped one another in a crazy-quilt jungle of conflicting authority and personal rivalries. Moreover, all the New Deal pump-priming spending and relief measures failed to overcome the depression. In 1939, on the eve of World War II, millions of people were still unemployed despite the expenditure of billions of dollars through the WPA and similar agencies. Roosevelt could never abandon his hope of returning to a balanced budget and could not bring himself to spend on the really gigantic scale necessary to eradicate the depression—that chance came with the national emergency created by the Second World War. Above all, he sought to preserve a modified capitalist structure, not destroy it. Clearly, as a practical politician he aimed his programs primarily to benefit the great middle class. Thus, although the New Deal helped a vast number of citizens, millions of blacks, slum dwellers, rural agricultural workers, and unemployed remained at the bottom of the economic ladder.

Yet even though the New Deal fell short of transforming American society, it still marked a bold new phase in American history. When judged against the past, its reforms remain impressive and enduring. The welfare-interventionist state had come to stay in America; New Deal reforms became a permanent part of the fabric of American life. In subsequent years, political debate raged not about whether gains such as Social Security, unemployment compensation, aid to agriculture, public power and conservation projects, and regulation of the economy should be kept, but about how to improve and better administer them. Thus, the Republican candidate in 1952, Dwight D. Eisenhower, declared, "Never again shall we allow a depression in the United States" and promised to mobilize the "full power" of government if necessary to that end. The New Deal had clearly marked an irreversible turning point in American life.

NOTES

1. David M. Kennedy, *Freedom from Fear: The American People in Depression and War, 1929–1945* (New York: Oxford University Press, 1999), p. 366.

2. Basil Rauch, *The History of the New Deal, 1933–1938* (New York: Capricorn Books, 1963).

3. Arthur M. Schlesinger, Jr., *The Politics of Upheaval, Volume 3: The Age of Roosevelt* (Boston: Houghton Mifflin, 1988).

4. Typically, it failed to challenge segregation in the South. See John A. Salmond, *The Civilian Conservation Corps, 1933–42* (Durham: North Carolina University Press, 1990).

5. Thomas K. McCraw, *TVA and the Power Fight, 1933–1939* (Philadelphia: Lippincott, 1971).

6. Irving Bernstein, *Turbulent Years: A History of the American Worker, 1933–1941* (Boston: Houghton Mifflin, 1970).

7. Theodore Saloutos, *The American Farmer and the New Deal* (Ames: Iowa State University Press, 1982).

8. John A. Hudson and George Wolfskill, *All but the People: Franklin D. Roosevelt and His Critics, 1933–1939* (New York: Macmillan, 1969).

9. Alan Brinkley, *Voices of Protest: Huey Long, Father Coughlin, and the Great Depression* (New York: Vintage, 1983).

10. William Ivy Hair, *The Kingfish and His Realm: The Life and Times of Huey Long* (Baton Rouge: Louisiana State University Press, 1996).

11. Melvyn Dubofsky and Warren van Tine, *John A. Lewis: A Biography* (New York: Quadrangle/New York Times Press, 1977).

12. George McJimsey, *The Presidency of Franklin Delano Roosevelt* (Lawrence: University Press of Kansas, 2000), p. 1.

13. Brian Balogh, "The Social Security Board as Political Actor," in *Federal Social Policy: The Historical Dimension*, edited by Ellis Hawley (University Park: Pennsylvania State University Press, 1988).

14. Robert A. Slayton, *Empire Statesman: The Rise and Redemption of Al Smith* (New York: Free Press, 2001).

15. William E. Leuchtenburg, "The Constitutional Revolution of 1937," in *The Great Depression*, edited by Victor Hoar (Vancouver, British Columbia: Copp Clark, 1969), pp. 31–83.

16. Kennedy, *Freedom from Fear*, p. 363.

17. Frank B. Freidel, *Franklin D. Roosevelt: A Rendezvous with Destiny* (New York: Little, Brown, 1991).

CHAPTER **3**

The Slow Death of Versailles

While the United States slid deeper into the slough of the Great Depression, the blight spread abroad, inflicting paralysis and despair on Europe and Asia. Only the rigidly controlled state economy of the Soviet Union remained relatively immune to the deadly disease that cursed the capitalist world. The depression not only inflicted incalculable loss and misery on millions of people across the globe, it wrecked the postwar system established at Versailles in 1919. Over the ensuing decade, its provisions held a tumultuous peace. At home, America was trying to pull itself out of the Great Depression but found its attention increasingly diverted to Europe and Asia where the rise of Adolf Hitler in Germany, Benito Mussolini in Italy, Joseph Stalin in the U.S.S.R., and ultra-conservative militarists in Japan spelled out a formula clearly anathema to American interests. The 1930s proved that America could not be protected by any self-imposed isolation and remain oblivious to what was happening in Europe. Thus, despite America's best efforts to concentrate on domestic efforts to end the Great Depression, the slow death of Versailles increasingly demanded Washington's attention.

FOREIGN POLICY WITHOUT A RUDDER

The collapse of the international economic system seemed to tip the balance almost everywhere toward irrationalism, violence, and war. In Germany, the frail democracy of the Weimar Republic crumbled as Adolf Hitler grasped dictatorial power; Italy already had succumbed to the posturing

Fascist dictator, Benito Mussolini; totalitarian parties on the left and right proliferated throughout Europe, even in the old democracies of Britain and France; and in the Far East, right wing, supernationalist, and militaristic groups surged to the fore with their plans for solving Japan's problems through imperialism and conquest.

At the same time as trouble was brewing abroad, the Great Depression had a profound impact on the conduct of American diplomacy. As one observer put it, "It palsied the hands of American statesmen and sent them searching for formulas and phrases in which to settle, so they hoped, the difficulty of the moment."[1] Part of the reason was that the depression intensified isolationist sentiment in the United States. Trying desperately to achieve domestic economic recovery and fearful of another series of wars in Asia and Europe, most Americans seemed more determined than ever to erect an isolationist wall around their country. The neutrality laws adopted in the mid-thirties served notice of that determination. A strange paralysis of will seemed to afflict not only the United States but also the great European democracies. Great Britain and France almost supinely observed the rise of totalitarian dictators who openly expressed their contempt for democracy and barely troubled to hide their plans to "rectify" the Versailles settlement. Only belatedly did the western democracies, the United States most tardily of all, recognize the peril and act to meet it.

East Asia had seemed to promise a new era of progress and stability during the twenties. The great powers had curbed the arms race and agreed to preserve the territorial status quo in the Pacific at the Washington Naval Conference of 1921–22. In Japan, moderates held power and pursued a policy of conciliation toward China and cooperation with the western powers. Meanwhile, at home they began to curb military expenditures and undertook a number of social reforms. Even China seemed to make progress toward unity and stability. By 1929, the heir to the Nationalist Party leadership, Jiang Jieshi (Chiang Kai-shek), had succeeded, at least outwardly, in unifying his country.

By the beginning of the 1930s, however, the region seethed with change, discontent, and conflict. Once again, the U.S.S.R., China, and Japan had become embroiled in a conflict over Manchuria, a fertile and strategically important frontier area that had long been a center of rivalry.[2] By 1937, Japan, a country now governed by anti-Western ultraconservatives and supernationalists, had driven back Chinese troops in Manchuria, pulled out of the League of Nations (1933), embarked upon an aggressive military buildup program that flagrantly contravened the London Naval Agreement of 1930, and had completely disregarded the territorial agreements of the Washington Conference. It confronted the United States, along with the other major powers that maintained interests in the region, with a direct and serious challenge.[3]

President Herbert Hoover differed rather sharply with his secretary of state, Henry L. Stimson, over Far Eastern policy.[4] Although not a narrow isolationist by any means, Hoover was determined to limit America's foreign commitments and to keep the nation at peace. Moreover, coping with the depression at home monopolized his time and energies. Hoover had not known Stimson well and decided on him for the State Department only after three other men had declined the post. Stimson, an old follower of Theodore Roosevelt and a former governor general of the Philippines, came from a stern mold. Confident, moralistic, and with a Roman sense of duty, he conceived of world relations as governed by strict standards of moral principles and mutual respect. He sympathized with China, but more importantly, he viewed Japanese aggression as threatening the entire world system established at Versailles and upon which, he was convinced, rested world peace. Contrasting with Hoover's views on Far Eastern policy, Stimson was at first inclined to trust the Japanese civilian leaders to restrain the military. Like many observers, he overestimated the strength of the moderates and underestimated the determination of the Japanese army.

The United States obviously lacked sufficient naval power and popular will to restrain Japan. Moreover, American moral gestures affronted one of its best customers. American trade with China, despite the old illusion of a vast potential market, was very small while Japan was the third largest purchaser of American exports. American policy toward Japan's aggression in Manchuria reflected a high degree of moralistic outrage and traditional missionary-nourished sympathy with China. Many Japanese, however, regarded Western condemnation as hypocritical at best. In the words of Yosuke Matsuoka, later Japan's foreign minister, "The Western Powers taught Japan the game of poker but after acquiring most of the chips they pronounced the game immoral and took up contract bridge." There was a realistic element also—Stimson feared that Japan had undermined the postwar settlement and if unchecked would stimulate aggression elsewhere.

Franklin D. Roosevelt's early foreign policy has aroused much debate, with critics characterizing it as a time of drift and inconsistency. Did he adhere essentially to the neo-isolationist course of his Republican predecessors, avoiding binding political commitments abroad? Or did he recognize American interests in a stable world and seek cooperation with other states to curb aggression and war?[5] Roosevelt took a great interest in international affairs, as his private correspondence amply reveals, reflecting his education and his earlier service in the Wilson administration. But in practice, at least through 1936, he followed a course not greatly different from that of Hoover. In part, this was because domestic issues of recovery and reform absorbed most of his energies. Furthermore, these were years of mounting withdrawal sentiment in America. A practical politician, Roosevelt well realized the need for caution in foreign affairs in order to obtain the support of powerful liberal isolationists in Congress for his domestic legislation. He once remarked, "It's a terrible thing to look over your shoulder when you are trying to lead—and to find no one there." But equally important, despite his internationalist or Wilsonian orientation, Roosevelt could not be completely impervious to the isolationist current of his day—to some degree, he too shared isolationist views and emotions.[6] Consequently, Roosevelt's first administration revealed drift and inconsistency, with isolationist and internationalist policies incongruously intermixed.

Cordell Hull, sixty-one years old when he took office, served longer than any other secretary of state—eleven years and nine months before he resigned at the end of 1944. A Tennessee politician and dedicated Wilsonian, Hull viewed world affairs from a Wilsonian perspective of idealistic and moral principles.[7] He had a rather simple panacea for world troubles: freer trade, revival of morality, and the application of international law. Hull's absorbing interest was to remove or reduce barriers to international trade. In other areas, he lacked specific solutions and was inclined to deliver moral lectures to erring foreign governments. Hull indeed resembled the great leader he so revered—like Wilson, he had a pronounced penchant for expressing moral indignation. He made his most significant contributions to New Deal foreign policy in trade reciprocity and the Good Neighbor Policy, but his naive view of power politics and his faith in moral exhortations poorly fitted him to deal with the threat of aggressions in Europe and the Far East. Although never close to Roosevelt and highly suspicious—with much justification—of the president's very able and sophisticated friend in the State Department, Undersecretary Sumner Welles, Hull nevertheless played an important part in American foreign policy until Pearl Harbor. Thereafter, he found himself increasingly by-passed.[8]

Roosevelt continued his predecessor's short-sighted course toward the League of Nations and the war debts question. During the 1932 election, Roosevelt had conciliated William Randolph Hearst and other isolationist die-hards when he assured an audience that the present League of Nations had fallen away from Wilson's ideal and the United States had no place in it. He even failed to name an ambassador to the league, the least that many internationalists expected, and he left it to Secretary of Labor Francis Perkins to get the United States into the International Labor Organization. Hoover had shown some interest in scaling down the war debts owed to America. Roosevelt, realizing this would be highly unpopular in the United States, continued to insist upon full payment of the debts. When all the European debtors except Finland defaulted in whole or in part, he signed the 1934 Johnson Act prohibiting private or governmental loans to foreign governments in default. Subsequently in 1940 and 1941 he regretted thus tying his hands in foreign affairs.

The World Disarmament Conference, finally convened in 1932 after years of planning, still limped along when Roosevelt entered office. The conference was large—some fifty-nine nations were represented—and it held grand ambitions. Yet it had become, as one observer has put it, "an un-mitigated nuisance."[9] France demanded security before reductions, and Germany wanted equality with France. Hoover previously had attempted to make the conference a success, first by suggesting the abolition of all offensive weapons and then by proposing one-third reduction in all armaments. Roosevelt also tried offering a package containing a pledge of nonaggression, overall arms reductions, and an American promise in case of crisis to consult with other powers; if the United States agreed on the designation of an aggressor, it would not interfere with any sanctions the league might impose. Roosevelt apparently dared not go further toward collective security. In any case, the conference ended in failure when Hitler ordered the German delegates to walk out of the meeting and announced that Germany would withdraw from the League of Nations.

Hull finally obtained the tariff reductions that he had desired to revive international trade and promote a more peaceful world. By the Reciprocal Trade Agreement Act of 1934, regularly renewed in subsequent years, the executive could negotiate agreements with other countries, reducing existing tariff rates by as much as 50 percent. The State Department completed sixteen agreements within the first three years under the act, most of them with Latin America. By 1940, the number had increased to twenty-two. Apart from winning some good will abroad, and some quickening of trade, especially in Latin America, the reciprocal trade approach fell lamentably short of Hull's liberal dream. Too many other countries, especially the dictatorships, preferred protectionism or governmental bartering.

Roosevelt realistically decided that the time had arrived to recognize the Soviet regime in the U.S.S.R. His Republican predecessors had continued Wilson's policy of nonrecognition, reflecting moral disapproval of Communist ideology, methods of government, and the Soviets' repudiation of foreign debts. While most Americans approved nonrecognition, a number of liberals always had been inclined toward tolerance, or even endorsement, of the Soviet system as an experiment for the improvement of mankind. Many Americans mistakenly viewed Lenin's New Economic Policy as indicating an abandonment of socialism and a return to the free enterprise system in the U.S.S.R. After Lenin's death in 1924, Americans observed with some pleasure that he was replaced by an obscure Joseph Stalin instead of that well-known and feared advocate of world revolution, Leon Trotsky. Moreover, many American businessmen subscribed to the illusion that recognition would bring increased trade with Russia, especially after most European countries recognized the former outcast and renewed their economic relations. The Great Depression heightened the lure of trade, which Soviet authorities cleverly exploited to facilitate diplomatic recognition.[10] Moscow initially sought recognition primarily for reasons of prestige. The growth of the fascist threat in Europe and Japanese expansion in the Far East also made recognition attractive for the security it might provide.

By 1933, a number of large American firms, such as General Electric, Ford, and International Harvester had entered the Soviet market. In 1930, the United States briefly surpassed all competitors in exports to the U.S.S.R. Stalin's first Five Year Plan, calling for increased mechanization of industry and agriculture, seemed to promise vast new opportunities for American exporters. They felt acute disappointment, therefore, when the volume subsequently fell off and Germany replaced the United States as the U.S.S.R.'s foremost supplier. Business spokesmen and politicians such as senators Hiram Johnson (R-CA) and William Borah (R-ID) argued that recognition would greatly facilitate the growth of American trade with the Soviets. Of course, many Americans remained opposed to recognition on moral and religious grounds. Patriotic groups such as the American Legion and the Daughters of the American Revolution, members of Protestant and Roman Catholic churches, the American Federation of Labor (AFL), and the chambers of commerce provided the bulk of the opposition. As long as Hoover occupied the White House, these negative viewpoints prevailed. As the El Paso *Herald* sneered at proponents of recognition on trade grounds, "A dangerous Red is any Russian who appears in America without placing an order for machinery."

Roosevelt favored formal diplomatic relations on the realistic grounds that whatever one thought of it the Soviet regime had existed for sixteen years; moreover, a restoration of official relations hopefully would bolster the status quo in the Pacific against Japan and would strengthen nonaggressive forces in Europe. After preliminary explorations, Soviet Foreign Commissar Maxim Litvinov arrived in Washington, making it clear that Moscow preferred unconditional recognition prior to negotiations on outstanding issues, in accordance with the pattern it had followed in establishing diplomatic relations with other countries. The American authorities, however, insisted on negotiations first. With Roosevelt taking a direct part in the conversations, recognition was completed on November 16, 1933. The arrangement established diplomatic relations, provided freedom of religious worship for Americans in the Soviet Union, and promised to halt Soviet propaganda and subversion in the United States. Roosevelt and his advisers insisted upon the religious provision, primarily because the American people took such issues seriously and had long objected to the Soviet regime as godless. Public opinion also required the promise that neither government would interfere "in any manner" in the internal affairs of the other. The U.S.S.R. dropped its claims for compensation for damages during the American intervention in North Russia and Siberia and promised further negotiations on the question of debts. American claims totaled over $630 million, including about $187 million owed by the former provisional government in bond issues, private loans, and property confiscations. In their "gentlemen's agreement," Litvinov mentioned a possible settlement for $75 million, while Roosevelt referred to a figure of $150 million.[11]

Most Americans approved the establishment of formal relations. Litvinov was honored at a farewell luncheon at the Waldorf-Astoria Hotel, attended by the representatives of such giant capitalistic firms as J. P. Morgan and the Pennsylvania Railroad. The president of International Business Machines even urged Americans to promote better relations in the future by refraining "from any criticism of the present form of Government adopted by Russia." Unfortunately for such enthusiasts, recognition of the Soviets proved a disappointment. Trade remained small, primarily because the Soviet Union lacked the necessary funds, and private long-term credits were deemed too risky by businessmen and financiers. The hoped-for diplomatic benefits also proved illusory, the two powers failing to achieve any notable collaboration either in regard to Japan or Europe. The debt negotiations also ended in deadlock. Moscow, in effect, refused to agree to any sum unless the United States provided double that amount in the form of long-term governmental loans or credits. Since such a settlement would merely increase Soviet indebtedness to the United States, the State Department rejected it. The Soviets, needless to say, continued their propaganda and subversion in this country. When Hull protested the continuation of revolutionary activities, trumpeted at the Seventh Congress of the Comintern at Moscow in 1935, the Soviet government blandly disavowed the private and separate international Communist apparatus that happened to be meeting on Soviet soil. Litvinov reportedly had told an American Communist when he made the agreement in 1933, "The letter [pledge] is a scrap of paper which will soon be forgotten." The State Department did not forget it, however, and lodged repeated protests. A growing number of Americans soon came to view recognition as a serious mistake.

RELATIONS WITH LATIN AMERICA

Long before the era of the New Deal, the American government had begun to cultivate better relations with Latin America. The Wilson administration and its Republican successors in the 1920s became aware of Latin American resentment of the Colossus of the North and tried to assuage it. Latin American critics cited a long list of Yankee "crimes" and blunders: the "rape of Panama"; armed interventions and military rule in the Caribbean; economic penetration and exploitation of Latin America; and the refusal of the United States to subject its actions to international restraints by joining the League of Nations. Above all, the Monroe Doctrine and its infamous Roosevelt Corollary—justifying preventive intervention in the Caribbean in the name of security—aroused hatred and fear among neighbors to the south. American businessmen, eager for new markets and investment opportunities, urged a more conciliatory course on the State Department. So did many other Americans, appalled at the often exaggerated accounts of harsh military rule by the marines in Haiti and the Dominican Republic. For these reasons, and because after 1918 the United States no longer felt insecure about the Panama Canal, the government began to abandon its benevolent imperialism.

Hoover made such notable contributions to Pan Americanism that some historians credit him with originating the Good Neighbor Policy. While president-elect, Hoover undertook a good will tour of Latin America in 1928 during which he tried to dispel distrust and several times used the phrase "good neighbor" in his speeches. In office, he refrained from further armed interventions, despite revolutionary disturbances in Panama; removed American troops from Nicaragua in 1933; and promised withdrawal in Haiti. He also abandoned the moralistic Wilson recognition policy for a return to the traditional practice of recognizing de facto regimes regardless of how they came to power. Yet like his predecessors, Hoover refused to pledge that armed intervention would never again be used. Treaty arrangements with several Caribbean states sanctioned the right of intervention, and he and his advisers felt the United States could not be certain that it might not again be necessary to intervene to protect foreign lives and property.

President Roosevelt, in his inaugural address, pledged a policy of the Good Neighbor toward the entire world, but the phrase soon came to be applied exclusively to his policies in Latin America. His contributions to hemispheric harmony constituted virtually a new policy and entitled his administration to primary credit as the originator of the Good Neighbor Policy. The policy paid handsome dividends in promoting the security and unity of the Western Hemisphere as the danger of another world war increased. Latin Americans hailed Roosevelt as *"el gran democrata,"* and many viewed his New Deal as a model for reform in their own countries. His accomplishments in Latin America, his role as leader of the Western world during the Second World War, and his role as the spokesman for the aspirations of the common man everywhere earned Roosevelt near deification in Latin America. While historians would long debate the "true" authorship of the Good Neighbor Policy, Latin Americans almost unanimously gave the credit to Roosevelt.[12]

The Good Neighbor Policy is best defined as noninterventionism and the multilateralization of the Monroe Doctrine from a U.S. doctrine into a hemispheric defense responsibility. Further, it supplanted the high protectionism of the Republican era with reciprocal trade agreements and was prepared to sacrifice when necessary private American economic interests in Latin America for the national interests of the United States. Cordell Hull delighted apprehensive Latin Americans at the Seventh Pan American Conference at Montevideo in 1933 when he voted for a resolution of nonintervention by armed force in the internal affairs of any Western Hemisphere state, except as sanctioned by international law. He reiterated this pledge without any reservation at the special Pan American Conference convened at Buenos Aires in 1936 that was personally opened by Roosevelt. Latin Americans cheered these renunciations by the United States. A Mexican delegate at the Montevideo conference expressed the conviction that "there is in the White House an admirable, noble, and good man—a courageous man who knows the errors of the past but who feels that the errors really belong to the past."

In the interval between these two conferences, the marines left Haiti as Hoover had promised, and in 1934, the State Department agreed to abrogate the so-called Platt Amendment with Cuba, a treaty that had given the United States the right to intervene in the island. The latter action came only after the United States twice perilously neared armed intervention during the overthrow of the Gerardo Machado dictatorship and its successor. Sumner Welles, American ambassador to Cuba, had encouraged Machado's fall, but he was greatly distressed when the next regime also was toppled and threatened armed intervention. Rejecting Welles's recommendation, an alarmed Roosevelt and Hull perceived the danger that diplomatic interference might culminate in armed intervention. These experiences made Roosevelt willing to renounce forceful measures unconditionally.

Alarmed at the threat of war in Europe and by fascist activities in Latin America, the United States sought to multilateralize the Monroe Doctrine from a U.S. unilateral policy into a collective defense system for the Western Hemisphere. Argentina, traditionally a rival of the United States for leadership in the Western Hemisphere and a country increasingly under strong fascist influences, repeatedly blocked Washington's proposals for a binding commitment for mutual measures to repel outside aggression. Hull finally managed to obtain a loose declaration at the Eighth Pan American Conference held at Lima in 1938, for consultation and co-operation against subversion or external threats to the peace of the hemisphere. Canada, a fully self-governing dominion within the British Commonwealth, remained apart from the Pan American movement in order to preserve its nationality and its ties to Britain. In effect, however, Roosevelt brought Canada under the scope of the inter-American system when at Kingston, Ontario, in 1938 he declared that the United States could not see Canada threatened by conquest. After the outbreak of the Second World War, Canada and the United States concluded joint defensive arrangements. The United States thus prepared the way for close collaboration during World War II and the creation of the Organization of American States after the war.

The Roosevelt administration revealed during these years that while it continued to be concerned with the legitimate economic interests of American citizens in Latin America, it would no longer act as a bond collector for

Wall Street. In fact, when necessary, the administration prepared to sacrifice substantial private interests for the sake of better political relations with Latin America. When Bolivia expropriated Standard Oil Company holdings and Venezuela demanded increased royalties from American oil companies operating in that country, the State Department refrained from threats or retaliation and sought to arrange equitable settlements. Mexico proved more difficult, but there too the State Department successfully applied the new tactics. President Lázaro Cárdenas, a leftist reformer, expropriated foreign-owned lands and oil properties in 1938. Although an exasperated Hull inclined toward retaliation, Roosevelt, at the inspiration of Ambassador Joseph Daniels, arranged settlements that left American investors highly displeased but avoided a serious crisis between the two countries. American oil companies had to accept compensation of $24 million for holdings they evaluated at half a billion dollars. A subsequent Import-Export Bank loan from the United States helped Cárdenas's successor pay for even these reduced compensations.

THE GROWTH OF ISOLATIONISM

By the middle of the 1930s, isolationist sentiment was growing. With economic distress at home and war clouds abroad demonstrating that the Great Crusade of World War I had all but failed, the conviction grew that the United States should shun foreign entanglements that might lead to war. As Senator Borah said in 1934, America was not and would not be isolated economically, "but in all matters political, in all commitments or any nature or kind, which may encroach in the slightest upon the free and unembarrassed action of our people, or which circumscribe their discretion and judgment, we have been free, we have been independent, we have been isolationist." Isolationism seemed particularly strong in the Midwest, though it was not limited to that region. The midwestern reaction was a reflection of a large number of German and Scandinavian-Americans and geographical remoteness, but above all of agrarian radicalism. Farmers looked with distrust upon eastern big business and financial firms as exploiters of rural folk. Many agrarian isolationists believed that big businessmen and financiers had brought about intervention in the recent world war, from which they had profited at the farmers' expense. Of course, isolationism appealed to those other than agricultural groups. It drew support as well from urban reformers and idealists and cut across political lines. Isolationism gradually became more conservative as liberals swung toward internationalism in the last years of the decade.

Antiwar novels, articles, movies, and revisionist histories reflected and contributed to the popular mood of pacifism, disillusionment, and withdrawal. Peace movements proliferated and flourished, and college students, like their counterparts in the late 1960s, demonstrated against war and demanded the expulsion of ROTC units from campuses. Novels by writers such as Erich Remarque—his *All Quiet on the Western Front* (1929) became a popular movie (1930)—Ernest Hemingway, and John Dos Passos depicted war as senseless and barbaric. Muckraking books by Helmuth C. Englebrecht, *Merchants of Death* (1937), and George Seldes, *Iron, Blood and Profits* (1934), strengthened the popular conviction that the common man fought so that bankers and munitions manufacturers might prosper. Some historians revised the previously accepted version that Germany had been solely responsible for the war in 1914 and for American involvement in 1917. Revisionist scholars sought not merely the truth about events in 1914 to 1917 but to influence current public discussions on foreign policy and to prevent intervention in another war injurious to liberal reform at home. Harry Elmer Barnes pioneered in revisionist studies during the mid-1920s. Barnes had been an ardent supporter of Wilsonian internationalism until disillusioned by the postwar settlement. His *Genesis of the World War* (1926), a Book-of-the-Month Club selection, and C. C. Tansill's *America Goes to War* (1938), also indicted the one-sided nature of American neutrality in 1914–1917. To a very large degree, the revisionists won the intellectual community to their views and helped create that climate of public opinion that explains passage of the neutrality laws in the 1930s. A Gallup Poll in April 1937, for example, revealed that 64 percent of the public regarded American intervention in the First World War as a mistake. In that same year, the emergency Peace Crusade observed the twenty-ninth anniversary of the 1917 war entry with a "no foreign war crusade," and those senators and representatives who had voted against war in 1917 were lavishly praised.

The Nye Committee hearings were symptomatic of the popular disillusionment. Responding to demands for federal regulation of the arms industry, from groups such as the Women's International League for Peace and Freedom, the Senate in 1934 authorized a special inquiry into the munitions industry. The administration, caught off guard, failed to block the selection of Republican Senator Gerald P. Nye of North Dakota, a rough-hewn arch-isolationist, to head the inquiry. Roosevelt probably could have made a greater effort to remind the nation that the country had fought for more serious reasons than profits in the recent war, but he failed to do so. Apparently Roosevelt shared popular aversion to arms profiteers, and he hoped to obtain controls over them. Nye's committee, heavily over-representative of rural isolationist viewpoints but also backed by urban pacifists and anti–big business liberals, staged a public circus in uncovering the huge profits made by eastern financiers and the munitions industry during the neutrality years. The committee's sensational releases helped convince many citizens that profit-hungry capitalists had dragged the United States into the First World War. As Nye summed it up, "When Americans went into the fray, they little thought that they were there and fighting to save the skins of American bankers who . . . had two billions of dollars of loans to the Allies in jeopardy." The investigation seemed almost as much anti–big business in bias as anti-war, and it reflected the widespread view that greedy bankers and industrialists encouraged international strife. Americans seemed periodically susceptible to "devil theories" of history, as the "military-industrial complex" stereotype of the late 1960s again indicated.

Ironically, Roosevelt suggested neutrality legislation to the Nye Committee in 1935 to bar American citizens from traveling on belligerent ships. A threatened conflict between Italy and Ethiopia offered the occasion. Roosevelt apparently hoped to avoid the risks of being involved in a future war by issues of neutral rights; American policy, freed of the burden that had plagued President Wilson, then could be based on more fundamental national interests. Roosevelt hoped that any ban against the arms trade would permit him to discriminate between aggressive and defensive nations, but he encountered a threatened filibuster by the pacifist and isolationist bloc in Congress. He accepted a substitute measure, prepared by senators Key Pittman (D-NV) and William Borah, that provided for a mandatory arms embargo. Upon a presidential proclamation of the existence of a foreign war, the sale or transportation of munitions to belligerent countries would be prohibited, and at the executive's discretion, citizens could be warned not to take passage on belligerent vessels. Roosevelt, to Hull's disappointment, signed the measure because it was due to expire in six months and he hoped at that time to obtain a more satisfactory law. Apparently he also thought that application of the 1935 Neutrality Act would hurt Italy in case of war with Ethiopia.

When Congress passed the Neutrality Act, Europe seemed once more on the threshold of a major war. As noted earlier, fascism, a peculiar blend of idealism, romantic nationalism, conservatism, and militarism, had come to power in Italy in 1922. Led by Benito Mussolini, the Fascists achieved some worthwhile reforms and social stability but at the price of a totalitarian dictatorship. Mussolini in general remained pacific in foreign policy until the Great Depression and the rise of Adolf Hitler in Germany began to undermine the Versailles settlement. Hitler adeptly exploited popular resentment of the Versailles Treaty, mass unemployment and economic distress, and the weaknesses of the postwar democracy in Germany. His National Socialist, or Nazi, Party espoused policies similar to Italian fascism and took power in early 1933, only a few weeks before Roosevelt's inauguration in the United States. Using violence and intimidation, Hitler fastened a brutal dictatorship on the German people. He began to rearm Germany, threatened to use force to rectify the 1919 settlement, and launched violently anti-Jewish persecutions within the Third Reich. The American ambassador, William E. Dodd, warned the president and the State Department about Hitler's plans for conquest, while the anti-Semitic Nuremberg Laws fully revealed the vile nature of the Nazi regime. A growing exodus of German Jews fled to the United States, among them the noted physicist Albert Einstein. (It should be noted, however, that the administration and Congress, owing to apathy and prejudice, failed to relax the immigration laws to permit large numbers of Jews to seek haven in America.) Yet until Mussolini's Ethiopian venture revealed the supineness of Great Britain and France, Hitler acted fairly cautiously in foreign affairs.

When Mussolini invaded Ethiopia in the fall of 1935, the Council of the League of Nations condemned the attack and invoked economic sanctions prohibiting loans and the export of arms and war materials to Italy. The alarmed British and French governments, however, anxious not to drive Italy into Hitler's arms, carefully left oil, vital to Mussolini's war machine, off the list of sanctions. This appeasement of dictatorship also led to a still-born attempt at compromise, the Hoare-Laval plan for giving Mussolini two-thirds of Ethiopia, but public wrath in Britain and France caused its repudiation. Meanwhile, Mussolini's legions, armed with advanced weapons and using poison gas, completed the conquest of primitive Ethiopia, the first victim to appeasement.

Roosevelt and Hull deemed it politically unwise to cooperate openly with League sanctions, but they invoked the Neutrality Laws even though Mussolini had not formally declared war. Unfortunately, and contrary to the administration's expectations, this action had little effect on Italy, which did not need to import arms, while hurting Ethiopia who did. The administration then called for a moral embargo against oil shipments to Italy, urging American firms not to increase supplies to Mussolini's war machine. The administration found it difficult to enforce the moral embargo, however, and its action failed to encourage the League of Nations to adopt sterner sanctions. Britain and France thereby missed a promising opportunity to involve the American government more closely with League efforts to defend the peace. Their timidity encouraged Hitler to reoccupy and fortify the Rhineland, to restore conscription, and to launch a large naval and military aviation program in defiance of the Versailles Treaty. Conclusion of the Rome-Berlin Axis in 1936 solidified the new alignment of fascist powers against the Western democracies, supplemented in the same year by German and Italian anti-Comintern pacts with Japan.

Congress approved the second Neutrality Act in February 1936, while Mussolini digested his Ethiopian conquest. The act prohibited loans as well as sales of arms to belligerents and directed the president to extend the ban to new belligerents entering a war, an obvious warning of noncooperation with League members that might be drawn into hostilities through sanctions against aggressors. The isolationist tenor of American sentiment and policy became even clearer when the Spanish Civil War broke out in the summer of 1936. Despite a nonintervention agreement among the major European powers, Germany and Italy actively supported the arch-conservative and fascist-tinged rebel forces of General Francisco Franco against the Spanish republican armies. Many American liberals and intellectuals sympathized deeply with republican Spain and several thousand American volunteers fought for the republic in the Abraham Lincoln Battalion and other units. Although the Communists were active in organizing pro-Loyalist committees in America, most American sympathizers simply admired the heroic resistance of the Republicans and viewed the civil war as a crucial struggle between democracy and fascism. Conversely, a minority of American conservatives and Roman Catholic spokesmen saw Franco as a bulwark against atheism, socialism, and communism in Spain. The majority of Americans, however, tended to be apathetic or neutral about the civil war. A poll classified 12 percent of the public pro-Franco, 22 percent pro-Loyalists, and the remainder either neutral or without an opinion.[13]

The Roosevelt administration gave full support to Anglo-French efforts to isolate the Spanish Civil War. Although normally a recognized government is permitted to import arms despite internal disturbances, Roosevelt and Hull treated the conflict virtually as one between two sovereign states. They proclaimed a moral embargo against shipment of war material to either the rebels or the legal government in Spain. Subsequently Congress formally extended the neutrality law to apply to the civil war. The Loyalists alone suffered from the Anglo-French and American attempts to isolate the conflict, for Germany, and especially Italy, cynically violated their nonintervention pledges to supply Franco with arms and "volunteer" troops. President Roosevelt was to contemplate raising the embargo against the Loyalists, but he desisted because of domestic opposition and the obvious hopelessness of the republican cause.

The third Neutrality Act, enacted in 1937, marked the final stage in the effort to immunize America from war. Although Roosevelt still desired more flexible provisions to permit him to discriminate between aggressors and their victims, he was deeply involved in the court packing fight and left the responsibility primarily to Senator Pittman of Nevada, the chairman of the Senate Committee on Foreign Relations. Pittman, not an ardent internationalist and anxious to preserve the independent role of his committee, repeatedly advised the administration to move cautiously in seeking modifications in the neutrality laws. The 1937 act renewed the ban on arms sales and loans to belligerents and prohibited travel on belligerent passenger and merchant vessels whenever the president should proclaim the existence of a foreign war. At the president's discretion, the exportation of nonmilitary goods to belligerents could also be prohibited during any war in the next two years unless done on a "cash and carry" basis. In a sense, the new measure represented a compromise, benefiting the Axis powers in case of war with an arms embargo and yet offering the Western democracies, who would control the seas, the opportunity to purchase vital raw materials for cash and to transport them away in their own ships. "Cash and carry" also reflected an agrarian bias against eastern industrialists and financiers, and a determination to keep open profitable markets for farm products in Europe.

The president found his freedom to maneuver sharply restricted by the neutrality law. Arms and loan bans would have to apply to aggressive and peaceful states alike. Underlying this act and the earlier neutrality laws were highly debatable assumptions that no basic moral issues were involved in the struggles taking place abroad, no fundamental American national interests were at stake, and that the nation could be secure in its hemisphere regardless of external developments. For the sake of isolation and peace, Congress had abandoned the nation's traditional policy of defending neutral trading rights on the high seas. As several commentators quipped, the neutrality acts appeared to be an attempt by Congress to legislate the United States post facto out of World War I.

THROWING OFF THE SHACKLES OF ISOLATIONISM

Prior to 1937, Roosevelt and Hull had not followed a consistent foreign policy. Not only had the administration accepted crippling neutrality legislation without putting up prolonged resistance, but Roosevelt sometimes sounded an isolationist note in public. The Democratic platform in 1936 reassured the electorate that the country would not be pulled into war by political or commercial entanglements. During the campaign, Roosevelt declared his resolve to insulate America from foreign conflicts and remarked, "I hate war. I have passed unnumbered hours, I shall pass unnumbered hours, thinking and planning how war may be kept from the Nation." But the situation in China and the crises in Europe pressured Roosevelt to take a more decided internationalist course. He hoped somehow to prevent a general war but, if that failed, to strengthen peace-loving states against their assailants. When Japan launched the "China Incident" in 1937, his concern involved more than sympathy with China; it seemed to him that the forces of order and security everywhere stood on the defensive. Japan's aggressions comprised only one aspect of this assault against world peace and decency. Roosevelt did not invoke the neutrality laws in Japan's undeclared war because he wanted to give China whatever aid possible.

In his "Quarantine Speech" in Chicago, on October 5, 1937, President Roosevelt tried to alert the American people and to prepare them for a more responsible foreign policy. Speaking in the heartland of isolationist America, he indicated that the nation's security depended on cooperation with other peaceful states: "Let no one imagine that America will escape, that America may expect mercy, that this hemisphere will not be attacked." After proclaiming the principle that international gangsters should be segregated as society quarantines the carriers of dangerous diseases, Roosevelt declared, "We are determined to stay out of war . . . but we cannot *insure* ourselves against the disastrous effects of war and the danger of involvement; we cannot have complete protection in a world of disorder in which confidence and security have broken down." The address aroused favorable response across the country, but it also ignited isolationist criticism and charges of war mongering. Some alarmed isolationists even muttered threats of impeachment. It soon became apparent, however, that the president had no clear policy changes in mind.[14] He may have contemplated some kind of collective neutrality whereby, without adopting economic or military sanctions, peaceful states would morally condemn aggressive powers. In subsequent remarks to reporters, however, he beat a hasty retreat and denied even the intention of passing moral condemnation on the aggressors. In retrospect, it seems clear that Roosevelt burnt his fingers in Chicago and thereafter felt more apprehensive than probably he should have about the strength of isolationism in America.

The League of Nations condemned Japan's aggression in China as a violation of the Kellogg-Briand and Nine Power pacts, and suggested a conference of signatories of the Nine Power Pact. Shortly before the United States and the other signers, plus Russia, met in Brussels in November 1937, Roosevelt made it clear that he did not favor vigorous measures against Japan; apparently he saw the role of the conference simply as bringing moral pressure to bear. Japan declined to attend, and only Russia advocated strong measures. Britain and France left the initiative to the Untied States, while Roosevelt and Hull recoiled from economic sanctions against Japan. Consequently, the conference achieved nothing beyond a pious reaffirmation of treaty principles. The Brussels Conference was not only a fiasco but a disaster. The fact that it met encouraged China to continue resistance in the hope of substantial aid, while its failure emboldened Japan's leaders to persist in their course.

The *Panay* incident in December 1937 further revealed the reluctance of the United States to risk conflict with Japan. Japanese warplanes deliberately attacked the American gunboat *Panay* and three Standard Oil Company tankers on the Yangtze River and strafed survivors in the water. Yet unlike the *Maine* incident in 1898, most Americans reacted mildly and wanted to withdraw all U.S. ships and men from the area to avoid future incidents. The government accepted Japanese apologies and reparations. The incident also quickened congressional support for the so-called Ludlow Amendment to the Constitution, prohibiting war except in case of actual invasion or with majority approval in a national referendum. The administration had to exert strong pressure, including a letter from the president that was read in the House of Representatives, to block the bill from coming to the floor for formal debate and action.

Encouraged by slowly increasing public support for a stronger course, the State Department began to deal more firmly with Japan. The Two-Ocean Naval Act of 1938 vastly increased naval construction, even

isolationists accepted the need for greater hemispheric defense. Meanwhile, Japan, heretofore apologetic for many of her acts, openly proclaimed
in 1938 a "New Order" for East Asia; no longer would it give even lip-ser-
vice to the principles of the Open Door in China. Hull strongly objected to
the "New Order" and reasserted American rights in China and the Far East.
The administration gave Jiang Jieshi a small loan in 1938 to bolster China's
currency and its morale and slapped a moral embargo against the sale and
shipment of aircraft to Japan. Roosevelt ordered the Pacific Fleet moved
temporarily to Pearl Harbor, a graphic reminder to Tokyo of American
power and will to resist. Finally, the State Department opened the way for
economic retaliation on July 26, 1939, when it gave notice terminating the
Japanese-American commercial treaty of 1911.

War between the United States and Japan was not yet inevitable, although clearly the two countries followed sharply diverging courses. From
the standpoint of practical interests, American policy has been viewed as
highly unrealistic. The American economic stake in China, as noted before,
fell far short of its trade with Japan. Moreover, Japan clearly ranked as the
strongest power in East Asia. Would Washington have been wiser merely to
lodge formal protests against the aggressions in China while patiently
working for greater moderation by Japan? Or, if that failed, to have acquiesced to Japanese control of China as inevitable? From the later perspective
of the cold war and the Japanese-American Security Treaty, U.S. policy in
the 1930s has seemed questionable to some scholars. Roosevelt and Hull,
however, not gifted with hindsight, believed that aggression must be opposed lest it spread everywhere. In short, they saw Japan's attack upon
China as part of the general breakdown in world security and peace. Moreover, the American leaders thought that a greater display of firmness offered a chance of restraining Japan. Even after the European war erupted in
1939, Roosevelt and Hull continued to hope that hostilities could be
avoided with Japan, while they concentrated American attention upon Hitler's conquest of Europe. They did not view Japan as an immediate threat to
American security until Tokyo concluded the Tripartite Alliance with the
Axis powers in September 1940.

Public opinion splintered under the impact of foreign events. Isolationists and noninterventionists feared involvement in war and were increasingly suspicious of Roosevelt's leadership, as the Ludlow Amendment
indicated. The internationalists, however, felt a growing apprehension
about the Axis threat in Europe and Japanese militarism in Asia, and they
supported the administration's movement toward collective security.
Many previously pacifist or isolationist liberals began to shift into the internationalist camp. Some professed to fear the dangers of fascism at home,
where anti-Semites rallied behind fascist organizations such as William
Dudley Pelley's Silver Shirts, the German-American Bund, and the Christian Front, movements that were inflamed by the growing numbers of Jew-

ish refugees fleeing Central Europe.[15] The formation of the House Committee on Un-American Activities in 1938 also disturbed thoughtful citizens. Headed by Representative Martin Dies (D-TX), the committee tended to ignore right-wing activities and concentrated on ferreting out Communist infiltration and front organizations. The Dies Committee permitted witnesses at its hearings to make unsubstantiated and reckless charges of communism against individuals who often had no opportunity for rebuttal. Some 640 organizations were denounced as controlled or infiltrated by the Communists.

Communism had become more respectable during a time of crisis when the Soviet Union had joined the Western democracies in opposition to fascist aggression. In the United States, Earl Browder, who replaced William Z. Foster as General Secretary of the American Communist Party, pursued the Popular Front strategy, playing down revolutionary jargon and urging a coalition of all democratic forces to oppose fascism. A number of organizations, such as the American League Against Fascism, apparently had been founded by the Communists as front organizations to rally intellectuals and other groups. Browder boasted of his Revolutionary War ancestry and described communism as merely twentieth-century Americanism. The Communist Party successfully penetrated various peace and youth groups and some Congress of Industrial Organization (CIO) labor unions. A few also found places in the executive government, but none in key policy-making positions, and their importance has often been grossly exaggerated.

During 1938, Nazi dictator Adolf Hitler took the first two steps in his *Drang nach Osten*, or drive to the east, by annexing Austria and the predominantly German sections of Czechoslovakia, prompting British Prime Minister Neville Chamberlain to pay two visits during mid-September 1938 to the German dictator in an effort to broker a peaceful settlement. His missions were in vain; the further Britain, France, and Czechoslovakia moved toward Hitler's demands, the more extreme Hitler's demands became. By the end of September, when Roosevelt entered the fray, the continent was on the brink of war. Roosevelt also joined with Chamberlain and French Premier Edouard Daladier in a plea to Mussolini to persuade Hitler to accept a peaceful settlement that would give him substantially all he asked for. Hitler yielded to the extent of agreeing to meet with Mussolini and the French and British premiers in Munich. There, on September 29, Hitler, Mussolini, Chamberlain, and Daladier agreed on a plan that the Czech government perforce accepted. It differed little from Hitler's ultimatum of a week before, merely allowing slightly more time for Czech withdrawal from the surrendered area. Thus, it was assumed, war had been averted. Chamberlain told the people of England that he had brought back "peace with honor. I believe," he added, "it is peace in our time."[16]

Americans greeted the Munich settlement with profound relief that war had been avoided. Thus the American government and people at this time obviously favored appeasement of the Nazi führer. As Hitler violated his pledges and anti-Jewish outrages multiplied in Germany, Roosevelt publicly voiced disapproval. After the violent *Kristallnacht* in Germany, a wave of anti-Jewish riots and stringent repressive measures that followed the assassination of a German diplomat in Paris by a Jew, Roosevelt recalled the American ambassador in Berlin, remarking that "I myself could scarcely believe that such things could occur in a twentieth century civilization."[17] Hitler fully reciprocated American dislike and recalled his ambassador. He viewed the United States as a racially mongrelized society that could not even cope with the economic depression. America need not be taken seriously, he told his intimates in 1938, because it was too impotent to fight and would not go beyond meaningless moral gestures in international affairs. The German military shared his opinion. Using "racial arithmetic," Hitler concluded that the polyglot United States was held together only by the glue of 20 million superior Anglo-Saxons or 60 million of valuable racial stock; therefore, Germany with its larger population of Aryans was far more powerful. The neutrality laws merely strengthened his contempt.[18]

The Munich settlement proved to be but the prelude to the complete extinction of Czechoslovakia as an independent nation. Hungary and Poland at once demanded and received slices of territory where Magyars and Poles were numerous. Internal dissension between Czechs and Slovaks afforded Hitler an excuse for taking control of the destinies of those two ethnic divisions of the former republic. In March 1939, Bohemia-Moravia and Slovakia became German protectorates. While Hitler was helping himself to territory in Central Europe, Mussolini seized the occasion to strengthen Italy's position in the Mediterranean. On April 7, 1939, Italian troops occupied the independent state of Albania, which was, a few days later, added to the realms ruled over by Mussolini in the name of King Victor Emmanuel III.

Hitler had declared at Munich: "This [Sudetenland] is the last territorial claim which I have to make in Europe." His absorption of Czechoslovakia had given the lie to that declaration, and by April 1939, he was pressing Poland for consent to annexation of the free city of Danzig and a sort of German corridor across the Polish corridor to give Germany freer access to East Prussia. By this time even Chamberlain had lost faith in Hitler's promises. He abruptly abandoned appeasement and, with France, gave guarantees of aid against aggression to Poland and later to Rumania and to Greece, the latter threatened by Italy's April occupation of Albania. Geography would make it difficult to implement these guarantees effectively, but they at least served notice on the Axis powers that further aggression against their small neighbors would mean war with the great Western democracies.

In Washington, the sympathies of the Roosevelt administration were unequivocally on the side of the European democracies and against the fascist and Nazi dictatorships. In his annual message to Congress on January 4, 1939, Roosevelt remarked that although the United States had no intention of using other than peaceful methods to discourage aggressors, there were "many methods short of war, but stronger and more effective than mere words, of bringing home to aggressor governments the aggregate sentiments of our own people." But "methods short of war," if that phrase meant material aid, were barred by the neutrality laws, which, as the president complained in the same message, "may actually give aid to an aggressor and deny it to the victim." Thus began a long campaign to have the neutrality law repealed or revised.

On April 15, a week after the Italian invasion of Albania, Roosevelt addressed a surprise message to Hitler and Mussolini. Referring to the fear of war that hung over the world, he suggested that the two dictators could dispel it by giving a ten-year nonaggression guarantee to their neighbors in Europe and the Near East—the president named thirty-one governments. He believed that he could, in return, secure similar promises from the governments named. If this were accomplished, he promised, the United States would gladly participate in discussions aimed at easing the burden of armaments and freeing the channels of international trade. To this communication, Mussolini made no reply. Hitler answered it two weeks later, in a speech to the Reichstag. He had, he said, inquired of all the thirty-one governments named by Roosevelt as to whether they feared aggression by Germany and therefore felt the need of such promises as the president had proposed. In each case, he said, the answer had been negative. Any fear of German aggression, he implied, must exist only in President Roosevelt's imagination.

As spring turned to summer and as European tension built up over the Polish question, Roosevelt and Hull became increasingly convinced that the neutrality laws, especially the arms embargo, served as an encouragement to aggression by assuring Hitler that in a general European war Great Britain and France could purchase no arms, ammunition, or implements of war in the United States. Repeal of the arms embargo, the administration reasoned, would give Hitler reason to pause before inviting war with the democracies. During June and July, therefore, the administration's allies in Congress attempted to secure repeal of that provision, while leaving the remainder of the law intact or slightly modified. The House passed a bill so mutilated as to be worthless. In a final effort, Roosevelt and Hull met with leading senators and sought to impress upon them the danger of war in Europe and the perils that would confront the United States if the Axis won, as it might well do. The surest road to security for America, they argued, lay in taking action that would assure Great Britain and France of access to American materials and so deter Hitler from starting a war. Senator William

Borah, always the isolationist, replied that he had sources of information in Europe more reliable than those of the State Department, and that his sources assured him that there would be no war. Isolationist sentiment was strong in the Senate, and the administration's friends were forced to admit that they did not have the votes to pass the repeal bill. Congress adjourned without taking action.

While Roosevelt asked in vain for legislation to strengthen the hands of the democracies, the British and French were seeking the only available means of making effective their guarantees to Poland and Rumania, namely, the support of the Soviet Union. Though Russia had been ignored at Munich, the Soviet dictator, Josef Stalin, in April 1939 offered to make with France and Great Britain a defensive alliance against further German aggression. Negotiations began in April and dragged on into August. The stumbling block was the refusal of Poland, Rumania, and the Baltic states to accept a Russian guarantee of their territory, which would imply a right to occupy it for protection against German aggression. To the Russians this right seemed an essential element in their plans for defense. To the small states lying between Germany and the Soviet Union, the eastern giant was at least as great a peril as the western. When the British and French baulked at forcing Russia's attentions upon its neighbors against their will, the Kremlin secretly opened parallel negotiations with Germany. On May 3, Maxim Litvinov, a friend of the West and of the League of Nations, was replaced as foreign commissar by that diplomat of ill omen Vyacheslav M. Molotov. For three months, Molotov shrewdly kept two paths open, one to Berlin, one to Paris and London. The first clue to the outcome was the announcement on August 20 that Russia and Germany had signed a trade agreement. Immediately thereafter Nazi Foreign Minister Joachim von Ribbentrop flew to Moscow and on August 23 signed with Molotov a nonaggression pact that assured Hitler of Soviet neutrality if he invaded Poland. Accompanying it was a secret agreement for the partition of Poland between Germany and the U.S.S.R. and for delimitation of their spheres of influence in the Baltic states.

Hitler now pressed peremptorily his territorial demands on Poland, hoping to avoid war with Britain and France but willing to face it rather than retreat. Last minute efforts at settlement by negotiation broke down, and on September 1, 1939, German armies crossed the Polish frontier, and German airplanes bombed Polish cities. The expectation that the subjugation of Poland would provoke only formal protests from London and Paris was shattered by their declaration of war on Berlin on September 3. The twenty-year armistice had expired; World War II had begun. But while isolationism remained powerful in America, the shock of recent events had weakened it badly. Various polls since 1937 had indicated that most Americans viewed Nazi Germany as morally wrong and that in case of a major war they favored supplying arms to the Western democracies despite the neutrality laws. Now as war raged in Poland, another Gallup poll indicated that 84 percent of the American people desired an Allied victory, and 76 percent, despite an overwhelming desire to remain at peace, expected America to become involved sooner or later. Although over two years more elapsed before the United States entered the war, public opinion had begun to adjust to that prospect by the fall of 1939.

NOTES

1. Robert H. Ferrell, *American Diplomacy in the Great Depression: Hoover-Stimson Foreign Policy, 1929–1933* (New Haven, CT: Yale University Press, 1957), p. 278.

2. The struggle for control of Manchuria had a long and important history. See, for example, Akira Iriye, *After Imperialism: The Search for a New Order in the Far East, 1921–1931* (Cambridge: Harvard University Press, 1965).

3. Dorothy Borg, *The United States and the Far Eastern Crisis of 1933–1938* (Cambridge: Harvard University Press, 1964).

4. There were also many points of personal difference that hampered their working relationship. See particularly Ferrell, *American Diplomacy in the Great Depression*, pp. 35–43.

5. See Robert Dallek, *Franklin D. Roosevelt and American Foreign Policy, 1932–1945* (New York: Oxford University Press, 1979); Warren F. Kimball, *The Juggler* (Princeton, NJ: Princeton University Press, 1991); and Frederick W. Marks, *Wind over Sand: The Diplomacy of Franklin Roosevelt* (Athens: University of Georgia Press, 1988).

6. Wane S. Cole, *Roosevelt and the Isolationists, 1932–1945* (Lincoln: University of Nebraska Press, 1983).

7. Donald F. Drummond, "Cordell Hull," in *An Uncertain Tradition: American Secretaries of State in the Twentieth Century*, edited by Norman A. Graebner (New York: McGraw-Hill, 1961), pp. 184–209.

8. Irwin Gellman, *Secret Affairs: Franklin Roosevelt, Cordell Hull, and Sumner Welles* (Baltimore, MD: Johns Hopkins University Press, 1995).

9. Ferrell, *American Policy in the Great Depression*, p. 194.

10. Joan Hoff Wilson, *Ideology and Economics: U.S. Relations with the Soviet Union, 1918–1933* (Columbia: University of Missouri Press, 1974).

11. Donald G. Bishop, *The Roosevelt-Litvinov Agreements* (Syracuse, NY: Syracuse University Press, 1965).

12. See Bryce Wood, *The Making of the Good Neighbor Policy* (New York: Columbia University Press, 1961); and Irwin Gellman, *Good Neighbor Diplomacy* (Baltimore, MD: Johns Hopkins University Press, 1979).

13. Allen Guttmann, *The Wound in the Heart: America and the Spanish Civil War* (New York: Free Press, 1962).

14. Dorothy Borg, "Notes on Roosevelt's 'Quarantine' Speech,'" *Political Science Quarterly* 72, 3 (1957): 405–33.

15. David Wyman, *Paper Walls: America and the Refugee Crisis, 1938–1941* (Amherst: University of Massachusetts Press, 1968); and David Wyman, *The Abandonment of the Jews: America and the Holocaust, 1941–1945* (New York: Pantheon, 1984).

16. Joseph M. Siracusa, "The Munich Analogy," in *Encyclopedia of American Foreign Policy*, 2nd ed., vol. 2, ed. Alexander de Conde, et al. (New York: Scribner, 2002), p. 444.

17. Quoted in Cyrus Adler and Aaron M. Margalith, *With Firmness in the Right* (New York: American Jewish Committee, 1946), p. 381. See also William R. Rock, *Chamberlain and Roosevelt* (Columbus: Ohio State University Press, 1988).

18. Arnold A. Offner, *American Appeasement: United States Foreign Policy and Germany, 1933–1938* (Cambridge: Harvard University Press, 1969).

CHAPTER 4

Call to Arms

The attack on the U.S. Navy at Pearl Harbor is perhaps history's most famous "surprise attack." Yet it was, in fact, the violent culmination of a long period of diplomatic conflict. Preceding the attack, with Europe at war and Japan posing an increasingly severe strategic threat to American interests in the Pacific, domestic isolationist sentiment wilted in the face of international realities. Despite Washington's efforts to maintain neutrality, its interests were directly challenged, first by Adolf Hitler, then by Japan's Tojo. In response, the United States moved inexorably toward war. Ultimately, Pearl Harbor gave America its final push to enter the fray, silencing isolationists along the way.

FROM NEUTRALITY TO A "SHOOTING WAR"

Faced with the outbreak of war in Europe, in Washington, President Roosevelt issued on September 5, 1939, the customary proclamation of American neutrality. In this instance, with war having been formally declared by all principal belligerents, he had no choice but to invoke the provisions of the neutrality laws, whose amendment he had earlier sought from Congress. The arms embargo and other features of the act were applied against both belligerent camps. There was, however, no repetition of Woodrow Wilson's appeal for impartiality in thought, nor was there any pretense of impartiality of deed on the part of the administration.

Roosevelt's first priority was to prevent an Axis victory, which in his mind would present a deadly peril to the United States. This he believed from the first but even more keenly after the German victories of 1940 revealed the frightful power of the Nazi war machine. An Axis victory, he believed, would mean eventual encirclement of the United States by the Berlin-Rome-Tokyo combination, followed by economic strangulation if not by military disaster. Second, there seems no good reason to doubt that he sincerely desired to keep the United States out of the war, unless American participation should become necessary to prevent an Axis victory. In that event, as he saw it, better war sooner with dependable allies than war later when those allies had been crushed by the Axis. At some point along the way, probably in the summer of 1941, he became convinced that only American entry into the war could ensure Allied victory. It should also be added that although believing participation in the war might be necessary to American security, Roosevelt never took the American people fully into his confidence. Third, unless or until America should enter the war, the president held that it should give all possible material and moral aid to the opponents of the Axis. Only thus was there hope of an Allied victory without American participation. This program meant scrapping the neutrality legislation so laboriously written in the 1930s. It meant also complete disregard of the old rules of neutrality, which prescribed impartial treatment of the belligerents and forbade a neutral government from aiding a belligerent. Thus, the United States moved from a status of neutrality to a newly recognized status known as a nonbelligerency—the status of a nation not at war but giving active aid to one belligerent. It was a juggling act from the start.

In Roosevelt's open stand for all-out aid for the Allies short of war, and in his unpublicized belief that war would be a lesser evil than an Axis victory, he had important segments of public opinion both with him and against him. The isolationist sentiment that had promoted the neutrality laws was still strong. It opposed aid to the Allies as a step toward war, and it felt that America's sharing in "Europe's wars" was the greatest of evils. It was organized most effectively in the America First Committee, with General Robert E. Wood of Chicago as president and Colonel Charles A. Lindbergh as leading orator. It received the support of, among other journals, the *Chicago Tribune* and the Hearst newspapers. The America First Committee was "going strong" up to the afternoon of the Pearl Harbor attack. On the other side, the most important organized vehicle for the expression of public opinion was the Committee to Defend America by Aiding the Allies, headed for some time by the well-known Kansas editor William Allen White and often referred to as the White Committee. Organized in the spring of 1940, it stood for all material aid to the Allies short of war; part of its membership favored outright participation in the war. Some persons sharing this latter view, from both within and without the White Committee, formed the Fight for Freedom Committee in April 1941. They held that, in asking others to do all the fighting, America was playing an ignoble role, and urged that America take its place as a full-scale belligerent in the "fight for freedom."

In a short time, the United States moved away from neutrality and nearer to war. The first step was a modification of the neutrality laws along the lines earlier proposed by the administration. Roosevelt called Congress to meet in special session on September 21 and asked for legislative permission to sell arms to the Allies. After six weeks of debate and by safe majorities, Congress passed a fourth Neutrality Act, which became law on November 4, 1939. It repealed the embargo on arms, ammunition, and implements of war and placed sales to belligerents of goods of all kinds on a cash-and-carry basis. It empowered the president to designate "combat areas," which American ships and American citizens would be prohibited from entering. Other restrictions of the earlier legislation were generally retained. The great importance of the new law was in opening the American market in war goods to the French and British, since they alone, of the European belligerents, could buy and carry away.

In Europe, a lightning German campaign against Poland was followed by months of comparative inactivity—the *sitzkrieg* or "phony war." But in a remarkable display of military power, in April 1940, the *sitzkrieg* suddenly became a *blitzkrieg* or "lightning war." Denmark, Norway, the Netherlands, and Belgium were quickly overrun by German airborne troops and motorized columns. The French armies were crushed, the Maginot Line taken in the rear. The British Expeditionary Force escaped, as by a miracle, from Dunkirk, but left on the beaches all its heavy equipment and most of its small arms. On June 10, Mussolini, who hitherto had preserved a nonbelligerent status in his partner's war, declared war upon stricken France. On June 22, France surrendered. All of northern and western France became occupied territory. Hitler left the south and east to a government established by Marshal Henri Philippe Pétain at Vichy.

President Roosevelt's response to these events was prompt and emphatic. Speaking at the University of Virginia, Charlottesville, on June 10, he remarked, with reference to Mussolini's attack on France: "The hand that held the dagger has struck it into the back of its neighbor." More important was his declaration: "In our American unity, we will pursue two obvious and simultaneous courses: we will extend to the opponents of force the material resources of this nation, and at the same time we will harness and speed up the use of those resources in order that we ourselves in the Americas may have equipment and training equal to the task of any emergency and every defense."

During the summer of 1940, Congress, at Roosevelt's request, took important steps toward strengthening the armed forces of the United States and stepping up production of war material for the use of the "opponents of force." The army was to be enlarged from an authorized strength of 280,000 men to 1,200,000 as soon as the men could be raised and trained, with other increments to follow. Army and navy air strength was to aug- mented by over 18,000 planes, and a production goal of 50,000 planes annu- ally was set. Authorization of an unprecedented naval increase of 1,325,000 tons laid the basis for a "two-ocean navy." The total defense appropriation of over $5 billion, more than the president had asked, broke all peacetime records—with authorizations for future construction contracts, the grand total came to some $16 billion. In September, Congress passed the first peacetime selective service act in American experience. Fear of Hitler had stimulated a tardy but impressive drive for rearmament.

The surrender of France soon after the president's Charlottesville speech left only two active "opponents of force" in the world, Britain facing Ger- many and Italy in the west and China facing Japan in the east. Roosevelt's most immediate concern was with Britain, now assailed from the sea and air. If Britain should fall, if her fleet should be destroyed or pass into hostile hands, the future for America would look dark indeed. Britain's most pressing need was for swift naval vessels for antisubmarine patrol and con- voy duty. The United States had fifty over-age destroyers, which in the president's mind would serve the United States better if put to active use by the British than laid up "in moth balls" in American harbors. Attorney Gen- eral Robert Jackson found ingenious ways through both domestic and in- ternational law to carry out the president's wishes, and on September 2, Roosevelt agreed to turn over the destroyers to the British Navy in return for the right, over a 99–year period, to set up and maintain American mili- tary bases in eight British possessions stretching from Newfoundland to British Guiana. The bases made possible a naval and air screen covering the approaches to·the Atlantic coast of the United States and to the Caribbean. In announcing the deal to Congress (he had not asked its consent), the pres- ident claimed: "This is the most important action in the reinforcement of our national defense that has been taken since the Louisiana Purchase." Congress and public opinion, for the most part, acquiesced in the presi- dent's startling *fait accompli*. The transfer of the destroyers to Great Britain was, as Winston Churchill later wrote, "a decidedly unneutral act by the United States," telling his Cabinet colleagues that by agreeing to transfer ships for bases, "the United States would have made a long step toward coming into war on our side." Hitler wasted no time before lodging official protests.

In July, the Democratic Party had broken precedent by nominating Roo- sevelt for a third term as president. The president's prior move of inviting into his Cabinet two prominent Republicans, Henry L. Stimson as secretary of war and Frank Knox as secretary of the navy, did nothing to appease the Republican Party. But the Republican candidate, Wendell L. Willkie, shared the president's belief in the importance of aid to Britain. Isolationism, there- fore, was not an issue in the campaign. Neither was its antithesis of joining in the war, for both platforms and both candidates declared emphatically against participation in "any foreign war," though the Democratic platform added the qualification "except in case of attack." The Republicans, however, painted Roosevelt as the war candidate, and the president found it expedient, as the campaign climaxed, to reassure the voters again and again that "your boys are not going to be sent into any foreign wars." Roosevelt won the election easily, though with a majority much reduced from that of 1936.

After re-election, the president received from British Prime Minister Winston Churchill a long letter setting forth Britain's financial crisis. That nation was struggling to pay for goods already ordered and would need "ten times as much" for the extension of the war. Churchill hoped that Roosevelt would regard his letter "not as an appeal for aid, but as a statement of the minimum action necessary to achieve our common purpose." The problem, as Roosevelt saw it, was how to aid Britain in the common cause without incurring such a breeder of ill will as the war debt problem after World War I. After brooding over the matter for days during a Caribbean cruise on the cruiser *Tuscaloosa*, he came up with the ingenious idea of lending goods instead of money. He wanted, as he told a press conference, to get away from that "silly, foolish old dollar sign," and he compared what he proposed to do to lending a garden hose to a neighbor to put out a fire that might otherwise spread to one's own house.

In a "fireside chat" on December 29, 1940, he described the United States as the "arsenal of democracy," and in his message to Congress a few days later, on January 6, he described the kind of world that the program was designed to make secure: "A world founded upon four essential human freedoms." These were freedom of speech and expression, freedom of religion, freedom from want, and freedom from fear, the last to be achieved by a worldwide reduction of armaments to such a point that no nation would be able to commit an act of aggression against a neighbor. The Lend-Lease Act, as it was approved by Congress on March 1, was in every sense the complete negation of old-fashioned neutrality. It empowered the president to make available to any country "whose defense the President deems vital to the defense of the United States" any "defense article," any service, or any "defense information." "Defense articles" might be manufactured expressly for the government that was to receive them, or they might (after consultation with top military and naval advisers) be taken from existing stocks in the possession of the United States. Launched on a modest scale, the lend-lease program eventually conveyed goods and services valued at over $50 billion to the friends and allies of the United States in World War II; and it left in its wake no such exasperating war debt problem as that of the 1920s.

From January to March 1941, while Congress was debating the lend-lease proposal, British and American military and naval officers were holding secret staff conferences in Washington. Their purpose was to plan coordination of the American and British effort, first on the basis of lend-lease while the United States remained nonbelligerent, and second in joint military and naval operations if and when the United States entered the war. The conferences reached the fundamental decision that if Japan entered the war, Germany was still to be regarded as enemy number one and its defeat was to be given priority over that of Japan. One reason for this decision was fear that the German scientists, if given time, might perfect new superweapons; there was no such apprehension as to Japanese achievement. After conclusion of the conferences, American officers went to Britain to select sites for future naval and air force bases.

Akin to this tie-up with belligerent Britain were contemporary arrangements with Canada, a country that was also a belligerent. In August 1938, a year before the outbreak of war, Roosevelt and Canadian Prime Minister Mackenzie King had exchanged assurances of mutual assistance in case of need; the president declaring that the United States would not "stand idly by if domination of Canadian soil is threatened by any other empire." Meeting at Ogdensburg, New York, August 17, 1940, while the Battle of Britain still hung in the balance, the two statesmen agreed to set up a Permanent Joint Board of Defense for the protection of their two countries. After the passage of the Lend-Lease Act in Congress, the two met again at Roosevelt's home in Hyde Park, New York, on April 20, 1941, and took steps to gear together the production facilities of the United States and Canada for their own defense and that of Britain. A Joint Defense Production Committee was established on November 5, 1941. Thus, months before the United States became a belligerent, it was working closely with Canada for a common objective: defeat of the Axis powers.

In August 1941, Roosevelt and Churchill met secretly for their first conference in Argentina, Newfoundland. The two statesmen discussed a variety of topics connected with the war, including means of deterring Japan from attacking the British or Dutch possessions in the Far East. But the most famous if not the most important achievement of the conference was the production of the document known as the Atlantic Charter. This pronouncement, which came chiefly from Churchill's pen, may be compared roughly to Woodrow Wilson's Fourteen Points during World War I. Like Wilson's formulation, it set up idealistic objectives that might be expected to appeal to liberals everywhere. That it brought the United States a step nearer to war was clearly seen and appreciated by Churchill, who wrote: "The fact alone of the United States, still technically neutral, joining with a belligerent Power in making such a declaration was astonishing. The inclusion in it of a reference to 'final destruction of the Nazi tyranny' . . . amounted to a challenge which in ordinary times would have implied war-like action."

In the Atlantic Charter, Roosevelt and Churchill joined in a declaration of their objectives, Churchill as head of a government at war, Roosevelt as head of a nonbelligerent government committed to all aid short of war. Notable among those objectives were the "desire to see no territorial changes that do not accord with the freely expressed wishes of the people concerned"; respect for "the right of the all peoples to choose the form of government under which they will live"; and the "wish to see sovereign rights and self-government restored to those who have been forcibly deprived of them." The charter contemplated also "the establishment of a wider and permanent system of general security." The fourth point of the charter, proposing for all states "access, on equal terms, to the trade and to the raw materials of the world which are needed for their economic prosperity," committed the signers to the principle of elimination of economic barriers, or the "open door," which Secretary of State Cordell Hull had considered vital to the preservation of world peace. While nominally idealistic, this principle was also undoubtedly conducive to the economic prosperity and growth of the United States. It was rarely lost from sight in American planning for the postwar world. The principles of the Atlantic Charter were endorsed by the Soviet Union, with an interpretative qualification, and were accepted by the governments signing the Declaration by United Nations of January 1, 1942. Thus they became, at least in theory, a part of the program of the nations allied against the Axis powers.

The lend-leasing of "defense articles" to Great Britain was worse than useless unless the articles could be delivered. The protection against German submarines of convoys from North America to British ports strained the resources of the British and Canadian navies. The problem was further complicated when Hitler turned on the Soviet Union on June 22, 1941, and the United States determined to make the U.S.S.R. a beneficiary of lend-lease. The northern sea route to Russia stretched around the northern tip of Norway to its terminus at Murmansk, and the British navy could not protect the Murmansk convoys unless it got relief elsewhere.

For the United States to convoy British shipping carrying lend-lease "defense articles" would have been stretching nonbelligerency to a point that even Roosevelt thought inexpedient. But a substitute method was found. A Conference of American Foreign Ministers at Panama in September-October 1939 had proclaimed the neutrality of a wide belt of the western Atlantic and had warned the belligerents against acts of war in these waters. Though neither Britain nor Germany had paid any heed to this declaration, Roosevelt decided, in the spring of 1941, to have the U.S. Navy patrol most of the North Atlantic and publish the position of Axis ships or planes it found. Thus British convoys would be warned of the positions of Nazi submarines located by the U.S. Navy.

Such "nonbelligerent" activity could not continue for long without bringing on clashes with German U-boats, and U.S. ships sometimes became targets of German torpedoes. On October 17, 1941, the destroyer *Kearny*, doing convoy duty, was hit by a torpedo with the loss of eleven men. On October 31, the *Reuben James* lost ninety-six men in a similar attack. In response, Roosevelt warned, "We have wished to avoid shooting. But the shooting has started. And history has recorded who fired the first shot."

With public sentiment in favor of the Allies growing, Roosevelt decided the time had come to get rid of as many as possible of the troublesome remaining restrictions of the neutrality laws. On October 9, 1941, he asked Congress for repeal of the section forbidding the arming of merchant vessels. "We intend," he said, "to maintain the policy of protecting the freedom of the seas against domination by any foreign power which has become crazed with a desire to control the world." In spite of large anti-interventionist blocks in both houses of Congress and in spite of warnings that repeal meant war, Congress passed and the president signed on November 17, 1941, a law that went further than he had asked. It not only permitted the arming of American merchantmen, but also repealed the cash-and-carry and combat area provisions of the law of 1939. American merchant ships were now free to arm themselves and to sail anywhere on the globe, carrying, if their owners wished, arms, ammunition, and implements of war for the British, the Soviets, or the Chinese. American destroyers and German submarines were already trading depth charges for torpedoes in the North Atlantic. With all restrictions removed from American merchant ships, it is impossible to know how long the country would have waited before an accumulation of "incidents" would have drawn a declaration of war from a reluctant Congress—or a reluctant Führer. The Japanese attack on Pearl Harbor eliminated any such period of waiting.

THE ROAD TO WAR

There can be little doubt that by the fall of 1941 Roosevelt had concluded that entering the war with Germany was in America's best interests; similarly, he had also concluded that the Axis could not be defeated without U.S. involvement. He never said so publicly nor, so far as the records have revealed, privately. He exasperated the more war-minded of his advisers, like Secretary Stimson, by his failure to share his apparent conviction that the road to national security lay through war. He feared, it may be assumed, to call for a declaration of war as long as the response of Congress and the public was in doubt. As late as November 5, 1941, a poll conducted by the American Institute of Public Opinion showed 63 percent answered 'no' to 26 percent 'yes' to the question: "Should Congress pass a resolution declaring that a state of war exists between the United States and Germany?" In Congress, the bill for arming merchant ships had carried by a vote, in the two houses, of 262 in favor, 231 against. A still more formidable opposition might be expected against a declaration of war, and a defeat on this crucial issue, in Roosevelt's view, would have been disastrous. A victory by such a slender margin would have been an inauspicious beginning of a war for survival. So, it would appear, the president tried to provoke Hitler into declaring war or into committing an overt act that would silence American opposition to war. The president's words and actions toward Germany, from August to November 1941, were not the words or actions of someone committed to staying out of the war.

Why, in the face of American "unneutrality," did Hitler shun war with the United States? From the time of the destroyer deal in September 1940, the United States had committed one unfriendly act after another. It was overtly aiding Hitler's foes in ways that a belligerent would hardly have stood for in any prior war. Yet Hitler issued no ultimatum, threatened no reprisals. He said merely, after Roosevelt's shoot-on-sight order, that German submarines would defend themselves. The reasons for Hitler's hesitation are clear enough. However irrationally he may have acted in other matters, in this one he was realistic and rational. He well remembered the result of American participation in the First World War. If possible, the führer was determined to avoid repeating the mistake of drawing America into the war, at least until he had won his war in Europe. When he had crushed the U.S.S.R. and defeated or cowed Britain, there would be time enough to reckon with America.

While the United States was drifting into an undeclared naval war with Germany in the Atlantic, it was approaching a crisis in its relations with Japan in the Pacific. Japan followed up its announcement of the "New Order for East Asia" by seizing, in February 1939, the large island of Hainan off the south China coast, and, a month later, the Spratly Islands in the South China Sea. Hainan, a Chinese island, was in the French sphere of influence; it also lay in close proximity to the British shipping lane between Singapore and Hong Kong. The Spratly Islands, claimed by France, were uncomfortably close to French Indochina and the American Philippines. Japan, in other words, while ostensibly fighting only China, was moving southward into an area where its forces constituted a potential threat to the possessions of France, the United States, and Great Britain, and even to those of the Netherlands. At the same time, Japan continued its policy of gradually closing the door of China to Western trade and Western culture. Ambassador to Japan Joseph C. Grew, at home in the United States during the summer of 1939, found, as he wrote, "an unmistakable hardening of the administration's attitude toward Japan and a marked disinclination to allow American interests to be crowded out of China." This hardening attitude took tangible form when, on July 26, 1939, the United States gave the required six month notice of the abrogation of its 1911 commercial treaty with Japan; thus it would be free, early in 1940, to restrict Japan's trade with the United States in any way it might deem expedient. "Methods short of war" were in the making and upon returning to his post in Tokyo, Grew publicly warned the people of Japan during a speech on October 19, 1939, that the policy of their government was alienating the friendship of the United States.

When this speech was delivered, Europe had been at war for seven weeks. The "phony war" of the following months had little effect on the Far Eastern situation, but the spring and summer of 1940 seemed to open lucrative opportunities to the ambitious Japanese. First the Netherlands and then France succumbed to German might; only the English Channel and the Royal Air Force and Navy barred Hitler from the conquest of Great Britain, and how long those barriers would hold, no one could foretell. French Indochina, the Netherlands East Indies, and British Malaya appeared as tempting prizes to Hitler's Asiatic partner. A new Japanese ministry, headed, like that of 1938, by Prince Konoye, proclaimed on August 1 a "New Order for Greater East Asia." This enlargement of Japan's prospective empire, also called the "Greater East Asia Co-prosperity Sphere," was chiefly the plan of the new Foreign Minister, Yosuke Matsuoka. Aggressive, boastful, and garrulous, pro-Axis and anti-United States, Matsuoka was described by Cordell Hull as being "as crooked as a basket of fishhooks." The Greater East Asia Co-prosperity Sphere was defined, under Matsuoka's inspiration, by a Liaison Conference consisting of cabinet and military leaders in Tokyo on September 19, 1940, as comprising the former German islands under mandate to Japan since 1920 (the Carolines, Marianas, and Marshalls), French Indochina and French islands in the Pacific, Thailand, British Malaya and Borneo, the Dutch East Indies, Burma, Australia, New Zealand, and India, "with Japan, Manchuria, and China as the backbone." An item conspicuously missing from this list, no doubt out of temporary deference to the United States, was the Philippines. To take care of such omissions, Matsuoka had added an "etc." at the end of his enumeration and in addition had commented that "this sphere could be automatically broadened in the course of time."

Matsuoka had also opened negotiations for an outright alliance with Germany and Italy. On September 27, 1940, representatives of the three powers signed in Berlin a Tripartite Pact, comprising mutual recognition by the three partners of the "new orders" instituted by them in Europe and Greater East Asia, respectively, and also a defensive alliance aimed at mutual defense against U.S. attack. Its purpose was to deter the United States from entering the war against either Germany or Japan by the warning that by so doing it would have to fight all three Axis powers. With American interference thus fended off, Matsuoka believed Japan could readily take possession of French, Dutch, and British colonies in greater East Asia. He hoped, too, that the pact would enable Japan to improve its relations with the Soviet Union and, by isolating China, to compel Jiang Jieshi to make a peace satisfactory to Japan. This was the bright mirage that dazzled Yosuke Matsuoka and led Japan along the road to disaster.

Far from intimidating the United States, the Tripartite Pact still further stiffened the American attitude toward the Axis. The threat of encirclement made the two wars one in American eyes and, in the mind of Roosevelt at any rate, strengthened the determination to aid Britain. Roosevelt followed up his re-election in November by proposing the lend-lease policy, which became law in March 1941. In a letter of January 21, 1941, to Ambassador Grew he explained the "global strategy" that he thought imperative in the interest of American security, involving supplying Britain with aid as well as keeping supply routes and sources open around the world. He referred specifically in this connection to the Dutch East Indies and British Malaya, sources of rubber, petroleum, and tin. A few weeks later, on February 14, 1941, the American embassy in Tokyo passed on this idea to the Japanese vice minister for foreign affairs, adding that the United States would not tolerate a Japanese threat to these commodity sources.

As the fateful year 1941 dawned, friction between the United States and Japan was increasing. Resentful of Japan's assaults upon China's independence and of violations of the open door policy, the United States was now seriously concerned about Japan's affiliation with the European Axis and its threatened appropriation of the rich raw materials of Southeast Asia. During 1940, the United States had begun to exert economic pressure upon Japan. The launching of the rearmament program in the spring and summer furnished a pretext for cutting off supplies from Japan on the grounds that they were needed at home. On July 25, 1940, the president prohibited the export without license of petroleum, petroleum products, and scrap metal. Six days later, he placed an embargo upon the export of aviation gasoline to all countries outside the Western Hemisphere, except for the use of American planes in the service of foreign countries. As an answer, presumably, to the Japanese landings in Indochina and the advance news of the signing of the Tripartite Pact, the president, on September 26, placed a similar embargo on exports of scrap iron and steel, making shipments to Britain the only exceptions. Other gestures designed as warnings to Japan were a $25 million loan to China through the Export-Import Bank, and a notice to all American citizens in the Far East urging that they return to America.

Such measures as these, and the possibility of still more drastic ones, without doubt gave Japan pause, and eventually led to the opening of negotiations. Serious talks began in April following the arrival in Washington of a new Japanese ambassador, Admiral Kichisaburo Nomura. Nomura's negotiations with Hull were complicated by the presence in Washington of two Roman Catholic clerics, Bishop James E. Walsh and Father James M. Drought of the Maryknoll Society. Through a complicated arrangement of unofficial diplomatic channels with the U.S. postmaster general Frank C. Walker at its center, Walsh and Drought returned from a visit to Japan bringing what they thought to be an offer from the Japanese government.

Japan, they reported, was ready to recall Japanese troops from China and to nullify the Tripartite Pact insofar as it was a threat to the United States. Hull soon discovered that this offer misrepresented Japanese intentions.

Actually, as the conversations with Nomura revealed, Japan was asking the United States to press Jiang Jieshi to accept Japan's terms, including merger of his government with the puppet government in Nanking and retention of some Japanese troops in North China and Inner Mongolia. Should he refuse, the United States should deprive him of any further aid. The United States was also to restore normal trade with Japan (insofar as articles needed by Japan were available) and to assist Japan in obtaining raw materials from Southeast Asia to meet its needs. In return, Japan would promise to use only peaceful means in seeking its ends in Southeast Asia and would reserve to itself the right to interpret its obligations under the Tripartite Pact; in other words, if the United States went to war with Germany, Japan would decide independently whether it was bound to assist its Axis partner.

The United States, for its part, asked Japan's acceptance of four general principles set forth by Secretary Hull: (1) respect for the sovereignty and territorial integrity of all nations; (2) noninterference in the internal affairs of other countries; (3) the open door, or equality of commercial opportunity; and (4) no disturbance of the status quo in the Pacific except by peaceful means. Specifically, the United States asked that Japan withdraw its armed forces from China and Indochina, accept the government of Jiang Jieshi as the only legitimate government of China, and disavow the Tripartite Pact as aimed at the United States. Each government adhered inflexibly to its set of demands, so by June 1941, an impasse had been reached.

The renewal of aggressive action by Japan in July, clearly designed as a prelude to armed attack upon Malaya and the Netherlands Indies, brought quick response from the United States, Great Britain, and the Netherlands. The Japanese excuse—that the occupation was a defensive measure against alleged British designs—was answered by Roosevelt with a proposal that Indochina be neutralized, a suggestion that was refused by Japan. In the meantime, the United States had broken off the discussions with Nomura that had been proceeding since April, and had announced the freezing of all Japanese funds in the United States. Within a few days, Great Britain and the Netherlands took similar action. This was the final stroke in cutting Japan off from its most important markets and sources of raw material.

There were those in both England and the United States who believed that Japan would retreat before a united front of the democracies. With this idea in mind, Winston Churchill, at the Atlantic Conference in August, urged Roosevelt to warn Japan that an attack on British or Dutch possessions in the Far East would compel the United States "to take counter-measures, even though these might lead to war between the United States and Japan." Although the message was toned down in the version Roosevelt delivered on August 17, the ultimatum was clear. It was accompanied by an offer to reopen the interrupted conversations and to institute a helpful economic program for the Pacific area if Japan were willing to suspend its expansionist policies.

Upon Roosevelt's return from the Atlantic Conference with Churchill, he found awaiting him a proposal for a Pacific Conference with Prince Konoye, the Japanese premier. Konoye had suggested that a personal meeting of the two statesmen might settle controversies that seemed otherwise insoluble. The proposal was heartily endorsed by Ambassador Grew. Grew believed that Japan was ready to make important concessions. As he saw it, the inconclusive and costly war in China, economic pressure from the democracies, and growing distrust of Germany had combined to convince the cabinet, the emperor, and many top military men that Japan was following a ruinous course. Retreat would be difficult and would meet strenuous opposition, but Grew believed, and the entire embassy staff shared his view, that a dramatic meeting of premier and president, productive of a promising economic program, even though at the cost of important concessions, would catch the popular imagination and overwhelm the opposition. Confidence in this outcome was strengthened by the assurance that such a program would have the full support of the emperor. Specifically, Grew believed that Konoye was ready to satisfy the United States in regard to the Tripartite Pact and to withdraw Japanese troops from Indochina and from China. Roosevelt was at first quite taken with the suggestion of a Pacific Conference. Secretary Hull, however, threw cold water on the idea. He doubted the ability of the premier, whatever his intentions, to gain the consent of the militarists to a program acceptable to the United States, and he insisted that the general lines of an acceptable agreement be sketched out before the meeting. Otherwise, he feared the meeting would result in a fiasco, which Japanese propaganda would then turn against the United States. On the necessity of a preliminary agreement, the president accepted Hull's position, and Konoye was asked to state Japan's terms. In a talk with Grew on September 6, Konoye stated that he accepted "conclusively and wholeheartedly" (the Foreign Office later added the words "in principle") the four principles of international behavior previously set forth by Secretary Hull. But on specific concessions that they were willing to make, the Japanese refused to commit themselves, possibly, as Grew believed, because they feared that leaks in the Foreign Office would reveal such proposals prematurely to Matsuoka and other extremists. In the absence of specific advance commitments by Japan, Roosevelt was unwilling to meet the premier. On October 16, the Konoye ministry resigned, and whatever chance there was for an agreement at the top level was lost. Konoye's successor was General Tojo, the minister for war. While Tojo announced that the change in cabinet meant no change in policy and that negotiations with the United States would continue, the Japanese military was quietly instructed to prepare for war.

During the next two weeks, operation MAGIC—the decoding and translation by Naval Intelligence of intercepted Japanese messages—picked up a steady stream of messages passing back and forth between Tokyo and the Japanese embassy in Washington. Through these intercepts Washington knew that Japanese envoys had been given two sets of proposals to lay before the American government, Plan A and Plan B, the latter to be presented if the former were rejected. Plan B represented Japan's final fallback position. It was known also that Japan had set a deadline for negotiations to be completed, first November 25 and later November 29. "After that," ran one intercepted message, "things are automatically going to happen." Washington knew, therefore, that unless the United States accepted Japanese Plan B by November 29, or persuaded Japan to take something less, "things" were "going to happen." Washington did not know what or where, but Japanese concentrations of troops and transports pointed to attacks on British Malaya, Thailand, the Dutch East Indies, or possibly the Philippines.

It was assumed in Washington that an attack on the British or Dutch possessions would, or at least ought to, bring the United States into the war. Roosevelt had, in fact, given secret assurances to this effect to the British. Such a course was in line with Roosevelt's "global strategy" and had been made plain to Japan. But neither the army nor the navy was prepared for war in the Pacific; both desperately needed time to prepare. Secretary of War Stimson, in particular, believed that in three months he could build up a force of B-17s (Flying Fortresses) in the Philippines that could block Japan's southward expansion. So the army and navy pleaded for a postponement of the showdown, for three months at least, and there was talk of a possible temporary *modus vivendi*, or way of getting along, if no permanent agreement could be reached.

After Japanese Plan A was rejected by Secretary Hull, the envoys brought in on November 20 their Plan B, which they described as a *modus vivendi*, presumably only temporarily. The proposals were as follows: (1) neither government was to send armed forces into the Southeast Asia or South Pacific area, except Indochina; (2) the two governments were to cooperate to secure needed commodities from the Netherlands Indies; (3) commercial relations were to be restored to their status before the freezing of funds and the United States was to supply Japan with "the required quantity of oil"; (4) the United States was "not to resort to measures and actions prejudicial to the endeavors for the restoration of general peace between Japan and China"; and (5) Japan was to move its troops in southern Indochina into the northern portion upon the conclusion of this agreement, and to withdraw all troops from Indochina upon the making of peace with China "or the establishment of an equitable peace in the Pacific area." With regard to Japan's relations with Germany, not mentioned in the document, Japan's special envoy, Saburo Kurusu, had told President Roosevelt on November 17 that Japan could not openly abandon the Tripartite Pact but "had no intention of becoming a tool of Germany nor did she mean to wait until the United States became deeply involved in the battle of the Atlantic and then stab her in the back."

The United States rejected these proposals on the basis that accepting them would have meant "abject surrender of our position under intimidation," as Cordell Hull later put it. But since the army and navy were pressing for time, Hull prepared a *modus vivendi* of his own. Thus, he thought of proposing to the Japanese a three-month truce, during which either a permanent agreement might be reached or, if not, the armed forces would have had that much more time to prepare for war. The new proposals comprised mutual pledges of peaceful policy; promises that neither would advance further in the Pacific area by means of force or threat of force; withdrawal of Japanese forces from southern to northern Indochina and limitation of those in that area to 25,000; resumption of trade with Japan on a limited scale; sale of petroleum to Japan for civilian use only; and any settlement between Japan and China to be "based upon the principles of peace, law, order, and justice."

The difference between these proposals and Japan's Plan B was not so wide as to rule out possible agreement. On the other hand, they provided so little for China—nothing but a "pious hope," in fact—that China, which, along with the United Kingdom, the Netherlands, and Australia, was consulted about them, protested bitterly. Since neither the British nor the Dutch greeted them with enthusiasm, and since their publication at home was sure to bring charges of "appeasement," Hull decided reluctantly, and after consulting with Roosevelt, to discard the *modus vivendi* entirely and to submit instead a ten-point program for a permanent settlement along strictly American lines. Since this program called for withdrawal of all Japanese troops from China and Indochina and for a virtual disavowal of the Axis Pact, Hull must have known when he presented it on November 26 that Japan would spurn it and that "things" would begin to happen. He made this clear the next day by telling Stimson: "I have washed my hands of it, and it [the situation] is now in the hands of you and Knox, the Army and Navy."

The American note of November 26, sometimes referred to as an ultimatum, was, more accurately, a rejection of Japan's ultimatum of November 20. As far as the United States was concerned, it left the door open for further negotiation. In fact, the army and navy still hoped for at least a postponement of hostilities. Intercepted messages from Tokyo, however, directing Japanese envoys in the democracies to burn their codes and destroy their code machines and referring to war as imminent, made it plain that Japan was bent on war. The movement of a large Japanese convoy down the China coast in the direction of Indochina pointed surely to a southern campaign. Its objective might be Thailand, British Malaya, the Netherlands Indies, or the Philippines—any or all of these. Prevailing opinion in Washington in these last days of peace held that Japan would not deliberately attack United States territory, and the problem that most exercised the minds of the president and his advisers was whether American opinion, in Congress and out, would support the administration in making war if the Japanese attack should fall only upon British or Dutch or Thai territory.

To meet this contingency, the president set his advisers to work drafting a message to Congress for the purpose of demonstrating to the legislators that any further Japanese advance in Southeast Asia would threaten the vital interests of the United States and thus justify armed resistance. But this message to Congress was to be preceded by a last ditch attempt to dissuade Japan from aggression—a direct appeal from the president to the emperor. The idea of an appeal to the emperor was deliberated over for at least a week before the message was sent. One draft revived the idea of a *modus vivendi*, with a ninety-day truce between Japan and China, as well as between Japan and the Western powers. The message actually sent, on the evening of December 6, too late to have any effect, contained no such proposal. It reviewed the long friendship between Japan and the United States and the current threats to it and described the occupation of Indochina as a threat hanging over the people of Malaya, the Netherlands Indies, Thailand, and the Philippines. It offered guarantees that no other power would occupy Indochina if Japan withdrew and promised: "Thus a withdrawal of the Japanese forces from Indo-China would result in the assurance of peace throughout the whole of the South Pacific area." Notably, this last appeal to Japan placed all the emphasis upon Southeast Asia, none upon China. This final attempt to stave off hostilities reached Ambassador Grew in Tokyo too late for delivery to the emperor until almost the moment of the fateful Pearl Harbor attack.

In late November a Japanese carrier force set sail for Hawaii with utmost secrecy. When Tokyo determined that negotiations had failed, it ordered the attack early in the morning of Sunday, December 7, and just before 8 A.M. that day waves of almost 200 Japanese planes bombed and strafed the American fleet in the harbor, focusing particularly on the eight battleships at anchor there. There were also coordinated attacks on American airfields in the area and in the Philippines and the British outposts of Malaya and Singapore. By the time the smoke cleared there were over 2,300 dead, over 850 missing, and almost 1,300 injured. Eight major ships had been sunk, including five battleships, along with many smaller vessels and hundreds of planes that were destroyed on the ground. Moreover, much of the remaining fleet was severely damaged. From the Japanese perspective, the attack clearly had been a dramatic success.

Coming before a declaration of war, the attack provoked outrage not just for the material destruction, but also for the manner with which it was carried out. The Japanese reply to the American note of November 26—a long complaint against American policy in the Far East ending with notice of the breaking off of the negotiations—was presented by the ambassadors to the secretary of state at 2:20 P.M., Washington time, on Sunday December 7, 1941. The hour set for its delivery had been 1:00 P.M., a few minutes before the first bombs were scheduled to fall on Pearl Harbor. Delay in decoding postponed the envoys' call upon Secretary Hull so that when they reached his office, he knew, as they did not, of the Japanese attack. After glancing at the note, the content of which he had already been apprised through MAGIC intercepts, Hull castigated it as "crowded with infamous falsehoods and distortions," and showed the ambassadors the door. Later in the day, word came that Japan had formally declared war, some two hours after the Pearl Harbor attack, though some elements in the government had fully intended to give a much clearer declaration than was contained in the memo but were overruled by the Japanese Navy, which was determined to maximize the element of surprise. Responding to Roosevelt's call to arms, during which he famously declared December 7 "a day of infamy," Congress declared war against Japan on December 8. The British government had done the same a few hours earlier. On December 11, Germany and Italy declared war according to an arrangement worked out with Japan less than a fortnight previously.

The phrase "sneak attack," however, was a convenient rationalization that helped to divert attention from the culpable negligence that made the surprise possible. There were several reasons why the attack should have been anticipated. In the "war games" of 1932, American carriers had launched a successful Sunday morning attack on the defending force at Pearl Harbor. This exploit gave the Japanese a perfect pattern but had apparently been forgotten by responsible Americans. As early as January 1941, Ambassador Grew reported to the State Department rumors he had picked up in Tokyo suggesting that Japan would open hostilities with an air attack on Pearl Harbor. From September 1941 to the eve of the attack, intercepted Japanese instructions to the Japanese consul general in Honolulu showed a suspicious curiosity about the exact location of ships at Pearl Harbor. In November, when negotiations were approaching a climax, Ambassador Grew warned that hostile Japanese action might come "with dangerous and dramatic suddenness," and Secretary Hull remarked to a meeting of the "War Cabinet" at the White House that the Japanese might rely on surprise and that they might attack at various points simultaneously; the Japanese habit of striking first and declaring war later was, after all, well known and had been most dramatically demonstrated in the outbreak of the Russo-Japanese War.

In considering culpable negligence, one may discard at once the discredited theory that President Roosevelt deliberately enticed the Japanese to attack Pearl Harbor in order to get the United States into the European war by the "back door." That Roosevelt would voluntarily have invited destruction of a major weapon, the Pacific Fleet, as a means toward involvement in a two-front war, which he did not want, stands the test neither of reason nor of the evidence.[1] The explanation for the disaster lies, not in a conspiracy of the president and a few close advisers, but in complacency and negligence, both in the administration in Washington and in the high command in Hawaii.

Certainly Washington was remiss in its failure to alert the Hawaiian commanders more emphatically to the possibility of surprise attack. "War warnings" were sent to the army and navy commanders there and in the Philippines on November 27, the day after the final note was handed to Japan. The warnings were not followed up as it seems clear they should have been when intercepted messages revealed that the zero hour was approaching. For reasons of security, knowledge of the MAGIC intercepts was limited to very few persons in Washington. Their content was not communicated to the commanders in Hawaii or the Philippines. Even if it had been, there is no certainty that Admiral Walter C. Short in Hawaii would have acted with more foresight than he actually exhibited. The intercepts showed unmistakably that war was coming—somewhere. The only item that pointed specifically to an attack on the fleet at Pearl Harbor was the display of Japanese interest in the precise location of the ships there; nevertheless, the Japanese were showing similar curiosity about ship locations in Panama, San Diego, San Francisco, Portland, Vancouver, and elsewhere.[2] Washington intelligence failed to see any special threat to Pearl Harbor (even though Pearl Harbor sheltered the prime target for Japanese attack). With the same information, Kimmel and Short might well have similarly failed in their interpretation. In the absence of more specific warnings from Washington, Admiral Kimmel and General Short took measures for protection against submarine attack and sabotage respectively. These measures apparently satisfied their superiors in Washington. They were not told to, nor did they, take special precautions against attack from the air.

Neither in Washington nor in Hawaii, it seems in retrospect, was there the alert imagination that imminent war with a tricky enemy called for. For Washington, the rather obvious explanation (certainly not a justification) of the blind spot is the fact that all eyes were fixed so intently on the Far East that earlier warnings of danger to Hawaii were forgotten. Japanese concentrations in Formosa (threatening the Philippines), large Japanese convoys heading for Malaya, other concentrations in the Carolines pointing toward the Netherlands Indies were all known as real threats and were watched with anxiety. No one had spotted Admiral Nagumo's task force, plowing through the North Pacific toward Hawaii. No one dreamed, apparently, that Japan could be aiming another major blow in addition to the several for which preparations were visible. In summary, the Pearl Harbor tragedy resulted not from high-level conspiracies but from plain stupidity and apathy by middle-echelon intelligence officers, grievous neglect of duty by the top commanders in Hawaii, and stunning faults in the uncoordinated, decentralized intelligence system.

There are other intriguing questions. Why did Roosevelt keep the Pacific Fleet at Pearl Harbor when its former commander, Admiral James O. Richardson, had advised that it would be both safer and more effective if operated from Pacific Coast bases? The probable answer is that Roosevelt, though recognizing the military soundness of Richardson's advice, took a calculated military risk rather than withdraw the fleet in a move that both Japanese and their Chinese victims would have viewed as a retreat by the United States. Why did the Japanese, aware of the greatly superior material and human resources of the United States, initiate a war in which the long-range odds were so heavily against them? The answer lies partly, of course, in their reliance upon the prowess of their German ally, but also in their drawing a false lesson from history. Records of prewar military discussions suggest that Japanese optimists expected to repeat the achievements of their fathers against Russia in 1904–1905. In that conflict, a succession of early and impressive victories had worn down the determination of a stronger foe and led to a favorable peace. Would not the same strategy work against America? Finally, why did the United States think it necessary to oppose Japan's program of expansion up to the point where Japan had either to abandon it or to fight for it? American policy may have been right or wrong, but it had historical roots and a logical pattern. The United States had objected from the beginning to Japan's step-by-step domination of China. It began to talk of forcible resistance only after Japan allied itself with Germany and threatened to absorb in its Greater East Asia Co-Prosperity Sphere areas considered vital to the free world. There may have been errors of judgment and missed opportunities for compromise, as Ambassador Grew judged; but the fact remains that Japan was bent upon expanding its empire in ways incompatible with Roosevelt's "global strategy," with his commitments to Great Britain, and with his moral commitments, at least, to Jiang Jieshi. The United States did not choose to fight; it blocked Japan's path and left the choice to fight up to the Japanese.

NOTES

1. For a particularly strong treatment of this issue, see Roberta Wohlstetter, *Pearl Harbor: Warning and Decision* (Stanford, CA: Stanford University Press, 1962).
2. Ibid.

CHAPTER 5

America at War

Pearl Harbor, in many ways the midwife of modern American internationalism, silenced the isolationist versus internationalist debate within the United States, and the nation entered the war with a vengeance, mobilizing manpower and machinery on a scale of immense proportions. While Allied forces fought in the Pacific and conquered the beaches of Normandy and beyond, the home front provided the manufacturing and financial support for the armed forces, in the process giving the whole spectrum of American society an opportunity to contribute toward the national cause. Finally, as victory loomed, the leaders of the Allied powers met to map out the postwar world.

WAGING WAR AT HOME AND ABROAD

Of all the wars America participated in during the twentieth century, World War II has always been regarded as the least objectionable. Drawn into it by a vicious surprise attack, and battling the tyrannies of nazism, fascism, and Japanese expansionism, public support was complete, and there was relatively little hysteria this time about so-called disloyal elements. Yet part of the immediate home front reaction led to one of the most objectionable episodes in the nation's history—the flagrant violation of Japanese-American civil liberties.

Anti-Japanese sentiment had, of course, long existed in the United States. Because of geography, those resentments tended to be concentrated within the western states, particularly in California, long the center of Japanese migration to America. Since the turn of the century, as Japan underwent modernization of its economy, its surplus rural population had caused a significant migration of Japanese workers to the West Coast of the United States, as well as to Hawaii, Australia, and Canada. This migration triggered adverse, and at times violent, reactions by so-called native Americans, especially in California. At the heart of anti-Japanese sentiment, not unlike the earlier experience of the Irish in Boston, lay fear of these recent arrivals as serious economic competition. Pearl Harbor presented the anti-Japanese elements with an opportunity to brand indiscriminately all Japanese, whether natural born citizens or not—there were 80,000 in the former category and 47,000 in the latter—as traitors and disloyal. They were accused of deliberately living near military and naval installations for purposes of future espionage and sabotage. Various agricultural, labor, and business groups, led by American Legionnaires and members of the Daughters and Sons of the Golden West, demanded, in the name of national security, the mass evacuation of Japanese Americans from the West Coast. More moderate citizens, especially members of the clergy and educators, vainly opposed such a demand. Even civil libertarians such as California's Attorney-General Earl Warren and journalist Walter Lippmann joined the chorus in arguing for evacuation.

Although the Justice Department sought to act with the utmost caution, distinguishing carefully between Japanese and American citizens, heavy pressure from the West Coast and the War Department, led by Secretary of War Henry Stimson, persuaded it to capitulate. On February 19, 1942, the War Department, at the direction of President Franklin Roosevelt, drew up Executive Order 9066, authorizing Stimson to designate military areas and to exclude from these areas anyone the War Department deemed a security threat. The forced evacuation of Japanese Americans from West Coast states commenced in March, culminating shortly in a full-scale program of internment under the direction of the newly created War Relocation Authority headed by Milton Eisenhower. Thousands of Japanese Americans, without regard to whether they were citizens or not or any other factors, soon were rounded up and transported to ten so-called relocation centers in seven western states. Of the 110,000 evacuees, approximately 17,000 were able to obtain leaves of one kind or another, the most notable of these being those who enlisted in the 442 Regimental Combat Team and distinguished themselves in battle in Italy. The Supreme Court upheld the policy of relocation in 1944 but did order the release of loyal citizens.

Despite this blight on America's wartime record, the business of war mobilization continued. Under the Selective Service Act of 1940, the nation raised mammoth armies in a short time. All males between the ages of eighteen and forty-five were required to register with their local draft boards; of these 40 percent were rejected for physical and mental disabilities or other deferrable causes. Altogether, the United States raised wartime forces totaling fifteen million men and women, the latter serving as volunteer corps adjuncts to the Army (WACs), Navy (WAVES), Coast Guard (SPARS), Army Air Force (WASPs), and Marines. Conscientious objectors also performed special war related work.

A vast increase in economic production was necessitated by the war effort. Only then, under the lash of mobilization, did the huge unemployment of the Great Depression disappear, moving from eight million unemployed persons in 1940 to an increase of the civilian work force by nearly seven million in 1945. Of these, more than six million women joined the nation's work force during the war, working in shipyards, aircraft plants, and munitions factories as cops, taxicab drivers, welders, electricians, and boilermakers. By 1943, women made up one-third of the work force. "Rosie the Riveter," the title of a popular song, became the generic term for women working in defense industries.

Roosevelt continued his New Deal approach of creating government-run agencies to solve national problems. As early as August 1939, Roosevelt set up the War Resources Board (in 1941 the Office of Production Management) to manage the conversion of civilian industry to war production. By early 1943, the Office of War Mobilization, under the direction of James F. Byrnes, a shrewd politician and a long-time Roosevelt political ally, assumed control over the economic side of the war effort. Recognizing the centrality of technology to that effort, Roosevelt established the Office of Scientific Research and Development in June 1941 headed by Vannevar Bush, an engineer by training, but one who had long experience dating back to World War I of integrating science with the military. Directed to coordinate the nation's scientific efforts, this agency assisted in the development of such innovations as radar, the proximity fuse, sonar, and the atomic bomb. Production reached prodigious heights. The output spoke for itself: The nation produced a total of 296,000 aircraft and 5,400 merchant vessels, in addition to 71,000 naval craft of various sizes. The latter included, by 1945, 28 aircraft carriers, 70 escort carriers, 72 cruisers, 373 destroyers, 365 destroyer escorts, 240 submarines, and 23 battleships.

To curb wartime inflation, prices, wages, and rents came under the control of the Office of Price Administration in 1942. By then, general prices had already risen by 25 percent, but the line was held thereafter. A system of rationing, which was comparatively mild in relation to the other wartime powers, controlled supplies of scarce commodities such as sugar, coffee, gasoline, and automotive tires. Since Japan had cut off the nation's accustomed source of raw rubber, American industry began to develop synthetic rubber for tires and other needs. Agriculture boomed under the war stimulus, further encouraged by very high parity prices and supports. Industrial production, too, reached new heights despite less manpower, as machinery and fertilizers were utilized in unprecedented ways. Between 1939 and 1945, manufacturing output doubled while agriculture rose 22 percent.

During the course of the war, labor was allocated by a War Manpower Commission. The National War Labor Relations Board, at first, preserved industrial peace and kept the number of strikes below normal. Even so, 1943 witnessed an increase in strikes as labor felt squeezed by wartime inflation. Although most of these labor disruptions were unauthorized "wildcat strikes"—with some notable exceptions such as when John L. Lewis led the United Mine workers out of the coal mines in 1943—labor's record on the whole was good, and disruptions did not seriously impair war productivity.

War finance posed another great challenge. By mid-1943, war costs ran at $8 billion per month—as much as the yearly New Deal budgets of the past. By the end of the war, the national debt had risen to $247 billion, from $48 billion in 1941. Increased taxes raised an estimated 40 percent of the total costs, a greater proportion than in any previous war; the remainder was met by the time-honored method of borrowing. Millions of Americans were encouraged, even coerced, by public pressure into investing in war bonds. The 1942 War Revenue Act instituted a novelty to Americans—the payroll deduction system—and sharply increased tax rates. The introduction of the payroll income tax deduction, proposed by Beardsley Ruml, chairman of the Federal Reserve Bank of New York, produced a veritable tax revolution as the number of people paying income taxes increased from four million in 1939 to nearly 50 million by 1945. Naturally, rates were raised most sharply on the upper income brackets and corporate earnings. The total war costs of $350 billion surpassed the record World War I costs by at least ten times the 1917–1920 totals.

World War II witnessed growing unrest in racial relations within the United States. African Americans were determined both to attain full equality and to share in the wartime prosperity. During the course of the war, over a million black Americans migrated from the Deep South in search of new opportunities, with figures reaching 60,000 in Detroit, 100,000 in Chicago, and 250,000 on the West Coast. Wherever blacks went, it seemed, they encountered discrimination, much of it of the ugliest variety. Tensions, fed by a number of factors including critical housing shortages, erupted into violence ranging from such places as Beaumont and Port Arthur, Texas, to Mobile, Alabama, and in the barracks at Fort Dix, New Jersey. The worst incident of the war years occurred in Detroit in June 1943, as tensions exploded into a race riot that required federal troops to suppress it and restore order. Before it was over, twenty-five blacks and nine whites had been killed. At the same time, Mexican Americans in Los Angeles, the so-called zoot suiters—the Spanish-speaking youths who dressed in zoot suits that emanated from Harlem—became the targets of white servicemen, while the local and military police turned the other way.

But in other respects, the war saw marked advances for African Americans. Lynchings declined, Georgia repealed the poll tax, and the white primary in Texas was outlawed by the U.S. Supreme Court. In these and in other ways, liberals of both races united in campaigns against Jim Crowism and on behalf of civil rights for African Americans. But perhaps black Americans made their greatest advances on the economic level. Under pressure of a threatened protest march on Washington, organized by A. Philip Randolph, president of the Brotherhood of Sleeping Car Porters, Roosevelt issued Executive Order 8802 declaring it to be the policy of the United States "that there should be no discrimination in the employment of workers in defense industries or government because of race, creed, color, or national origins." To enforce this policy, the president established a Fair Employment Practices Committee (FEPC) to investigate any complaints of discrimination and to take the necessary measures to redress grievances. The FEPC worked effectively after 1943, and as the war ended, approximately two million African Americans had found employment in war industries. Although it is no doubt true that the critical labor shortage played the large role in this development, the gains were nonetheless real.

Politics continued as usual during the war. Making a determined bid to recapture Congress in the 1942 election, Republicans gained forty-six seats in the House and nine in the Senate. Moreover, Republican Thomas E. Dewey won the governorship of New York, the first member of that party to head the Empire State since 1920; altogether, Republicans controlled the governorship in twenty-six states by 1944. This resulted in increasingly bitter struggles between the White House and Congress over domestic issues, though both parties continued to support the war effort. Although Wendell Willkie was theoretically the titular head of the Republican Party, his star faded rapidly due to his lack of rank and file support and to his close identification with the Roosevelt administration's foreign policies. After suffering a defeat in the Wisconsin primary, Willkie, early in 1944, withdrew from the campaign, leaving the way open to Dewey, who brought strong assets to his quest for the GOP nomination—youthful vigor, moderate liberalism, and proven vote-getting ability. Not unexpectedly, he easily defeated his principal rivals, including Governor John W. Bricker of Ohio, to gain the nomination at the June 1944 Republican convention in Chicago.

Having already flouted the third-term tradition, Roosevelt announced in July that "as a good soldier" he would accept a fourth nomination to the presidency. Despite the lack of enthusiasm on the part of some of the party's leaders to his decision, none dared to challenge him as he still enjoyed a vast popularity at the grassroots level across the nation. Accordingly, the Democratic National Convention renominated Roosevelt on July 20 in Chicago. The only matter in doubt was the struggle over the vice-presidential nomination.

At one side of the intraparty divide was Henry A. Wallace, vice president in Roosevelt's third term and the undisputed choice of party radicals. He had the support of organized labor and the more liberal New Deal elements but was strongly opposed by the professional politicians and party bosses. Although Roosevelt publicly endorsed Wallace, he refused to fight for his nomination. In fact, Roosevelt had apparently decided upon South Carolina's James "Jimmy" Byrnes. Byrnes, however, met growing opposition from liberal Democrats and organized labor. Sidney Hillman of the Congress of Industrial Organization (CIO) had organized the Political Action Committee (PAC) in 1943 to gain an increased voice for labor, and he warned the president that the former senator from South Carolina was unacceptable to organized labor. At this point, Roosevelt's support shifted to Senator Harry S. Truman, a second-term Democrat from Missouri. Although elected to the United States Senate in 1934 at the age of fifty, it was not until America entered World War II that Truman truly distinguished himself, reaching national prominence as chairman of the Senate Committee to Investigate the National Defense Program, a body charged with auditing military contracting procedures. His blunt manner, which later earned him the nickname "give-'em-hell-Harry,"[1] also earned him the respect of Washington correspondents who, according to the *New York Times* voted him as "the civilian who, next to President Roosevelt, 'knew most about the war.'" From his Senate position and because of his record, Truman was able to weather the bitter political contest for the Democratic vice-presidential nomination. Truman was chosen on the third ballot; his victory, though, was unconvincing, and he could not escape being labeled by some as "the second Missouri Compromise."

In the campaign that followed, Dewey fought hard but could not overcome certain severe handicaps. As Allied forces won victories in Europe and the Far East, he faced an electorate reluctant to change leadership in the midst of the greatest foreign war ever fought by the United States. Moreover, suspicions about Roosevelt's ill health were overcome by his vigorous campaigning. Roosevelt promised voters a full continuation of progressive New Deal programs and policies after the war. The PAC performed ably in mobilizing the nation's workers on his behalf. Hence, on Election Day, Roosevelt scored a sweeping victory, defeating the challenger by 25.6 to 22 million popular votes and an overwhelming Electoral College victory of thirty-six to twelve states. In Congress, the Democrats lost one Senate seat while gaining twenty in the House.

DEALING WITH ALLIES

The strengthened mandate gave Roosevelt even more room to maneuver in the international sphere. Upon entering World War II, the United States did not, as in 1917, hold itself aloof from its associates. In 1917–18 the United States had described itself as an "associated power," not one of the Allies. In the later war, although it made no formal treaty of alliance, it took the lead in drawing up and signing, on January 1, 1942, the Declaration of

United Nations, which for practical purposes amounted to the same thing. Barely a voice was heard against the declaration, even though Roosevelt had in effect committed the United States to a military alliance without so much as consulting Congress. Drawing heavily upon the spirit and word of the Atlantic Charter, the declaration committed its signatories to full material commitment to the war effort and pledged them not to sign a separate peace.

The members of this grand alliance contributed to the common war cause in proportion to their abilities, combined with their enthusiasm, the contributions of many being purely nominal. The brunt of the fighting was borne by the "Big Three," the United States, the United Kingdom, and the Soviet Union, with China a poor fourth. The British Dominions, the Yugoslav guerrillas, and the Free French under General Charles de Gaulle did their full share. All the allies that contributed to the war, and some that did not, received the benefits of the lend-lease program of the United States.

The most intimate cooperation was that between the United States and the United Kingdom. This cooperation originated at the highest level. Within a few hours after receiving the news from Pearl Harbor, Winston Churchill was planning a visit to Washington. He spent several weeks at the White House in December and January, with excursions to Ottawa and to Palm Beach. This conference, which was given the code name of "Arcadia," was the first of a notable series of meetings in which the president and the prime minister and their advisers made decisions on matters of high strategy, both political and military. Not always did they see eye to eye, but they always resolved their differences amicably. The president, commanding the greater resources in men and material, had his way more often than did the prime minister. Between conferences, Roosevelt and Churchill kept in touch through frequent letters, telegrams, and telephone conversations. Roosevelt's friend, Harry Hopkins, was frequently in Britain and was in Churchill's confidence. In these various ways, regular diplomatic channels were largely by-passed.

On one basic matter there was never any difference of opinion between the two men: Hitler's Germany was the primary enemy. This decision had been reached in staff conferences nearly a year before the United States entered the war. Both nations agreed that ultimately Germany presented a more dangerous threat than Japan; therefore, its defeat must have priority. From the British point of view, this was an obvious truth. To an American, after Pearl Harbor, it was less obvious, particularly to American commanders such as General Douglas MacArthur and Admiral Ernest King, who had the task of fighting Japan. Even General George Marshall, the chief of staff, sometimes wavered. Yet Roosevelt adhered consistently to the Germany-first policy and would have had the satisfaction, had he lived, of seeing Japan surrender three months after the defeat of Germany. On some other important aspects of the war there were differences. Roosevelt rated much more highly than Churchill the importance of China and of assisting Jiang Jieshi, perhaps because he expected that China would follow the American lead in international policy. This difference was not of too great practical importance, since available aid for Jiang was severely limited. The war against Japan was won not on the Chinese mainland, but by sea and air attacks upon the Japanese homeland.

In the strategy of the war in Europe, such differences as arose were usually between the two men's military advisers rather than between Roosevelt and Churchill. The Americans, anxious to deliver a knockout blow to Germany at the earliest possible moment, urged a crossing of the English Channel by Anglo-American forces in the spring of 1943, with a possible preliminary crossing still earlier. The British, with tragic memories of the trench warfare of World War I, would not agree to such a crossing until assured of possession of overwhelming force and adequate landing equipment, and until Germany had been further worn down by blockade, bombing, and attrition on the Eastern front—Churchill insisted that 1943 was too early. In the face of this refusal, General Marshall proposed shifting the main American effort to the Pacific, but Roosevelt at once vetoed this suggestion. A compromise was found in TORCH, the North African landing in November 1942; followed by the advance into Sicily and Italy in 1943; and OVERLORD, the Normandy landing in June 1944. The dispute had been over timing, not over the final objective. A proposal of Churchill's in 1944 that troops in Italy, earmarked for southern France, be sent instead across the Adriatic into Yugoslavia and perhaps as far as Vienna and Hungary, where they might have anticipated the Red Army, was vetoed by Roosevelt. Churchill, disturbed by the advance of the Red armies was more concerned for the political future of Central Europe than were Roosevelt and his advisers, who tended to think in strictly military terms.

One real difference in outlook between the two men persisted throughout the war. Roosevelt, an anti-imperialist, had no enthusiasm for preserving or restoring the colonial holdings of the French or the British and occasionally urged upon Churchill the claims to independence of India or other British possessions. Churchill, not unexpectedly, took a dim view of such ideas. Proud as Rudyard Kipling of his nation's imperial achievements, he proclaimed in the House of Commons, soon after the Anglo-American landing in North Africa: "I have not become the King's First Minister in order to preside over the liquidation of the British Empire." The anticolonialism of Roosevelt and Cordell Hull was traceable in principle to Woodrow Wilson's preaching of self-determination, but it had, too, an important economic significance. Colonial empires, even the liberal British Commonwealth, were associated with "imperial preferences," that is, with partially closed economic systems. These were contrary to the nondiscriminatory, or "open door," principles that Hull had tried to promote through the reciprocal trade treaties and the terms of the lend-lease arrangements.

The best assurance of the end of "imperial preference" would be the end of empires. Here, as in some other matters, American principles were in harmony with American economic interests.

One consequence of the Arcadia Conference between Churchill and Roosevelt was the set up in Washington of a body known as the Combined Chiefs of Staff. Formed in January 1942, This group was made up of the Joint Chiefs of Staff of the United States (the army, navy and air force chiefs, together with, later on, the chief of staff to the president) and deputies of the corresponding British chiefs, the deputies being quartered in the Pentagon in offices adjacent to those of the American chiefs. This body was charged with making and executing plans for the strategic conduct of the war, for meeting war requirements in material, for allocating munitions and transportation facilities, all of which was conducted, of course, under the general direction of the president and the prime minister.

Further machinery for Anglo-American collaboration took the form of a number of combined boards created in 1942 and consisting of American and British members. The most important of these were those for raw materials, munitions assignments, shipping adjustment, production and resources, and food. On the last two, Canada also was represented. The purpose was to direct all materials and services available to the United States into channels where they would contribute most to winning the war. There was, of course, friction between Americans and British at various levels, but on the whole, the branches of the English-speaking world cooperated with gratifying smoothness and success.

If a lack of cordiality characterized Soviet-American relations until 1939, despite Roosevelt's moves to recognize the Soviet regime, the events of that year and of 1940 turned American sentiment violently against the Soviets. Josef Stalin's pact with Hitler was quickly followed by the Red Army's occupation of eastern Poland. The Baltic states of Lithuania, Latvia, and Estonia were first required to admit Soviet troops for their "protection" and then quietly were incorporated into the U.S.S.R.'s territory. When Finland refused to grant in full the Kremlin's demand for bases on Finnish territory and was attacked and invaded in consequence, it put up a brave but hopeless fight, which won the sympathy of the democracies and led to the expulsion of the U.S.S.R. from the League of Nations, the League's last, futile gesture against aggression. All of these Soviet acts alienated whatever sympathy American non-Communists may have felt for the U.S.S.R. and were poor preparation for wartime partnership.

When Hitler turned his arms against his former partner on June 22, 1941, the United States joined Great Britain in welcoming the Soviet Union into the fellowship of the nations engaged in combating totalitarianism. Secretary Hull, ill at home, phoned the president: "We must give Russia all aid to the hilt. We have repeatedly said we will give all the help we can to any nation resisting the Axis." Roosevelt stated at once that the United States was prepared to give all possible assistance to the Soviet Union. Convinced through on-the-spot investigations by Harry Hopkins, Averell Harriman, and others that the U.S.S.R. would hold out if adequately supplied, he informed Stalin on October 30 that military equipment and munitions to the value of $1 billion would be supplied under lend-lease. A week later, he instructed the lend-lease administrator that he now found the defense of the U.S.S.R. as vital to the national security of the United States and that therefore Moscow qualified for immediate lend-lease aid. This was the first installment of lend-lease goods to the amount of $11 billion to be supplied to the Soviet Union during the war. Shipments went via Murmansk, via Vladivostok (under the noses of the Japanese), and via the Persian Gulf and Iran.

In return, the Soviet armies and people, through their heroic resistance, played an indispensable role in defeating Nazi Germany. Apart from this, the Soviet government made certain gestures of good will that soft-pedaled, for the time being at least, the basic antagonism of Soviet communism for the capitalist world. On the American side, there was much wishful thinking to the effect that the collaboration of wartime would survive the destruction of Hitler. Neither Roosevelt nor his advisers, whether civil or military, seemed aware of the danger of a too powerful postwar U.S.S.R.; or, if the danger occurred to them, their remedy was to integrate Stalin's aims with those of the West. If faith in Stalin's good intentions wavered, there was another motivation sustaining the collaboration: fear that Russia might turn again to Hitler and make a separate peace, or fear that Russia would not aid in defeating Japan after Germany had been crushed. The idea prevailed in Washington that the United States needed the Soviet Union more than the Soviet Union needed the United States. Therefore, Stalin could name his price and sometimes got even more than he asked. Lend-lease aid, for example was sometimes pressed upon indifferent Soviet recipients.

The Soviet Union, for its part, showed no such naive trust in its Western allies. It was not without grounds for suspicion, for a common British hope had been to see Germany and the U.S.S.R. tear each other to pieces while the West stood by. So now, almost from the time the United States entered the war, Stalin demanded the opening without delay of a second front in Europe, to relieve the pressure on the massive but tiring Red armies. Misleading assurances about a second front in 1942 were given to Vyacheslav Molotov on a visit to Washington in May and June of that year, and Churchill later had difficulty in persuading Stalin that the landing in North Africa (November 1942) was the only offensive possible to the Western Allies at that stage. Up to the Normandy landing in June 1944, there were periodic complaints from Moscow that the Anglo-American forces were dragging their feet. As late as March 1945, Anglo-American negotiations for the surrender of German troops in northern Italy brought from Stalin angry accusations that his allies were planning a separate peace.

In the meantime, there was endless friction in negotiations over comparatively minor matters—over the use of bases in Soviet territory, over liberated prisoners of war, even over the details of lend-lease, where the Soviets were given to haggling over prices of goods for which they would never be called upon to pay. One frustrating difficulty arose from the almost invisible amount of discretion allowed to Soviet negotiators at all but the top levels; virtually all decisions had to be referred to higher authority. When Soviet authorities made concessions on paper, they too often failed to implement them in practice. When the president and the secretary of state met with their corresponding Soviet officials, as they did on several occasions, superficial harmony was generally achieved, but in these meetings, the Soviets generally had their way, and such concessions as they made to the American or British point of view were too often forgotten when the time came to apply them.

By its Good Neighbor Policy of the 1930s, the United States had laid the basis for New World solidarity in confronting Axis aggression. Axis sympathizers were influential in Argentina and, to a lesser degree, in Chile. The rest of Latin America cordially supported the United States during both its nonbelligerency and its participation in the war. Following the outbreak of war in Europe, the foreign ministers of the American republics met in conference in Panama in September and October 1939. There they approved a General Declaration of Neutrality of the American Republics and announced rules of neutral conduct that, like the U.S. Neutrality Act of 1939, favored the European democracies. In the Declaration of Panama, they undertook to prohibit any belligerent act in the waters adjacent to the American continents (south of the Canadian border) and delimited those waters as extending on the average three hundred miles to sea. It was in this declaration that President Roosevelt found justification for patrolling North Atlantic waters for the detection of Axis submarines.

The German victories over the Netherlands and France in the spring of 1940 raised the question of the fate of the French and Dutch possessions in the Caribbean. The possibility that they might be claimed or seized by Germany called forth reassertions by the secretary of state and by Congress of the nontransfer principle long associated with the Monroe Doctrine. It led also to another conference of American foreign ministers in Havana in July 1940. There, by the Act of Havana, the foreign ministers provided that an "emergency committee," one member from each republic, might set up a "provisional administration" for any European colony in the American area that might be threatened with a change of sovereignty. In urgent cases, a single American republic might act without waiting for a meeting of the committee. Upon the ending of the danger, the colony in question should either become independent or return to its former status. A convention, giving permanent form to the provisions of the act, also signed in Havana, was ratified and proclaimed early in 1942.

Such drastic action as that contemplated in the act and the Treaty of Havana ultimately proved unnecessary. The landing of American troops in Greenland and Iceland was done with the consent of the Danish minister in the first case and the Icelandic government in the second. By arrangement with the Dutch government, U.S. and Brazilian troops aided in the protection of the bauxite mines in Surinam, from which came 60 percent of the ore for the American aluminum industry. In the spirit of Havana, however, the United States informed the American republics of its action in Surinam, and declared open to the use of any of them the bases acquired through the arrangement with Great Britain securing bases in exchange for allowing the British Navy to lease American destroyers.The attack on the United States at Pearl Harbor and the declarations of war by the Axis powers brought the real test of inter-American solidarity. The results were in the main gratifying. All of the Central American and Caribbean republics (many of them former objects of intervention by the United States) promptly declared war against the Axis powers and were on hand to sign the United Nations Declaration, January 1, 1942. Mexico, Colombia, and Venezuela severed diplomatic relations with the Axis. The other republics without exception sent friendly messages to the United States. Not one subjected it to the restrictions that normally would have been imposed upon a belligerent.

For a third time, the foreign ministers or their deputies met in January 1942, this time in Rio de Janeiro. Here they declared that an act of aggression against one was aggression against all and recommended that all member states that had not yet severed relations with the Axis powers to do so without further delay. This recommendation met with prompt compliance, except by Chile, which delayed until January 1943, and Argentina, which continued to harbor Axis diplomats until January 1944. Eventually all the American republics declared war against Germany or Japan or both, although Argentina did not do so until March 27, 1945. All except Argentina and Panama received lend-lease assistance. Brazil sent an expeditionary force to Europe. Brazil, Cuba, Ecuador, and Panama permitted the United States to establish military bases within their territory. Otherwise, except in the furnishing of raw materials at good prices, their positive contributions to the war effort were not great. Nevertheless, the assurance that enemy agents would not find harborage in neighboring territory was an advantage of no small consequence to the United States.

SHAPING THE POSTWAR WORLD

Plans for ending the war and arranging for the peace to follow it began many months before the United States became a belligerent. The chief planners were the United States and the Soviet Union. American plans were highly publicized in Roosevelt's pronouncements, which were idealistic in the main but not altogether neglectful of American material interests. Stalin talked little but moved quietly to safeguard the Soviet future. Winston Churchill, a poor third in the possession of power, accepted the American program with skepticism and watched Soviet strategy with misgiving.

By his actions during 1939 and 1940 in Finland and the Baltic, Stalin was clearly violating the spirit of self-determination encapsulated in the Anglo-American Atlantic Charter. Anthony Eden, the British foreign secretary, visiting Moscow in December 1941, was confronted with a demand that Great Britain recognize the Soviet Union's annexation of the Baltic States and a slice of Finland. Eden agreed to pass on the Soviet proposal to Great Britain and the United States. The United States rejected this demand as in conflict with the Atlantic Charter, despite Churchill's argument in favor of expedient concessions to the Kremlin. Both powers, furthermore, refused to accede to Molotov's demand, a few months later, that they recognize Soviet claims on eastern Poland and a part of Rumania. Molotov settled for a twenty-year treaty of alliance with Britain, in which both governments agreed to "act in accordance with the two principles of not seeking territorial aggrandizement for themselves and of non-interference in the internal affairs of other States." This phraseology accorded well with the Atlantic Charter, but at the Teheran Conference (November–December 1943) Stalin informed Roosevelt that the status of the former Baltic States was not open to discussion, since they had voted to join the Soviet Union. At the same conference, the Western powers agreed to the Soviet proposals for the boundaries of Poland. Here, as elsewhere, the principles of the Atlantic Charter yielded, first to the urgent need of holding the U.S.S.R. as an ally and, later, to the persuasive presence of victorious Red Army.

The frequent meetings of Roosevelt and Churchill were concerned very largely with the conduct of the war. As military prospects improved, however, their meetings and those that they held with Stalin and Jiang Jieshi dealt increasingly with the shape of the peace and with postwar problems. In January 1943, two months after the successful landings in North Africa, the president and the prime minister met in Casablanca, on the Atlantic coast of Morocco. Premier Stalin was invited to attend the meeting but, in the words of the official communiqué, "was unable to leave Russia at this time on account of the great offensive which he himself, as Commander-in-Chief, is directing." The principal business of the conference was the planning of campaigns to come, in the Mediterranean theater and elsewhere, but in his remarks to the press correspondents at the close of the conference on January 26, 1943, the president used a momentous expression. Recalling the phrase "unconditional surrender" used by General Ulysses S. Grant in the American Civil War, Roosevelt informed the reporters: "The democracies' war plans were to compel the 'unconditional surrender' of the Axis." The use of this phrase, which had been approved in advance by Churchill and the British War Cabinet, was apparently designed to convince Stalin that America and Britain were determined to fight the war to a finish. In the opinion of most analysts, it had the unintended and unfortunate effect of stiffening enemy resistance and postponing the day of surrender, certainly of Germany and Japan, and perhaps of Italy. Conducive to the complete destruction of German and Japanese military potential, it helped to ensure the collapse of the balance of power and the military ascendancy of the Soviet Union in Europe and Asia.

Similarly unfortunate in its hardening effect on German resistance was the endorsement by Roosevelt and Churchill, during their meeting in Quebec in September 1944, of the so-called Morgenthau Plan. Named for its author, Secretary of the Treasury Henry Morgenthau, Jr., the plan called for the forcible conversion of Germany "into a country primarily agricultural and pastoral in its character." It was vigorously opposed by Secretary of State Hull and Secretary of War Stimson. The bitter debate that erupted upon Roosevelt's return to Washington was more than a turf war; Roosevelt and Churchill soon had their eyes opened to the preposterous nature of a program that would have eliminated the most productive industrial workshop in Europe, leaving a void in the European economy and starving millions in western Germany. The plan was quietly shelved but not before it had "leaked." To Joseph Goebbels, minister of information in Berlin, it had obvious propaganda value.

Roosevelt met Stalin for the first time in November 1943. But a month before that, Hull, despite his seventy-two years and frail health, had flown to Moscow to confer with Vyacheslav Molotov and Anthony Eden. Italy had surrendered to Anglo-American forces in September, and the German divisions that still held much of the peninsula were being steadily pushed back. The Soviet armies, too, had taken the offensive. The tide of war had turned, and it was none too soon to consider postwar arrangements. At the close of a twelve-day conference, held October 19–30, 1943, the foreign ministers of the Big Three issued a communiqué and a number of declarations. They had agreed upon setting up in London a European Advisory Commission to study and make recommendations upon questions that might arise as the war developed. An Advisory Council for Italy, to include a representative of the French Committee of National Liberation, and eventually representatives of Greece and Yugoslavia, was to make recommendations for coordinating Allied policy in Italy. A declaration regarding Italy promised a government "made more democratic by the introduction of representatives of those sections of the Italian people who have always opposed Fascism." It also promised to the Italian people restoration of freedom of speech, the press, political belief, public meeting, and religious worship. A declaration on Austria promised liberation from German domination and recorded the wish of the three governments "to see re-established a free and independent Austria."

At the urging of Secretary Hull, China was invited to join in what thus became a Declaration of Four Nations on General Security. In this, the four governments pledged that the united action of wartime would be "continued for the organization and maintenance of peace and security" and recognized "the necessity of establishing at the earliest practicable date a general international organization" for that purpose. Here was the first definite international commitment to the idea of a postwar substitute for the League of Nations. In Secretary Hull's mind, having secured a Soviet pledge to cooperate with the Western powers in a postwar security organization was an important achievement. In reporting on the work of the conference to a joint sitting of Congress, he prophesied, "As the provisions of the Four-Nation Declaration are carried into effect, there will no longer be need for spheres of influence, for alliances, for balance of power, or any other of the special arrangements through which, in the unhappy past, the nations strove to safeguard their security or to promote their interests."

In Moscow, the foreign ministers also issued a declaration on German atrocities over the signatures of Roosevelt, Churchill, and Stalin. This declaration promised punishment for crimes committed against nationals of the countries occupied by German armed forces but said nothing about Nazi atrocities against their own Jewish nationals. Merciless persecution of German Jews had begun immediately upon Hitler's accession to power in 1933. It had been promptly extended into the countries annexed or occupied by the Third Reich. While such racial persecution was deplored in the United States, the American people, with some millions unemployed, showed no disposition to make places for refugees from the Nazi terror, and the State Department, partly out of fear that spies might slip in as refugees, displayed a surprising indifference to the sufferings and death of millions of European Jews and to the plight of thousands of Protestant and Catholic Christians who were also victims of Nazi persecution. Contrary to precedent, the department, with Roosevelt's approval, took the position that the United States had no right to interfere with the German government's policy toward its own nationals. Even after receipt in August 1942 of conclusive evidence that Hitler's "final solution" of the Jewish question was the extermination of all European Jews, the State Department declined to protest.

Omission of all mention of the plight of the Jews from the Moscow Declaration aroused deep indignation among Jews in the United States and Britain. In the ensuing month, however, Secretary of the Treasury Morgenthau and members of his staff were able to convince Roosevelt that some effort should be made to save those European Jews who had not yet been sent to the gas chambers. On January 20, 1944, the president set up the War Refugee Board, which acted vigorously and with some success to save many thousands of Jews remaining in satellite countries. In a strong statement two months later, Roosevelt described the Nazi treatment of the Jews as "one of the blackest crimes of all history" and gave assurance of American determination that none who participated in these acts of savagery shall go unpunished. The new policy bore some fruit. It should have been tried years earlier, although the threats of punishment owed their efficacy to the growing conviction that Hitler was doomed to defeat.

During the Moscow conference, arrangements had also been made for a meeting of Roosevelt, Churchill, and Stalin at Teheran, the capital of Iran. This was as far from his own borders as Stalin could be induced to journey. Jiang Jieshi, by contrast, did not hesitate to fly to Cairo to confer with Roosevelt and Churchill as they stopped there en route to Teheran. From Cairo, the three statesmen issued a declaration (released December 1, 1943) calling for the withdrawal of Japan to its borders as they had been at the beginning of 1914, the restoration of Chinese territories, and a commitment to the independence of Korea.

In Teheran, where the Big Three leaders and their advisers conferred from November 28 to December 1, 1943, Roosevelt, as he reported to Congress, "'got along fine' with Marshal Stalin," and on the basis of this experience predicted "that we are going to get along well with him and the Russian people—very well indeed." The meeting was, in fact, quite harmonious. Important military decisions were reached; notably that the cross-Channel invasion, known as OVERLORD, should be launched in May or June 1944, with a supporting landing on the south coast of France and a simultaneous Soviet offensive in the east. Stalin repeated the promise, made to Hull in Moscow, that as soon as Germany was defeated, the Soviet forces would enter the war against Japan. He mentioned no price for such intervention, but Churchill expressed sympathy with the Soviets' desire for an ice-free port, and Roosevelt suggested that access to Dairen in South Manchuria would meet the need. It was agreed that in Yugoslavia all aid should be given to Tito and his partisans—a decision that ensured Communist, though not necessarily Soviet, domination of that country.

On the political side, the most important questions debated were the boundaries of Poland and the future of Germany. The three leaders were in general agreement that Poland's eastern boundary should be the Curzon Line, a supposedly ethnographical demarcation proposed in 1919. Poland would thus lose some White Russian and Ukrainian areas that it had held from 1921 and 1939. For these losses in the east, it was to be compensated in the west by accessions of German territory up to the Oder River. Neither Churchill nor Roosevelt betrayed any moral scruple about these territorial changes to be made, contrary to the principle of self-determination espoused in the Atlantic Charter, although Churchill did insist upon Polish boundaries that he could defend to the Polish government in exile in London.

Nor did either Roosevelt or Churchill reveal any uneasiness over the proposed elimination of Germany as a military factor and the consequent destruction of the balance of power in Europe. Both agreed with Stalin that the revival of German military must be made impossible. Roosevelt proposed that Germany be partitioned into five independent states, excluding the Ruhr-Saar and Kiel areas, which should be internationally controlled. Churchill preferred to isolate Prussia on the one hand and, on the other, to construct a Danubian Confederation along lines resembling those of the former Austro-Hungarian Empire. Stalin preferred Roosevelt's solution to Churchill's. No decision was reached, but the debate showed to what extent the Nazi peril had blinded Roosevelt, and even Churchill, to the menace of Soviet expansion.

Roosevelt and Stalin did not meet again until the celebrated Yalta Conference in February 1945. In the interval, Churchill paid a visit to Moscow in October 1944, a meeting code-named "TOLSTOY," with the principal object of seeking an understanding on the affairs of Poland and the Balkan States. The latter problem proved the easier to solve temporarily and superficially. It existed because of the advance of the Soviet armies into Rumania and Bulgaria and a threatened conflict between Russian and British interests, especially in Greece and Yugoslavia. A temporary arrangement of the previous June, giving to the U.S.S.R. predominance for three months in Rumania and to Britain the same in Greece, had been acceded to by Roosevelt over the objections of the State Department. Now Churchill proposed and Stalin accepted (at least he made a blue check mark on Churchill's memorandum) an extension of this arrangement on a mathematical formula. According to Churchill's notation, as amended by Molotov, the Soviet Union should have 90 percent predominance in Rumania, and Britain (presumably in accord with the United States) 90 percent in Greece. Russian influence should predominate 80 to 20 percent in Bulgaria and Hungary, while in Yugoslavia, the proportion was to be 50–50. It seems clear that this exercise in arithmetic had no binding force, particularly since Roosevelt had cautioned Stalin that he would not be bound by a tête-à-tête agreement made in his absence; but it is useful in indicating the thinking of Stalin and Churchill at the time.[2]

The three leaders next met at Yalta in the recently liberated Crimea. Here the statesmen, with their diplomatic and military staffs—700 British and American were flown in a night from Malta to Yalta—met from February 4 to 11, 1945. Four principal subjects occupied the time of the conference: (1) details of the proposed United Nations Organization; (2) the treatment of defeated Germany; (3) restoration of self-government in the countries of eastern Europe, now occupied in whole or in part by Russian armies; and (4) the terms of Russia's entry into the war against Japan. The future of Germany was left undecided. The governments of the United Kingdom, the United States, and the Soviet Union were declared to possess "supreme authority" to "take such steps, including the complete disarmament, demilitarization, and dismemberment of Germany as they deem requisite for future peace and security." Study of the procedure of dismemberment was referred to a committee consisting of the British foreign secretary and the American and Russian ambassadors in London, who might at their discretion bring in a French member. In the meantime, Germany was to be divided into four zones of military occupation, a French zone to be formed out of previously agreed upon American and British zones.

Germany was to pay reparations in kind, in the first instance to the nations that had borne the main burden of the war, suffered most heavily, and "organized victory over the enemy." Reparations were to be of three categories: (1) removal, over a two-year period, of capital goods located either within or without German territory, "chiefly for the purpose of destroying the war potential of Germany"; (2) "annual deliveries of goods from current production for a period to be fixed"; and (3) "use of German labor." A reparations commission representing the three governments was to be set up in Moscow. The American and Soviet delegations agreed in recommending that the commission should take, "as a basis for discussion," a total reparations figure of twenty billion dollars, one-half to go to the Soviet Union. The British delegation was opposed to naming any figure, pending consideration by the commission. The question of punishment of major war criminals was left for inquiry and later report by the three foreign secretaries. At one stage, Churchill proposed that all German war criminals should be shot without trial. The conference also agreed that a new Polish Provisional Government of National Unity should be established, constituted by including with the existing (Communist) Provisional Government at Lublin "democratic leaders from Poland itself and from Poles abroad." The new government should be "pledged to the holding of free and unfettered elections as soon as possible on the basis of universal suffrage and secret ballot." The "three heads of Government" considered that Poland's eastern boundary should be the Curzon Line, with some deviations in favor of Poland, and that Poland should receive "substantial accessions of territory in the north and west." These accessions were not defined.

Both the American and British governments had for some time considered Soviet aid indispensable against Japan if the war in the Far East were to be brought to an early conclusion. Stalin had promised such aid to Hull in Moscow, to Roosevelt in Teheran, and to Churchill during his visit to Moscow in October 1944. Beyond specifying that he would need to stockpile over a million tons of lend-lease goods for the campaign in the Far East, Stalin had hinted in October 1944 that there were political questions that should be "clarified" before he directed his forces to enter the Pacific war. In an interview between Stalin and Ambassador Averell Harriman in December 1944, the questions became demands. Harriman telegraphed these demands to Roosevelt on December 15. The president knew of them, therefore, six weeks before setting out for Yalta and had ample time to consider them. They were embodied almost word for word in the Yalta agreement. By that agreement, Stalin promised, subject to several important conditions being met first, that the Soviet Union would enter the war against Japan "in two or three months" after the German surrender.

No single act of President Roosevelt's career has been more harshly criticized than this group of agreements with Stalin at Yalta. The least excusable of the agreements made at Yalta was that concerning the Far East. The pretense that it restored to the Soviet Union rights of which Japan had robbed it was hollow. Russia had been the most active aggressor in the Far East between 1895 and 1904, and its moral claim to Dairen, Port Arthur, and the Manchurian railroads was no better than Japan's. All had been exacted from China by the threat of force. To restore to the U.S.S.R. these rights and properties, with recognition of its "preeminent interest" in Manchuria, was a contradiction of American policy since the turn of the century. It was paying Moscow for its assistance with Chinese coin. With hindsight, the tragic irony is that Soviet aid was not needed. The postwar U.S. Strategic Bombing Survey concluded that without the Soviets' entry into the war, without invasion of the homeland, and without use of the atomic bomb, Japan would have surrendered before December 31 and probably before November 30, a month after the date set for the first Anglo-American invasion of the home islands. This estimate, of course, was not known to Roosevelt or his advisers in Yalta, but it is to be noted that both the navy and the commander of the Strategic Air Force were skeptical about the need for invasion or Russian assistance. It was the army that misjudged the situation and was chiefly responsible for Roosevelt's decision to pay Stalin's price.

NOTES

1. Truman unwitting gave himself this nickname when he fed it to reporters on his 1948 whistle-stop campaign. See Robert J. Donovan, *Conflict and Crisis: The Presidency of Harry S Truman, 1945–1948* (New York: W. W. Norton, 1977), p. 420.

2. Joseph M. Siracusa, *Into the Dark House: American Diplomacy and the Ideological Origins of the Cold War* (Claremont, CA: Regina, 1998), pp. 1–30.

Chapter 6

The Transition

By 1945, the United States was on the verge of victory in both military theaters, and the Great Depression was all but vanquished. The tumult of the previous decade seemed to be giving way to a tangible promise of peace and prosperity; but realizing that promise would not be easy. When Harry S. Truman assumed the presidency upon Franklin Roosevelt's death, he was relatively ill-prepared for the office—and America was equally unprepared for a new president—yet circumstances dictated that he would oversee a period of extraordinary transition. Victory in Europe and ultimately in the Pacific, the conversion of a wartime economy to a peacetime one, the beginning of the cold war, the dawn of the nuclear age, the massive demobilization of the armed forces, and the rapid infiltration of technology and new-found affluence into everyday life were just some of the challenges—and opportunities—that America faced in the postwar years. For better or worse, the decisions Truman made and the actions he took reverberated through American society and policy for decades to come.

VICTORY ON BOTH FRONTS

By the spring of 1945, the race for Berlin was on. The Western allies had liberated France and pushed east across the Rhine in a final drive into the heart of the German Third Reich. Simultaneously, Marshal Georgi Zhukov's Red Army forces surged westward; by March, a million Soviet troops were within thirty miles of Berlin. Acutely aware of the political prestige that would accrue to the conqueror of the Nazi capital, British

Prime Minister Winston Churchill and Field Marshal Bernard Law Montgomery sought a quick drive in order that the Western allies reach Berlin before the Soviets. "We should shake hands with the Russians as far to the east as possible," Churchill told Allied Supreme Commander General Dwight D. Eisenhower.[1] Eisenhower disagreed on the basis of military expediency and provoked the outrage of Churchill, the British chiefs of staff, and even American General George S. Patton, Jr., by informing Stalin that he would leave the capture of Berlin to the Red Army and would direct Allied forces away from the city and toward the Bavarian Alps to head off the establishment of a German national redoubt, a much-rumored attempt by the Nazi regime to relocate to remote mountain bunkers from where it could conceivably prolong the war for months. To absolutely no one's surprise, Stalin readily agreed. In vain, Churchill implored Roosevelt to overrule Eisenhower. With the capture of Vienna imminent, he cautioned, "if they [the Soviets] also take Berlin will not their impression that they have been the overwhelming contributor to our common victory be unduly imprinted in their minds, and may this not lead them into a mood which will raise grave and formidable difficulties in the future?"[2] As it happened, on April 7, the Red Army captured Vienna. On May 2, Zhukov's forces secured Berlin. Prague and Budapest quickly followed.

At this fateful moment of the war, with the Anglo-American-Soviet alliance on the verge of military victory in Europe, Roosevelt died suddenly on April 12, 1945, of a massive cerebral hemorrhage. His death came as a shock. "We had no idea that he was ill," remembered John Kenneth Galbraith, then head of the Office of Price Administration. "We thought he would live forever."[3] Eisenhower, who had never met Truman and heard the news of Roosevelt's passing while listening to British Broadcasting Corporation radio, was apprehensive about what the change in the White House would mean for the war. "It seemed to us," Eisenhower wrote, "to be a most critical time to be forced to change national leaders. We went to bed depressed and sad."[4] The U.S. armed forces magazine *Yank* observed without exaggeration that Roosevelt had been commander-in-chief not only of the armed forces but also of a whole generation. He was the only president younger Americans had ever known; his New Deal legislation, with its clear humanitarian spirit of government, was the only political program they had experienced. During World War I, the federal government was still a comparatively small enterprise; by the time Roosevelt died, it touched in one way or another almost every facet of American life. The question of government intervention in the American economy to promote the welfare of the people—the hallmark of the New Deal—had become settled. Equally significant, Roosevelt gradually broke down the nation's interwar isolationist psychology and prepared for the nation's participation in World War II. Pearl Harbor, together with Roosevelt's diplomacy, made certain that things would never be the same again.

Roosevelt's influence went well beyond America's shores. Not since Woodrow Wilson had an American president played such a vital role on the world stage. To the Soviets, Roosevelt was friend and "the personification of enlightened American liberalism," as the Moscow correspondent of *The Times* of London put it. Finding it difficult to find hyperbole strong enough to convey the sense of loss felt all over the free world, the *British Economist* summed it up this way: "Never before in a statesman of another country and rarely for one of our own leaders have the outward pomp of ceremonial mourning and also the inward and personal lamentation of the public been more universal and heartfelt." The most telling comment came from the man to whom the mantle of American leadership had fallen along with the hopes and expectations of the nation: vice president of a mere eight months, Harry Truman. "No man," Truman wrote, "could possibly fill the tremendous void left by the passing of that noble soul." All in all, to contemplate the career of Franklin D. Roosevelt and his impact on the course of American and world affairs was to come to grips with the very problem of "great men" in history, regardless of one's view of his politics.

By contrast, Truman was self-consciously—and proudly—of the "common people." With his colorful language, direct manner, and celebrated lack of pretension, Truman appeared at first glance to be everything Roosevelt was not. Acutely aware that he was untested on the world stage, the new president could nevertheless take some comfort in having the confidence of the nation. Truman was a man of his times, an avowed internationalist and an accomplished politician, and he soon demonstrated that he could wield his new powers with considerable executive ability. Fully determined to be president in his own right, Truman made clear that he would be wholly responsible for the decisions he would have to make, famously adopting an old poker phrase to underscore the point: "The buck stops here." Nevertheless, his first months in the Oval Office were consumed by trying to continue Roosevelt's policies while struggling to keep pace with rapidly changing events. Being driven by events during these first few months, Truman later wrote, convinced him that "being a president is like riding a tiger. A man has to keep on riding or be swallowed."[5]

While the world grieved Roosevelt's passing and tried to take the measure of the new president, Soviet shells rained down on Berlin. Facing the inevitable, Adolf Hitler committed suicide in his subterranean bunker below the streets of Berlin on April 30, 1945. His death only formalized the disarray of his regime, and V-E (Victory in Europe) Day finally came when Eisenhower accepted the German army's unconditional surrender at Reims on May 7, to go into effect the next day.[6] Thus, the Third Reich, which was supposed to endure a thousand years, was destroyed after only twelve. When Eisenhower flew into Washington in the presidential plane "Sacred Cow" on June 18, 1945, he was welcomed as a hero in every way. More than thirty fighters and bombers escorted the plane to its landing at

National Airport in Washington, D.C., and more than a million men and women thronged to greet him.[7]

But there was business still to be done. As Roosevelt had prophesied at Yalta, the Big Three—Great Britain, the United States, and the Soviet Union—met next in Berlin, at Potsdam, an outer suburb of the city. Convening on July 17 and adjourning on August 2, 1945, the aptly code-named TERMINAL conference was attended by a new cast of characters. In Roosevelt's place sat Truman; at his shoulder sat Secretary of State James Byrnes, a long-time Roosevelt supporter and Truman's disappointed rival from the 1944 vice presidential nomination. Truman had appointed Byrnes believing that it would provide continuity of U.S. policy, but in truth, Byrnes had not been so privy to Roosevelt's thinking or the key Yalta discussions as Truman imagined. Midway through the conference, Winston Churchill's Tory Party suffered defeat in the national elections, and his place was taken, both at 10 Downing Street and at the conference table at Potsdam, by Clement Attlee of the Labour Party. He was accompanied by his foreign minister, Ernest Bevin.

Among the most contentious issues was the future of Poland. The composition of the government of the re-emerging Polish state remained the great stumbling block, symbolizing in Western eyes Stalin's expansionist aims. Also at issue was the establishment of a Council of Foreign Ministers to prepare treaties for Italy and the lesser Axis states of Rumania, Hungary, Bulgaria, and Finland. A German peace treaty, however, remained elusive. More controversial in the immediate discussion was the issue of reparations. Stalin insisted that Germany help pay for rebuilding the Soviet economy. The Allies were determined to learn from the mistakes of the Versailles treaty and resisted moves to impose an overly harsh peace on the conquered nation. A compromise was reached whereby each occupying force would obtain its share of reparations from its own zone, with the Soviet Union to be compensated for its greater losses by 25 percent of the capital goods located within the western industrialized zones, a part of which in turn was to be exchanged for food shipments from the largely agricultural areas occupied by the Soviets. Finally, as a purely temporary arrangement, Germany was divided into four occupation zones. France, Great Britain, and the United States would occupy the three western zones, and the Soviets would control the eastern zone. Each occupation force was responsible for implementing in its own zone the overall program to denazify, decentralize, disarm, and democratize Germany until such time as it was deemed fit to rejoin the family of nations. Berlin, which was deep inside Soviet territory according to the zonal boundaries agreed upon earlier, would also be divided and jointly occupied. In this temporary and arbitrary division of Germany lay the seeds of some of the most dangerous confrontations of the cold war.

For the moment, however, the cold war remained undeclared. Potsdam, like the Yalta Conference before it, ended on a note of apparent friendship and continued cooperation. Truman was impressed after his first face-to-face encounter with Stalin, recording in his diary that "he is honest—but smart as hell." Many years later, Truman had the opportunity to look back on the Potsdam conference: "What a show that was! But a large number of agreements were reached in spite of the set up—only to be broken as soon as the unconscionable Russian Dictator returned to Moscow! And I liked the little son of a bitch."

Unaware that in his last days Roosevelt had been having second thoughts about how best to deal with Stalin, Truman initially adhered to Roosevelt's official policy of collaboration with the Soviet Union. It was not long, however, that Truman, like his advisers, came to recognize that Moscow viewed conciliatory gestures as a sign of weakness. For some time, the American ambassador to the Soviet Union, W. Averell Harriman, had been warning that the Soviets were increasingly confusing Washington's "generosity" with weakness. "There is every indication the Soviet Union will become a world bully wherever their interests are involved," he warned.[8] By the time Vyacheslav Molotov, the Soviet foreign minister and Stalin's deputy, arrived for talks in Washington in April 1945 en route to the founding conference of the United Nations to be held in San Francisco, Truman had served notice that he considered U.S.-U.S.S.R. relations up to that point to have been overwhelmingly one-way and that he expected more from the Soviets. Moreover, the president made it clear that his patience was rapidly running out. In their celebrated meeting of April 23, Truman rebuked Molotov for Soviet behavior, all in the roughest Missouri language. The Soviet foreign minister, a dour, humorless man, yet a universally respected diplomat, defended his nation's interpretation of the Polish accord worked out at Yalta in February, adding that he had never been spoken to in such terms. According to Truman's interpreter, Charles Bohlen, these were "probably the first sharp words uttered during the war by an American President to a high Soviet official."[9]

While the cold war loomed on the horizon, there were more pressing matters to deal with and primary among them was convincing the Japanese leaders to surrender unconditionally. Having successfully executed the "Europe first" part of U.S. war strategy, American military might was diverted to the Pacific. At Potsdam, Stalin, who was then still technically at peace with Tokyo, agreed to enter into the war in the Pacific on August 15, making good a pledge given earlier that the Soviet Union would do so three months after the war in Europe had been won. Also at Potsdam, the British, Chinese, and the United States (since the U.S.S.R. was not technically yet at war with Japan, Stalin took no part in discussions concerning the war in the Pacific) reissued their ultimatum of the unconditional surrender of Japan. Since late 1944, American long-range B-29 bombers had been conducting the greatest air offensive in history. In total, approximately 160,000 tons of bombs were dropped upon Japan toward the end of the war, including fire-bomb raids that destroyed downtown Tokyo and a number of other large Japanese cities. These raids alone killed 333,000 Japanese soldiers and civilians and wounded half a million more. As a consequence, by July 1945, the Japanese war economy was all but destroyed. But still Japan refused to surrender.

Although there were elements within the Japanese government that had long recognized the war was lost, official Allied policy continued to be that nothing less than unconditional surrender was acceptable. So, while the Japanese government and Emperor Hirohito favored suing for peace, the militarists, led by the army, resisted. Faced with such determined resistance, the Joint Chiefs of Staff estimated that the cost of invading the Japanese home islands would be no less than one million American and Allied casualties. Deeply troubled by such a prospect, Truman sought alternatives. Soon after assuming the presidency, Truman had been briefed by Secretary of War Henry Stimson on the Manhattan Project, an extraordinary collaboration of international scientists headed by J. Robert Oppenheimer and backed by the enormous resources of the U.S. government. The project was focused upon the objective of developing a new type of weapon harnessing the power generated by splitting the atom. Roosevelt had initially authorized the program in 1942 to ensure that the Allies perfected the technology before Nazi scientists did, but it was not until after the German surrender that the Manhattan Project bore its intended fruit. While at Potsdam, Truman had been informed that the first test, on July 16 at Alamogordo, New Mexico, had been successful. The United States now had in its arsenal a weapon capable of unparalleled destruction; Stimson even suggested that it would create "a new relationship of man to the universe."[10] Truman's advisers agreed that the atomic bomb could end the war in the Pacific, but they could not agree on the best way to use it. Some, such as scientist James Franck who chaired an important committee investigating the matter, proposed a public demonstration on an uninhabited region. Others argued that it should be used against Japanese naval forces. Others argued that it should be used against Japanese cities. Still others argued that the objective was not so much to defeat Japan as to issue a warning shot for Stalin's benefit.

After considering the various proposals, Truman concluded that the only way to ensure that the bomb had its maximum effect was to use it against Japanese cities. On the morning of August 6, 1945, shortly after 8:15 A.M., a lone B-29 bomber named the *Enola Gay* dropped a single bomb, dubbed the "Fat Boy," over the city of Hiroshima, Japan's second most important military-industrial center. Approximately 70,000 people were killed instantly in the blast. Three days later another, larger bomb with a destructive force equivalent to the collective load of 4,000 B-29 bombers, was dropped on Nagasaki killing at least 20,000. With Japanese doctors at a loss to explain why many civilian patients who had not been wounded were now wasting away, in the following weeks the death counts in both cities rose as the populations succumbed to radiation-related illnesses.

The shockwaves were felt well beyond the Japanese home islands. Western newspapers struggled to explain to a triumphant but mystified public how thousands of American, British, and Canadian scientists had managed to harness the power of the sun to such deadly effect. No easier to explain was that the U.S. government could undertake a military and scientific program as massive and prolonged as the Manhattan Project, employing more than 65,000 people, with such absolute secrecy. This paradoxical view of the government's achievement was typical of the American public's response to the bomb. The elation at the prospects of imminent peace was tempered by a growing recognition of the awesome responsibility of possessing such a powerful weapon. The impact of the new weapon spread well beyond the military and scientific circles in which it had been developed; to an extent unprecedented, it began to seep into the popular imagination as images of mushroom clouds became symbolic of the new destructive potential that had been developed. What Truman called "the greatest scientific gamble in history" had paid off with devastating effectiveness, and there was no doubt that a turning point in the history of the contemporary world had been reached. Indeed, "the bomb," as it was quickly dubbed, quickly became a defining feature of the post–World War II world.[11]

With a Japanese surrender imminent, and recognizing that if it was going to play a part in postwar Asia it would need to enter the fray quickly, the Soviet Union declared war on Japan on August 8, a week sooner than Stalin had pledged Truman at Potsdam. Nine minutes after its declaration, the Soviet Union's Far Eastern Army and Air Force attacked Japanese troops along the eastern U.S.S.R.-Manchuria borderlands. Yielding to the reality of the situation, Emperor Hirohito, supported by civilian advisers, finally overcame the Japanese militarists and ordered a surrender on August 14. For its part, the United States agreed to retain the institution of the emperor system, stripped of pretension to divinity and subject to American occupation headed by General Douglas MacArthur. On September 2, thereafter known as V-J Day, a great Allied fleet sailed into Tokyo Bay. Aboard the USS Missouri, General MacArthur accepted the Japanese surrender on behalf of the Allies. With a simple ceremony, World War II was finally brought to a close.

Even in small wars, counting casualties becomes an inexact science. Tallying the dead in the global destruction of World War II could never have been otherwise. Over 400,000 Americans had died. But this paled beside the casualties suffered in Europe and Asia where noncombatant deaths were disproportionately high. Of the estimated 55 million people killed, approximately 30 million were civilians, without including more than 5 million Jews killed in the Holocaust. In the Soviet Union, between 20 and 30 million, or one in every eight citizens, had died, almost half of which were civilians. China lost approximately 15 million, two-thirds of which were civilians; Germany lost approximately 7 million of which roughly half were civilians; and Poland lost almost 5 and a half million, all but about 120,000 of which were civilians; Japan lost around 2 million, most of which were military. While the American mainland had largely been spared the physical effects of the war, Europe had not. Farmlands were destroyed or littered with unexploded munitions. Disease and starvation ravaged millions of displaced persons. In Poland, three-fourths of the horses and two-thirds of the cattle were gone. The destruction of the dykes holding in China's Yellow River meant that much valuable farming land was submerged, as was much of the Dutch countryside.[12] Although the populations turned immediately to reconstruction, it was clear that the economies of Europe and Asia would neither quickly nor easily return to normal.

POSTWAR RECONSTRUCTION

In contrast to the European and Asian experiences, where destruction and fragmentation prevailed, the American experience immediately following the Second World War was characterized by renewal and staggering growth. In the last months of 1941 as war approached, army spending hit $2 billion a month; in the first six months of 1942, military spending rocketed to $100 billion. In 1939, the federal budget was $9 billion; by 1945 it had ballooned to $166 billion. These massive increases in government spending had profound—and for the most part positive—effects on American society. Almost overnight the crippling unemployment of the Great Depression had been wiped out; in fact, the labor market significantly increased with the war ultimately creating 17 million new jobs. Women and minorities, especially African Americans, entered the industrial marketplace on a scale previously unknown and became integral parts of the American industrial economy. The wave of thousands of African American workers who migrated from the agricultural South to the industrialized North helped redistribute the economic weight of the nation, in the process placing highly publicized and often resented demands on the local northern communities.

Despite fears that the small gains won by the civil rights movement of the war years would be quickly reversed in the postwar period, the new American passion for national values measured in ideological terms—especially when contrasted with those of Nazi Germany or later Communist Russia—proved an unexpected ally to the civil rights movement, although not before a wave of violence against returning African American servicemen in the South captured national and international headlines.[13] For a growing number of Americans, the issue of domestic racial segregation became linked to the battle against tyranny overseas. Although it would take at least a decade for this sentiment to begin to be manifested in meaningful changes to the Jim Crow laws of segregation, the process of breaking down racial barriers was begun. At the same time that African Americans such as baseball star Jackie Robinson of the Brooklyn Dodgers were breaking down the cultural walls of segregation, African American families began their own assault on the economic front, and for the first time, large portions of the African American community were able to share in the bounty of American capitalism. With employment figures in the postwar years reaching new heights and reducing the competition for jobs, many whites forgot that they had once felt their economic security threatened by competition from black workers. The result was that in the two decades following 1940, blacks almost doubled their median income, sharing in the nation's renewed prosperity. Convincing Congress to translate these small but important economic and cultural gains into political ones, however, would prove more difficult.

What were people to do with this new-found affluence? Enterprising businessmen were quick with suggestions, building on the gains they had made during the war. By persuading military administrators that Coca-Cola was essential to armed forces personnel, that company's president, Robert W. Woodruff, ensured that the soda would remain the most widely available consumer item in the United States and in the process gained exclusive access to armed forces sugar supplies and priority shipping for the company's equipment. Equally remarkably, Wrigley's chewing gum was touted by the company to ease tension, promote alertness, help clean teeth, and was a substitute for smoking in cases where cigarettes were dangerous or unavailable. To ensure that sufficient quantities of this panacea were on hand for America's armed forces, military administrators granted the company privileged access to raw materials and reserved military shipping space. The hucksters also had their day, but more was involved here than Madison Avenue dreaming. New products evolved and markets were created often simply by the emergence of a new consumer item as the promise of a better world increasingly became synonymous with material affluence. Detroit's gleaming new automobiles, General Electric's air conditioners, hi-fidelity sound systems, television, and dishwashers, were symptomatic of the new, seemingly insatiable, consumerism born of a decade of deprivation followed by postwar affluence.

There was more to a strong economy, however, than short-term demand for consumer items. The true challenge lay in sustaining the wartime boom over the long-term peace. Less than a week after the Japanese surrender, Truman delivered a special message to Congress presenting a twenty-one point program for the reconstruction period ahead. With no illusions that the process of reconversion would be an easy one, the president outlined a number of policies that would govern the transition of American society from war to peace: demobilizing the armed forces as soon as possible, canceling and settling war contracts, clearing war plants to make way for peacetime production, holding the line on prices and rents until fair competition could be restored to prevent inflation and undue hardship on consumers, keeping wages in line so that their increase would not precipitate price rises, removing all possible wartime government controls with a view toward facilitating reconversion and expansion while retaining only those that were deemed absolutely necessary, and preventing rapid decrease of wages or purchasing power. Among other things the special message signaled the inevitable return of politics to the domestic front. Put succinctly by the *New York Times*, "Some Democrats saw in it [the president's message] a great state document; others viewed it as a belated recognition of Congress as a co-equal branch of the government. Republic spokesmen found in it a continuation of the New Deal and a sign that the Truman administration had decided to go to the left."

The demobilization of the armed forces was a logistical challenge, but it ultimately proved no real difficulty. By the spring of 1946, seven million servicemen, not to mention large numbers of servicewomen not subject to the Selective Services Act, had returned home, determined to pick up where they had left off. To cushion the return to civilian life—and also to cushion the effect on the national economy—numerous laws were enacted that provided, among other things, job recruitment, unemployment pay, insurance, home loans, and educational opportunities. The latter category alone gave twelve million veterans access to technical and university education. By 1947, more than four million Americans were taking advantage of the Servicemen's Readjustment Act, otherwise known as the GI Bill, to receive a government subsidized tertiary education.

Congress also complied with the president's request for early action on a full employment bill. The Employment Act of 1946 required the chief executive to submit an annual economic report; established a council of economic advisers to bring wisdom to presidential economics; and declared the intention of the federal government to promote maximum employment, production, and purchasing power. Though it did not specifically endorse the economics of John Maynard Keynes, the act clearly foreshadowed policies of deficit spending and unbalanced budgets. In other areas, a spate of wartime agencies was abolished by executive order.

Between September 1945 and January 1946, $35 billion in contracts were cancelled, and hundreds of war plants, previously owned by the government, were sold off, mainly to the corporations that had been running them. Within this time more than 90 percent of the war plants had been reconverted to peacetime uses, bringing high employment and prosperity. The specter of another Great Depression, with estimates of as many as eight million unemployed, never materialized. Controlling inflation was another matter. Americans emerged from the war with unprecedented savings of approximately $145 billion, which they were determined to spend on homes, automobiles, and the many gadgets that the American people regarded as their birthright. The Office of Price Administration (OPA) had been created during the war to curb wartime inflation, the movement of prices, wages, and rents. By mid-1946, business, labor, and farmers clamored for the end of these controls so that each could claim a bit more of the American economic pie. Trying to balance the continuing prospect of prosperity with the duty to curb inflationary pressure, the president vetoed a much-amended follow-on version of the OPA in the hope that a compromise might yet be worked out. For twenty-five days, the prices of commodities and residential rents were allowed to find their own levels, while political passions ran high. The chairman of the Republican National Committee, Carroll Reece, summed up the feeling of the opposition: "Having long since lost all semblance of control over the Congress in which his party has majorities in both houses, the President now, apparently, lost control of himself." On July 25, the president reluctantly signed a measure revalidating the OPA, with specific exemptions; in the interim, prices jumped 25 percent and threatened to go even higher. In November, shortly after the election of what he called the "do-nothing, good-for-nothing 80th Congress," Truman abandoned all price, wage, and salary controls, with the exception of ceilings on rents and sugar. "In one swoop," noted one observer, "the President virtually cut the American economy loose from the shaky moorings of a four-year-old stabilization program." Now it was labor's turn.

Within weeks of V-J Day, a half-million American workers went on strike; by the end of the year, strikes had disrupted the production of steel and automobiles. The auto workers finally settled in March 1946 for a wage increase of 18.5 percent. More ominously, John L. Lewis led the country's 400,000 soft coal miners out of the pits at 12:01 A.M. on April 1 over a series of deadlocked issues involving health and welfare programs and wages. Truman in turn seized the mines, retaining control when the bituminous operators failed to accept a contract that the United Mine Workers (UMW) had negotiated under federal auspices. A second strike called by Lewis in late November in defiance of a court order resulted in his being held in contempt of court at the federal level. He was personally fined $10,000 and the UMW was fined $3,500,000, later reduced to $70,000. The miners returned to work in early December, having won most of their demands. Earlier in May, Truman, angry about the disruption the strikes were causing the economy and himself, had appealed directly to Congress for authority to draft striking rail workers into the army. The railroad strike, which had paralyzed America's commerce and marooned 90,000 passengers, was settled on the president's terms.[14]

Complaints of inflation, anti-union sentiment, and voter dissatisfaction with Truman's policies—according to a Gallup poll his approval rating had plummeted from 87 percent to 32 percent within a year—translated themselves into a conservative Republican victory in the midterm congressional elections of 1946. With a gain of thirteen seats in the Senate and fifty-six seats in the House, the GOP controlled the Congress for the first time in fourteen years. The 80th Congress, led by Republicans and conservative southern Democrats, managed to antagonize farmers, westerners, and ethnic groups. Most significantly, Congress managed to antagonize unionists to the point where labor gladly re-embraced the president, whose previous calls for the seizing of coal mines and railroads were forgiven if not forgotten. Nevertheless, the results did not bode well for the Democrats in the 1948 election.

In a determined effort to put labor in its place, Congress passed the Taft-Hartley Act on June 23, 1947, over Truman's veto. Among other things, the new law banned the closed shop, which had prohibited the hiring of nonunion workers; allowed employers to sue unions either for broken contracts or damages resulting from strikes; established a Federal Mediation and Conciliation Service; required employers to submit a sixty-day notice or "cooling off" period in termination of contract; authorized the federal government to obtain injunctions imposing a cooling off period of eighty days on strikes threatening the national well-being; mandated that unions make public their financial statements; prohibited union contribution to political campaigns; and allowed union officials to take an oath that they were not members of the Communist party. Truman remonstrated in his veto that this particular piece of legislation reversed the basic direction of the nation's labor policy, injected the government into private economic affairs on an unprecedented scale, and conflicted with important principles of a democratic society. Moreover, he concluded that its provisions would cause more strikes rather than fewer. With the return of labor to the Democratic fold in 1948, one of the first electoral victims of the Taft-Hartley Act was Representative Fred Hartley, Jr., of Minnesota.

If the 80th Congress was in no mood to help labor, neither was it in the mood to help the nation's African Americans. For reasons of their own, Republicans and southern Democrats joined forces to block civil rights legislation of any kind. Prompted by protests against the outbreak of racial murders in the South in 1946, which included the cold-blooded murder of two young blacks and their wives by an unmasked band of twenty whites in Monroe, Georgia, the president appointed a special Committee on Civil Rights in July. After ten months of deliberation, the committee, headed by Charles E. Wilson, president of General Electric Company and future secretary of defense, issued its report entitled "To Secure These Rights." "The pervasive gap between our aims and what we actually do," suggested the report, "is creating a kind of moral dry rot which eats away at the emotional and rational bases of democratic belief." On February 2, 1948, Truman requested Congress to implement the report's recommendations, including legislation to outlaw lynching and Jim Crow practices while establishing a nationwide system for monitoring civil liberties. As a further step, and in the face of Republican-controlled Congress and in the full knowledge that he would alienate many southern Democrats, in July 1948 the president issued Executive Order 9981 barring segregation in the armed forces—really, a pragmatic recognition of the new realities spawned by World War II. In 1949, a federal law further barred discrimination in federal civil service positions.

The 80th Congress moved more positively in the sphere of governmental reorganization. The President Succession Act of 1947 revised the law of 1886, making the speaker of the House of Representatives first and the president *pro tempore* of the Senate second in line of succession behind the president and vice-president, followed by the secretary of state and other cabinet members according to rank. The year 1947 also witnessed the inception of the Twenty-Second Amendment to the Constitution—essentially an anti-Roosevelt gesture limiting the president to no more than two terms in office—as well as the establishment of the Commission on the Organization of the Executive Branch of the government under the direction of former president Herbert Hoover. The amendment was ratified on February 26, 1951. The final report of the commission proved extremely influential: almost two hundred of the report's recommendations were fully or partially accepted. In late July 1947, President Truman signed legislation for the unification of the armed forces and named James V. Forrestal, then secretary of the navy who had made his fortune on Wall Street, as the secretary of defense, with cabinet status. The act further established the National Security Council and under it the Central Intelligence Agency (CIA), which was to correlate and evaluate intelligence activity relating to the nation's security.

THE EMERGENCE OF THE COLD WAR

Although signs of an impending clash of interests and ideology between the West and the Soviet Union had been evident for some time, the absence of a common enemy accelerated the process. America was in the process of demobilizing its massive military machine and reshaping its industrial and economic power into domestic prosperity. The Selective Service Act, which had governed the induction of over ten million servicemen since 1940, expired on March 31, 1947, though provisions were made for the maintenance of records and conscription in emergency situations. While relations with the Soviet Union appeared tranquil enough on the surface, policymakers at the highest levels had moved well in the direction of locating and identifying the Soviet Union as the most serious threat to international peace, despite Truman's half-hearted efforts to convince the American public otherwise. Returning from the Potsdam Conference, Truman told the American people that "there was a fundamental accord and agreement with the objectives ahead of us," an assertion that hardly reflected the deep-seated Soviet-American differences over such matters as reparations and the future of Germany and Austria. On October 5, 1945, in a radio broadcast originating from Washington, Secretary of State Byrnes announced to the nation that the first session of the Council of Foreign Ministers, which had met in London in September, had closed in stalemate. The conference had broken up mainly over the unexpected Soviet refusal to allow China and France to participate in the drafting of peace treaties with Italy and the lesser Axis nations.

Other difficulties included the joint Anglo-American refusal to recognize the pro-Soviet governments of Bulgaria and Rumania. The Americans based their refusal squarely on the ground that freedom of speech and assembly were still being denied to the Bulgarian and Rumanian people, basic rights without which political self-determination could not be realized. Draft treaties for Italy, Rumania, Hungary, Bulgaria, and Finland were finally arranged by the time a peace conference of twenty-one nations assembled in Paris in July 1946. They were signed and went into effect on February 10, 1947, but not before the cold war rivalry that would animate Soviet-American relations for the next generation and beyond had taken root.

Despite late efforts to assuage Soviet fears, and in a manner that foreshadowed the administration's hardening attitude toward Stalin in the wake of a fruitless second meeting of the Council of Foreign Ministers, the State Department vigorously continued to object to the Soviet establishment of totalitarian political regimes and economic control over the countries of Eastern and Central Europe. In full conformity with the American position of self-determination and equality of commercial opportunity, State Department planners argued that America should use its great influence to break the Soviet grip. The method chosen to resist the Soviets lay principally in the economic sphere, a natural choice given the dominance of the American economy in the postwar period. Through a combination of encouraging Eastern European nations to resist Communist control and trying to persuade the Kremlin to loosen its grip over those same countries, the United States hoped to buy political independence—and ultimately allegiance to the West—for nations in the Soviet sphere. With the proverbial battle line drawn, the Truman administration began to abandon hope of accommodating Stalin's fears and plans for expansion by early 1946. "I'm tired of babying the Soviets," President Truman was alleged to have told his secretary of state.

Seen from Washington and London, Soviet foreign policy in the postwar period seemed insatiably expansionist. Churchill warned as much in a widely publicized speech on March 5, 1946, at Westminster College in Fulton, Missouri. In front of an audience that included President Truman, Churchill called on the West to defend against Soviet expansion, and in words flashed around the globe by international wire services, warned that "from Stettin in the Baltic to Trieste in the Adriatic, an iron curtain has descended across the Continent" of Europe. For the American government, the timing was propitious. Just two weeks earlier, in response to a State Department request for an interpretive analysis of the significance and meaning of Stalin's and other related pronouncements, the American chargé in Moscow, George F. Kennan, formulated an assessment of Soviet foreign policy that captured the mood of the Truman administration's determination to resist the perceived threat of Stalinist policies to world peace. Known as the Long Telegram, Kennan's missive of February 22, 1946, became a watershed in the administration's thinking about the Soviet threat. Not only was Kennan able to explain the basis of Soviet foreign policy, he also had a remedy: containment. What "we have here," argued Kennan persuasively, is "a political force committed fanatically to the belief that with the [United States] there can be no permanent *modus vivendi*, that it is desirable and necessary that the international harmony of our society be disrupted, our traditional way of life be destroyed, the international authority of our state be broken, if Soviet power is to be secure." What to do about it was compounded by the fact that Soviet leadership was "seemingly inaccessible to consideration of reality in its basic reaction," though not in the same sense that informed Hitler's reckless ambitions. "Impervious to logic of reason," concluded Kennan, "it [U.S.S.R.] is highly sensitive to the logic of force. For this reason it can easily withdraw—and usually does—when strong resistance is encountered at any point." Kennan became permanently and unwittingly identified with this policy in his famous "X" article published in the influential journal *Foreign Affairs* in 1947. At that time, he refined what has since become the classic definition of containment: "Soviet pressure against the free institutions of the western world is something that can be contained by the adroit and vigilant application of counterforce at a series of constantly shifting geographical and political points, corresponding to the shifts and maneuvers of Soviet policy, but which cannot be charmed out of existence." On November 24, 1948, the doctrine of containment was officially adopted by the Truman administration, although by then the doctrine had so fundamentally changed that its original author would not have recognized his creation.

Throughout 1946, Soviet actions tended to confirm the administration's worst fears. While pursuing obstructionist policies in the occupation control councils in Germany and Austria, the Soviets continued to retain forces in Manchuria and northern Iran, in the latter area preventing government troops from intervening against Communist-organized rebels in the province of Azerbaijan. In March 1946, Iran protested to the United Nations Security Council, demanding the evacuation of the Red Army from the disputed territory. By early May, Soviet troop withdrawal had been completed but not before the United Nations had shown its powerlessness in the face of the Kremlin's veto power. The Iranian crisis, together with Soviet threats against Turkey at the same time, prompted Washington to begin to plan for war with the Soviet Union, suggesting the extent to which early cold war diplomats were prepared to play power politics.

With memories still strong of the appeasement of Hitler at Munich, the United States concluded that the U.S.S.R. could only be checked by policies initiated by Washington. Accordingly, the Truman administration was determined to resist what it regarded as Soviet aggression the next time it reared its head, although the actual form and timing of that resistance were much in doubt. The immediate background of the pronouncement of the Truman Doctrine was the official disclosure in February 1947 that the British government would shortly be terminating its military and economic support of the existing Greek and Turkish regimes. The president's response both to the plight of the British and to the deteriorating situation in Greece and Turkey was swift and unequivocal. Requesting urgent economic and financial assistance for the relief of these countries, Truman declared to a joint session of Congress on March 12, 1947: "I believe that it must be the policy of the United States to support free peoples who are resisting attempted subjugation by armed minorities or by outside pressures. I believe that we must assist free peoples to work out their own destinies in their own way." The exact meaning of these words, although Truman specifically qualified them to mean "that our help should be primarily through economic and financial aid," has been the subject of much historical and political debate. But whatever the president meant, there can be little doubt that his speech was a major turning point in modern American foreign policy. Significantly, this was a policy that had the support of Republicans and Democrats alike, the former organized under the direction of Senator Arthur Vandenberg of Michigan, the leading Republican spokesman on foreign policy in the Senate and one of the earliest supporters of a bipartisan approach to postwar international relations. The only element left to argue about was tactics.

By late May 1947, it had become alarmingly apparent that the administration had grossly underestimated the destruction of the European economy in the aftermath of World War II. From France to China, much of the Eurasian land mass was wracked by famine and disease. Hundreds of thousands of persons had to be integrated back into the national economies. "Europe is steadily deteriorating," observed Under Secretary of State William L. Clayton; furthermore, "the political position reflects the economic." As the fate and well-being of the United States were invariably bound up with the fate and well-being of Western Europe, it was only natural that Washington would seek to repair the fortunes of its natural allies.

The situation begged U.S. intervention. During commencement exercises at Harvard University on June 5, 1947, the eminent soldier and new secretary of state, George C. Marshall, observed that in the name of enlightened self-interest, "it is logical that the United States should do whatever it is able to do to assist in the return of normal economic health in the world, without which there can be no political stability and no assured peace." Marshall called for the reconstruction of Europe by Europeans and so was born the Marshall Plan or, more accurately, the European Recovery Program, signed into law by Truman on April 3, 1948. Two weeks later, the sixteen Western European nations involved met in Paris to set up the necessary machinery for economic cooperation, the Organization for European Economic Cooperation. From that time until the Marshall Plan officially came to an end in December 1951, the United States pumped $13 billion into the economy of Western Europe, providing a solid foundation for the long-term revival of the continent and committing, in Churchill's phrase, "the most unsordid act in history."

POSTWAR POLITICS

Despite the bipartisan support for his cold war policies, Truman found his domestic political support ebbing. With the growing prospect of a GOP victory in the fall, the Republican National Convention, meeting in Philadelphia in June 1948, nominated Thomas E. Dewey, the moderate-to-liberal governor of New York, on the third ballot. Dewey, who had polled 4.58 percent of the popular vote in 1944 against Roosevelt, gladly accepted his party's nomination, adding that he had come to the convention "unfettered by a single obligation or promise to any living person, free to join with you in selecting to serve our nation the finest men and women in the nation." As his running mate, he chose the even more liberal Governor Earl Warren of California. Joining ranks with his erstwhile antagonists, such as Senators Robert L. Taft of Ohio and Arthur H. Vandenberg, Dewey ran a subdued campaign.

The Democratic National Convention meeting in July, also in Philadelphia, was a different story. Truman was nominated by default, for lack of serious challengers. Senator Alben W. Barkley of Kentucky was Truman's selection for vice president. Several southern delegates bolted the convention in protest against the strong civil rights plank, and shortly afterward nominated Governor J. Strom Thurmond of South Carolina to run for president on a states' rights or Dixiecrat ticket. To make matters worse, the disgruntled followers of the controversial Henry Wallace, the secretary of commerce who had been dropped from Truman's cabinet in September 1946 for challenging the president's get-tough policy with the Soviets, organized the Progressive party to run for the presidency. With the Democrats splintered and the Republicans united, the election of the confident

Dewey seemed a foregone conclusion, if one could believe the pollsters and pundits. Truman, however, refused to play dead.

Truman literally took his campaign to the people, traveling 23,000 miles and making 272 speeches on his so-called whistle-stop campaign. In town after town, he made the performance of the "do-nothing, good-for-nothing" 80th Congress the target of his attack. His message was simple and unequivocal: Were the special privilege boys or the people going to run the country? "How far," he asked the voters in Springfield, Illinois, "do you suppose the real estate lobby would get with Abraham Lincoln?" On the eve of the election, Truman waited at his home in Independence, Missouri, convinced that he had developed a hidden groundswell to carry him into the presidency on his own merits. To the surprise of everyone but himself, the president won handily, receiving a popular vote of 24,105,695 (49.3 percent) to Dewey's 21,969,170 (45 percent). The electoral victory was even more impressive at 303 to 189. Significantly, the Democrats regained control of the Senate and the House. Never had the political prophets been more perplexed.[15]

Finally president in his own right, Truman sought to extend and enlarge upon the New Deal legislation of his predecessor. In his State of the Union message to Congress, broadcast nationally on January 5, 1949, the president announced that "every segment of our population and every individual has a right to expect from our Government a fair deal." Interpreting the presidential election of 1948 as a mandate from the people, he began, "We have rejected the discredited theory that the fortunes of the nation should be in the hands of a privileged few. We have abandoned 'the trickle-down' concept of national prosperity." In its place, he said, "we believe that our economic system should rest on a democratic foundation and that wealth should be created for the benefit of all." Translated into specifics, the Fair Deal argued for a series of anti-inflationary measures enacted at the national level; special attention to rural problems; the development of natural resources with a view to conservation; and raising the standard of living through social security, health, education, and civil rights.

The program was ambitious, and the 81st Congress met the president halfway, enacting more liberal legislation than any Congress during the previous decade: It increased minimum wages from forty to seventy-five cents per hour; expanded social security benefits while extending coverage to ten million more people; expanded public welfare through rural electrification, soil conservation, and flood control developments; extended immigration quotas under the Displaced Persons Act; set up a National Science Foundation; provided for some slum clearance and low-cost housing; and granted the chief executive power to deal with inflation.

In most other areas, however, the Fair Deal ran into a stone wall. While some programs were deemed too costly, others, such as civil rights and national health insurance, encountered the resistance of southern Democrats and special interest groups, particularly the American Medical Association. There were also other problems. In response to recommendations made by the Presidential Commission on Employee Loyalty, established in November 1946, Truman issued an executive order in March 1947 calling for an immediate investigation of the loyalty and intentions of every person entering civilian employment in any department or agency of the executive branch of the government. Those already holding positions were to be scrutinized by the Federal Bureau of Investigation, their fate resting essentially on the decision of their department heads, who were willing to pledge personal responsibility for their subordinates. Done generally in moderation, the procedure passed over millions of employees, with only a few thousand closely examined. The final effort resulted in several hundred dismissals, mostly based on guilt by association. Of course, the real targets were Communists and Communist sympathizers. To parry accusations that his administration was "soft" on communism (mainly the repercussion of establishment support for former State Department employee Alger Hiss who was found guilty of perjury during a highly publicized trial in 1950), Truman went a step further in January 1949 when the nation's leading twelve Communists—later, eleven—were called to trial on charges of violating the Smith Act of 1940, making it a criminal offense to advocate the forceful overthrow of the government. Convicted, the eleven challenged the constitutionality of the Smith Act. In 1951, in *Dennis et al. v. US*, the Supreme Court upheld the law, with justices Hugo Black and William Douglas dissenting. In September 1950, Congress passed, over the president's veto, the McCarran Act, providing for, among other things, the registration of Communists and Communist-front organizations, as well as for the internment of Communists during national emergencies.

In this atmosphere, it was learned that Dr. Klaus Fuchs, a German-born scientist working for the British and someone who had been deeply involved in the Manhattan Project and postwar atomic research, had provided atomic secrets to the Soviets; furthermore, he implicated a number of Americans, including Julius and Ethel Rosenberg, who had transmitted classified information to Moscow from 1942 to 1947. Both Rosenbergs were consequently executed. These events, together with the "loss of China"—the defeat of Jiang Jieshi's pro-Western forces by Mao Zedong's Chinese Communist Party in 1949—and the news just months earlier that the Soviets had broken the U.S. atomic monopoly, gave extremists their chance. One of these extremists was Joseph R. McCarthy, the Republican senator from Wisconsin. McCarthy declared in a speech at Wheeling, West Virginia, in early 1950 that 205 (later revised to 57) Communists had infiltrated the State Department. Though McCarthy's accusations gained wide publicity, a special subcommittee of the Senate Foreign Relations Committee found the allegations to be baseless. In the midst of the national emergency proclaimed later in the year resulting from the outbreak of the

Korean War, the senator's accusations increased while partisan attacks against the Truman administration were stepped up, in the process taking on some of the most prominent American patriots such as George C. Marshall. Before McCarthyism would spend itself in 1954, incalculable damage would be done to the careers and lives of many innocent Americans as the loyalty oath overshadowed common sense.[16]

GLOBAL CHALLENGES

Abroad, what had started as a political contest with the Soviet Union became dangerously close to military conflict. Resolved to an approach of what Secretary of State James Byrnes called "patience and firmness" to resist Communist expansion, the United States firstly became drawn into political struggles in Europe. For its part, the Kremlin resolved to do everything possible to defeat the program of American "imperialism." Communist-inspired strikes in France and Italy sought in vain to deter these countries from accepting Marshall Plan aid. Treaties of defensive alliance linking the Soviet Union with Finland, Bulgaria, Hungary, and Rumania were added to treaties previously negotiated with Czechoslovakia, Poland, and Yugoslavia. With the United States already committed to sustaining pro-Western governments in Greece and Iran, the threat of a Communist electoral victory in the Italian elections of 1948 prompted the Truman administration to authorize CIA covert involvement to the tune of $10–20 million.[17] In February 1948, a Communist coup overthrew the democratic government of Czechoslovakia and installed one firmly attached to the Kremlin. This blow to the West was partly compensated for when, later in the year, Yugoslavia, under Marshal Tito, broke with Moscow.

But it was the German problem that would come to dominate the early cold war. While the objective for all parties was ostensibly a unified Germany, both sides took action that made such a result more remote.[18] The repeated failure of the Council of Foreign Ministers to reach agreement on Germany by late 1947 led to moves by the Western powers toward the creation of a unified and self-governing West Germany. The Anglo-American-French elements had already taken one large step in that direction by the economic merging of their zones in creating what was referred to first as Bizonia and then later Trizonia with the addition of the French zone. Consultations in London in the spring of 1948 resulted in agreements, announced June 7, proposing the creation of a West German government with some safeguards planned for the control of the Ruhr industries. The Germans of the Western zones would elect members of a constituent assembly, which in turn would draw up a constitution for a federal state that might eventually include the Eastern Zone. Complaining that such moves flagrantly violated the quadripartite control of Germany established by the Potsdam Protocol, the Soviets set out to eject their erstwhile allies from jointly occupied Berlin, a city which, because of shortsighted agreements made during the war, lay 110 miles within the Soviet zone. Berlin, with no guaranteed surface corridor of communications with the West, had restrictions upon the movement of persons to and from the city imposed in April 1948, followed in June by the prohibition of all surface transportation between Berlin and the Western Zone. Although the Soviets never said as much, in truth it amounted to a blockade. The Western powers were faced with the prospect of withdrawing their small but symbolic garrisons from Berlin in defeat or of supplying not only them, but also the two million inhabitants of West Berlin. Despite the initial impression in some quarters that the Western forces might consider leaving the former German capital if the suffering of the populace became too great, Truman decided to take a stand, promising that Western forces would stay put "come what may."[19]

Rejecting advice that he open the road by military force, the president, in consultation with the British, resorted to air transport to temporarily alleviate the situation until a means of resolution could be found. The Berlin airlift, initially conceived only as a temporary measure, commenced at once, and by September, American and British planes were flying in 4,000 tons of supplies daily. Since air corridors were the only form of access to the city for which formal agreement had been reached in the chaotic days following Germany's defeat in 1945, and Stalin recognized that interfering with the airlift would likely bring war with the West, Soviet planes occasionally threatened but never ventured to attack. Allied persistence and patience finally paid dividends as the Soviets ended the blockade in May 1949. Faced with capitulation or war, Stalin folded.

Shortly thereafter, in September 1949, the Western powers established the German Federal Republic with its capital at Bonn. Military government officially terminated, although occupation forces remained. The Federal Republic was soon made eligible for Marshall Plan aid and, under its first chancellor, Konrad Adenauer, showed a spirit of willing cooperation with the West. Following suit, the Soviets established the German Democratic Republic with its capital in Pankow, an outer suburb of Berlin. Like its competitor in Bonn, East Germany rested upon a constitution dedicated to the unification of all Germany, although it is clear that Stalin would not have been displeased with the cold war status quo. With West Germany dependent on the Western powers for protection and thus locked into the status quo, it was unlikely to be able to resume its now traditional place as a primary threat to the Soviet Union.

The Communist coup in Czechoslovakia and the Berlin blockade greatly alarmed the Western powers. There was, after all, no guarantee that the Soviets, with their preponderance of conventional forces, might not renew efforts to oust the Western allies from Berlin or to strangle the German Federal Republic in its infancy. "Containment" of Soviet Russia, until then dependent mainly upon economic and political means, appeared in need of more military backing. For if the U.S.S.R. could be certain that an act of aggression against any one of the free nations of Western Europe would mean a conflict with the others and also with the United States, it might be deterred from such acts. Neither America's nuclear monopoly nor the U.N. Security Council, because of the Soviet veto, could supply such a deterrent. It was in this context that the West turned to Article 51 of the United Nations Charter, which legalized "collective self-defense" by groups within the United Nations. In the Americas, the Rio Pact of September 1947 had already invoked Article 51 in a hemispheric collective-security agreement; in Europe a beginning had been made in March 1948 when Britain, France, and the Benelux countries signed in Brussels a fifty-year treaty of economic, social, and cultural collaboration and collective self-defense.

Support for the treaty was promptly proposed by Truman in an address to Congress in March 1948. The president spoke frankly of the danger from Moscow, calling for the adoption of a universal military training program (which Congress defeated), and temporary re-enactment of selective service legislation. The buildup of American armed forces strength, which had been allowed to disintegrate since 1945, began with the Draft Act of June 1948, requiring military service of men from nineteen to twenty-five years of age. With the aid of this, and later under the stimulus of the Korean War, the combined strength of the American armed forces grew from 1,350,000 in 1948 to 3,630,000 in June 1952. The way for collective action was cleared when the Senate, in the Vandenberg Resolution of June 17, 1948, articulated the proposition that the United States should associate itself, "by constitutional processes, with such regional and other collective arrangements as are based on continuous and effective self-help and mutual aid, and as affect its national security."

The Vandenberg Resolution was the prelude to the North Atlantic Treaty (1949), a significant and profound venture in search of meaningful collective security. The treaty—a fundamental departure from principles established by George Washington a century and a half previously of "no entangling alliances"—was signed by twelve nations of the northern Atlantic and western European areas, a number increased to fifteen in 1955 with the inclusion of West Germany, Greece, and Turkey. The parties agreed to settle all disputes peacefully among themselves and to develop their capacity to resist armed attack. But the heart of the treaty was Article 5 with its "Three Musketeers" pledge that an armed attack upon any one of the members in Europe or North America would be considered an attack upon all; furthermore, the treaty pledged each member to assist any attacked party "by such action as it deems necessary, including the use of armed forces." Thus originated the North Atlantic Treaty Organization, or NATO.

Two other events in 1949 greatly shaped the direction of the United States defense effort. The first was the revelation in September that the U.S.S.R. had exploded its first atomic bomb; the second was the completion

of the Communist conquest of all of mainland China, followed by the proclamation of the People's Republic of China at Beijing in October. The latter
event was regarded as a major triumph in the Kremlin's program of world
revolution; the former a potential mortal danger to the continental United
States. One top secret document, Policy Paper Number 68 of the National
Security Council (NSC 68), approved by Truman in September 1950, went
so far as to estimate, in the "period of peril" motif so often employed in
modern times, that within the next four years the Soviet Union would be
capable of seriously damaging vital centers of the United States provided
that it struck first. Although Paul Nitze, the primary drafter of the document, concluded that existing American retaliatory capability was adequate to deter the Soviets from launching a direct military attack, he also
warned that the time was fast approaching when the power would not be
sufficient. Washington, therefore, had little choice but to increase drasti-
cally both its atomic stockpiles and to invest in a new generation of weapon
predicted to be hundreds—if not thousands—of times more powerful than
the Hiroshima bomb: the hydrogen bomb, or "super." To fund such an increase, as to provide an argument for raising the Defense Department's
budget of $13.5 billion, Nitze recommended a more rapid buildup of politi-
cal, economic, and military strength than had been previously contemplated. Only such a program, concluded NSC 68, could provide long-term
security for the United States.[20] Such a buildup, however, would clearly require a massive diversion of government funds from domestic priorities—a particularly sensitive proposal while the national economy had not
yet fully recovered from the recession of 1949 and unemployment rates
were climbing to the highest they had been since World War II.[21] Secretary
of Defense James Forrestal had been warning since 1948 that the postwar
demobilization had gone too far but had been unable to convince Truman
to undertake anything on the scale he considered necessary. The "selling"
of NSC 68 to the American people, however, came from unexpected quarters.

With Stalin's blessing and Mao's acquiescence, on June 25, 1950, North
Korean forces launched a well-organized surprise attack along the entire
width of the 38th parallel, the postwar dividing line between the So-
viet-supported Democratic People's Republic of Korea headed by Kim
Il-Sung and the American-supported Republic of Korea, or South Korea,
headed by Syngman Rhee.[22] Within a few hours of receiving the news, Truman requested a meeting of the U.N. Security Council, and later that afternoon, the United Nations adopted a U.S.-sponsored resolution declaring
the North Korean action a "breach of peace," demanding that the aggressor
withdraw beyond the 38th parallel and calling upon all members of the
United Nations to assist in the enforcing of the resolution. Owing to the absence of the Soviet delegate—who had boycotted the session because of
U.N. refusal to seat the representative of Communist China in place of the

member of the Taiwan regime—the resolution passed the Security Council by a vote of 9–0 (Yugoslavia abstaining). On June 27, the Security Council recommended that U.N. members provide military assistance, and two weeks later, General Douglas MacArthur was named commander of all U.N. forces serving in Korea.

Truman acted promptly and properly in throwing the weight of America into the balance. On June 27, he announced that he had ordered U.S. air and sea forces to provide Korean government troops with cover and support. Three days later in Tokyo, the president authorized the use of American ground troops in Korea, ordered a naval blockade of the Korean coast, and authorized the air force to attack targets in North Korea. In his announcement, Truman also revealed other action that constituted a distinct change of policy: "Communism had passed beyond the use of subversion to conquer independent nations and will now use armed invasion and war." Under the circumstances, the president felt justified in accelerating military assistance to French forces fighting Ho Chi Minh's independence movement in Indochina and to the Philippines, as well as stretching the nation's "defensive perimeter" to include Taiwan, the refuge of the defeated nationalist Chinese forces who had fled from the mainland. But despite the rapid deployment of U.S. forces under U.N. auspices, the response to the Security Council's call to arms was less than universal. In addition to the United States and South Korea, fifteen other nations, from Australia to Britain, participated in the fighting. Yet such was the superiority of the North Koreans in equipment and preparations that they were able to push back the South Koreans and the first U.N. troops to the extreme southeast corner of the Korean peninsula, an area that fortunately included the important port of Pusan.

The tide of war turned abruptly on September 15 when General MacArthur undertook a risky maneuver by landing U.N. forces far behind North Korean lines at Inchon. Large elements of the North Korean army were either destroyed or captured, with the remainder driven beyond the 38th parallel. Supported by the authority of a U.N. General Assembly resolution reiterating the objective of a "unified, independent and democratic Korea," U.N. forces crossed the 38th parallel on October 7, twelve hours before the U.N. resolution was passed, and pressed forward to the Yalu River, Korea's northern border. Urged on by MacArthur, Truman backed the decision to cross the parallel as a calculated risk because he reasoned that a reunified Korea would not only inflict a momentous defeat on Soviet ambitions of world revolution, but also would guarantee for Koreans the right of national self-determination. Communist China had other plans; it felt called upon to prevent the extinction of North Korea. After a skillful buildup, whose significance eluded the American command, Chinese armies, under the banner of the Communist People's Volunteers, launched a massive attack in late November. Within a few weeks, Beijing had driven the U.N. armies back below the 38th parallel and recaptured the South Korean capital of Seoul. By early 1951, however, the line had been stabilized, and the U.N. forces counterattacked, pushing the Chinese and North Koreans again beyond the parallel.

On April 11, 1951, Truman relieved General MacArthur of his command. Increasing friction between MacArthur and Truman had resulted from the general's impatience at the restraints placed upon his military activities and his irritating habit of publicly voicing his disagreements with administration and U.N. policy. In particular, MacArthur had complained about the prohibition against bombing enemy sources of supply and communications in what he termed the "privileged sanctuary of Manchuria." His recall caused a firestorm of political debate in the United States, a debate that continued in muted tones until well after the Korean War. The issue for many was whether to limit the war to Korea or to go all out for victory against Beijing at the risk of provoking the Soviet Union. For his part, Truman gave Europe first place and deferred to the opinion of allies in the United Nations, in sharp contrast to MacArthur and his supporters who believed Asia to be the decisive theater in the struggle with communism and who would have had the United States "go it alone if necessary." A long investigation by two Senate committees ended inconclusively, and the administration adhered to its policy of limited war.

With costs escalating on both sides—in military and economic terms—and neither side seeing victory in sight, on June 23, 1951, in New York, the head of the Soviet delegation to the United Nations, Yakov A. Malik, responded to a secret inquiry from Washington by stating publicly that the Korean conflict could be settled if both parties so desired. The Soviet delegate's statement led to the opening of armistice negotiations on July 10 at Kaesong, just north of the 38th parallel. There, and later at Panmunjom, the negotiations proceeded with a number of interruptions until July 27, 1953. The questions that proved the most troublesome were the location of the cease-fire line, machinery for enforcing the armistice terms, and repatriation of prisoners. By the spring of 1952, agreement had been reached on all but the last point. The People's Republic of China demanded that all prisoners of war be repatriated, but the United Nations would not agree to compulsory repatriation of thousands of Chinese and North Korean prisoners who were simply unwilling to return to communism., The negotiations stuck on this issue until after the 1952 presidential election.[23]

The repercussions of the Korean War on America were profound. The war had claimed 54,000 American lives and had all but destroyed what were already poor relations with Communist China. Defense expenditure increased rapidly from $22.3 billion in fiscal year 1951 to $50.4 billion in fiscal year 1953; put differently, defense spending absorbed 5.2 percent of the nation's gross national product in 1950 and 13.5 percent of a much expanded national product in 1953. The Korean War also inflamed the already aroused anti-Communist sentiment in the nation and exacerbated political tensions. What had begun as a promise of peace and prosperity had all too quickly become a period of uncertainty.

NOTES

1. *The Papers of Dwight D. Eisenhower: The War Years*, ed. Alfred D. Chandler (Baltimore, MD: Johns Hopkins University Press, 1970), 4:2579 n.1.

2. *Churchill and Roosevelt: The Complete Correspondence*, ed. Warren F. Kimball (Princeton, NJ: Princeton University Press, 1984), 3:603–05.

3. Quoted in *The Australian*, 10 July 1999.

4. Dwight D. Eisenhower, *Crusade in Europe* (Garden City, NY: Doubleday, 1948), p. 409.

5. Harry S. Truman, *Years of Trial and Hope, 1946–1952* (New York: Doubleday, 1956), p. 1.

6. The political imperative of ensuring that the German surrender was ratified by the Western Allies and the Soviet Union at the same time meant that the press was instructed initially to withhold the story until a Russian signature could be added to the surrender document. That took place in Berlin on May 9. See Eisenhower, *Crusade in Europe*, p. 427.

7. Steven Neal, *Harry and Ike: The Partnership that Remade the Postwar World* (New York: Scribner's, 2001), p. 1.

8. Harriman to Harry Hopkins, 10 September 1944, box 157, Harry Hopkins Papers, Franklin D. Roosevelt Library, Hyde Park, New York.

9. Charles E. Bohlen, *Witness to History, 1929–1969* (New York: W. W. Norton, 1973), p. 213.

10. Notes on the Stimson Interim Committee Meeting, 31 May 1945, "The Decision to Drop the Atomic Bomb" Collection, Harry S. Truman Library, Independence, Missouri.

11. See Richard Rhodes, *The Making of the Atomic Bomb* (New York: Simon and Schuster, 1986); and Paul Boyer, *By the Bomb's Early Light: American Thought and Culture at the Dawn of the Atomic Age* (New York: Pantheon, 1985), especially pp. 3–26.

12. Melvyn P. Leffler, *A Preponderance of Power: National Security, the Truman Administration, and the Cold War* (Stanford, CA: Stanford University Press, 1992), pp. 1–2.

13. Robert Weisbrot, *Freedom Bound: A History of America's Civil Rights Movement* (New York: W. W. Norton, 1990), p. 10; and Mary L. Dudziak, *Cold War Civil Rights: Race and the Image of American Diplomacy* (Princeton, NJ: Princeton University Press, 2000), pp. 23–24.

14. Robert J. Donovan, *Conflict and Crisis: The Presidency of Harry S. Truman, 1945–1948* (New York: W. W. Norton, 1977), pp. 209–18.

15. On the 1948 campaign, see particularly Zachary Karabell, *The Last Campaign: How Harry Truman Won the 1948 Election* (New York: Knopf, 2000); Gary A. Donaldson, *Truman Defeats Dewey* (Lexington: University Press of Kentucky, 1999); and Harold U. Gullan, *The Upset that Wasn't: Harry S. Truman and the Crucial Election of 1948* (Chicago: Ivan R. Dee, 1998).

16. Arthur Herman, *Joseph McCarthy: Reexamining the Life and Legacy of America's Most Hated Senator* (New York: Free Press, 2000).

17. Leffler, *A Preponderance of Power*, pp. 195–97.

18. For the centrality of the German problem to the cold war, see particularly Marc Trachtenberg, *A Constructed Peace: The Making of the European Settlement, 1945–1963* (Princeton, NJ: Princeton University Press, 1999). For the contours of the debate over responsibility for the division of Germany, see Carolyn Eisenberg, *Drawing the Line: The American Decision to Divide Germany, 1944–1949* (Cambridge, MA: Cambridge University Press, 1996); John Lewis Gaddis, *We Now Know: Rethinking Cold War History* (New York: Oxford University Press, 1997), pp. 113–51; and John H. Backer, *The Decision to Divide Germany: American Foreign Policy in Transition* (Durham, NC: Duke University Press, 1978).

19. William Hillman, ed., *Mr. President: Personal Diaries, Private Letters, Papers, and Revealing Interviews of Harry S. Truman* (London: Hutchinson, 1952), pp. 119–20.

20. Joseph M. Siracusa, *Into the Dark House: American Diplomacy and the Ideological Origins of the Cold War* (Claremont, CA: Regina, 1998), pp. 57–90.

21. Richard J. Carroll, *An Economic Record of Presidential Performance: From Truman to Bush* (Westport, CT: Praeger, 1995), pp. 53–54.

22. Sergei N. Goncharov, John W. Lewis, and Xue Litai, *Uncertain Partners: Stalin, Mao, and the Korean War* (Stanford, CA: Stanford University Press, 1993), p. 213. See also William Stueck, *The Korean War: An International History* (Princeton, NJ: Princeton University Press, 1995).

23. See Max Hastings, *The Korean War* (New York: Simon and Schuster, 1987).

Herbert Hoover.
Library of Congress
[LC-USZ62-111716]

A Bonus Marcher and his family pose with their makeshift home on the Anacostia mud flats in 1932. The hardship of the Great Depression forced many Americans to look to the federal government for help with their plight. Library of Congress [LC-USZ62-115568]

During the press conference at the conclusion of their meeting at Casablanca, French Morocco, in January 1943, President Franklin Roosevelt and British Prime Minister Winston Churchill demand the "unconditional surrender" of the Axis powers. University of Virginia Library

General Dwight Eisenhower gives orders to American paratroopers in England on D-Day, June 6, 1944. Library of Congress [LC-USZ62-25600]

Soviet premier Joseph Stalin and President Harry Truman, Potsdam Conference, July 1945. When the Allied powers met in Potsdam, Germany, to decide the fate of defeated Germany, Truman met Stalin for the first time. Truman's first impression of Stalin was favorable—"I liked the little son of a bitch" Truman later wrote. Before long, however, the Cold War would cast the Soviet Union and the United States as bitter enemies. Library of Congress [LC-USZ62-91781]

Factory workers make gas masks during World War II. Women and minorities become vital contributors to the American war effort, a development that would have profound social, political, and economic ramifications for postwar America. University of Virginia Library

The founding fathers of the anti-communist hysteria of the late 1940s and early 1950s, members of the notorious House Committee on Un-American Affairs during 1948. Richard Nixon (right), then a young Congressman from California, would repeatedly remember the HUAC's prosecution of State Department official Alger Hiss as a model of political behavior. Others would accuse HUAC of fabricating evidence and worse. Library of Congress [LC-USZ62-119692]

U.S. Marines watch as air support uses napalm against Communist Chinese forces during the Korean War. Library of Congress [LC-USZ62-96779]

John F. Kennedy visiting West Berlin, 1963, with Cold War allies West Berlin Mayor Willy Brandt (standing, center) and West German Chancellor Konrad Adenauer (right). John F. Kennedy Library

U.S. District Court judge Sarah T. Hughes administers the Oath of Office to Lyndon Johnson aboard the Air Force One of the tarmac of Love Field, Dallas, less than two hours after President Kennedy's assassination. The slain president's wife, Jacqueline Kennedy, stands beside the new President. Lyndon B. Johnson Library

An African American protester reacts to strikes from a group of policemen wielding night sticks following a failed sit-in demonstration in Chester, Pennsylvania, in 1964. Library of Congress [LC-USZ-62-127368]

The Reverend Dr. Martin Luther King addresses followers after their aborted march on Selma, Alabama, 1965. Library of Congress [LC-USZ62-111158]

Students picket the White House in their campaign for U.S. withdrawal from Vietnam, 1965. For all the efforts of officials to paint the anti-Vietnam movement as the radical fringe, President Lyndon Johnson's 1965 decision to escalate American involvement prompted a rapidly growing portion of the middle class to mobilize in the antiwar effort. Library of Congress [LC-USZ62-122600]

CIA Director George Bush briefs President Gerald Ford (standing, far right) on the evacuation of Americans from Beirut as White House Chief of Staff Dick Cheney (standing, far left) and Secretary of State Henry Kissinger (sitting, right) listen. June 1976. Gerald R. Ford Library [B0246-33]

Jimmy Carter is sworn in as President as the outgoing President, Gerald Ford, looks on, January 1977. "Let us create together a new national spirit of unity and trust," Carter urged the nation during his inaugural address, but by the end of his first term the American voters firmly rejected Carter's leadership. Library of Congress [LC-USA7-43173]

Ronald Reagan and White House Chief of Staff Donald Regan in Geneva, Switzerland, during a summit meeting with Soviet leader Mikhail Gorbachev, November 1985. Library of Congress [LC-USZ62-117700]

CHAPTER 7

Navigating the Middle Road

The Eisenhower years were a time of consolidation, a time when America was affluent and outwardly confident; "the fifties" would forevermore evoke nostalgia for simpler times. Stability seemed to radiate from the Oval Office across the nation. Domestically, the turbulence of the postwar transition was giving way to moderation and a level of middle class comfort that augured well for future peace and prosperity. Overseas, the cold war was still vigorously contested but had largely solidified between the forces of noncommunism and communism. But staying on the middle road was not always easy, as beneath the calm exterior lay the seeds of the protest movements and international crises that would rock the nation in the next decade.

GENERAL IN THE WHITE HOUSE

Played out against a backdrop of rising inflation, stalemated armistice talks in Korea, and revelations of graft and corruption in high places, the presidential campaign of 1952 proved long and bitter. There were also some political surprises. In March, President Truman announced that he would not be a candidate for nomination by the Democratic Convention. Ostensibly concerned with restoring the two-term tradition, Truman conceded that eight years as president had been "enough and sometimes too much for any man to serve in that capacity"—an opinion shared by much of the public and most of his critics; a Gallup poll of Truman's approval rating in the fall of 1951 was just 23 percent, the lowest number measured by that respected polling organization for any president before or since. This, together with the shocking loss of the New Hampshire Democratic primary contest to Senator Estes Kefauver of Tennessee, who had gained national attention as the chairman of the Special Senate Subcommittee to Investigate Interstate Crime, probably persuaded Truman to return to his beloved Independence, Missouri. In any case, the Republicans could feel fairly confident of regaining the White House, as well as the House and the Senate, particularly if their success in the 1950 midterm elections was any indication. All that remained was to agree on a candidate.

The Republican National Convention, which met in Chicago during the second week of July, was divided between the supporters of Senator Robert A. Taft of Ohio and the supporters of General Dwight ("Ike") D. Eisenhower. Lawyer, politician, and the son of former president William Howard Taft, Senator Taft rose to prominence as a consistent critic of the New Deal and Fair Deal policies, succeeding the late Senator Arthur Vandenberg as the GOP's chief spokesman in the Senate. Unlike Vandenberg, however, who supported the Truman administration's bipartisan foreign policy in the immediate postwar period, Taft opposed American commitments to Europe as unrealistic, disapproved of the White House's handling of the Korean War, and generally gave credence to the extremist charges of Senator Joseph McCarthy of Wisconsin. All of these and other views strongly endeared Taft to the conservative wing of the party, particularly among those located in the midwest.

The liberal-internationalist wing of the party, located in the East and the far West, looked to another kind of man as the candidate most likely to return the presidency to the heirs of Herbert Hoover. In turning to General Eisenhower, these Republicans chose a man who had not run for nor held any public office and had, in fact, not voted until 1948, when he was fifty-eight years old. His entire adult life had been spent in the U.S. Army, principally as an executive and staff officer until his appointment as supreme commander of the Allied Expeditionary Force in World War II. He was subsequently appointed army chief of staff, president of Columbia University, and the first supreme commander of the North Atlantic Treaty Organization (NATO) forces. For these accomplishments alone Eisenhower had already become one of the most admired men of his generation. Both parties, Republican and Democrat, had made overtures to him to run on their ticket, and Eisenhower conceded that he could have run either as a conservative Democrat or a moderate Republican. His reason for choosing the Republican Party, he explained, was that after twenty years of Democrat rule, the American people wanted—and deserved—a change. Casting himself as a reluctant candidate, Eisenhower agreed to accept a Republican nomination.[1] After a series of convention maneuvers, Eisenhower secured victory over Taft on the first ballot. The vice-presidential nomination went to Richard Nixon from California, a rising star in the GOP, an aggressive anti-Communist who as a member of the House Un-American Activities Committee achieved national recognition for leading the investigation of State Department official Alger Hiss, an experience that would provide Nixon's personal benchmark for the rest of his political career. In addition to attacking the administration's policies on China and Korea, the Republican platform supported a balanced federal budget, reduced national debt, and progressive tax relief. The platform also advocated the retention of the Taft-Hartley Act.

After failing to lure Eisenhower into the Democratic fold, Truman's personal choice to succeed to the presidency and continue the Fair Deal was Adlai Stevenson, the popular reform governor of Illinois, elected in 1948 by an unprecedented half-million vote plurality. Lawyer and New Dealer, Stevenson seemed ideally suited to the task. After the necessary prodding, Stevenson traveled from Springfield to Chicago in the third week of July to challenge the Kefauver delegates at the Democratic National Convention; after trailing Kefauver on the first two ballots, Stevenson was elected on the third. Senator John Sparkman of Alabama, a civil rights moderate, was nominated for vice president. The Democratic platform advocated, among other things, the continuation of the domestic and foreign policy of Roosevelt and Truman, as well as the repeal of the Taft-Hartley Act and federal legislation to secure civil rights.

During the course of the next several months, both standard-bearers campaigned long and hard, Stevenson covering a total of 32,500 miles and making over 200 speeches while Eisenhower covered 33,000 miles and made 270 speeches, doing his best to spread the ubiquitous "I like Ike" campaign slogan. Republican Party orators charged that the Democratic Party was spending the country into bankruptcy, was riddled with graft and corruption, had let too many Communists into important posts in Washington, had been in office too long, and had once again become the party of war. Democrats replied in kind, charging that the GOP would neither help farmers nor unions, was the party of the rich and the privileged, was without a plan for the defense of Europe against Soviet expansion, was the party of yesterday, and was likely to bring another depression with bread lines and millions of unemployed. The campaign was especially bitter, and Eisenhower, whose differences with Senator Taft were glossed over, soon shed his image of the proverbial nice guy. Inveighing against "the wasters, the bunglers, the incompetents" and the whole "top to bottom mess" in Washington, Eisenhower not only cast aspersion on Truman's integrity but virtually accused the administration of inviting the Communist attack in Korea through inept diplomacy.

The Democrats were vulnerable on two counts. First, they had been in power a long time, since 1932; and, second, the Korean War and the rapid rise of Soviet military power symbolized by Moscow's acquisition of the atomic bomb—one of the great espionage coups in modern times—placed the Democrats on the defensive. The Republican strategy was summed up in the simple formula: "K1C3 = Korea, Crime, Communism, Corruption." Urbane, wealthy, and sophisticated, Governor Stevenson attracted a wide following in liberal and academic circles, causing yet another kind of problem in a nation traditionally suspicious of intellectuals. Referring to both Stevenson's physical appearance and his intellectual sensibilities, the Alsop brothers, well-known newspaper columnists, coined the term "egghead" to describe Stevenson and his followers. In the hands of GOP advertising executives "egghead" quickly became synonymous with effete manners, pretentious refinement, weak-kneed policies, and socialism. Throughout, Stevenson suggested talking "sense to the American people. Let's tell them the truth." But, discussions of "a long, costly, patient struggle against the great enemies of men—war, poverty and tyranny"—were not messages likely to appeal to an electorate surfeited with war and economic depression.

As the campaign moved into autumn, GOP fortunes took an unexpected and dangerous turn. The *New York Post* released a story under the headline "Secret Nixon Fund!" alleging that Eisenhower's running mate enjoyed a high lifestyle paid for out of a secret "millionaires' club" account established for the vice-presidential candidate. Republican strategists panicked as Eisenhower prepared to demand Nixon's resignation. With little room to maneuver, the Republican National Committee sent word to Nixon that it had managed to purchase a half-hour of television time; the cost was $75,000 for prime viewing after the popular "Milton Berle Show." In the so-called Checkers speech of September 23, 1952, which critics contended was pure hokum, Nixon ably defended himself.

The speech began simply enough, seeking to demonstrate that this was not a man with a million dollars in the bank. According to Nixon, he owned a 1950 Oldsmobile, some life insurance, and was buying two houses, one in California and one in Washington, for both of which he owed $30,000. The touch of genius, the final touch that would make the speech a landmark in the brief history of television, came as Nixon concluded:

I should say this—that Pat doesn't have a mink coat. But she does have a respectable cloth coat. And I always tell her that she looks good in anything.

One other thing I should probably tell you, because if I don't they'll be saying this about me, too. We did get something, a gift, after the nomination. A man down in Texas heard Pat on the radio mention the fact that our two youngsters would like to have a dog and, believe it or not, the day before we left on this campaign trip we got a message from Union Station in Baltimore, saying they had a package for us. We went down to get it. You know what it was?

It was a little cocker spaniel dog in a crate that he had sent all the way from Texas—black and white, spotted, and our little girl, Tricia, the six-year-old, named it Checkers. And you know, the kids, like all kids, love that dog, and I just want to say this, right now, that regardless of what they say about it, we're going to keep it.

The impact of the speech was stunning. Sixty million Americans had watched the vice-presidential candidate choking back the tears in close-ups. Before the night was over, the Republican headquarters had received a million telegrams in support of Nixon, as well as $60,000 in contributions. This, together with General Eisenhower's late campaign promise to travel to Korea and review the nation's policy there if he were elected, set the stage for what was to be the heaviest election turnout in American history.

Eisenhower won in an electoral vote landslide with an impressive popular majority as nearly 62 million Americans went to the polls. With 33.8 million votes (54.9 percent) to 27.3 million (44.4 percent), Eisenhower out-scored Stevenson in the electoral vote category 442 to 89, smashing the traditionally Democratic South. Interestingly, both presidential candidates received the highest popular vote for a winner and loser respectively in the nation's history. At the legislative level, and despite Eisenhower's obvious popularity, the Republicans barely managed to capture the House and the Senate. The significance of the election defied simple analysis, for it soon became clear that it was the man and not necessarily the party for which the people had voted. What President Eisenhower would do with this overwhelming "mandate for change" remained to be seen. In any case, Americans looked forward to the first GOP inauguration since 1929.

In his inaugural address of January 20, 1953, Eisenhower uniquely captured the mood of the American people. "We sense with all our faculties," he observed, "that forces of good and evil are massed and armed and opposed as rarely before in history." In the face of a tumultuous half-century of change and violence, the president exhorted his fellow citizens to summon their collective wit and will to meet the question of the age: "How far have we come in man's long pilgrimage from darkness toward the light. Are we nearing the light—a day of freedom and of peace for all mankind? Or are the shadows of another night closing in upon us?" Having said that, Eisenhower then set out the rules of conduct by which the United States would be known to all peoples. Among these were: "We hold it to be the first task of statesmanship to develop the strength that will deter the forces of aggression and promote the conditions of peace; . . . we stand ready to engage with any and all others in joint effort to remove the causes of mutual fear and distrust among nations, so as to make possible drastic reduction of armaments; . . . we shall never try to placate an aggressor by the false and wicked bargaining of trading honor for security" and, finally, "we shall strive to help" proven friends of freedom "to achieve their own security and well-being," though "we shall count upon them to assume, within the limits of their resources, their full and just burdens in the common defense of freedom." While his words faithfully echoed the sentiments of the strictures found in the New Testament, the president, once in power, surrounded himself with the best minds to be found in the boardrooms of the nation's leading corporations.

In what was clearly meant to be seen as a businessmen's administration, Eisenhower appointed, among others, the president of General Motors, Charles E. "Engine Charlie" Wilson, as his secretary of defense; the president of M.A. Hanna and Co., George Humphrey, as secretary of the treasury; and one of the country's highest-paid corporate lawyers and a long-time Republican foreign policy advisor, John Foster Dulles, as secretary of state. Dulles, who was shortly to become one of the most influential men to hold that office in modern times, was also one of the most experienced in the ways of diplomacy, with service dating back to the Paris Peace Conference of 1919. Dulles gave Eisenhower the impression, in the president's words, that he "seems to sense the intricacies of what those people are driving at better than anyone I have listened to." Unfortunately for some, Dulles's apparent high-mindedness and moralistic rigidity made the otherwise logical appointment a difficult pill to swallow. Furthermore, Dulles' brother, Allen, the epitome of the "gentleman spy," was appointed director of Central Intelligence. Others in the cabinet included several automobile distributors, a manufacturer from New England, a conservation specialist in agriculture, and the wife of a prominent Texas publisher. The one exception in the cabinet was the secretary of labor, Martin Durkin, who was both a Democrat and president of a plumbers' union, prompting the *New Republic* to proclaim the cabinet "eight millionaires and a plumber." The administration's principal theme at home was, as Secretary of Defense Charles Wilson put it in his confirmation hearing, "What's good for our country is good for General Motors and vice versa."

Unlike Truman, whose induction into the presidency brought with it a sense of awe and a public plea for the prayers of his fellow citizen, Eisenhower approached the duties of the Oval Office with a sense of relative equanimity, recording in his diary of his first day at the president's desk, "Plenty of worries and difficult problems. But such has been my portion for a long time—the result is that this just seems like a continuation of all I've been doing since July 1941—even before that." Not unlike his predecessor, Eisenhower rapidly identified himself with the national forces of moderation. In 1949 in a speech to the American Bar Association as president of Columbia University, the future chief executive declared: "The path to America's future lies down the middle of the road between the unfettered power of concentrated wealth . . . and the unbridled power of statism or partisan interests." During the course of his presidency, Eisenhower seldom if ever deviated from his moderate principles, his middle-of-the-road position, on most questions. Perhaps such an approach to politics satisfied neither the liberals nor the conservatives; it did, however, satisfy the majority of Americans who were in no mood to witness the dismantling of major New Deal and Fair Deal legislation, particularly social security.

COMMUNISM AT HOME AND ABROAD

True to his campaign pledge, Eisenhower visited Korea in December 1952, letting it be known that he advocated the U.N. position on the prisoners of war. He was in fact determined to bring the war to an end and after his inauguration allowed Secretary of State Dulles to spread the word that unless an armistice were declared soon, Washington might find it necessary "to blast Manchuria north of the Yalu if the stalemate continued." To this covert threat to use atomic weapons against China, and his removal of Truman's ban on operations from Taiwan against the mainland in early 1953, the president later attributed the decision of Beijing to accept U.N. terms. Armistice negotiations were resumed in April after a suspension of six months. For reasons of their own, the Communists were now prepared to make concessions on the thorny issue of the prisoners of war, and in spite of the violent opposition of South Korean president Syngman Rhee, an armistice agreement was signed at Panmunjom on July 26, 1953, to go into effect the next day, bringing to an end a "police action" in which almost three million Koreans lost their lives (1.3 in the South and 1.5 million in the North) as well as a million Chinese and over 54,000 Americans.

Meeting in Berlin in early 1954, the Big Four foreign ministers agreed that a conference on the Korean question, among other things, should be held in Geneva in April. There, South Korea and fifteen of the nations that had participated in the U.N. police action confronted North Korea and its allies China and the Soviet Union. A U.N. proposal for the unification of the Korean peninsula after supervised free elections could be held throughout the country was rejected by the North Koreans, and no agreement was reached. In the absence of settlement, or even the prospect of one, the armistice continued to prevail. A treaty of mutual defense, similar to others then being negotiated by Washington in the Pacific region, had been signed by representatives of the United States and the Republic of Korea a year earlier, with South Korea consenting to the stationing of American armed forces "in and about" its territory. Two American army divisions remained in Korea technically under the auspices of the United Nations.

With the Republicans in control of the White House, Wisconsin senator Joseph R. McCarthy, perhaps the most formidable, gifted, and hated American demagogue of the century, proceeded to step up his crusade to purify the American body politic of any and all traces of communism, real or otherwise. Though few would care to admit it, McCarthy had behind him at the height of his power many of the nation's most respected politicians, Republicans as well as some conservative Democrats; the powerful Hearst newspaper network was also solidly for him. More significantly, according to a Gallup poll of January 15, 1954, 50 percent of the American people had a "favorable opinion" of the senator. At the root of McCarthyism lay American disillusionment with the aftermath of World War II, particularly growing evidence of Soviet betrayal of the lofty aims of the war in Eastern

Europe and, on a more sinister level, the discovery of evidence of Soviet espionage in the United States.

Eisenhower showed little inclination to confront the senator publicly, although it is equally clear the president harbored a strong dislike for the man and his methods. In the opening months of the administration, McCarthy attacked the presumably subversive elements in the Voice of America and the Overseas Book Programs, demanding the removal of works even remotely associated with Communists. Without mentioning McCarthy by name, Eisenhower warned against joining the book burners. McCarthy also sought unsuccessfully to stop the nomination of Charles E. Bohlen as ambassador to the Soviet Union on the grounds of his close connections with the foreign policies of Roosevelt and Truman. As chairman of the Senate Permanent Investigating Subcommittee of the Government Operations Committee, McCarthy then conducted a series of hearings, lasting to 1954, on the role of presumed Communist influence in government and in other areas. Congressional committees simultaneously investigated communism in the fields of education and entertainment. Again, careers in and out of Washington were ruined through the device of accusation and guilt by association.

In early 1954, the administration finally found itself forced to take a tougher public position against McCarthy. When the army failed to take punitive action against Major Irving Peress, a dentist accused of Communist activities (Peress was granted an honorable discharge), McCarthy inveighed against the major's commandant, General Ralph Zwicker, as a coddler of Communists and demanded that Zwicker be relieved of his command. After some hesitation in the direction of placating the senator, Secretary of the Army Robert Stevens remonstrated that he would "never accede to the abuse of Army personnel . . . never accede to their brow-beating and humiliation." The stage was now set for the final act in the senator's crusade against communism. After an investigation of Communist subversion at Fort Monmouth, New Jersey, in late 1953 and early 1954, the Senate Permanent Subcommittee on Investigations, with the senator from Wisconsin in the role of a witness, convened in April to examine allegations made by the secretary of the army that McCarthy and the subcommittee's counsel, Roy M. Cohn, sought by improper means to obtain preferential treatment for a committee consultant, Private G. David Schine. The subcommittee also agreed to look into McCarthy's countercharges that Secretary of the Army Stevens and several of his associates had engaged in a campaign to discourage further investigation of alleged Communist subversion at Fort Monmouth. The proceedings were televised over a period of thirty-five days lasting from April 22 to June 17; the featured speakers in what soon became called the Army-McCarthy hearings featured the senator and Special Army Counsel Joseph N. Welch.

In a nation increasingly addicted to television viewing, the Army-McCarthy hearings became compelling drama, the audience at times reaching twenty million people. After thirty-five days of public exposure, the American people had seen and heard enough to be persuaded that McCarthy, sinister-looking with his black, bushy eyebrows and five o'clock shadow, had indeed used improper means in trying to get preferred treatment for Private Schine, despite the subcommittee's majority report exonerating the senator from charges of improper influence. McCarthy's popularity among the American public plunged from 50 percent to 34 percent, according to a June 1954 Gallup poll. Some, including Republican committee member Senator Charles E. Potter of Michigan, were convinced that the principal accusation of each side was borne out and that perjury had indeed been committed. In August, the Senate established a select committee to investigate McCarthy's own activities in the Senate. On December 2, 1954, McCarthy became only the fourth member in the history of the United States to be formally "censured," with a final vote of 62 to 22. The resolution of condemnation—the word *censure* was not used in the official language—found that McCarthy's actions were "contrary to Senatorial ethics and tend to bring the Senate into dishonor and disrepute, to obstruct the constitutional processes of the Senate, and to impair its dignity." His own reputation in tatters, McCarthy's influence rapidly declined until his death in May 1957. The political witch hunt led by McCarthy had come to an end.

The war of words against McCarthy in no way indicated a lesser desire on the part of the Eisenhower administration to deal harshly with the perpetrators of the Communist conspiracy at home. Within his first two years in office, Eisenhower signed into law numerous pieces of antisubversive legislation. Various provisions of this body of legislation imposed legal, political, and economic penalties on Communist party members and took away the rights, privileges, and immunities that otherwise legal bodies ordinarily have under the federal government; granted immunity from prosecution to certain suspected persons in order to obtain the conviction of Communists; provided for the loss of citizenship by those advocating the overthrow of the government by force and violence; and increased penalties for those harboring or concealing Communists who were fugitives from justice. In August 1954, the president boasted that as a result of administration enforcement of antisubversive laws, "41 top communist leaders have been convicted, 35 more are indicted and scheduled for trial, and 105 subversive aliens have been deported." A year earlier, in June, the president adamantly refused to save convicted atomic-secret spies Julius and Ethel Rosenberg from death in the electric chair. "The execution of two human beings is a grave matter," remarked Eisenhower shortly before their deaths and in his second refusal of executive clemency, "but even graver is the thought of the millions of dead whose deaths may be directly attributable to what these spies have done." Two very probable spies went to their deaths without flinching or showing remorse.

"MIDDLE AMERICA"

Despite the political upheaval of the domestic war on communism, the 1950s were an era of stunning prosperity, especially for the upper 20 percent of a population, which grew by more than 28 million during the decade. Millions of Americans, continuing the traditional westward movement, migrated to California and the southwest. California had surpassed New York as the most populous state in the nation, with all the attendant political clout. Other immigrants doubled the population of Florida, a destination made more attractive by the widespread production of the air conditioner. Even the recessions of late 1953 and 1958 proved manageable, mainly through the exercise of the administration's strict monetarist policies and fiscal restraint that involved controlling the money supply and holding down federal appropriations. The swelling ranks of the American middle class were on the whole becoming content with their own way of life, perceived as an ideal blend of private initiative and government regulation, with provision for a limited program of social welfare. Not only were people becoming prosperous, but the fruits of wartime technology were now reaped by the general public in the form of supercars, superhighways, and inexpensive housing, mainly in the suburbs—the faceless dormitories of the middle class who commuted to the city to work.

The administration played its own role in determining these developments. The Housing Act of 1954 provided for the construction of 35,000 units in one year, allowing preferential refuge for those displaced by slum clearance and other public improvements. Subsequent housing acts raised maximum permissible mortgage amounts but required cash payments and generally liberalized the terms of down payment. For farmers, Eisenhower sought to construct a farm program aimed at bringing food and fiber supplies into line with demand without undercutting federal price supports; accordingly, Secretary of Agriculture Ezra Taft Benson turned to the establishment of a sliding scale of price supports to curb unbalanced farm production flowing from the price-depressing effect of $2.5 billion worth of farm products housed in federal storage.

Though Congress had already made a high-speed federal highway system eligible for federal funds in 1944, it was not until 1956 that much was done about it. Senator Albert Gore, Sr., (Democrat-Tennessee) and Representative George H. Fallon (Democrat-Maryland) drafted a congressional bill to provide substantial federal aid for the construction of a nationwide network of highways. Eisenhower had been an outspoken advocate of improved public roads since 1952, when he had declared that "the obsolescence of the nation's highways presents an appalling problem of waste, danger, and death" and also claimed for good measure that a modern high-way network was essential to the nation's security. With the White House's collaboration with Democratic congressmen, the Federal-Aid Highway Act of 1956 was enacted. Essentially, it provided for the spending of $32 billion over a thirteen-year period for the construction of a 41,000–mile interstate highway system (1,944 more miles were authorized later) and for completing construction of the federal aid system of highways, the government contributing 90 percent to the former and 50 percent to the latter to be financed by new taxes on gasoline and other highway-use items.

In other domestic landmarks, the administration established the Department of Health, Education and Welfare, with Oveta Culp Hobby as the first secretary in 1953; authorized the establishment of the U.S. Air Force Academy in Colorado Springs, Colorado, in 1954; and provided funds for the construction of the St. Lawrence Seaway, a twenty-seven-foot-deep channel between Montreal and Lake Erie, in the same year. The year 1954 also witnessed the enactment of the Atomic Energy Act, which opened the door to private enterprise in producing and marketing electric power generated from nuclear reactors. The act, which also allowed for the transfer of atomic weapons secrets to America's Western European allies, marked the first major revision of the basic law governing atomic energy since 1946.

Despite the legislative activity and the popularity of the administration, the congressional elections of November 1954 went badly for the GOP, proving once again that the chief asset of the Republican Party was the president himself. The Democrats overturned the Republican majority in Congress with a margin of twenty-nine in the House and a margin of one in the Senate. In 1955, even the president seemed in mortal danger from a coronary thrombosis he suffered in September. Though he resumed some duties within a week, it required months of good care before he was up to full strength. By early 1956, the president felt confident enough physically to declare that he would seek the renomination of his party later in the year.

In addition to living in houses and driving automobiles that looked alike, Americans in the 1950s were conditioned to think alike, the result mainly of the invasion of the television into the family home. Unlike radio, which also had its place in the family unit, television required little if any energy to watch and no imagination at all. Commercial television began in the United States in the late 1940s, though experiments in transmitting picture signals through the air waves had begun in Britain in the late 1920s. Despite its later omnipresence as the centerpiece of every American living room, television was not an overnight success. Until about 1951 or even later, commercial radio competed successfully for big network entertainment. The main problem was that television reception was relatively poor. Large home antennas were required to receive even local stations as viewers complained of the "snowstorm" effect, which often made viewing nearly impossible. But, of course, bad reception or not, people did watch.

The television age had been born, and by the end of the century, each American household was tuned into television for an average of over seven hours, a phenomenon with profound cultural and social ramifications.[2]

What did Americans watch? For the more discerning, television was, as a federal communications commissioner would later say, a "wasteland," though few would deny the merits of such first-class live drama as the celebrated *Playhouse 90*. For those less discerning, television fare was entertaining if at times dismal. A few of the top-rated shows of the 1950s included *Sid Caesar, Milton Berle, Jack Benny* (all done live), *Ozzie and Harriet, Our Miss Brooks*, and *Dragnet*. For the children there was *Howdy Doody, Pinky Lee*, and *Hopalong Cassidy*. The real power of television was not, however, revealed in the programs, most of which proved less than memorable, but in other areas, namely, the stunning impact of television commercials replete with their hidden persuaders. Indeed, the ad-man in his grey flannel suit and buttoned-down shirt became a kind of hero of the 1950s, at once a con artist and a brilliant student of his culture. The public was seduced, and they loved it. The television advertisements created minor legends, and the best of them passed into Madison Avenue folklore. Americans knew that Viceroy cigarettes were the thinking man's filter, that Geritol cured tired blood, that you could always tell a Halo girl, and that you should see the U.S.A. in your Chevrolet.

Even more indicative of the things to come was the revelation of the enormous potential of television to intrude into people's lives by bringing them face-to-face with real-life drama. The first such drama focused on the hearings into organized crime conducted by Senator Kefauver who proved to be the star of his own show; his co-star was New York underworld figure Frank Costello. The Costello interviews in March 1951 scored 70 percent in the influential television ratings, better than baseball's World Series. General Douglas MacArthur's tearful farewell to a packed Congress, Nixon's "Checkers" speech, and the Army-McCarthy hearings all involved the casual viewer in a manner previously thought impossible.

The debate about the merits of television has raged unabated since those early days. Social commentator and writer E. B. White once observed that television could either become a great boon or an inordinate distraction, perhaps the most perfect opiate the world has ever seen. For children, it was the veritable invasion of the body snatchers. Between the ages of six and eighteen, the average American child spent approximately fifteen to sixteen thousand hours in front of a television set, in contrast to approximately thirteen thousand hours in school. During this time, the same average child witnessed two hundred thousand acts of violence, including 50,000 murders, and 500,000 advertisements. Some critics of the medium argued that television tended to damage a child's critical abilities; others disagreed. What could not be doubted was the extent to which television homogenized Americans—regional dialects, outlooks, even the difference between adulthood and childhood tended to be blurred as all adult secrets came under the scrutiny of youthful observers.

The book that best conceptualized the American way of doing things in the 1950s was William H. Whyte's *The Organization Man* (1956), the perfect complement to the centrifugal forces of the culture makers of the time. *The Organization Man* served both as hero and model of young men everywhere, though to be sure there were rebels without a particular cause opting out of the system albeit in as conspicuous a fashion as possible. Whyte, an editor of *Fortune* magazine, read the times well. The one thing that struck Whyte about the U.S. economy in the 1950s was the increasing decline of small business; equally significant, the decline was unlamented. Small business had been replaced by big business, but not the big business of the robber barons of an earlier period. Rather, small business was replaced by the gentle, giant Big Brother organization, which really "cared" about society, its environment, and its employees.

Who was the Organization Man? For one thing, he was young, in his thirties; for another, he was a veteran of World War II who subsequently obtained a university education courtesy of the GI Bill. He was unmistakably dressed in his grey flannel suit, snap brim hat, narrow dark tie, and shirt with a button-down collar. An aspiring executive in a large corporation, he was upwardly mobile and determined to be a corporate success; in fact, it was the attraction of working in a large company that appealed to him and was his distinctive characteristic. As for his aspirations, the principal bestower of gratification and success was the Organization, whether a corporate giant, federal agency, or a great university. Whyte observed that with few exceptions all these institutions were as alike as the attitudes and expectations of their executives. The ultimate goal of the Organization Man was to be seen as a good team player, for there was no place for the individual or the genuinely creative genius unless, of course, he was prepared to play on the team. The Organization Man was a familiar if indistinguishable face in suburbia, played a community role, bowled on Friday evenings, and attended church (preferably Episcopalian or Presbyterian) regularly. Put another way, he sought to be Everyman. The trick of success, however, was to play Everyman so well that he could eventually reach the top—the reward reserved for one who was most like everyone else. Moreover, the Organization Man was constantly monitored to make certain he continued to be a team player, subjecting himself to a battery of "personality" tests designed to detect deviation from the norm. To round out the family requirement, the Organization Wife was supposed to look like Doris Day, while the children attended an Organization School. Whyte reproduced the personality test used to screen prospective executives for Sears Roebuck, considered a model corporation of its kind in the 1950s. Typical of the questions asked were: "Who did you love most: your father or your mother?" Or, "Which would you rather do: read a book or go bowling?" Men who chose their father, and preferred bowling to reading were assured every opportunity to succeed. The ascendance of the Organization Man in his Brooks Brothers suit led many social commentators to celebrate the so-called American consensus, which tended to highlight the values the majority of Americans shared rather than those on which they diverged. Less sanguine critics of consensus tended to perceive a darker, more sinister side. In his study *The Power Elite*, published in 1956, C. Wright Mills found cold comfort in the doctrine of consensus, perceiving in it a new and frightening version of the totalitarian state. As part of a new elite, Mills contended, the Organization Man was more interested in furthering his own interests than in the interests of the people as a whole. Whatever position one took on the matter, Whyte's *Organization Man* and Mill's *Power Elite* became classic expressions of the decade.

THE RISE OF THE PROTEST MOVEMENTS

Middle-class serenity was not the whole story, however, as growing protest movements sought to make political headway. Having failed in their bid to assassinate President Harry Truman in November 1950, Puerto Rican extremists campaigning for that country's complete independence from U.S. hegemony opened fire in the U.S. House of Representatives chamber on March 1, 1954, wounding five congressmen in the process. More profound was the discontent expressed by the civil rights movement, a movement that gained momentum during the Eisenhower presidency, in particular after the celebrated U.S. Supreme Court decision in the case of *Brown v. Board of Education of Topeka* handed down on May 17, 1954, a decision that galvanized the hitherto disparate campaigns for improving the plight of African Americans into a single civil rights movement. The unanimous decision was delivered by Chief Justice Earl Warren, whose appointment Eisenhower came to regret. The Supreme Court reversed its ruling of 1896 of *Plessy v. Ferguson*, which sanctioned segregation of the races under the doctrine of "separate but equal." The Court upheld the plaintiff's contention that segregated public schools were not "equal" and could not be made "equal," and that hence they had been deprived of equal protection of the law. The highest court in the land faced the question squarely: "Does segregation of children in public schools solely on the basis of race, even though the physical facilities and other 'tangible' factors may be equal, deprive the children of the minority group of equal educational opportunities?" Finding in the affirmative, the Court held that the "segregation of white and colored children," mainly as "the policy of separating the races is usually interpreted as denoting the inferiority of the Negro group." The message to the American people was unequivocal: "We conclude that in the field of public education the doctrine of 'separate but equal' has no place." In a ruling a year later, the Court ordered southern states to proceed with the desegregation of their school districts, "with all deliberate speed." The South's lower courts were entrusted with the responsibility of effecting these changes. Southern critics of desegregation fought with every weapon at their disposal, bringing intense pressure to bear on southern politicians, from the municipal to the federal level. While some rode the high ground of states' rights to oppose "forced" integration, much of the opposition was of the ugly variety, up to and including threats of physical violence. The first African American to register at the University of Alabama in early 1956 was driven from the campus by a mob of angry students, a scene to be repeated in Texas and Tennessee. A showdown was in the works.

Against a background of massive resistance in the Deep South, where not a single school had been integrated since the Supreme Court decision, a federal district court in 1957 nullified an Arkansas court injunction prohibiting the school board from commencing integration beginning with senior high school students. On the eve of the fall semester at Little Rock's Central High School, Governor Orval E. Faubus, hardly the ignorant and racist hillbilly the national media of the 1950s made him out to be, called out the National Guard to maintain law and order there, a pretext aimed at *preventing* nine black students from attending classes. In spite of a meeting with the president at Newport, Rhode Island, in September, Governor Faubus failed to remove the Guard until he was served with a federal injunction barring him from obstructing the entry of the black students. Shortly afterward, on September 23, violence broke out. There is strong circumstantial evidence that the onetime racial liberal provoked the mob violence to justify his tactics.

Though he had taken a Delphian position on the Supreme Court ruling of 1954—"I refused to say whether I either approved it or disapproved it"—Eisenhower showed not the slightest hesitation in enforcing the letter of the law. Accordingly, on September 24 he dispatched a thousand paratroopers from the crack 101st Airborne Division from nearby Fort Campbell, Kentucky, while federalizing the Arkansas National Guard. Within days, the African American students were attending school under guard. The people of Arkansas responded by re-electing Governor Faubus who, in turn, brought the matter to the Supreme Court. In September 1958, the Court held its ground, declaring that "the constitutional rights [of the black children] are not to be sacrificed or yielded to the violence and disorder which have followed the actions of the [Arkansas] Governor and legislature." Though further progress would be disappointingly slow, a start had at least been made.

On other matters, blacks took the lead in breaking down the dubious legal barriers and Jim Crow statutes that separated the races in the South. Segregated transportation came under fire when, on December 1, 1955, a 43–year-old black seamstress, Rosa Parks, refused to move to the designated "colored" section of a bus in Montgomery, Alabama; under the city's

municipal segregation ordinance, African Americans rode in the back of
the bus while whites rode in the front. Thousands of blacks boycotted the
bus company until the Supreme Court found in their favor in November; a
month later unsegregated bus services commenced. The policy of passive
resistance conferred the mantle of southern black leadership on a young
Baptist minister, the Reverend Martin Luther King, Jr., while in the North,
Roy Wilkins of the National Association for the Advancement of Colored
People (NAACP) and Floyd McKissick of the Congress on Racial Equality
developed strategy there. By the end of the Eisenhower era, sit-ins, and
freedom rides had broken down such discriminatory southern practices as
segregated lunch counters and facilities on interstate highways.[3] Moving in
yet another direction, the administration's civil rights acts of 1957 and 1960
went a long way toward bringing southern African Americans closer to
their ballot by creating new voting rights protections. Like others, the laws'
limitations became painfully obvious in the face of racial hostility and generations of conditioning. Still, the laws represented the most significant
civil rights legislation since the days of Civil War reconstruction.

A REPUBLICAN FOREIGN POLICY

Overseas, things were not going so well. By 1954, Washington was bearing 70 percent of the cost of French military effort directed against the nationalist insurgency of North Vietnam's Communist leader Ho Chi Minh.
In spite of such massive material aid and after eight years' effort, the war
went badly for the French, reaching crisis proportions in the spring when a
combined army of twenty thousand French and loyal Vietnamese found itself surrounded and isolated by a superior force of Viet Minh troops in the
frontier fortress of Dienbienphu. In urgent appeals to Washington, Paris
warned that without direct American military intervention all was lost,
and the way was paved for the Communist conquest of Indochina, perhaps
all of Southeast Asia. To Eisenhower, who likened the situation to the falling of a row of dominoes, and even more so to Secretary of State Dulles,
such a challenge merited a response. Congress, as well as the president,
strongly opposed unilateral intervention, however, and the British were reluctant to undermine the forthcoming international conference meeting in
Geneva to deal with the problems of Korea and Indochina. Consequently,
the French capitulated on May 7.

Having failed to reach agreement on Korea, the Geneva Conference
(April 26 to July 21, 1954) turned to Indochina with greater expectations.
Dulles took little part in this phase of the proceedings. The armistice terms
ended the fighting in Indochina and divided Vietnam at the 17th parallel of
north latitude. The Viet Minh, officially the Democratic Republic of Vietnam, was to take the north; South Vietnam was to take all lands south of the
line. The division was temporary until the country was to be united after

general elections scheduled for July 1956. Though the elections never took place, few doubted that Ho Chi Minh would have won.[4]

Since it appeared that only international action would prevent the further advance of communism in the region, Dulles initiated the creation of a Southeast Asia Treaty Organization (SEATO) to serve as a barrier to Communist advances in Southeast Asia, as NATO served in Europe. The only Asian nations that could be counted upon were the Philippines, Thailand, and Pakistan. Delegates from these three countries, together with representatives of the United States, Great Britain, France, Australia, and New Zealand, met in Manila in September 1954. The ensuing collective defense treaty followed the pattern of the Australia-New Zealand and Philippines treaties rather than the Three Musketeers' language of the NATO treaty, that is, a promise to "act to meet the common danger in accordance with its constitutional processes." Among other things, the treaty declared through an attached protocol that "the free territory under the jurisdiction of the state of Vietnam" should be eligible for both protective features and economic benefits deriving from the treaty. Within a year, the newly proclaimed Republic of Vietnam (South Vietnam), under the leadership of Ngo Dinh Diem, would draw closer to American sponsorship.

In its concern over the threat of communism in Asia and elsewhere, Washington had largely ignored troubling conditions in Latin America, where the need for economic and social reforms was imperative. Before long, dramatic happenings alerted the Eisenhower administration to the urgency of the Latin American situation. The first of these critical events was the adoption of an openly leftist line in both domestic policy and in alignment with the Soviets in the United Nations by President Jacobo Arbenz Guzman of Guatemala. To Secretary of State Dulles, any leftist beach-head in the Americas, no matter how small, seemed a direct threat to the security of the United States and its sister republics. Accordingly, in June 1954 Guzman was overthrown by a fellow countryman, Colonel Carlos Castillo Armas, who was assisted by American arms and several planes provided by the Central Intelligence Agency.[5] If the brief apparition of Communist power in Guatemala shocked the Eisenhower administration, a ruder shock was the series of violent demonstrations against Vice President Nixon during his tour of South America in the spring of 1958. Nixon departed for South America in April, announcing that the purpose of his journey was to show "that these countries are not only our neighbors but our best friends." The vice president's reception varied from country to country, but in Lima, Peru, and in Caracas, Venezuela, his life (and that of Mrs. Nixon) was in peril. Though Nixon attributed his problems in part to Communist elements, there was also a wide-spread popular impression that Washington had become too friendly to dictatorships in Latin America; indeed, the United States traditionally made no distinction between dictatorial and democratic regimes in its official relationships as long as they were anti-Communist.

The year 1956, a presidential election year, witnessed two major foreign policy crises, both of which tested the leadership of the Eisenhower administration to the limit. The first crisis was produced by Soviet suppression of an attempted anti-Communist revolution in Hungary; the second crisis was precipitated by an attack on Egypt by Israel, France, and Britain.

The death of Josef Stalin in March 1953 was the prelude to the rise of power in the Kremlin of a leader whose aims were identical to Stalin's but whose methods were more flexible, more seductive, and perhaps more dangerous. Stalin's first successor as premier, Georgi M. Malenkov, was promptly sidelined in favor of Nikolai A. Bulganin, while Nikita S. Khrushchev, the crude but brilliant Communist Party secretary, emerged as the effective Soviet leader. By 1958, Khrushchev also assumed the duties of premier. In foreign policy, the new regime set out to entice the uncommitted nations instead of frightening them; another important characteristic was a degree of relaxation in Moscow's control of Communist parties and governments in the Soviet sphere of Europe.

In Hungary, dissatisfaction took a more fundamental turn. Anti-Soviet and antigovernment riots led to the installation, on October 24, 1956, of a new regime headed by Imre Nagy. Several days later, the Communist Nagy admitted non-Communists to his government. On November 1, Budapest repudiated the Warsaw Alliance, declared Hungary a neutralist state—like its neighbor, Austria, which reemerged as an independent state in 1955—and appealed to the United Nations for assistance. By this time, the Soviet leadership, fearful of appearing weak, had had enough. Temporarily withdrawing its tanks and troops from the Hungarian capital, it sent them back in force, quelled the popular uprising in the city, and stage managed the installation of a new Communist regime headed by Janos Kadar, who obediently invited Soviet assistance into Hungary. Nagy, who had been granted a safe conduct by the Kremlin, was executed. A virtually unarmed citizenry proved no match for Soviet tanks. No aid came from the West, despite Secretary of State Dulles's brave talk of the "liberation" of peoples under the yoke of communism. Within two weeks, thousands of Hungarians died fighting, while several hundred thousand fled into exile. Even if the United States, or NATO for that matter, had wished to intervene, it would have been seriously hampered by contemporary events in the Middle East.

The Eisenhower administration pursued its containment policy in the Middle East in three ways: first, by attempting to resolve disputes that otherwise might tempt Soviet interference within the region, particularly the quarrel between Israel and its neighbor, and controversies between Egypt and Iran on the one hand and Britain on the other; second, by raising living standards through developmental assistance; and third, by strengthening the area's military potential, as well as its willingness, to resist Soviet-sponsored subversion. This third line of approach received its main impetus from Dulles, whose general policy was to encircle the U.S.S.R. with military alliances. What NATO did for Europe and SEATO did for Southeast Asia, the Baghdad Pact was supposed to do for the region stretching from Pakistan to Turkey. An alliance of "northern tier" states—Turkey, Pakistan, Iran, Iraq, and Britain—was set in place by early 1955, but with the United States reserving formal membership. Before the ink was dry, Egypt announced a barter deal of cotton for Czech arms followed by news of an alliance and a joint command between Egypt, Syria, and Saudi Arabia.

Washington and London attempted to recover their forfeited goodwill in Cairo by proposing to aid President Gamal Abdel Nasser in financing a new high dam at Aswan on the Nile. When Nasser's ambassador traveled to Washington in July 1956 to accept the loan, he was told abruptly that the offer had been withdrawn. To Dulles, Nasser had become a poor economic and political risk. Nasser was infuriated while the British were annoyed at not having been consulted on what had been a joint offer. The Egyptian leader responded dramatically on July 26 with the nationalization of the Suez Canal, owned chiefly by British and French stockholders and the vital link between Western Europe and the Middle Eastern oil fields. The Egyptian government proposed to collect the tolls and apply part of the proceeds to the construction of the Aswan Dam. Negotiations to arbitrate the difference led nowhere and were compounded by the fact that neither London nor Paris had any confidence in Nasser whose pan-Arab nationalism was seen as abetting rebellion against France in Algeria and British influence in Arabia.

Fearful for its very existence, Israel was the first nation to act. On October 29, 1956, less than a week after the start of the Hungarian revolt, Israeli forces struck without warning at Egyptian positions in the Gaza Strip and the Sinai Peninsula. The Egyptian armies were overwhelmed, great stores of arms were captured, and the invaders pushed on across the Sinai toward the Suez Canal. Officially, and in collusion with the Israelis, Britain and France requested Israel and Egypt to accept a cease-fire, and when Cairo predictably refused, Britain and France announced they would occupy positions along the canal to separate the belligerents and keep the canal open—the pretext for intervention. Their real purpose was to bring Nasser down. On November 5, Anglo-French troops parachuted into the canal area, followed a day later by a naval invasion at Port Said. Eisenhower reacted angrily to these resorts to force in violation of the United Nations Charter by one friendly state and two important allies; he made it clear to his allies that he was fully committed to support the victims of aggression and that, under the circumstances, he would not be bound by traditional alliances. The president also made it clear that he did not care in the slightest whether he was re-elected or not. On November 5, the U.N. General Assembly recommended the creation of an Emergency Force for Palestine, which was plainly perceived as a face-saving mechanism. Under combined international pressure, the British, the French, and the Israelis agreed the next day to a cease-fire. London and Paris had suffered a humiliating retreat. Nasser, in spite of a crippling military defeat and loss of territory to the Israelis, had been saved from complete disaster by the intervention of the United Nations, backed by the superpowers. Aid for the Aswan Dam was ultimately provided by Moscow. What did the United States hope to achieve? According to one senior Middle East correspondent, "President Eisenhower's insistence that the rule of law be obeyed was one of the high points of his presidency."

EISENHOWER'S SECOND TERM

The road to the 1956 presidential election held few surprises. Not unexpectedly, the Republican National Convention renominated Eisenhower and Nixon, although plainly the president was still more popular among the electorate than the party he represented. Again, the Democratic National Convention nominated Adlai Stevenson. The vice-presidential nominee, Senator Kefauver of Tennessee, was chosen in an open contest by the delegates after a spirited challenge by young Senator John F. Kennedy of Massachusetts. The impact of the Hungarian uprising and the Middle East crisis notwithstanding, the most remarkable aspect of the campaign was the absence of an issue. Economically, Americans were better off than they had ever been; inflation, after a spike at the beginning of the decade caused partly by the Korean War expenditures, averaged less than 1.4 percent a year in the Eisenhower years, was hardly a cause of concern, and the unemployment rate had stabilized since the 1954 recession.[6] On the whole, Stevenson was less impressive than he had been during the 1952 campaign. In the absence of any compelling need for domestic reform, Stevenson ended the campaign with a last-ditch effort to take on Eisenhower's foreign policy record by making proposals to reduce the draft and to suspend hydrogen bomb tests, but neither issue seemed persuasive.[7] The only real difference between the candidates, reported one observer, was that "the incautious Mr. Stevenson is promising the millennium tomorrow; the more cautious President Eisenhower promises it the day after." In any case, Eisenhower won by a landslide, the most spectacular victory since Franklin Roosevelt's triumph over Alfred M. Landon in 1930. Eisenhower won 457 electoral votes to Stevenson's 73, and 35,581,003 (57.4 percent) popular votes to Stevenson's 25,738,765 (41.5 percent). There were also a number of historic firsts: Eisenhower became the first Republican in the twentieth century to win two successive presidential elections; the first president in the nation's history to be legally debarred from a third term of office; and more ominously, the first president-elect since 1848 who failed to carry either the

Senate or the House. The Democrats won resounding victories in Congress with margins of 234 to 201 in the House and 49 to 47 in the Senate; in the midterm elections of 1958, the opposition improved these margins to 282 to 154 and 64 to 34, respectively.

Fully conscious of his one-man victory, the president, in his State of the Union address of January 1957, called on labor and business to exercise caution in wage and price policies; urged the conservation of the nation's natural resources; and exhorted people in all sections of the country to support him in moving closer to the goal of fair and equal treatment of citizens without regard to race or color. Given the revolution in civil rights that occurred during his administration, the president's comments in this respect amounted to classic understatement.

The situation abroad was becoming increasingly unstable as an acceleration of the arms race and increasing reliance upon nuclear weapons ushered in a new era of international crises. Eisenhower entered office committed at once to taking a "New Look" at national security and to pursuing a policy of fiscal restraint; in effect, he sought to cut the size of the armed forces without jeopardizing America's defense commitments. By October 1953, a new planning document, known as National Security Policy Planning Paper Number 162/2, had been approved by the president, and three months later, Dulles publicly unveiled the new policy of "massive retaliation." The United States, Dulles explained, had decided "to depend primarily upon a great capacity to retaliate, instantly, by means and at places of our own choosing" and it would no longer feel committed to fight what he called "brushfire wars" around the globe. To explain the strategy to the voters, Dulles used a simple analogy of municipal police: "We keep locks on our doors, but we do not have an armed guard in every home. We rely principally on a community security system so well equipped to punish any who break in and steal that, in fact, would-be aggressors are generally deterred. That is the modern way of getting maximum protection at a bearable cost."[8] Accordingly, the United States would no longer constrain itself to meet Communist military probes with a conventional weapons response as it had in Korea. The policy had a dramatic effect; increasing the relative emphasis on nuclear technology as opposed to maintaining large standing conventional forces allowed the administration to cut defense expenditures by about 25 percent compared to the late Truman years, leading Secretary of Defense Charles Wilson to declare proudly that the Pentagon now had "more bang for the buck."

Having adopted massive retaliation as a long-term cold war strategy, Eisenhower and Dulles found that strategy tested in the short term by a series of crises. Nevertheless, Eisenhower threatened massive retaliation in times of crisis sparingly and deliberately. In a series of confrontations with Communist China ranging from bringing an end to the Korean War in 1953 to the Taiwan Straits crisis of 1958, Eisenhower several times threatened nuclear attack. The primary focus of U.S. foreign policy, however, remained Europe. The struggle for Germany continued to manifest itself in crises over Berlin, which in turn presented U.S. foreign policy with perhaps its most serious test. Given the superior strength of Soviet conventional forces in Europe and the location of West Berlin deep inside Communist territory, that city was militarily indefensible. The situation was, as Senate Foreign Relations Committee chairman J. William Fulbright put it, "a strategic nightmare." The only viable option available to the United States short of thermonuclear war was to deter the Soviets from moving against the city.

With the overwhelming superiority of American forces, massive retaliation seemed to many to make sense. But by the end of the decade, with missile technology meaning that nuclear Armageddon was literally possible within minutes, many came to rethink U.S. nuclear strategy. The catalyst was the Soviet launching of *Sputnik*, the first artificial satellite, into space. *Sputnik* itself was harmless, being nothing more than a basketball-sized aluminum sphere filled with nitrogen and fitted with a rudimentary transmitter that emitted a distinctive "beep" every few seconds. Nevertheless, as amateur ham radio operators across America began picking up the signal, it became clear that an important milestone had been reached, and to the ire of the West, it was the Soviets who reached it first.

The effect on American thinking was both dramatic and humbling, particularly as it struck a blow at the presumed superiority of American technology. Eisenhower's response was twofold: the acceleration of the United States' own earth satellite program, which resulted in the launching of *Explorer I* in January 1958; and the adoption of an $877 million education aid bill, the National Defense Education Act (NDEA), in September 1958, aimed at strengthening the American education system so that it would meet the broad and increasing demands imposed upon it by consideration of basic national security. The NDEA, designed as an emergency undertaking to be terminated after four years, provided loans, fellowships to future college teachers, and grants to states to help locate and guide able students, as well as to provide equipment for teaching science, mathematics, and modern foreign languages.

The ushering in of the missile age had other, more serious implications. The addition of intercontinental ballistic missiles (ICBMs) to the Soviet strategic arsenal not only exposed the United States directly to massive nuclear attack for the first time, but also substantially increased the vulnerability of American strategic forces to a surprise attack, fulfilling the technical requirements of the presumption of a Soviet first-strike mentality envisaged by the national security debates of 1950. Clearly, nuclear vulnerability undermined the fundamental basis of the doctrine of massive retaliation. Despite charges, first, of a "bomber gap" and then of a "missile gap," the Eisenhower administration proceeded cautiously with the continued development and deployment of new generations of long-range nuclear missiles. Unbeknownst to all but a very select few at the top levels of the U.S. government, secret U-2 reconnaissance flights over the Soviet Union had confirmed that that the United States still held a massive superiority in nuclear forces.

But it was clear that Moscow could threaten U.S. interests without using the bomb. Although Moscow had shown that outright military conquest was not its preferred method of operation in the Middle East, Washington feared that states under Soviet influence might resort to violence to extend the boundaries of communism; the principal objects of this fear were Egypt and Syria, both of which had developed strong ties with the Soviet bloc. To guard against possible incursions into the area, Eisenhower secured from Congress, on March 9, 1957, a joint resolution setting forth what eventually became known as the Eisenhower Doctrine. Essentially, it empowered the president to use the armed forces of the United States, at the request of any nation in the Middle East, to protect it against overt armed aggression from any nation controlled by international communism. Though no nation of the region made the kind of request envisaged in the resolution, the administration found two occasions to act at least in the spirit of it. The first, a few weeks after the passage of the resolution, was on behalf of pro-Western King Hussein of Jordan, who was threatened by Egyptian and Syrian-supported leftist agitators. Among moves that included the showing of the American Sixth Fleet and a grant to Hussein of $30 million in economic and military aid, the situation brought forth from the president a declaration that he considered the independence of Jordan vital to American security. The second occasion occurred in the wake of a violent revolution in Iraq in July 1958 when the king, the crown prince, and all friends of the West were assassinated. A new government—not Communist, but friendly to the Soviet Union—took control and withdrew Iraq from the Baghdad Pact. The immediate Western reaction to the Iraq revolution was that it had been orchestrated by Nasser, who would then turn on Jordan and Lebanon. In Lebanon, in fact, there was already an armed rebellion in progress. After news of the Iraqi revolution, Lebanon and Jordan appealed for military protection to Washington and London respectively. Both appeals met swift response. The United States landed 14,000 marines and airborne troops in Lebanon, as Britain landed three thousand paratroopers in Jordan. After the situation had settled, American troops were withdrawn from Lebanon in October, and the British left Jordan in November.

The most serious crisis in Soviet-American relations during the second Eisenhower administration concerned Berlin. In a speech in November 1958 and in a series of notes to Washington, London, and Paris, Khrushchev demanded an end to the occupation of West Berlin by the Western powers. He insisted upon a solution within six months, threatening otherwise to make a separate peace with East Germany and leave the Allies to negotiate their rights in Berlin and their access there with a government they did not recognize. In December, the Allies joined in an unqualified rejection of the Soviet ultimatum. Faced by a determined and unified West, Khrushchev softened the tone of his demand by letting it be known that the six-month time limit was not to be taken literally. After two meetings of the Big Four foreign ministers in Geneva failed to make headway on the problem, Eisenhower invited the Soviet leader to visit him at Camp David, his mountain retreat in Maryland. Their meeting there, on September 25–27, 1959, climaxed ten days in which Khrushchev's touring of America—including a trip to Disneyland—and his sensational proposal at the United Nations of general and complete disarmament dominated the media. Despite the so-called spirit of Camp David and an invitation to the president to visit the U.S.S.R. the following spring, the troublesome Berlin question remained unresolved.[9]

In December, after the Camp David meeting, the Western Allies proposed a summit meeting of the Big Four for the coming May in Paris. The Soviets accepted, with Eisenhower's visit to the Soviet Union to follow in June. Prospects of agreement on Berlin, growing dimmer in the months prior to the Paris meeting, were completely destroyed by Khrushchev's reaction to the so-called U-2 incident. On May 1, a high-altitude U.S. reconnaissance plane of the U-2 type was shot down while on an espionage flight across the U.S.S.R. from Pakistan to Norway. The pilot, Gary Powers, was captured unharmed, along with his photographic and other equipment. After some internal skirmishing, Eisenhower accepted responsibility for such flights as a necessary safeguard against nuclear surprise attacks. The Kremlin seized upon the incident to wreck the summit conference, which ended abruptly on May 17, one day after its opening. The Soviet invitation to Eisenhower to visit the U.S.S.R. was withdrawn.[10]

Closer to home, the administration witnessed the successful overthrow of Cuban dictator Fulgencio Batista on New Year's Day 1959 by Fidel Castro. Initially, the American press and policymakers did not know what to make of Castro; Batista's regime had hardly been a model of democracy, and there were hopes that Castro's reforms might actually be positive. By 1961, however, Castro had tied himself to the Communist bloc. He repudiated early promises of free elections and a free press; confiscated foreign property, including American property worth $1 billion; and welcomed large-scale economic and military aid from the Soviet Union. Cuba, in the Eisenhower administration's view, had become the fountainhead of Communist propaganda and training school of revolutionaries for Latin America. For lack of regional support, Washington could only take unilateral action against Castro in retaliation for the latter's wholesale confiscation of American property and his continued propaganda abuse of the United States. In July 1960, Eisenhower cancelled about 95 percent of Cuba's remaining quota of sugar imports for the year, some months later canceling entirely the quota for the first quarter of 1961. An embargo on all shipments to Cuba save foodstuffs and medical supplies followed. On January 3, 1961, the president cut off all diplomatic and consular traffic with Havana. Meanwhile, secret plans were developed by the CIA to overthrow the Castro regime, but the decision on whether to act on them would ultimately fall to Eisenhower's successor.

As the Eisenhower administration approached its two-term limit, assessing its record remained problematic. Contemporary criticism of Eisenhower ranged from the mild to the extreme. Disaffected speech writer Emmet John Hughes judged the Eisenhower years to be both a personal and political tragedy: personal in the sense that the president had the support and resources to bring about great changes and did not, and political in the sense that he possessed the strength to revitalize the two-party system and failed to do so. Critics of a more liberal persuasion judged Eisenhower lazy (citing his obsession for golf very visible evidence), tongue-twisted, and frankly out of his depth in the White House, "a five-star babe in the woods." Sensitive to criticism of his "style" of leadership—or alleged lack of it—Eisenhower showed keenness in defending his achievements in office. In a letter written in 1966 to his former press secretary James C. Hagerty, he listed his accomplishments to include, among others, the statehood of Alaska and Hawaii; the building of the St. Lawrence Seaway; the ending of the Korean War; the largest reduction of taxes to that time; the first civil rights law in eighty years; the containment of communism in Iran, Guatemala, Lebanon, Formosa, and South Vietnam; the initiation of the most ambitious interstate highway system in history; the launching of a space and a ballistic missile program; starting federal medical care for the aged; and using executive power to enforce the order of a federal court in Arkansas with no loss of life. Interestingly, the president left off the one item for which most Americans have since come to remember him: his poignant warning of the danger of the military-industrial complex.[11]

In his farewell address to the American people delivered on January 17, 1961, Eisenhower noted that the conjunction of an immense military establishment and a large arms industry, each in itself necessary, was new in the American experience. Recognizing the imperative need for this development, he warned his fellow citizens that they must not fail to comprehend its grave implications. Specifically, he went on, "In the councils of government, we must guard against the acquisition of unwarranted influence whether sought or unsought, by the military-industrial complex. The potential for the disastrous rise of misplaced power exists and will persist." In the circumstances, the president concluded, "Only an alert and knowledgeable citizenry can compel the proper meshing of the huge industrial and military machinery of defense with our peaceful methods and goals, so that security and liberty may prosper together." Eisenhower was a citizen as well as a soldier. Because of his experience in both the army and the presidency, he knew firsthand the connection between industrialists and bureaucrats. His message was clear; his remedy, less so.

NOTES

1. Steven Neal, *Harry and Ike: The Partnership that Remade the Postwar World* (New York: Scribner, 2001), pp. 226–27; and Dwight D. Eisenhower, *Mandate for Change, 1953–1956* (New York: Doubleday, 1963), pp. 4–25.

2. For a discussion of the social and cultural effects of television, see John Leonard, *Smoke and Mirrors: Violence, Television and Other American Cultures* (New York: New Press, 1997).

3. Robert Weisbrot, *Freedom Bound: A History of America's Civil Rights Movement* (New York: W. W. Norton, 1990), pp. 19–44.

4. On the Eisenhower administration's struggle with the Indochina problem, see Robert Mann, *A Grand Delusion: America's Descent into Vietnam* (New York: Basic Books, 2001), pp. 77–224.

5. Nick Cullather, *Secret History: The CIA's Classified Account of Its Operations in Guatemala, 1952–1954* (Stanford, CA: Stanford University Press, 2000).

6. Richard J. Carroll, *An Economic Record of Presidential Performance: From Truman to Bush* (Westport, CT: Praeger, 1995), pp. 64–65.

7. John Bartlow Martin, *Adlai Stevenson and the World: The Life of Adlai Stevenson* (New York: Doubleday, 1977), pp. 379–86.

8. U.S. Department of State, *Bulletin*, 25 January 1954.

9. See Marc Trachtenberg, *History and Strategy* (Princeton, NJ: Princeton University Press, 1991), pp. 169–234.

10. Michael Beschloss, *MAYDAY, the U-2 Affair* (New York: Harper & Row, 1986).

11. The subsequent release of White House documents led to a more balanced assessment of the Eisenhower administration than that portrayed by contemporaries. For one of the most important books in this process, see Fred I. Greenstein, *The Hidden-Hand Presidency: Eisenhower as Leader* (New York: Basic Books, 1982).

CHAPTER 8

The Promise of Greatness

The short presidency of John F. Kennedy promised to take America to a "new frontier." After eight years of the relatively stable, yet uninspiring Eisenhower administration, Kennedy's youth and energy promised to revitalize American society. During the early 1960s, forces of reform that had begun to take root the previous decade, such as the civil rights and feminist movements, were beginning to find their political voices, creating a time of turbulence and opportunity. Overseas, the cold war was never hotter, with a series of crises taking the world to the brink of nuclear disaster. Gunned down after only three years in office, Kennedy left a powerful legacy. Yet it was ultimately left to his successor to make good on the promise.

A NEW GENERATION

The presidential election of 1960 marked the changing of the guard in the United States, bringing to the forefront the first generation of politicians to be born in the twentieth century. At the Democratic National Convention meeting in Los Angeles in early July, Senator John F. Kennedy, the suave young man from Massachusetts, swept a first-ballot nomination and, in the process, overwhelmed his nearest rival, Senator Lyndon B. Johnson of Texas, the Senate majority leader. Only forty-three years old in 1960, Kennedy was a cultured man of intellectual leanings, the scion of a well-known and wealthy Boston Irish family. A Roman Catholic, a hero in World War II (although not in the same league as Eisenhower on that score), and having written a Pulitzer prize-winning bestseller, *Profiles in Courage* (1956), Kennedy had served fourteen years in Congress, eight of them as the junior senator from Massachusetts. His election to the Senate in 1952 had provided a high profile political upset when Kennedy defeated Henry Cabot Lodge from one of the nation's most powerful political families. Since then, the combination of his good looks (along with those of his young wife, Jacqueline), his personal charisma, and his privileged family connections had firmly established him as the favorite political son of the nation's media.

Ostensibly to placate the South, which unsuccessfully resisted the adoption of the strongest civil rights planks in the party's history, in a controversial move Kennedy by-passed a number of leading personalities, including senators Hubert Humphrey of Minnesota and Stuart Symington of Missouri, to select Johnson as his running mate. The move angered many African Americans, but during the campaign, Kennedy was able to overcome Republican candidate Richard M. Nixon's initial appeal to black voters by insisting on the insertion of strong civil rights measures in the Democratic platform.[1] In addition to strong civil rights measures, the Democratic platform argued in favor of placing medical care for the aged under the auspices of the social security program and argued against the Eisenhower administration's tight fiscal policies. Taking the best of Stevenson's 1952 and 1956 campaigns, and casting himself as a liberal in the mold of Franklin Roosevelt, Kennedy promised to lead America out of what he called the "conservative rut" into which the Eisenhower administration had driven the nation.

Several weeks later at the Republican National Convention meeting in Chicago, Vice President Richard Nixon also swept a first-ballot presidential nomination, having long beforehand eliminated the challenge of Governor Nelson Rockefeller of New York. Of humbler origins than Kennedy, the 47-year-old Nixon was born into a California Quaker family, attended public schools, received an undergraduate degree from Whittier College in 1937, and completed his law studies at Duke University three years later. After a brief stint with the Office of Price Administration, he served in the navy for four years, reaching the rank of lieutenant commander. In 1946, he was elected to the 80th Congress where he made his reputation in the Alger Hiss investigation. He was the first vice president in the history of the modern two-party system to win the presidential nomination in his own right, and he chose Henry Cabot Lodge, chief U.S. delegate to the United Nations, as his vice-presidential running mate. Despite losing the nomination ballot to Nixon, Rockefeller continued to influence the domestic and foreign policy planks of the party platform. The platform on which the Republican Party campaigned reaffirmed the policies and tone of the Eisenhower White House, pledging more funds for national defense, a contributory health program, and a stronger stand on civil rights.

A Gallup poll in late August confirmed what most political analysts had already concluded: It was going to be a very close race. According to the poll, Nixon and Kennedy were tied at 47 percent each, with 6 percent undecided. As in most presidential campaigns, the personalities of the candidates weighed more heavily in the balance than the programs and the party platforms they espoused. Both were comparatively young; both possessed an inner ruthlessness. Neither had the comforting image that had swept Eisenhower into office eight years before. Republican critics assailed the wealthy and Harvard-trained Kennedy as an irresponsible smart aleck, quoting former President Truman to the effect that Kennedy was not ready to be president and the country was not ready for him. Critics of candidate Nixon questioned both his credentials and his integrity; the majority of liberals simply did not like anything about him.

There was also Kennedy's religion. The only other Roman Catholic to head the Democratic ticket, Al Smith, was swamped by Herbert Hoover in 1928. The "Catholic question" had been raised in the course of the West Virginia primary and would not go away. Accordingly, Kennedy met the issue head on, appearing before an influential gathering of Protestant ministers in Houston in September. "I believe in America," he told them, "where the separation of Church and State is absolute—where no Catholic prelate would tell the President (should he be a Catholic) how to act, and no Protestant minister would tell his parishioners for whom to vote—where no church or church school is granted any public funds or political preference—and where no man is denied public office merely because his religion differs from the president who might appoint him or the people who might elect him." The move was a political masterstroke; by bringing the issue out in the open and answering his critics directly, Kennedy succeeded in neutralizing the religious question.

Particularly noteworthy were the four, face-to-face encounters between the candidates on national television in late September and October. In the first television debates of their kind—actually, newsmen questioned the candidates and they in turn were allowed to challenge each others' comments—the widespread public view was that the telegenic Kennedy came out ahead; at the very least, he showed he could handle himself, though his aggressive attitude toward Cuba and the lack of support for the Nationalist Chinese-held islands of Quemoy and Matsu managed to irritate many. In particular, Nixon regarded Kennedy's call for American support of an anti-Castro revolution in Cuba as dangerously irresponsible and shockingly reckless, contrary to the nation's treaty commitments with Latin America and its obligations under the U.N. Charter. And yet, as one observer has noted, Kennedy's harsh anti-Castro rhetoric during the campaign "revealed neither personal adventurism nor animus but rather formed a belated salute to political necessity."[2] For his part, Nixon advocated instead an economic "quarantine" of Cuba. Other presidential issues dealt with matters of Soviet-American relations, U.S. prestige abroad, education, and welfare, yet some of the most pressing issues of the day were conspicuously absent from the debate.

After a strenuous campaign, which included thousands of miles of travel on both sides, Senator Kennedy won the election from Vice President Nixon by the astonishing margin of just under 120,000 votes out of a record of 68.8 million votes cast, a plurality of less than .05 percent of the total vote. This was the smallest percentage difference in the popular vote category of two presidential candidates since 1880; put another way, the margin amounted to less than two votes per voting precinct. The final count showed Kennedy receiving 34,107,646 (49.7 percent) to Nixon's 34,227,096 (49.5 percent). The electoral column was a different story with a Kennedy margin of 303 to 219, and even here the results could have been reversed if only 11,869 voters in five states had voted the other way. At most Kennedy's religion cost him 2 percent of the total popular vote but was probably the key factor in swaying blocks of Catholic voters (78 percent) and sympathetic minority groups in crucial industrial states where a great number of electoral voters were at stake. Kennedy was convinced that "it was TV more than anything else that turned the tide." He was probably right.

The election was close and there were suspicious results on both sides. In Chicago, Democratic Mayor Richard Daley had somehow delivered an unusually good result for Kennedy, a result that came under scrutiny when Kennedy won the state by less than 9,000 votes. There were also suspicions over Texas and elsewhere. Kennedy was initially believed to have won California, but after absentee ballots had been counted the state's electoral votes were eventually declared for Nixon. Citing voting irregularities, the Republican National Committee unsuccessfully challenged the Illinois vote in Federal Court, although Nixon himself carefully distanced himself from the various legal challenges presented by his party and supporters.

The election of John Kennedy broke a number of precedents. For one thing, at forty-three years old, he was the youngest man ever elected to the presidency; for another, he was the first Roman Catholic to win the office. For good measure, the Democrats retained control of Congress, although with slightly reduced margins. Divided government in Washington came abruptly to an end, yet Republicans and southern Democrats in Congress (the conservative coalition) still outnumbered moderate and liberal Democrats, not to mention southern domination of committees in Congress because of the seniority system.

As early as his acceptance speech at Los Angeles in July, Kennedy made it clear that his goal was to "get the country moving again." Americans, he said, stood "on the edge of a New Frontier—of the 1960s—a frontier of unknown opportunities and perils—a frontier of unfilled hopes and threats." His purpose was to offer the nation a set of challenges that appealed to its pride. In this regard, like Roosevelt, he envisaged the White House as the national center of action, with the president actively leading the country and Congress. Furthermore, what could not be accomplished by legislative action might just as well be achieved by executive action. But just how much latitude the American people were willing to give Kennedy remained to be seen. Few could argue that the voters had given him anything like a clear mandate. Even African Americans were not quite certain what to make of him, despite the Kennedy campaign's innovative use of African American church communities to spread its message among black voters, and also despite Kennedy's late-October phone call to Mrs. Martin Luther King, Jr., whose husband had recently been jailed in connection with a demonstration to end racial segregation in Atlanta's department stores. The dramatic intervention of the president's brother, Robert, when he managed to arrange bail for Dr. King—the most influential symbol of the sit-in-movement—must certainly have raised hopes though.[3] But despite this public ambivalence, once in office Kennedy behaved as though he had won a clear mandate, and he soon captured the public's imagination.

In his inaugural address, on January 20, 1961, the president spelled out his challenge to the American people in unequivocal terms. "We observe today," he told the nation, "not a victory of party but a celebration of freedom—symbolizing an end as well as a beginning—signifying renewal as well as change." Asking his fellow countrymen to remember their own revolutionary origins, he continued: "Let every nation know, whether it wishes us well or ill, that we shall pay any price, bear any burden, meet any hardship, support any friend, oppose any foe to assure the survival and success of liberty." From the Soviet Union, to which he referred as "our adversary," the president called for an exploration of the problems that united the superpowers rather than the ones that divided them. In this sense, he observed, "Let us never negotiate out of fear. But let us never fear to negotiate."

To achieve these goals, Kennedy surrounded himself with liberal intellectuals espousing the belief that technology and social planning could overcome any problem and remake any society into the likeness of the United States.[4] For his secretary of state the president selected Dean Rusk, a former assistant secretary of state in the Truman administration and president of the Rockefeller Foundation since 1952; for secretary of defense, he chose Robert S. McNamara, a former president of the Ford Motor Company; and for national security adviser, he recruited McGeorge Bundy from the East Coast academic establishment. In a move that sparked considerable controversy, he chose his brother Robert, who was ten years his junior, for attorney general. A stream of young, rich, and professional elite, dubbed the New Frontiersmen, poured into Washington, each to add to the tone of a White House unafraid to play host to the best and the brightest. Enhancing this image was the president's elegant wife, Jacqueline, and their energetic young family. Surely, this was an administration poised to "get the country moving again."

Things started inauspiciously. Kennedy had been in office only two months when he suffered a foreign policy disaster. What made it even worse was the fact that it was right on America's doorstep. As part of the Cuban problem, Eisenhower had handed over to the young president a secret plan to deal with the troublesome Fidel Castro. By the spring of 1960, the U.S. government had decided to sponsor an invasion of Cuba by anti-Castro refugees, of which there seemed to be no end. Kennedy soon endorsed the plan, assured by his own military advisers and the Central Intelligence Agency (CIA) that the probable chance of success was good. In the early hours of April 17, 1961, an "army" of approximately 2,000 CIA-trained and equipped Cuban refugees landed at Bahia de Cochinos (Bay of Pigs) on Cuba's southern coast. The plan was ill-conceived and poorly executed. In the absence of the anticipated American air cover and supplies of ammunition, Castro's forces quickly overwhelmed the army of refugees. The expected popular uprising, which American intelligence confidently predicted, failed to materialize. Kennedy expected Castro's nerve to break and important elements of the Cuban armed forces to defect. This, too, failed to happen. To make matters worse, the administration's cover story collapsed immediately, and it was clear that despite the president's denial of U.S. involvement, Washington was indeed behind it.

From there the matter deteriorated. To a message from Moscow threatening all-out war if the United States should invade Cuba, Kennedy replied that America intended no military invasion but made it clear that, in the event of outside military intervention, he would honor existing obligations under the inter-American system to protect the Western Hemisphere against external aggression. Secretly, the CIA and Defense Department wrote new plans for another, even larger, military invasion; although they were never acted upon. As for Castro, the target of the invasion and subsequent CIA assassination attempts, he was politically strengthened and emboldened by his success in crushing the invasion and responded by cracking down on those suspected of disloyalty at home. In the following year, he further embarrassed the United States by calling for a continental civil war to topple governments in Latin America. Kennedy's misadventure, which even the CIA's own internal post-mortem concluded had exceeded the agency's capabilities and responsibilities, cost American prestige dearly.[5] As well, the president took the failure personally, harboring a sensitivity to the issue for the remainder of his presidency, and it became an important factor in how he viewed his options in the foreign policy crises of the remainder of his time in office. Distrustful of the Pentagon and disdainful of the State Department—he once remarked to a group of advisers that the State Department was just a "tub of butter" and the Foreign Service was full of "fellows . . . who don't seem to have cojones"[6]—Kennedy learned from the experience to keep tight control from the Oval Office and remain skeptical of military advice.

The administration's other Latin America policy was less dramatic. The Latin American aid program launched in the closing months of the Eisenhower administration was taken over and expanded by Kennedy in his Alliance for Progress (*Alianza para el Progreso*). Essentially, the president envisaged a ten-year plan of economic development and social progress and reform that many characterized as a sort of Marshall Plan for Latin America. Without mentioning figures, Secretary of the Treasury C. Douglas Dillon, speaking at an Inter-American Economic and Social Conference in Punta del Este, Uruguay, in August estimated that at least $20 billion could be available from outside sources—North America, Europe, and Japan—during the next decade, mostly from public agencies. The conferees then proceeded to adopt a charter defining the aims and procedures of the Alliance for Progress and a "Declaration of the Peoples of America," both signed on August 17, 1961. For its part, Washington pledged to provide a major part of the $20 billion, principally in public funds. Cuba was represented at Punta del Este by its leading Communist theoretician, Ché Guevara, who did not sign the charter. Furthermore, Secretary Dillon made it clear that Cuba could expect no aid from the United States as long as it remained under Communist rule.

Despite the fanfare, the Alliance for Progress got off to a disappointingly slow start. Two years after its inauguration at Punta del Este, the United States had committed a total of $2.1 billion to the program and had disbursed over $1.5 billion, mainly for such items as residential housing, hospitals, and schools; overall, it made a relatively small contribution to the self-sustaining economic growth on which the eventual success of the program would depend. Private capital tended, moreover, to be frightened away by political insecurity. Entrenched resistance to reforms in landholding and taxation similarly took their toll, adding little to the promotion of political democracy in the Western Hemisphere.

An initiative that probably played a more important role was the Kennedy administration's Peace Corps, the inception of which was both a product of the cold war struggle and a reaction to the growing spirit of humanitarian activism evident throughout the Western world by the beginning of the 1960s, a spirit which had manifested itself in volunteer humanitarian programs already implemented in Canada, Australia, Britain, France, and Japan. The proposal to create a similar U.S. program had first been placed on the national political agenda by Democratic candidates during the 1950s, notably by Adlai E. Stevenson in his failed presidential campaigns of 1952 and 1956. During the course of the 1960 campaign, Kennedy championed the cause, reaping the electoral benefits of the program's appeal to young liberals. Once in office, Kennedy continued to challenge Americans to contribute to national and international public service, calling in his inaugural address for Americans to form a "grand and global alliance" to fight tyranny, poverty, and disease. On March 1, 1961, he temporarily established the Peace Corps through Executive Order 10924 under the auspices of the Department of State and appointed his brother-in-law, R. Sargent Shriver, Jr., to act as the corps' first director at a token salary of $1 per year. In September 1961, shortly after Congress formally endorsed the Peace Corps by making it a permanent program, the first volunteers left to teach English in Ghana, the first black African nation to achieve independence (in 1957) and whose government had since become an outspoken advocate of anticolonialism. Contingents of volunteers soon followed to Tanzania and India. By end of the twentieth century, the Peace Corps had sent over 170,000 American volunteers to over 135 nations.[7]

THE NEW FRONTIER AT HOME

At home, the New Frontier was launched in the depths of the fourth major recession since World War II. "We take office," observed Kennedy a little more than a week after taking office, "in the wake of seven months of recession, three and one-half years of slack, seven years of diminished economic growth, and nine years of falling farm income." To make matters worse, business bankruptcies had reached the highest level since the 1930s, farm incomes had been squeezed 25 percent since 1951, and 5.5 million people were looking for work. The economy was in trouble. Essentially, the Kennedy economic program consisted of protecting the unemployed, of increasing the minimum wage, of lowering taxes, and of stimulating the economy, particularly in the business and housing sectors. Like most presidents, Kennedy met with stiff opposition from Congress. In 1961 the administration managed to expand social security benefits. The minimum wage was increased in stages to reach $1.25 per hour, benefiting more than twenty-seven million workers. Nearly $5 billion was allocated for an omnibus housing bill. More controversial was the Area Redevelopment Act, which authorized loans, grants, and technical assistance to depressed industrial and rural areas. As a consequence of pumping money into the economy both by domestic and military spending, the recession faded by the end of the president's first year in office. In 1962, Kennedy's legislative program met with mixed results. On the positive side of the ledger, the president requested and received intact the Trade Expansion Act. Pronounced the most significant international economic legislation since the Marshall Plan, the act gave him authority to negotiate for the reduction and removal of tariffs, as well as creating a new program of "adjustment assistance" aid to industries and workers especially hard hit by competitive imports. Congress also enacted an accelerated Public Works Act and the Manpower Retraining Bill. The Communications Satellite Act, which authorized a privately owned and financed corporation, was also enacted in 1962.

Closer to home, and on the negative side of the ledger, the administration's legislative program found rough sledding in the Congress. Its social welfare, agricultural, and civil rights proposals met strong opposition from southern as well as northern conservatives—including the powerful American Medical Association, which assailed national health insurance as little more than "socialized medicine." Several significant pieces of welfare legislation, however, did see the light of day. Among these were the Higher Education Facilities Act, which authorized a five-year federal program for the growth and continuation or improvement of public and private higher education facilities; the Drug Industry Act, which established additional safeguards in the processing and prescription of drugs; and aid for research into mental illness and retardation.

There can be no question that the president gave much thought and energy to the problem of inflation. For, "If recession is . . . one enemy of a free economy—inflation is the other." Kennedy firmly believed that the first line of defense against inflation was the good sense and public spirit of business and labor working together to keep their total increases in profits and wages in line with productivity. According to the administration, the nation's basic national security policy rested on a "wage-price-productivity" triangle, the stability of which affected America's ability to grow economically, to export competitively, and to provide an adequate defense and foreign policy.

Against this background, it is easy to understand the president's anger when U.S. Steel Corporation, the nation's pre-eminent producer, suddenly announced price increases averaging $6 a ton on April 10, 1962, only five days after the company had signed a new two-year, "noninflationary" contract with the United Steelworkers of America. The administration had spent almost a year persuading both sides to exercise restraint. Feeling betrayed, the president accused the major steel corporations (five other big steel companies moved in step with U.S. Steel the next day) of "irresponsible defiance" of the public interest and of "ruthless disregard" of the common good. Roger M. Blough, chairman of the U.S. Steel Corporation, remonstrated with the argument that the increases amounted to no more than a partial "catch-up" adjustment, a mere three-tenths of a cent per pound. The president, who recalled his father's words "that all businessmen were sons-of-bitches, but I never believed it till now," swung into action, using all the power of his office to force a rollback. In addition to denouncing the companies involved, the White House announced the opening of grand jury proceedings leading to possible antitrust action and threatened to divert federal purchasing orders to companies that had not raised prices. After seventy-two hours of this kind of pressure, combined with the decision by several other large companies not to proceed further, U.S. Steel Corporation backed down and rescinded the increase. The president had proved his point, but business criticism of the administration reached an intensity not seen since the New Deal days of Franklin Roosevelt.

In other ways, Kennedy demonstrated that the White House was not afraid to blaze a trail. Cribbed and confined by opponents of civil rights legislation in Congress, Kennedy made extensive use of executive powers to improve the plight of African Americans, particularly those facing difficulties in the Deep South. Interstate transportation systems with their related terminals were effectively desegregated. A number of African Americans were appointed to high office, most notably Thurgood Marshall to the U.S. Circuit Court, Carl Rowan as ambassador to Finland, and Robert Weaver to the Housing and Home Financing Agency. Through the president's Committee on Equal Employment chaired by Vice President Johnson, the administration succeeded, in part, in combating racial discrimination in the employment policies of firms holding government contracts. Also, much effort went into strengthening the basic rights of blacks to vote, mainly in southern states that employed literacy tests and poll taxes. Robert Kennedy led the way in the area of voting reform, bringing over fifty suits in four states on behalf of African Americans seeking to cast their ballots. Finally, the Executive Order of November 20, 1962, went a long—though imperfect—way toward eliminating racial (as well as religious) discrimination in housing financed with federal aid. In these, as in other cases involving racial discrimination, persuasion sometimes worked; other times, it did not.

In January 1961, black Mississippian James Meredith, a veteran of eight years in the U.S. Air Force, applied for admission to the University of Mississippi, where no black had ever been enrolled; his application was rejected on the grounds that the black school from which he was attempting to transfer was not properly accredited and that his application lacked letters of recommendation from five alumni of "Ole Miss." In May, Meredith filed suit in the U.S. District Court of Appeals for southern Mississippi, contending that his admission had been denied squarely on racial grounds. Sixteen months later, in the fall of 1962, the federal courts ordered Meredith's admission. The governor of Mississippi, Ross Barnett, a states' righter and white supremacist, chose to defy the order and bar enrollment. Knowing that there would come a time when, to quote candidate Kennedy, "The next President of the United States cannot stand above the battle engaging in vague little sermons on brotherhood," the White House tried persuasion with Barnett, federalized the Mississippi National Guard, and ordered an escort of federal marshals to accompany Meredith to the campus. On October 1, 1962, Meredith was allowed to enroll during an ugly riot that took thousands of guardsmen and soldiers fifteen hours to quell. Hundreds were injured and two died, including a French journalist who said in his last article, "The Civil War has never ended." Meredith was graduated the next year.[8]

By the spring of 1963, the civil rights movement, together with broadly based support for black equality, took on life of its own. Both the North and the South witnessed civil rights demonstrations on a massive scale. Led by Dr. Martin Luther King, Jr., blacks had reached the point where "we're through with tokenism and gradualism. . . . We can't wait any longer." Slowly, inexorably, racial barriers came down in the hotels, universities, and recreational facilities of southern cities. Where progress or even the prospect of progress seemed distant, African Americans marched in the streets. In Birmingham, Alabama, King and his followers were met by the stereotypical southern police chief, in this instance "Bull" Connor, complete with cattle prods, police dogs, and fire hoses. Nothing could have been better calculated to bring the Kennedy administration into the foreground of the struggle for racial equality. When the governor of the State of Alabama, George C. Wallace, threatened to bar the entry of black students to the University of Alabama, he met the same fate as Governor Barnett of Mississippi, as Kennedy once again federalized the state National Guard. Moving a step further, the administration called on Congress to enact comprehensive legislation to protect and guarantee blacks their basic rights, measures supported by a huge "March on Washington" in June 1963, with a quarter of a million people in attendance. Unlike Eisenhower, Kennedy gave the marchers his moral support and left no one in doubt about his administration's position. But still, the president could not force the Congress to enact his legislative program nor could he prevent the senseless murder of the leader of the Mississippi branch of the National Association for the Advancement of Colored People, Medgar Evers, or the killing of four children in a bomb attack on a Birmingham church in September 1963. In the same year, the Reverend King admitted that while Kennedy had probably done a little more than his predecessor, the plight of the overwhelming majority of African Americans remained the same.

COLD WAR CRISES

While the drama unfolded at home, the international situation was no less unstable. Crises during 1961 and 1962 over Berlin and Cuba came frighteningly close to erupting into nuclear war. During the election campaign, Kennedy had persistently criticized the Eisenhower administration's defense strategy, claiming that in the era of missiles and thermonuclear weapons the strategy of massive retaliation was dangerously rigid and, furthermore, as a deterrent was undermined by a lack of credibility. In its place, Kennedy proposed to place a new approach, one that became known as "flexible response." By reducing the reliance upon nuclear weapons, Kennedy promised to continue to protect U.S. national security and revitalize the credibility of the nuclear deterrent, all while reducing the chance of nuclear war.

The first test of the new strategy came in the form of a renewed Berlin crisis. With the settlement of the German question much in his mind—along with the complex web of issues that involved—the Soviet Union's Nikita Khrushchev looked forward to dealing with a Democrat in the White House, for he plainly hoped to find Eisenhower's successor more yielding. In June 1961, Chairman Khrushchev and President Kennedy met for a two-day conference in Vienna. Although the meeting was superficially cordial and businesslike, behind the scenes was a tense situation. At the heart of the discussions were the two most pressing international confrontations of the day: Berlin and Laos. While the Laos situation seemed close to resolution, the Berlin problem was not. Khrushchev managed to resurrect the Berlin crisis on much the same terms as before, and again imposed a six-month deadline. Unless the four occupying powers could agree on a peace treaty or treaties with Germany within that time, Khrushchev said, the Kremlin would conclude a separate treaty with Walter Ulbricht's East German regime and would terminate the West's rights to traverse East German territory to access West Berlin, a move that would completely undermine the viability of West Berlin as a Western outpost and a symbol of Western resolve. *New York Times* writer James Reston, who had spoken with Kennedy immediately following one of the sessions in Vienna, reported that the new president felt that Khrushchev had tried to intimidate Kennedy and that the Soviet premier had mistaken Kennedy's poor judgment in the Bay of Pigs imbroglio for a general weakness of resolve. In truth, however, Khrushchev thought no such thing.

Nevertheless, Kennedy responded forcefully. During a post-summit report to the nation in July, Kennedy reaffirmed the Western commitment to West Berlin, declaring that NATO countries would not allow the Communists to drive them out of the city, an enclave of two million people living in freedom. Remarking that "we do not want to fight, but we have fought before," the president asked Congress for a $3.2 billion increase in the defense budget, for an increase in military manpower, and for authority to activate various reserve units. By increasing conventional forces at home and abroad, the president sought to broaden his options; in his words, "to have a wider choice than humiliation or all-out nuclear action." While thousands of Americans built fallout shelters, being less confident of presidential options than the commander in chief, Congress gave Kennedy everything for which he asked. To bolster the president's ability to respond flexibly, an additional 45,000 troops were moved to Europe. This, together with a French and West German build-up in NATO forces, brought the Western alliance up to twenty-five divisions. The Soviets cancelled their time limit but, in the early hours of August 13, began sealing the border between East and West Berlin with barbed wire and other fortifications. Over the coming months, a wall was built. Khrushchev's move had the desired effect of ending West Berlin's role as an escape hatch from Communist East

Germany, but it did not constitute a threat to U.S. interest per se; consequently Washington responded by protest only, much to the distress of the West Germans. As a follow-up move, Khrushchev initiated a new series of nuclear tests in the atmosphere, ending an informal moratorium begun in 1958. By the end of the year, the Kremlin publicly announced a large increase in its defense budget. In this acrimonious atmosphere, the cold war dangerously threatened to heat up.

It was in this tense environment that the United States and U.S.S.R. came face to face—or, as Secretary of State Dean Rusk aptly put it, "eyeball to eyeball"—in what has often been regarded as the moment when the world was in most peril of nuclear disaster.[9] In May 1962, Khrushchev and Castro had conspired to ship Soviet nuclear missiles to Cuba, only ninety miles from Florida, ostensibly to protect Cuba from a much-rumored U.S. invasion, but more accurately to serve a variety of Soviet objectives, among which was to neutralize the massive American nuclear superiority, which, in turn, would bolster the Soviet negotiating position on other issues such as the Berlin problem. During September, U.S. intelligence detected signs of a buildup of defensive conventional weapons on the island, including advanced air defense systems and several thousand Soviet "technicians" but did not yet have any firm evidence to back up Cuban refugee reports that the Soviets were installing nuclear missiles on the island. To quell the brewing political storm, Kennedy issued a statement that if any offensive weapons were found, "the gravest consequences would arise." Nevertheless, unbeknownst at the time to U.S. intelligence, 42,000 Soviet troops were arriving in Cuba along with nuclear-capable bombers, battlefield nuclear weapons, and nuclear missiles capable of reaching most of the continental United States. Not until November, when the crisis was ostensibly over, would Washington come to realize the full extent of the Soviets' military commitment.

Thus, no sooner had the administration settled the University of Mississippi civil rights crisis than it was confronted with a more dangerous emergency. When, in mid-October, American U-2 planes flying at high-altitude and outfitted with special surveillance camera equipment finally delivered hard evidence of Soviet missile installations on the island, Kennedy summoned to the White House his top advisers to devise a response. Meeting in absolute secrecy, this group, which later became known as the ExComm (Executive Committee of the National Security Council), debated Kennedy's options. Most of the group, including the president, was initially inclined toward some kind of military action ranging from air strikes on the missile sites themselves to a full-fledged invasion of the island. By October 21, however, Kennedy had settled on an interim response: a naval "quarantine" (in reality a blockade) accompanied by an ultimatum. On the evening of Monday, October 22, 1962, President Kennedy announced the existence of the missiles to a startled world. Their purpose, he explained in a televised address to a spellbound nation, could be "none other than to provide a nuclear strike capability against the Western Hemisphere." Some of the sites were designed for medium-range ballistic missiles with a range of over a thousand miles; others not yet completed appeared to be designed for intermediate-range missiles with a capability of reaching as far as Hudson's Bay, Canada, to the north, or Lima, Peru, to the south.

Denouncing the cloak of secrecy and deception under which the missiles had been spirited into Cuba, President Kennedy voiced a grave warning to the Kremlin: The United States would "regard any nuclear missile launched from Cuba against any nation in the Western Hemisphere as an attack by the Soviet union on the United States requiring a full retaliatory response upon the Soviet Union." On October 24, as American strategic nuclear forces were placed on DEFCON 2, the highest alert status below actual nuclear war, and school children practiced civil defense drills, the world waited anxiously for the Soviet response to the quarantine. As the world watched anxiously on television, some Soviet ships en route to Cuba voluntarily turned back or stopped dead in the water; others, known to be carrying inoffensive cargoes, were allowed to proceed. To maintain his credibility and to set a precedent, Kennedy ordered the search of a tanker that he knew was not carrying military supplies. On October 25, the U.S. ambassador to the United Nations, Adlai E. Stevenson, famously confronted the Soviet ambassador to the United Nations, Valerian Zorin, with photographic evidence and declared his intent to "wait until hell freezes over" for a Soviet explanation. At U.S. insistence, the Organization of the American States officially condemned the Soviet-Cuban action and thereby formalized Cuba's hemispheric isolation. In some of the most dramatic diplomacy that the United Nations had engaged in, acting Secretary-General U Thant became a valuable mediator of peace.

The world literally held its breath. Washington, with the support of its Latin American and major European allies, prepared for war. Khrushchev, however, did not challenge the blockade; Kennedy's strategy had worked. In a series of complex exchanges with the president, which lasted until Sunday, October 28, Khrushchev agreed to withdraw the "offensive weapons," in exchange for an American guarantee against a future invasion of Cuba. During secret talks between Robert Kennedy and the Soviet ambassador to the United States, Anatoly Dobrynin, Kennedy also secretly agreed to remove obsolete American Jupiter missiles in Turkey, although, ironically, Kennedy need not have made this concession to close the deal.[10]

The settlement rested on two key parts. First, Kennedy insisted that the nuclear capable IL-28 bombers that had also recently been deployed in Cuba by the Soviets also fell under the description of "offensive weapons" and therefore had to be removed on the terms of the agreement reached on October 27 and 28, although Khrushchev quite correctly pointed out that these were obsolete bombers that posed no serious threat to American air defenses. Second, Kennedy insisted that the removal of the offensive weapons had to be verified by on-the-ground inspections. It soon became clear that Castro would never allow on-the-ground inspection and when Khrushchev finally agreed on November 20 to remove the IL-28 bombers Kennedy seized the opportunity to end the crisis and lift the naval quarantine. Thus, the final settlement removed the long-distance missiles, the nuclear-capable IL-28 bombers, and several thousand Soviet "technicians," but left thousands of Soviet combat troops on the island equipped with advanced fighter-bomber MiG aircraft, sophisticated surface-to-air missile installations and short-range, nuclear-capable FROG (Free Range Over Ground Missiles). Kennedy himself never really had to answer publicly for these remaining troops. Indeed, for the most part these Soviet forces went undetected by the public eye for almost two decades, until President Jimmy Carter would be confronted by the "revelation" in 1979 of a Soviet brigade in Cuba.[11]

In terms of nuclear arms control, the Cuban missile crisis produced major yet contradictory effects. It provided renewed momentum for arms control as both Moscow and Washington recognized that they might not be so fortunate next time. After discovering the difficulty of communication in times of crisis, the White House and the Kremlin negotiated the so-called Hot Line agreement, signed in July 1963, providing for special crisis communication satellites between the superpowers. More significantly, at the same time the United States and the Soviet Union, together with Great Britain, concluded the Partial Nuclear Test Ban Treaty, which prohibited nuclear testing in the atmosphere, in outer space, and under water. This treaty has correctly been cited as the first real success in limiting the arms race. On the negative side of the ledger, the crisis provided impetus for yet another escalation in the arms race. Policymakers in the Soviet Union, not unreasonably, concluded from their Cuban experience that nuclear superiority provided the critical edge in diplomatic bargaining and resolved to enlarge their strategic arsenal both in qualitative and quantitative terms. During the mid- and late sixties, the Kremlin substantially increased its defense expenditures for offensive and defensive strategic weapons systems. Accordingly, a succession of new long-range missiles were developed by Soviet Strategic Rocket Forces; by 1970, the U.S.S.R. managed to surpass the United States in operational intercontinental ballistic missiles (1,100 to 1,054), although America still possessed more separate warheads.

While the Berlin and Cuban crises had both come to flashpoint and then faded away, developments in Asia ultimately proved more disastrous for the United States over the long term. The Geneva settlement of 1954 had left Laos's Communist forces, the Pathet Lao (Lao nation) in occupation of two northeastern provinces, adjoining North Vietnam and the People's Republic of China. Attempts by the neutralist faction to integrate these forces and their leaders into the Laotian army and government invariably aroused rightist opposition. Successive attempts by the Pathet Lao led to armed resistance, putatively supported by Communist regulars from Hanoi. A civil war between the left and the right threatened to escalate into a major conflict between Washington and Moscow: The United States, which had assumed the task of training and supplying the Royal Laotian Army, aided the right while the Soviet Union aided the Communists. As the Royal Army proved unequal to the Communist offensive, it became increasingly apparent in Washington that only some kind of intervention from the outside world could preserve even a semblance of a neutral Laos.[12]

Its efforts stimulated by the joint statement of Kennedy and Khrushchev made at their Vienna summit reaffirming their support of a neutral and independent Laos, a fourteen-nation conference met in Geneva in May 1961. The only neutralist solution for Laos, all agreed, was to be found in a coalition government representative of Laos's three main factions. Agreement among them required a year of hard bargaining, during which time yet another Communist offensive in the region threatened to spill over into Thailand, a SEATO (South East Asia Treaty Organization) ally of the United States. The landing in Thailand of eighteen hundred marines from the Seventh Fleet, followed by token forces from Britain, Australia, and New Zealand, headed off any such danger and probably expedited a Laotian settlement. By June 1962, a coalition had been constructed, with the new government committed to neutrality and nonentanglement in any alliance of military coalition (i.e., SEATO), and the transaction was completed in Geneva on July 21, 1962, when the fourteen nations of the conference signed the documents and agreed to respect the independence, sovereignty, neutrality, and territorial integrity of the Kingdom of Laos while setting forth rules for an international commission that presumably was to supervise the settlement. Intermittent pressure by Communist forces upon neutralist and rightist elements made it plain that the Laotian settlement would never be more than a shaky armistice waiting for trouble. In any case, in the matter of Vietnam, the administration proved much less inclined to compromise.

Kennedy had been in office only a few months when he received an appeal for increased military spending from President Ngo Dinh Diem of South Vietnam. For the previous several years, Diem's government had been engaged in guerrilla war with the Viet Cong, who had established their control of many rural areas. Whether this conflict was a war of aggression by the North against the South, or a genuine civil war with Ho Chi Minh of North Vietnam coming to the aid of his Communist brethren, there could be little doubt that guerrilla warfare was erupting all over Vietnam. To make matters worse, American military advisers provided the native army with training only for a conventional war based on the Korean model, while political advisers were unable to persuade Diem to adopt reforms that might have rallied the peasantry.

It was in these circumstances that Kennedy sent Vice President Lyndon B. Johnson on a fact-finding mission to Vietnam and elsewhere in Asia. Johnson, who as Senate majority leader had opposed intervention to save Dienbienphu in 1954, found the Communist threat in Vietnam serious, echoing President Eisenhower's famous "domino theory." According to General Maxwell D. Taylor, whom Kennedy had sent on a similar mission a few months earlier, Diem would particularly welcome American personnel to assist in logistics and communications, but he did not, at this time, request U.S. troops. Accepting the proposition that Hanoi orchestrated the terrorist campaigns in violation of the Geneva settlement, Kennedy promised to increase American assistance.

This promise began a new phase of United States aid to South Vietnam, which for the period from 1955 to 1962 exceeded $2 billion and by 1963 approached the rate of $500 million annually. A dramatic indicator of the Kennedy policy was the arrival at Saigon, on December 12, 1961, of an American escort carrier bearing helicopters, training planes, and requisite crews numbering about 400 men. This event served as the prelude to the so-called helicopter war in which American personnel were to participate throughout the next three years by flying Vietnamese troops over jungles and rice fields in an attempt to seek out the Viet Cong or Communist guerrillas. In addition, the United States had undertaken to train the Vietnamese in antiguerrilla tactics and had persuaded the Diem regime to launch a program isolating the peasantry from the Viet Cong by resettling them in fortified villages—a technique the British had found successful in fighting Communists in Malaya. Persuaded that Vietnam represented "the cornerstone of the Free World in Southeast Asia, the Keystone of the arch, "the finger in the dike," Kennedy steadily expanded the American presence there. The number of U.S. "advisers" in Vietnam rose from 650 when Eisenhower left office to 16,500 before the end of 1963. By May 1964, more than 200 Americans had been killed, about half of them in battle.

The administration's task was made even more difficult by a growing rift between non-Communist elements in the population and President Diem, whose government was in reality a shambles. Spurred on by his family and intolerant of criticism from any quarter, Diem resented Washington's suggestions for alleviating popular discontent. Meanwhile, the war against the Viet Cong dragged on with no end in sight. Dissatisfaction with Diem reached a crisis point in the summer and fall of 1963. With the writing clearly on the wall—and with the knowledge of the State Department—on November 1, a group of army officers overthrew the government and killed Diem and his brother. Kennedy promptly recognized the new provisional government, hoping for a more united and renewed effort against the Viet Cong. For the administration, Communist-led wars of national liberation remained fraudulent, despite the tenacity of the enemy; the possibility that the Viet Cong had strong indigenous roots in the south was not considered.

This was the Kennedy legacy in what would become America's longest war. By the time his administration was abruptly and tragically brought to an end, however, Kennedy seemed to be looking for alternatives to escalating involvement ahead of the 1964 presidential campaign. Tragically, however, such a path was remain one of the great "what ifs?" of recent history.

PRESIDENCY CUT SHORT

On November 22, 1963, while riding through downtown Dallas in a motorcade, President Kennedy was shot and killed by an assassin, later identified as Lee Harvey Oswald. Oswald, who had once defected to the Soviet Union and had been active in the pro-Castro Fair Play for Cuba Committee, was subsequently arrested by Dallas police after a brief struggle in a nearby theater prior to which a policeman had also been slain. Within thirty minutes of the shooting, 75 million Americans had heard the news; by late afternoon 90 million Americans, or 99.8 percent of the adult population, had heard of the president's death.

There then followed a bizarre turn of events. While still in police custody, Oswald was himself shot and killed by an obscure Dallas nightclub owner, Jack Ruby, the entire drama of which was captured on national television. Theories of conspiracies filled the air. The official Warren Report, the study of the presidential commission headed by Chief Justice Earl Warren in 1964, concluded that Oswald alone killed the president and that there was no conspiracy. The commission also found that Ruby acted alone in killing Oswald. Subsequent studies of the event make it difficult not to believe that Oswald pulled the trigger. As Norman Mailer put it thirty years later, Lee Harvey Oswald "had the character to kill Kennedy, and that he probably did it alone."[13] Immediately after his assassination, thanks especially to some doting accounts written by former aides,[14] President Kennedy was linked with Abraham Lincoln in the pantheon of great presidents. Kennedy's popularity among Americans continues despite the various historical assessments that range from the stricken knight from the legends of Camelot and King Arthur of the 1960s to the more complex political personality of the 1990s. There was pure tragedy in the death of someone of such style, wit, and grace at the hands, it appeared to most, of someone so lacking in these qualities.

It is now known that the "best and the brightest" were not generally the wisest. The prelude to the Cuban missile crisis was, after all, the disaster at the Bay of Pigs, prompted by paranoia, arrogance, and bad intelligence within an immature administration. The revelation that the King of Camelot had a taste for hookers and Hollywood starlets has tended to tarnish what remains of the shining myth.[15] What would he have accomplished had he lived longer? What history is left with, to quote the French ambassador of that time, is "a brilliant maybe," the perfect epitaph. In any case, as the nation mourned the loss of its youthful leader, a very different kind of man assumed the reins of power.

NOTES

1. Taylor Branch, *Parting the Waters: America in the King Years, 1954–1963* (New York: Simon and Schuster, 1988), pp. 375–77.

2. Robert Weisbrot, *Maximum Danger: Kennedy, the Missiles, and the Crisis of American Confidence* (Chicago: Ivan R. Dee, 2001), p. 31

3. Ibid., pp. 372–75; and Robert Weisbrot, *Freedom Bound: A History of America's Civil Rights Movement* (New York: W. W. Norton, 1990).

4. On this latter point, see particularly Michael E. Latham, *Modernization as Ideology: American Social Science and "Nation-Building" in the Kennedy Era* (Chapel Hill: University of North Carolina Press, 2000).

5. Peter Kornbluh, ed. *Bay of Pigs Declassified: The Secret CIA Report on the Invasion of Cuba* (New York: New Press, 1998), p. 99.

6. Timothy Naftali, ed., *The Presidential Recordings: John F. Kennedy, Volume 1* (New York: W. W. Norton, 2001), p. 47; and Timothy Naftali and David Coleman, eds., *The Presidential Recordings: John F. Kennedy, Volume 4* (New York: W. W. Norton, forthcoming).

7. Elizabeth Cobbs Hoffman, *All You Need Is Love: The Peace Corps and the Spirit of the 1960s* (Cambridge: Harvard University Press, 1998); and Gerard Rice, *The Bold Experiment: JFK's Peace Corps* (Notre Dame, IN: Notre Dame University Press, 1985).

8. Branch, *Parting the Waters*, pp. 633–72.

9. See Philip Zelikow and Ernest May, eds., *The Kennedy Tapes: Inside the White House during the Cuban Missile Crisis*, concise ed. (New York: W. W. Norton, 2002); and Aleksandr Fursenko and Timothy Naftali, *"One Hell of a Gamble": Khrushchev, Kennedy, and Castro 1958–1964* (New York: W. W. Norton, 1997).

10. Khrushchev had already ordered his agents abroad to back down before the message arrived in Moscow that Kennedy was secretly offering to remove the Turkish missiles. See Fursenko and Naftali, *"One Hell of a Gamble,"* pp. 278–87.

11. See David D. Newsom, *The Soviet Brigade in Cuba: A Study in Political Diplomacy* (Bloomington: Indiana University Press, 1987); and Naftali and Coleman, *The Presidential Recordings: John F. Kennedy, Volume 4*. The presence of the Soviet troops and their extensive military hardware did not go totally unnoticed by the press, however. See particularly the reports by Marguerite Higgins in the *New York Herald Tribune* on November 19 and 20, 1962.

12. Lawrence Freedman, *Kennedy's Wars: Berlin, Cuba, Laos, and Vietnam* (Oxford: Oxford University Press, 2000), pp. 293–304.

13. Norman Mailer, *Oswald's Tale: An American Mystery* (New York: Random House, 1995).

14. See particularly Arthur M. Schlesinger, Jr., *A Thousand Days: John F. Kennedy in the White House* (Boston: Houghton Mifflin, 1965); and Theodore C. Sorensen, *Kennedy* (New York: Harper and Row, 1965).

15. Seymour Hersh, *The Dark Side of Camelot* (Boston: Little, Brown, 1997). For a more balanced historical view, see the essays in *Kennedy: The New Frontier Revisited*, edited by Mark J. White (New York: New York University Press, 1998).

CHAPTER 9

The Great Society

With Kennedy's presidency ending so abruptly under such tragic circumstances, Lyndon B. Johnson was forced to make what he could of Kennedy's legacy. But after a generation of concentration on problems of the cold war, President Johnson made it clear that he was reviving the tradition of domestic reform. In laying the foundations of the "Great Society," Johnson supported affirmative action and attempted to break down many of the traditional social barriers. Yet the emergence of a new radicalism challenged his reforms and resulted in widespread violence. The most controversial action of his presidency, however, was the escalation of the American involvement in Vietnam, a move that divided the nation and resulted in long-term political and social upheaval.

PICKING UP THE PIECES

Vice President Lyndon B. Johnson, who had been riding in the third car in the fateful Dallas motorcade, was sworn in as the thirty-sixth president of the United States within two hours of Kennedy's assassination. In contrast to the privileged upbringing of his predecessor, the 55-year-old Johnson had come to prominence in Washington via a very different route. The new president was born in 1908 in a three-room house, in poor farming country near Stonewall, Texas. The impoverished Texan worked his way through Southwest State Teachers College in San Marcos and afterward taught speech and debate in the Houston public school system. Working as state director of the National Youth Administration in the mid-1930s, and thereby demonstrating a connection to Franklin D. Roosevelt, Johnson made his political move in 1937 when he was elected to fill a congressional vacancy. With a brief leave of absence for naval duty in 1941–1942, he served in the House of Representatives until 1949; from that time until his selection as Kennedy's vice president, Johnson served with distinction in the Senate, finally attaining the position of majority leader in 1955, an acknowledged master of the art of legislative persuasion.

Throughout his political career, Johnson remained a staunch defender of the New and Fair Deals, with a commitment to the common welfare and an appeal to the middle ground of American political life. Physically imposing, irrepressible, and homey in manner, the president possessed a reputation as a consummate politician. He also had a legendary appetite for gossip and an earthy sense of humor. He often put these traits to use in subjecting difficult politicians to the celebrated "Johnson treatment."

In his first State of the Union Address to Congress, delivered on January 8, 1964, Lyndon Johnson showed every sign of carrying forward the plans and programs of Kennedy, "Not," he said, "because of our sorrow or sympathy, but because they are right." In addition to retaining his predecessor's cabinet, Johnson guided two key pieces of Kennedy's legislative program through to fruition. The first was the Tax Reduction Act, in February; the second, the Civil Rights Law of 1964, in July. In the tax law, which was designed to stimulate the economy, personal income tax rates were reduced from a 20–91 percent scale to a 14–70 percent scale over a two–year period, while corporate tax rates were reduced from 52 to 48 percent. The civil rights law was the most far-reaching civil rights legislation since the era of Reconstruction. It prohibited discrimination in areas of public accommodation, publicly owned facilities, employment, union membership, and federally aided programs. It also authorized the attorney general to institute suits to desegregate schools or other public facilities, and it outlawed discrimination in employment on the basis of race, color, religion, sex, or national origin. An Equal Employment Opportunity Commission was established to monitor compliance by industries or unions involved in interstate commerce that employed more than twenty-five workers. The impact of this law, which received the bipartisan support of more than two-thirds of the members of both the House and Senate, was profound. Any organization or body could now be held accountable for discriminatory behavior. The purpose of the law was to ensure equality of opportunity; preferential treatment to any individual or to any group on account of perceived imbalances, "which may exist with respect to the total number or percentage of persons of any race, color, religion, sex, or national origin employed by any employer," was expressly prohibited.

Other major legislative accomplishments in 1964 included the Urban Mass Transportation Act, also signed into law in July, and the Wilderness Preservation Act ratified in September. The Transportation Act provided

$375 million in federal grants over a three-year period for the construction and rehabilitation of commuter bus, subway, and train facilities and was the nation's first program of its kind to give massive aid to urban transportation systems. The Wilderness Act set aside 9.1 million acres of forest and mountain preserves, adding some protective barrier around the last of America's fast-disappearing wilderness.

LAUNCHING THE GREAT SOCIETY

Moving beyond the New Frontier reforms of the Kennedy administration, Johnson set out to stamp his own imprint of reform on the American people. Essentially, the former poor boy from West Texas declared unconditional war on human poverty and unemployment in the United States. The outcome of this offensive, he hoped, would be a Great Society, "a place where the city of man serves not only the needs of the body and the demands of commerce but the desire for beauty and the hunger for community." Johnson seemed deeply troubled by the existence of poverty in the midst of plenty, "the invisible poor" described in Michael Harrington's influential 1962 study, *The Other America*. Harrington estimated that as many as 35 million Americans, or almost 18 percent of the population, lived in poverty, too poor even to publicize their plight.[1] Johnson took up the challenge.

The embodiment of the Great Society took the form of the Economic Opportunity Act of late August 1964 as well as other related legislation. Together they attacked the presumed root causes of poverty—particularly illiteracy, unemployment, and inadequate public services. Within a short time, nearly $1 billion was appropriated for ten separate programs conducted by the Office of Economic Opportunity. Among these were the Job Corps; Volunteers in Service to America (VISTA), a domestic Peace Corps; Upward Bound, a program to send underprivileged children to college; Project Head Start, a program for preschool children; work-training and work-study programs; and incentives to small businesses. Other equally ambitious legislation would have to await the outcome of the 1964 presidential election.

The Republican National Convention, meeting in San Francisco in July nominated Barry M. Goldwater on the first ballot. A senator from Arizona and the champion of a new American conservatism, Goldwater was born in the territory of Arizona three years before its statehood. The son of a devout Episcopalian mother, he became a strong opponent of "Big Government," challenging both the Great Society as well as what he called the "dime store New Deal" of the Eisenhower administration. His message was simple, and it appealed to the many Americans who had imagined the passing of a simpler life: The danger to freedom, according to his campaign biography *Conscience of a Conservative* (1960), came from the intervention of the federal government into the lives of individuals, from the graduated income tax to the social security system, both of which he saw as unnecessary intrusions into the private sector. The senator also favored militant anticommunism abroad and a tougher stand in Vietnam. Congressman William E. Miller of New York was chosen as his running mate. Their principal target was Lyndon Johnson, whom Goldwater indicted as "the biggest [civil rights] faker in the United States," and the "phoniest individual who ever came round." The Goldwater-Miller theme was "Extremism in the defense of liberty is no vice. Moderation in the pursuit of justice is no virtue." The conservative Republicans finally got their way over their moderate colleagues.

Meeting in August in Atlantic City, the Democratic National Convention nominated Johnson for a term of his own; the president then smashed tradition by stepping before the delegation to name Senator Hubert H. Humphrey of Minnesota as his personal choice for running mate. Against the lurid image of a demagogic Goldwater with his finger on the "Bomb," all Johnson had to do was look normal. The major polls, Gallup and Harris, predicted a landslide result for the Texan and the effervescent Humphrey. They were right, as the Texan and the "Happy Warrior" from Minneapolis-St. Paul were elected by a landslide with 486 to 52 electoral votes and 42.8 to 27.1 million popular votes (61.41 to 38.7 percent, respectively). The Democrats were further strengthened in Congress with a gain of thirty-eight seats in the House and two in the Senate. The GOP, wracked and ruined by the reactionary wing of the party, would require the next four years to rethink its strategy.

"We are only at the beginning of the road to the Great Society," Johnson declared in his January 1965 message to Congress on the State of the Union. "The Great Society," he continued, "asks not how much, but how good; not only how to create wealth but how to use it; not only how fast we are going, but where we are headed." To prove his point, Johnson and his supporters in the 89th Congress pushed through the most significant social legislation since the days of Franklin Roosevelt's New Deal. The Elementary and Secondary School Act provided $1.3 billion in aid to public schools under a formula designed to aid the neediest; in addition, it provided $100 million to purchase textbooks and library materials for both public and parochial school children—the first time federal funds had been authorized to assist nonpublic schools even indirectly. Medicare, a federal program of health insurance for the elderly under social security first proposed by President Truman in 1945, was passed, as was Medicaid, subsidized medical care for the poor. The Voting Rights Act of 1965 struck down literacy and other such tests used in the South to deny African Americans the vote and allowed federal examiners to register all eligible voters. The Omnibus Housing Act, costing $7.5 billion, was directed toward rent subsidies for low-income families and aid to small businesses displaced by urban renewal. The Clean

Air Act amendments required all 1968 and later automobiles to meet federal control standards. Subsequent years of the Johnson administration witnessed a Model Cities program aimed at encouraging the rehabilitation of city slums; the creation of the Department of Transportation, and legislation creating a nonprofit public corporation (Public Broadcasting Corporation) to accelerate the growth and improve the quality of noncommercial television. The Great Society also attempted to reorient American behavior. An "affirmative action" policy emerged in the form of an executive order in 1965 requiring federal contractors and institutions to give a better deal to women and nonwhites in employment opportunities. The Truth-in-Lending Act of 1968 required full disclosure to consumers of information related to credit transactions. The newly established National Foundation for the Arts and Humanities financially assisted painters and performing artists, and a revision of the immigration laws, repealing racial quotas that Congress had set in the 1920s, rounded out the legislative landscape of the Great Society.

Expansive and broad minded, the reforms embodied in the Great Society reflected the dreams, aspirations, and financial priorities of Lyndon Johnson, a domestic reformer of the highest order. Like other reformers before him, Johnson would shortly have to decide between guns and butter; experience proved beyond any doubt that no one could have both, not even the president of the United States of America.[2]

OVERSEAS INVOLVEMENT

Johnson had been in office only six months when he was confronted with his first foreign policy crisis: relations with the Republic of Panama. The immediate cause was some student dispute over rival flags at a high school inside the Canal Zone; before long it turned dangerous, culminating with an attempted invasion of the zone by a Panamanian mob in January 1964. The mob was finally repulsed by American troops but not before the deaths of three American nationals and an unknown number of Panamanians in the commotion. By April, diplomatic relations, which had been broken off by Panama, were restored. More than anything else, the incident demonstrated the extent to which the Panamanians were determined to renegotiate a new Canal Zone treaty with Washington, preferably one that would oversee the passing of American sovereignty and special privileges on Panamanian soil.

Johnson's handling of the Panama crisis was, on balance, considerate and tactful and was well received in Latin America. Quite different was the reception of his intervention in the Dominican Republic in the spring of 1965. There, according to most observers, he overreacted to a danger that was partially imaginary. To preserve the position of a military junta of strong anti-Communists who opposed the revolt by a group of young offi-

cers several days earlier, Johnson announced on April 28, 1965, that he had
ordered the landing of U.S. marines in the Dominican Republic in order to
give protection to hundreds of Americans who were presumably in mortal
danger. The 556 marines landed at Santo Domingo were soon reinforced by
more marines and airborne troops to a total of 21,000. To explain the sending of such a large force, the administration said that the revolutionary
movement, originally democratic in purpose, had fallen under the control
of Communists trained in Cuba and elsewhere and that intervention alone
could prevent turning the Dominican Republic into another Cuba. What
was clear was that the American intervention posed a direct violation of the
charter of the Organization of American States, despite the subsequent,
nominal participation of several other Latin American countries. Right or
wrong, the Dominican intervention did bring comparative peace to the island, which witnessed the departure of the last of the so-called peace force
in September 1966. By then, some troublesome events halfway around the
world had begun to consume the energy of the Johnson cabinet.

The overthrow and death of South Vietnam's President Diem was followed in less than three weeks by President Kennedy's assassination. Johnson wasted no time in reaffirming the policy objectives of his predecessor
regarding Vietnam and called upon all government agencies to support
that policy with full unity of purpose. The stability and efficiency that had
been hoped for from the new government of military officers did not materialize; in fact, military coups followed one another at frequent intervals
until June 1965 when General Nguyen Van Thieu emerged as chief of state
with Air Vice-Marshal Nguyen Cao Ky as premier.

Through a drawn-out process beginning in the summer of 1963 and finally resolving in the winter of 1965, Johnson eventually found it necessary
to make the decision that he had foreseen in 1961—"Whether we commit
major United States forces to the area or cut our losses and withdraw."
Through a long series of decisions complicated by an array of domestic bureaucratic and political maneuvers, Johnson chose to escalate U.S. involvement, with each decision usually triggered by an allegedly provocative act
by the enemy.[3]

The first such episode was an attack by North Vietnamese PT-boats on
American destroyers cruising in international waters in the Gulf of Tonkin,
August 2, 1964, and again, so it was claimed, on August 4. The administration retaliated by bombing North Vietnamese naval stations, and Congress,
at the president's request, passed a joint resolution authorizing the president "to take all necessary measures to repel any armed attack against the
forces of the United States," or "to assist any member or protocol state" (for
example, South Vietnam) of the SEATO treaty "requesting assistance in defense of its freedom." This Tonkin Gulf Resolution, as it came to be called,
passed the House of Representatives unanimously and the Senate by a vote
of 92 to 2. Described by the State Department as "a functional equivalent of

a declaration of war," it gave the president congressional backing for such escalation of the war as he might choose to carry out. Its passage was later bitterly regretted by some of its sponsors, notably Senator J. William Fulbright, chairman of the Committee on Foreign Relations, who had originally sponsored the bill but soon came to believe that the provocative incidents had been distorted or magnified and used by the president to secure a wide grant of powers.[4] In point of fact, there was no North Vietnamese attack on the night of August 4.

The Gulf of Tonkin incident, as it happened, came in the thick of a presidential campaign in which the Republican candidate, Senator Barry Goldwater, was urging a more vigorous participation in the war by the United States. In defending his more restrained course, Johnson gave repeated assurances that American soldiers would not be sent "nine or ten thousand miles away from home to do what Asian boys ought to be doing for themselves." His sweeping victory in the election was presumably due in part to such assurances. In any case, some senators questioned whether the attacks had really been unprovoked and thought that, in any event, the U.S. response (sixty-four air sorties) was excessive. Would the truth have changed anything? If reports from the Gulf of Tonkin had not prompted Johnson to strike out against North Vietnam in August 1964, something else probably would have done so within a few months; that much is fairly certain.

The decision to "Americanize" the war was not the result of a single provocation—or even a series of provocations—but rather was a convergence of a myriad of factors and accumulation of decisions. And the sum total of these factors and decisions was by no means a foregone conclusion. Serious and sustained doubts were expressed by informed and influential people. Senator Mike Mansfield (D-MT), the Senate majority leader, repeatedly urged Johnson to resist the pressure to escalate. The distinguished Harvard economics professor and confidant of former President Kennedy, John Kenneth Galbraith, told Johnson in no uncertain terms that "much official crap to the contrary . . . Vietnam is of no great intrinsic importance. Had it gone Communist after World War II we would be just as strong as now and we would never waste a thought on it."[5] Richard B. Russell (D-GA), the chairman of the Armed Services Committee, and J. William Fulbright (D-AR), chairman of the Senate Foreign Relations Committee, both expressed similar doubts in private, demonstrating during the early 1960s a good appreciation of the difficulties of the conflict. For the most part, however, these early voices of dissent were heard only in private and so in mid-1965 the "Americanization" of the war passed the point of no return.[6]

By early 1965, there were some 23,000 American troops serving as advisers and only incidentally exposed to the risk of combat in South Vietnam. Attacks by the Viet Cong on American barracks in February altered the pic-

ture completely, with American retaliation for specific hostile acts transforming itself into a regular bombing campaign against North Vietnamese
military targets. The air war, with all its risks, was carried to within ten
miles of the Chinese border. The landing of two Marine battalions at
Danang on May 6, 1965, marked the introduction of the first American
troops actually deployed for combat in Vietnam; it also marked the Americanization of the war with mostly young American soldiers—average age,
nineteen—taking over an increasingly heavy share of fighting on the
ground. From there, the numbers grew: 180,000 by the end of 1965, 380,000
a year later, and 542,000 in 1969.

American involvement in Vietnam was, by any standard of judgment,
the most disastrous episode in the history of U.S. foreign policy. The loss in
national treasure and blood was staggering. From 1961 until the collapse of
the Thieu regime in late April 1975, U.S. expenditures in Indochina
amounted to a total in excess of $141 billion or, to put it another way, $7,000
for each of South Vietnam's twenty million people. After finally breaking
their silence after 1965, civil rights leaders pointedly observed that it cost
something near $30,000 to kill a single enemy soldier, about three times
what was spent to rehabilitate a Job Corps trainee.[7] The loss of life was
equally staggering. From the time of the death in 1961 of Specialist 4 James
Thomas Davis, of Livingston, Tennessee, the man later designated by Johnson as "the first American to fall in defense of our freedom in Vietnam," until the Paris Peace Accords of 1973, American casualties alone reached a
figure of 350,000 with approximately 58,000 killed, 40,000 of which were
killed in combat. Vietnamese casualties (North and South) reached a figure
of more than two million, with more than 241,000 South Vietnamese combat deaths and more than one million combined North Vietnamese and Viet
Cong combat deaths. In addition to the known dead, there are 300,000
North Vietnamese MIAs, in contrast to the famous 2,000 Americans still
missing. The war, which was daily televised and made napalm and
"free-fire zones" household words, witnessed a number of dubious precedents, including bombing tonnage (more than three times the tonnage
dropped in World War II) and the first known use of weather warfare. There
was always something tragically surrealistic about it.

At home, as well as on the battlefield, the Vietnam imbroglio left its
mark. The economy was racked by severe inflation, university campuses
were politicized; a generation of unpardoned and unpardonable draft refugees were exiled to Canada and other foreign lands; and the traditional security of the office of the executive was shaken to its roots. In these and
countless other ways, the Vietnam experience affected the lives of all who
survived it, from the president and his policymakers to the proverbial man
in the street. In the Vietnam era, nearly 27,000,000 American men came of
draft age; of that number there were 570,000 apparent draft evaders. Another 15,000,000 were deferred, exempted, or disqualified, including

Sylvester Stallone, the actor who would eventually play the all-American Vietnam War hero in the Rambo series of movies, who spent his time as a coach at a private girls' school in Switzerland and then as an acting student at the University of Miami. At the height of the conflict, draftees were getting killed at twice the rate of enlistees, with the result that avoiding the draft became the preoccupation of an entire male generation or at least that part of it which had the means and wit to manipulate the Selective Service System to its advantage. Particularly devastating was the effect on the African American community. Without the array of political defenses against the draft available to whites, young blacks made up a disproportionate number of U.S. conscripts (and casualties)—20 percent of the conscripts fighting in Vietnam, a figure that was twice their percentage in the general population.[8] The war and the draft that served it broke up American society.

For his part, Johnson argued that the defense of Vietnam was essential to the containment of Chinese communism, a test of Beijing's theory of the inevitable success of Communist guerrilla warfare. It was also the test case of American determination to hold the line against the forces of international communism. "It became increasingly clear," observed the president subsequently in his memoirs, "that Ho Chi Minh's military campaign against South Vietnam was part of a larger, much more ambitious strategy being conducted by the Communists. What we saw taking shape rapidly was a Djakarta-Hanoi-Beijing-Pyongyang axis, with Cambodia probably to be brought in as junior partners and Laos to be merely absorbed by the North Vietnamese and Chinese." Given the presumed correctness of these assumptions, concluded the Texan who more than once likened Vietnam to the defense of the Alamo, "The members of this new axis were undoubtedly counting on South Vietnam's collapse and an ignominious American withdrawal."

Americans who argued for continuation of the war or, as some of them did, for waging it more relentlessly were labeled "hawks"; in August 1965, the Gallup poll indicated that six out of ten Americans approved of U.S. involvement there. Those who opposed the war were called "doves." These included Senator Fulbright of Arkansas, the Democratic chairman of the Senate Foreign Relations Committee, who had sponsored the original Gulf of Tonkin Resolution; Senator Mike Mansfield, Senate majority leader; and veteran journalist Walter Lippmann, who thought it was a mistake to ask the armed forces to do what was not possible for them to do, that is, to fight armed peasants who were willing to die. Others opposed the war on the grounds that the United States had no legal obligation under SEATO to defend a regime that was in any case unpopular and repressive.

The war outraged the world as it divided the American people and wasted American resources, starving the Great Society. A victory by North

Vietnam, the doves conceded, might make all Vietnam Communist, but clearly, a Communist Vietnam, with its ancient hatred and fear of China, would never be a puppet of Beijing. Quite apart from the calculations of geo-political strategy, the grim spectacle of hundreds of thousands of young American men returning home with physical and psychological wounds was simply too much for many Americans to bear, leading to a dramatic swelling of support for the antiwar movement. The movement had first found voice in "teach-ins" on college campuses but rapidly expanded into the wider population with Johnson's decision to escalate. By 1965, when some prominent civil rights leaders such as Dr. Martin Luther King, Jr., and Bayard Rustin abandoned their silence to speak out against "Johnson's war," the commonality of interests between the antiwar and civil rights movements compounded not only the political strength but also the experience in the methods of dissent of both movements. Initially, the peace movement generally aimed at building public consensus through legitimizing the dissent movement, and the preferred method was nonviolent protest of the kind first mastered by Mohandas Gandhi in India. But by 1967, some antiwar activists were resorting to increasingly drastic methods, and civil disobedience gave way to urban unrest punctuated by violence. Over the weekend of October 21–22, 1967, approximately 100,000 antiwar protesters converged on Washington threatening to escalate their expressions of opposition from dissent to resistance by disrupting the U.S. military machinery and attacking the Pentagon building if possible. For the first time since the 1932 Bonus March, U.S. troops and marshals were deployed in Washington, D.C., to protect against domestic protesters. Similar mass protests were staged in San Francisco and New York. Despite the increasingly extreme measures being adopted by the protest movement, the longer the war dragged on with no end in sight, the stronger grew the appeal of the doves to an already disillusioned public. Much to the administration's consternation, the antiwar protesters could not simply be dismissed as fringe "riff-raff"; rather, CIA investigations ostensibly into the foreign elements supposedly pulling the protesters' strings concluded that there was no simple way to identify an antiwar activist and that in fact the movement was remarkable for its appeal across the entire spectrum of American society.[9]

By 1968, the Vietnam War had reached a stalemate. The Viet Cong and North Vietnamese troops could not force the Americans out or destroy the Saigon government; U.S. troops and their allies, on the other side, could not destroy the Viet Cong or, despite heavy bombing, prevent North Vietnamese supplies and reinforcements from reaching the battle area via the so-called Ho Chi Minh Trail through Laos or through Cambodia. Nor could the Americans prevent attacks on South Vietnamese cities either by rocket-borne bombs or by occasional infiltration. The most significant illustration of the apparent vulnerability of the government-held area of South

Vietnam was the Tet (Lunar New Year) offensive of January-February 1968. Notwithstanding high-level assessments, by U.S. commander General William Westmoreland and others, in November 1967 that the United States was winning a war of attrition and that "there was light at the end of the tunnel," and that American forces could begin the process of withdrawal within two years, the Viet Cong stunned American public opinion with simultaneous surprise attacks on as many as forty provincial capitals, as well as on a number of American-Vietnamese airfields and bases in the early morning of January 31, 1968. The most dramatic episodes were the seizure and six-hour occupation of the American embassy compound in Saigon by a suicidal Viet Cong unit and the capture of the capital city Hue by North Vietnamese regulars, from which the invaders were driven out only after weeks of fighting. The Viet Cong took advantage of the occupation of Hue, furthermore, to murder an estimated 3,000 supporters of the Saigon regime. The Viet Cong and their allies were eventually expelled from all the towns and cities that they had seized, and Johnson proclaimed the Tet offensive a complete failure, which in military terms it surely was. From the standpoint of Washington, according to Walt Rostow, special assistant to President Johnson, "The surprise was not the scale of the Viet Cong forces revealed but the bold imprudence of the effort: an unlikely diffusion of resources that resulted in a disaster from which the Viet Cong (and their political cadres) never recovered." Still, from this time forward, talk of victory ceased.

In addition to producing widespread disillusionment with the war in general, the Tet offensive accelerated opposition to the president's war policy within the Democratic Party. In March, Senator Eugene McCarthy of Minnesota, running on an antiwar platform, won 42 percent of the vote in the New Hampshire Democratic presidential primary; shortly afterward, Senator Robert F. Kennedy of New York, President Kennedy's brother and a most formidable war critic, entered the presidential race. Meanwhile, a new consensus was emerging within the administration. Led by the new secretary of defense, Clark M. Clifford, who succeeded Robert McNamara on March 1, 1968, arguments prevailed that it was useless to press for military victory in Vietnam and that the bombing should be halted as a step toward a negotiated peace. Accordingly, in a television address on the night of March 31, 1968, President Johnson announced that the bombing would be ended the following day over all of North Vietnam except the sparsely populated southern portion that contained the access routes to South Vietnam. In the same address, and with no hint in the air, the president announced that he would not seek nor accept his party's renomination for the presidency.

To the surprise of many, Hanoi responded positively to the president's overture to negotiate. After weeks of wrangling about finding a place for the talks, both sides accepted Paris, and there on May 10, 1968, delegations headed by veteran diplomats Averell Harriman for the United States and Xuan Thuy for North Vietnam at last met. The results were disappointing, for now Hanoi refused to discuss terms of settlement until all bombing of the North was stopped. This was done on October 31, five days before the presidential election.

Meanwhile, the arms control movement failed to move much beyond the 1963 agreements during the remainder of the 1960s, though Moscow and Washington managed to agree in January 1967 to internationalizing and denuclearizing the use of outer space, the moon, and other celestial bodies. The only other proposal with impact comparable to that of the Partial Nuclear Test Ban Treaty of 1963 was the Nuclear Nonproliferation Treaty, signed in July 1967, which prohibited nuclear states from transferring nuclear weapons or control of such weapons to nonnuclear states and, correlatively, nonnuclear states from manufacturing or otherwise acquiring nuclear weapons and from receiving assistance in the manufacturing of nuclear weapons. Thus, the superpowers saw it to their advantage, if only in a negative way, to preserve the relatively simple but familiar nuclear balance. The treaty's significance was, however, diminished by the refusal of France, China, and India to sign.[10] Further progress was prevented by the Soviet invasion of Czechoslovakia in August 1968 and American involvement in Vietnam.

THE PROTEST MOVEMENTS GAIN MOMENTUM

Within less than a week of the signing into law of the Voting Rights Act of 1965, the first of the major ghetto riots of the 1960s broke out in the Watts section of Los Angeles, an abject slum and home to a sixth of that city's 523,000 blacks. On August 11, a hot and unusually muggy night in the city, a routine traffic arrest in Watts turned into a riot, with rioters spreading out into the surrounding area, breaking windows, looting stores, and going on a rampage. For the next several days, the rioting continued throughout the entire 154 blocks of Watts, as well as in other areas of the city. Not until the fifth day of rioting did authorities, spearheaded by 15,000 National Guard troops, gain the upper hand; by then losses from fires and looting had run into hundreds of millions of dollars. Thousands had been arrested and injured while twenty-eight African Americans were dead. Similar violence spread across the country, to Chicago, Illinois, and Springfield, Massachusetts. In the former, a street corner civil rights rally turned into a two-day battle, the worst outbreak of racial violence in Chicago in over a decade. In the latter, rioting erupted after police arrested civil rights demonstrators blocking the steps of City Hall.[11]

In July 1966, street rioting broke out again on Chicago's largely black West Side, ostensibly over the police decision to turn off fire hydrant water that children were using; again National Guard units were summoned to restore order. In this instance, two African Americans were killed and six policemen wounded by snipers. The situation eased somewhat the next month when Dr. Martin Luther King, Jr., chairman of the Southern Christian Leadership Conference, who had challenged Alabama to put an end to racial discrimination in the famous march from Selma to Montgomery in March 1965, announced an agreement with civic leaders and real estate interests in a program to end discrimination in residential renting and sales, paving the way for the Federal Open Housing Law of 1968. But the worst was yet to come. The summer of 1967 brought with it racial rioting in, among other places, Detroit, Michigan, East Harlem, New York, and Newark, New Jersey. Death and destruction lay in the wake of the riots. The assassination of the 39-year-old Nobel Prize-winning Dr. King by James Earl Ray on a motel balcony in Memphis on April 4, 1968, set off a week-long wave of urban disturbances in 125 cities encompassing 29 states. Dr. King once quoted an old slave preacher, who said, "We ain't what we ought to be and we ain't what we want to be and we ain't what we're going to be. But thank God we ain't what we was." Because of Martin Luther King's life, the lives of America's African Americans would never again be the same.

In the aftermath of the 1967 riots, President Johnson established a National Advisory Commission on Civil Disorders, chaired by Governor Otto Kerner of Illinois. Fourteen hundred pages in length and one-half year in the making, the "Kerner Report," told Americans mostly what they already knew: "Our nation is moving toward two societies, one black, one white—separate and unequal." Furthermore, the report warned, unless drastic and costly remedies were begun at once, there would be a "continuing polarization of the American community and, ultimately, the destruction of basic democratic values."

Who was to blame for this state of affairs? As far as the commission was concerned, "white racism" lay at the heart of the explosive conditions that ignited riots of the last few summers, civil disorders that were neither caused nor organized by plan or conspiracy. Nonetheless, the report cautioned against a policy of separatism advocated by "Black Power" militants such as Huey Newton's Black Panthers and Stokely Carmichael's increasingly radicalized Student Non-Violent Coordinating Committee, for it could, "only relegate Negroes to a permanently inferior economic state." Among the sweeping recommendations made at the federal and local levels were changes in law enforcement, welfare, employment, education, and news media. Although no attempt was made to put a price tag on the panel's recommendations, it was abundantly clear that they went far beyond further proposed legislation of the Great Society. Answering the "guns versus butter" quandary, a *New York Times* editorial expressed a sentiment shared by a majority of the American people in 1968: "The first necessity (for national action on the racial problem) is for a long overdue reordering of priorities in Washington—a turn toward de-escalation of the military combat in Vietnam and escalation of the war against poverty and discrimination at home." The growing migration of rural blacks to urban areas by 1970—16.8 million out of a total black population of 22.5 million—attested to the urgency of the task ahead. At the same time, other Americans set out to reorder their own priorities.

In protesting the war in Vietnam, poverty and racism at home, and the traditional patterns of education and employment, a new radicalism in social thought emerged in the 1960s, known sometimes as the "counterculture." Although often identified as a revolt of the young, it was, as historian Robert Allen Skotheim has argued,[12] both less and more than that, for while nearly 14 million souls swelled the ranks of the youth population in the 1960s, only a minority of them participated directly in or expressed sympathy for political dissent and the search for a new lifestyle. But as is often the case among intellectuals in relation to the whole society from which they were estranged, the young radicals, whose motto was "You can't trust anyone over thirty," had an influence out of proportion to their numbers. Their favorite philosophers ranged from Herbert Marcuse whose *One Dimensional Man* (1964) helped them locate totalitarianism in the government and society of the United States, to Jean Paul Sartre whose play *No Exit* (1958) said it all. Their favorite historians were Barton Bernstein of Stanford University and Howard Zinn of Boston University; their favorite musicians were Joan Baez and Bob Dylan; their favorite films were *The Graduate* (1967) and *Easy Rider* (1969); and their favorite highs were marijuana and the psychedelic high of LSD (lysergic acid diethylamide).

The New Radicalism or New Left, as it was sometimes called, was a pluralistic, amorphous grouping, embracing among others the Free Speech Movement, the Students for a Democratic Society, and the various antiwar organizations composed mainly of white, middle-class youth. Furthermore, the New Radicalism, according to one close student of the subject, Jack Newfield, operated essentially on three levels. On the political level, it was an anti-establishment protest against all the obvious inequities of American life; on a more complex level, it was a moral revulsion against society that was perceived as being increasingly corrupt; and on the last level, it was an existential revolt against remote, impersonal forces that were not responsive to human needs.[13] For some, solutions to those problems required figuratively reaching out and grabbing their university administrations by the throat, forcing the termination of such practices as armed forces recruitment and the curtailment of Pentagon-related research on campus, or the introduction of a more "relevant" curriculum. The result was turmoil and violence at universities from California to New York, culminating with the shooting to death of four students on the campus of Kent State University by the National Guards in May 1970. By the end of the decade, "The Movement" was gone, the victim of its own infighting. More and more, its most extreme exponents turned further and further in a leftward direction, appealing to violence and losing touch with the dreams and aspirations of their natural constituencies. Others became insurance salespeople and stockbrokers. In the end, the New Radicalism could not justify the political supremacy of a minority of intellectuals who could not even shape their own academic institutions, much less persuade the majority of Americans that the culture in which they lived was a form of fascism.

Not to be outdone, Hispanics, American Indians, and women created their own liberation movements, each hoping, in its own way, to throw "the man" off their back. Hispanics, or Spanish-speaking Americans, numbered nearly twenty million, making the United States the fourth-largest Spanish-speaking nation in the world. Hispanics came from such places as Cuba, Puerto Rico, and, of course, Mexico. Almost eight hundred thousand Puerto Ricans alone lived in New York, accounting for one-third of that city's welfare recipients. Six million Mexican Americans, resident largely in the Southwest, suffered unemployment at twice the national level. Many eked out an existence as migrant laborers in California's "farm factories." Their leaders, including Cesar Chavez whose National Farm Workers association championed the migrants' cause, adopted the term "Chicano" to describe their cultural identity. They demanded bilingual instruction in the public schools and sought legal remedy to rectify perceived past injustices in the workplace and marketplace. They were only partially successful.

Well outside the mainstream of national life were the American Indians. Though their population grew at four times the national rate in the 1960s, reaching nearly eight hundred thousand in 1970, their prospects were dim: Their unemployment was the highest in the nation, as was their infant mortality, alcoholism, and suicide rates; the only thing less than average was life expectancy—forty-six years compared with the national average of sixty-nine. Worse yet, the Department of the Interior's Bureau of Indian Affairs had done little to alleviate horrendous conditions on federal reservations. In protest to these and other grievances, particularly claims to recover ancestral land, the American Indian Movement was formed, drawing attention to its people's conditions by temporarily occupying public places linked to their vanishing past. Some actions were peaceful; others were violent. All had little impact.

More successful was the feminist movement, a movement that had become revitalized during the 1960s and reaped the benefits of its activists' participation in other protest movements. There were at least three strains, or groups, of women who merged in the late 1960s to become known as the women's liberation movement: the group of mature, professional women such as sociologist Alice Rossi and Democratic congresswoman Martha Griffiths of Michigan, who had been working behind the scenes in the late 1950s for legislation benefiting women (favorable clauses in the Social Security Act as well as antidiscriminatory legislation in general); the college-educated white, middle-class housewives who lived in the suburbs at the opening of the decade and who responded dramatically to Betty Friedan's *Feminine Mystique* published in 1963; and the new generation of college-age women who represented the largest single group of women ever to gain higher education. Many in this latter group worked in the civil rights movement at the beginning of the decade and the anti-Vietnam movement in the middle of the decade. It was after 1967 that they moved on to form the radical wing of the women's movement. These three, distinct groups came together at the end of the decade because they recognized that they shared more complaints than they had ever imagined, principally that the "oppression of women" was universal and not restricted to one class or race and that expressive politics—demonstrations, rallies, and confrontations—that had characterized all of the other social movements of the decade could well be applied to women's issues.

The leaders of the movement were drawn from all three groups: Betty Friedan became the spokeswoman for the frustrated suburban housewife; Alice Rossi, Esther Peterson, and Martha Griffiths became the representatives of the professional woman; and Shulamith Firestone, Robin Morgan, and Kate Millett became key speakers for the militant women's liberationist. Gloria Steinem and Jane Fonda, attractive celebrities with reputations established in other areas outside women's liberation, also became speakers for women's issues. The speeches and writings of these and many other women were widely circulated and received a great deal of headline and front-page coverage by the end of the decade and into the early 1970s. They all generally agreed that women had been segregated into the lowest-paying jobs in the marketplace; that many had been consigned to the role of domestic servant and baby machine; and that neither universities, businesses, nor the government took women seriously as equal human beings with the same rights and opportunities as men.

They differed, however, in their methods and ultimate goals for the women's movement. While the radicals preached separatism and lesbianism, the liberal middle, including the National Organization for Women, advocated legislative remedies, scrupulous advocacy of equal opportunity laws, and the improvement of man-woman relations. Some women in the movement identified with the "equal pay-equal work" slogan; others insisted on equal admission of women into professional schools; still others experimented with new marriage relationships in which men shared the homemaking and child-rearing tasks with women and in which they shared paid employment (either both part-time or alternating full-time work). Still others insisted that men and women could never live harmoniously in Western, capitalistic culture. Some radical feminists shared the Marxist critique of Western society and, though they were often hard-pressed to find a desirable alternative in the Socialist world, they envisioned a more ideal future. Some feminists espoused Maoism in the 1960s and defended China's Mao Zedong's versions of the egalitarian society until the drastic consequences of the Cultural Revolution made this claim impossible to hold any longer.

The climate within which the women's movement thrived after 1967 was one in which a wide variety of social reforms were promulgated. Feminism has always had the most success in times when other social reforms have been proposed (the Progressive period is the closest example; the Abolitionist period the most distant example). Criticism of American foreign policy in Vietnam, the well-organized protests of the civil rights movement, the critique of higher education, and the ecology movement that was getting underway provided a sympathetic environment for a discussion and examination of women's role in American life. After all, women were the numerical majority in the country, yet they seemed more deprived culturally and legally than any minority whose rights were being vigorously espoused.

Even before these three groups merged into an uneasy coalition at the end of the decade (and the coalition did not last beyond the mid-1970s), there was evidence in the national administration of concern over women's issues. At the beginning of the decade, President Kennedy had appointed a number of prominent women, including Eleanor Roosevelt and Esther Peterson (assistant secretary of labor), to the Commission on the Status of Women. This illustrious commission investigated the working conditions of women in government, industry, and education as well as the prevailing laws regarding women's opportunities in higher education, and it prepared a major report called "American Women" that was published in 1963. In particular, the report called attention to the fact that one of the worst discriminators against women was the federal government, and Kennedy called for all federal agencies to examine their practices and procedures and eliminate all discriminatory forms.

In 1963, Congress passed the Equal Pay Act sponsored by Representative Edith Green (Democrat, Oregon), a fighter for women's rights for many years. Indeed, the few women in the House of Representatives joined by the few in the Senate (particularly Maurine Neuberger, Democrat, Oregon) worked against great odds in the late 1950s and early 1960s to secure legislation favorable to women. The word "sex" was introduced into the Civil Rights Law of 1964, and Congress thereby forbade discrimination in employment on the basis of gender as well as race and religion. Through the offices of the Equal Employment Opportunities Commission, women sought legal remedies more and more. The publicity that accompanied the Civil Rights Law and the coupling of civil rights for African Americans with all women served to educate Americans on the common needs of both groups, and indeed, one of the greatest accomplishments of the women's movement in the 1960s was acquainting everyone with the issues of feminism. Women educated themselves in new groups called "consciousness raising sessions" where they discussed their experiences and examined them for evidences of sexism. The American vocabulary was enlarged by feminism: Words such as "sexism" and "male chauvinism" were introduced into common usage. Though hostility to men was not characteristic of the movement as a whole, most feminists were not averse to labeling particular men who exhibited sexist attitudes toward women as "male chauvinists." The goal was for men also to do some soul searching and consciousness raising, and many did.

Another social movement that became very popular toward the end of the decade contributed in no small measure to the mood and ethos of the women's movement; this was the mental health movement. Part of the general re-examination of American society that so invigorated many young Americans in the 1960s was the effort to democratize the psychiatric profession. Group therapy became common and flourished in this period and beyond. "Consciousness-raising" sessions shared many characteristics with group therapy sessions. Both sought to examine the individual's life history, with the support and help of the group (and sometimes the professional aid of the leader), and to give advice for short-term problems. The assumption underlining this process of self- and group-education was a very American assumption: Knowledge will set you free. Before women could go into places of power where they had never trod before—before women could assert themselves with their husbands and auto mechanics—they had to understand how their diffidence, their self-image, and their adult roles had come to be. Before they could challenge the male establishment, they had to develop the self-confidence that was essential to a successful confrontation. Thus, assertiveness training courses for women became extremely popular too.

Typical of one of the most exciting reform periods of American history, the 1960s and the women's liberation movement existed in a time when education, legislation, judicial change, occupational changes occurred simultaneously. The 1960s witnessed the coming of age of the first group of baby boomers. Colleges burst at the seams, welcoming larger and larger numbers of students for the first time in American history. The economy, until the end of the decade when Vietnam soured it, was prospering with minimal levels of inflation. The mood was one of frustration and optimism, mixed uneasily together. But, with change, the phenomenon of rising expectations also developed. As Congress responded to African-American demands, their demands increased; as students protested the draft, the war heated up. As women began organizing in their own behalf, they kept expanding their goals. The 1970s would see many of the issues raised in the 1960s persist as vital concerns. There would be a re-examination and reassessment of many issues as well. But the enthusiasm, the demonstrations, and the coalescing of various social reform movements remained unique to the 1960s. Television played a major role in publicizing the issues and the personalities of the movements in the sixties in an unprecedented way. No war would ever again not be a television war; no demonstration would go unnoticed. Though coalitions formed in the 1960s were destined to disintegrate in the 1970s for lack of a common focus, many of the leaders and articulators of the key women's issues would remain for years to come as leaders in the movement.

POLITICS OF DIVISION

The Republican National Convention, gathering in Miami in early August 1968, nominated former Vice President Richard M. Nixon for the presidency on the first ballot. This was something of a second-wind for Nixon; after his razor-thin loss to Kennedy in 1960, and more substantial loss to Democrat Pat Brown for the governorship of California in 1962, many—including apparently Nixon himself—had concluded that his political career was over. The day after his loss to Brown, Nixon had struck out against the press, telling them: "You won't have Nixon to kick around anymore, because, gentlemen, this is my last press conference." Initially, he seemed true to his word, moving to New York and practicing law, but after Goldwater's debacle, Nixon had proved himself the politician's politician, cultivating Republicans at the grassroots level. The favorite of party professionals, big contributors, and the rank-and-file who controlled the party machinery in the conservative Middle West and South, Nixon easily pushed aside the challenges of Governor Nelson Rockefeller of New York and Governor George Romney of Michigan. "The time has come for us to leave the valley of despair and climb the mountain so that we may see the glory of the dawn of a new day for America, a new dawn for peace and freedom to the world," declared the Republican presidential nominee in his acceptance speech. Promising to end "the long dark night for America," Nixon proclaimed that, on the foreign front, he would make the end of the war in Vietnam his first order of business; on the domestic front, he would solve the nation's internal problems by combining a firm approach to law and order with innovative remedies to poverty that would depend less on federal aid and more on private enterprise. Specifics were kept purposely vague. As his running mate, Nixon chose Governor Spiro Agnew of Maryland, a conservative public administrator and the son of a Greek immigrant and restaurant owner in Baltimore.

The Democratic National Convention, meeting in Chicago in late August, nominated Vice President Hubert Humphrey for the presidency. Humphrey was the beneficiary of a series of events that would otherwise have made his nomination problematical: President Johnson's decision to withdraw from politics, the assassination of challenger Senator Robert F. Kennedy in June, and the inability of Senator Eugene J. McCarthy to sustain the momentum of his unexpected success in the New Hampshire primaries. Humphrey was clearly the choice of labor unions, city machines, black organizations, and farm groups. He had also managed the difficult task of mollifying southern conservatives without alienating northern liberals. His hand-picked vice-presidential running mate was Senator Edmund S. Muskie of Maine, the son of a Polish immigrant. Confident and assured in his own way that he could find a way out of the Vietnam War—he had no peace plank—Humphrey had all but lost touch with the young antiwar protestors whose presence in Chicago led to violent street clashes with the local police within a few blocks of the convention center and within full view of the American television audience.

Inside, the Democratic Convention delegates appeared as bitterly divided on the issue of Vietnam as the protestors and the police in the street. Ugly scenes, name calling and nastiness, in both places, were there for all to see. The nomination of segregationist Governor George C. Wallace of Alabama and Vietnam hardliner General Curtis E. LeMay as presidential and vice-presidential candidates of the American Independent party, with the real threat of throwing the election into the House of Representatives, rounded off the principals in an already extraordinary presidential campaign. As the election neared, the major public opinion polls predicted a very close outcome, and they were right.

Nixon, bringing to a climax one of the most amazing personal comebacks in American political history, edged out Humphrey in a close and tumultuous presidential campaign. In the popular vote column, victory held the barest of margins: 31,710,470 votes (43.4 percent) to 30,898,055 (42.3 percent), or put differently, only four-tenths of a percentage point. In the electoral column, a different story emerged with 302 electoral votes to 191, with one elector voting for Wallace. Joining the ranks of Thomas Jefferson and Andrew Jackson, Nixon became only the third man to be elected to the White House after having been previously defeated for the presidency. Although many distrusted his personality, even Nixon's severest critics recognized the president as intelligent and able, essentially a moderate conservative. He would in fact require all of these qualities in dealing with a Democratic-controlled Congress. The 37th president of the United States controlled neither the House (243–192) nor the Senate (58–42) at the time of his inauguration. In any case, Richard Nixon finally had the job that he desperately wanted, and the American people had the change of government they thought they needed. The New Frontier and Great Society now seemed a million light years away.

NOTES

1. Michael Harrington, *The Other America: Poverty in the United States* (New York: Macmillan, 1962). See also Michael Harrington, *The New American Poverty* (New York: Holt, Rhinehart, and Winston, 1984); and Richard J. Carroll, *An Economic Record of Presidential Performance: From Truman to Bush* (Westport, Connecticut: Praeger, 1995), pp. 112–17.

2. For a detailed discussion of Johnson's struggle with this dilemma, see Irving Bernstein, *Guns or Butter: The Presidency of Lyndon Johnson* (New York: Oxford University Press, 1995).

3. Fredrik Logevall, *Choosing War: The Lost Chance for Peace and the Escalation of War in Vietnam* (Berkeley: University of California Press, 1999). See also Mann, *A Grand Delusion: America's Descent into Vietnam* (New York: Basic Books, 2001); and David Kaiser, *American Tragedy: Kennedy, Johnson, and the Origins of the Vietnam War* (Cambridge: Harvard University Press, 2000).

4. Logevall, *Choosing War*, pp. 203–4; and Randall Woods, *J. William Fulbright, Vietnam, and the Search for a Cold War Foreign Policy* (New York: Cambridge University Press, 1998).

5. Quoted in Mann, *A Grand Delusion*, p. 452.

6. Ibid.; and Logevall, *Choosing War*.

7. Robert Weisbrot, *Freedom Bound: A History of America's Civil Rights Movement* (New York: W. W. Norton, 1990), p. 247.

8. Ibid., p.247.

9. Charles DeBenedetti, *An American Ordeal: The Antiwar Movement of the Vietnam Era* (Syracuse, NY: Syracuse University Press, 1990); Walter Hixson, ed., *The Vietnam Antiwar Movement* (New York: Garland, 2000); Walter Hixson, "A CIA Analysis of the Anti-Vietnam War Movement: October 1967," in *The Vietnam Antiwar Movement* edited by Walter L. Hixson (New York: Garland, 2000), pp. 115–26.

10. Rebecca Craig-Smith, "America, Nuclear Non-Proliferation, and the Cold War" (Ph.D. diss., University of Queensland, 1999).

11. Taylor Branch, *Pillar of Fire : America in the King Years, 1963–65* (New York: Simon and Schuster, 1998).

12. Robert A. Skotheim, *American Intellectual Histories and Historians* (Princeton, NJ: Princeton University Press, 1966).

13. Jack Newfield, *A Prophetic Minority* (New York: New American Library, 1966).

CHAPTER 10

White House under Siege

Richard M. Nixon, the consummate politician, brought to the presidency many years of political experience, experience that was to serve the nation well in its foreign relations. By extricating America from the Vietnam imbroglio, engaging both China and the Soviet Union as part of détente, and pursuing arms limitation, the administration played a generally positive role. Domestically, however, historical judgment has been more ambivalent. While social unrest first provoked by anti-Vietnam protesting spread to other complaints, Nixon battled the economy. An American walked on the moon, yet the United States faced domestic oil shortages due to conflict in the Middle East. However, the Nixon administration is best remembered for Watergate, an abuse of presidential power that ultimately tested the relationship between the government and the people and cast a long shadow over American politics.

NIXON IN THE WHITE HOUSE

"We cannot learn from one another," declared Richard Nixon uncharacteristically in his inaugural address of January 20, 1969, "until we stop shouting at one another—until we speak quietly enough so that our words can be heard as well as our voices." Eschewing the hawkish, political, and combative Nixon of the past, President Nixon positioned himself to listen and "to listen in new ways—to the voices of anguish, the voices that speak without words, the voices of the heart, to the injured voices, the anxious voices, the voices that have despaired of being heard." For those who had been left out of participating in the American Dream, he would try to bring them in; for those who had been left behind, he would help them to catch up. In an apparent reference to winding down the Vietnam War, the president observed that "we shall plan now for the day when our wealth can be transferred from the destruction of war abroad to the urgent needs of our people at home," though it was equally clear that he foresaw that there were limits to what government alone could do. To the Soviet Union, Nixon offered peaceful competition instead of conflict. The times were, he supposed, on the side of peace.

Not surprisingly, perhaps, hawkish Republicans felt betrayed by the emergence of this supposedly new Nixon; many opposition Democrats remained cynical. Was it really possible for this self-acknowledged political man, this genius of political opportunism, to avoid the temptation of extremism? Had he not gone out of his way to praise the Democrats, enlist youth, and reach out to the African Americans? "I know America," he said, "I know the heart of America is good."

President Nixon surrounded himself with competent if undramatic personalities. For his secretary of state he chose William P. Rogers, a lawyer who had served as attorney general in the Eisenhower administration; for secretary of defense, Congressman Melvin R. Laird of Wisconsin, a member of the House Armed Services Committee and a strong supporter of the war in Vietnam; and as attorney general, John N. Mitchell, presidential campaign manager and the president's New York law firm associate. Despite his poor image among the nation's intellectuals, the president was able to attract two distinguished members of the Harvard University faculty into his administration: Daniel P. Moynihan and Henry A. Kissinger. Flamboyant and innovative, Moynihan sought to assist Nixon in transforming the nation's welfare program into a work-rewarding system, whereby instead of federal welfare grants, the government would make a cash grant to guarantee a minimum income level; the proposal and its controversial provisions became known as the Nixon-Moynihan Family Assistance Plan and managed to alienate so many politicians and constituencies that it was eventually abandoned.

Kissinger, a German Jew who had emigrated to the United States in 1938, was named assistant to the president for national security affairs. Among other things, Kissinger served as the administration's formulator of détente, a diplomatic strategy designed to manage relations with the Soviet Union and China. In particular, he sought to engage Moscow in an intricate network of commercial and other relations, with a view to increasing the Kremlin's stake in peace. As part of the carrot-and-stick approach—or "linkage" as it became known—it was necessary to make clear to the Soviets that there was an iron link between their external behavior and the West's willingness to deal economically with them; in this sense, trade was perceived as a technique for opening the way to other agreements, establishing a continuing process of negotiation, and advancing peaceful change within the Soviet sphere of influence. A brilliant strategy in many respects, détente as conceived and played out by the administration would enjoy a number of spectacular if limited successes.

NIXON AND VIETNAM

While still hoping to end the war through negotiations, which had stalled over conflicting peace proposals, President Nixon attempted to assuage criticism at home by a process of "Vietnamization," that is, the gradual withdrawal of American forces and their replacement by South Vietnamese troops with improved training and equipment. An announcement on June 8, 1969, that 25,000 U.S. troops would be withdrawn during July, to be replaced by South Vietnamese, marked the beginning of the end of American involvement. The president's first comprehensive exposition of the new policy came in a television address to the nation on November 3, less than a month after a quarter of a million antiwar protesters descended on Washington. All U.S. combat forces, explained Nixon, reaching out to what he perceived to be "the great silent majority" of his fellow Americans, would be withdrawn and replaced by South Vietnamese on an orderly, scheduled timetable. The timetable, in turn, would depend on the progress of the peace talks, the scale of enemy activity, and progress in the training of South Vietnamese troops. He warned Hanoi, whose leader Ho Chi Minh had died in September, that any increase in violence would be met by strong and effective response—renewed bombing of the North. An announcement in December that 50,000 additional American troops would be withdrawn in April 1970 went a long way toward taking the steam out of the antiwar movement, an effect noted on the nation's uneasy campuses.

Such comparative harmony came to a sudden halt on April 30, 1970, with Nixon's declaration that American and South Vietnamese forces were carrying the war into Cambodia in order to destroy Communist bases there. For years, areas adjoining South Vietnam had been employed as Viet Cong sanctuaries with the tacit consent of nominally neutralist Prince Norodom Sihanouk, the Cambodian chief of state. Washington had long tolerated this breach of neutrality rather than taking action that might have otherwise driven the prince into the enemy's camp, but a new situation had arisen with the emergence of a pro-West leadership that found itself threatened by the presence of thousands of North Vietnamese ensconced in the sanctuaries. Faced with this threat, the new Cambodian government of General Lon Nol requested the urgent assistance of the United States and other allies. Going to the presumed "heart of the trouble," Nixon responded with an intense ground and air attack against the enemy-held sanctuaries, promising to remove the forces no later than June 30.

208 Depression to Cold War

The thrust into Cambodia looked to many Americans plainly like an expansion of the war, producing yet another round of demonstrations on university campuses. The most violent of the campus protests occurred on May 4, 1970, when four unarmed students were killed in a skirmish between the Ohio National Guards and antiwar protesters at Kent State University in Ohio, an episode that sparked its own protest movement when over four million students nationwide participated in college protests against the killings. A fifth of the nation's campuses were shut down for periods ranging from a day to the rest of the school year. "It was easily," remarked one observer, "the most massive and shattering protest in the history of American higher education."[1]

Still the war raged. From the Senate came the introduction of several resolutions designed to prevent the administration from widening hostilities in Indochina without the consent of Congress. Upon completion of the June 30 sweep through the Cambodian sanctuaries, Nixon issued a report claiming outstanding success for the operation, even though the "key control center" of the Communist command had not been located. In November, the administration turned its attention to the large buildup of military supplies in North Vietnam, the problem being one of preventing their movement southward. To meet the challenge, the United States in February 1971 launched what was to be the last major offensive of the war; with American air cover only, the South Vietnamese were provided with their first real test at fighting on the field alone. Though not very successful, it did appear that Vietnamization of the war was well underway. Thereafter, until the Paris Ceasefire Agreement was finally signed in January 1973, the administration resorted to increased bombing raids in the North to meet increased fighting in the South and as a means of prodding Hanoi to the peace table.

The last American troops were withdrawn in March 1973, two months after the ceasefire and eight years after the first formal commitment of military forces. Hanoi regarded the agreement as a scrap of paper and completed its goal of reunifying the two Vietnams by force of arms in April 1975. The collapse of Saigon together with the defeat of pro-Western elements in Cambodia (and subsequently Laos) marked the end of American influence in the area, giving some substance to the row of falling dominoes alluded to by Eisenhower in the 1950s.

Long before the collapse of U.S. foreign policy in Southeast Asia, in April 1975, the lessons of Vietnam were being translated into politics at the highest levels. The Nixon Doctrine, the logical corollary to Vietnamization, was foreshadowed by the president at a news conference on the island of Guam on July 25, 1969, and reiterated on numerous occasions. In a subsequent report to Congress, Nixon spelled out the administration's intentions in terms the war-weary American public could well comprehend: There were "lessons to be learned from our Vietnamese experience—about unconventional warfare and the role of outside countries, the nature of commitments

[and] the need for public understanding and support." The result was the so-called Nixon Doctrine. In the case of non-nuclear aggression, Nixon went on record, "We shall furnish military and economic assistance when requested in accordance with our treaty requirements." Manpower would, however, come from the nation under threat. Though some argued that such a policy in fact raised the nuclear threshold, none could doubt that the president's words accurately reflected the mood of the nation. On June 13, 1971, the *New York Times*, in collaboration with other major newspapers such as the *Washington Post*, began publishing installments of the so-called Pentagon Papers, a classified, 7,000–page study formally known as "The History of U.S. Decision-Making in Vietnam, 1945–1968," commissioned by Secretary of Defense Robert McNamara in 1967 and completed the following year. This history of the "lessons" of the Vietnam decision-making process since the end of World War II dispelled once and for all that U.S. involvement in Vietnam had been unavoidable.[2] The attempt of Attorney General Mitchell to block the release of further information from this source on the legal ground that it would cause "irreparable injury to the defense interests of the United States"—ultimately rejected by the Supreme Court in *New York Times v. United States*—produced further disillusionment with the administration and raised the prospect of Congress cutting off funding for the war.[3] None could doubt that militarily the United States failed in Vietnam: that the military failed to assess its technical problems and that the White House foolishly left the issue to the military.

On the positive side, the Vietnam debate enlarged and encouraged congressional participation in the foreign policy process, a long overdue adjustment to the use and abuse of executive power in this field since 1945; it was precisely this participation that averted a recrudescence of "McCarthyism" and "stab in the back" theories, the latter propagated by no less than former South Vietnamese President Nguyen Van Thieu. Senate Majority Leader Mike Mansfield observed much to his credit at the end of the conflict, "There is not profit at this time in hashing over the might-have-beens of the past. Nor is there any value in finger-pointing." Most Americans concurred.

DÉTENTE

Meanwhile, the cold war détente with the Soviet Union was beginning to bear fruit. Since the peaceful resolution of the Cuban missile crisis and the signing of the Partial Test Ban Treaty and the Nuclear Non-Proliferation Treaty, the United States and the Soviet Union had each pursued two contradictory courses. On the one hand, both invested in safeguards against nuclear war—a White House to Kremlin direct hotline and controls on nuclear testing, for example. On the other hand, however, subscribing at least in part to the argument that America's vast nuclear superiority had led to "victory" in the missile crisis, both sides also poured enormous amounts of money into a new arms race. By the beginning of the 1970s, the nuclear forces of the Soviet Union and the United States were at relative parity. In terms of the sheer explosive power, the U.S.S.R. had surpassed the United States and was in the process of developing weapons with even larger pay-loads and greater accuracy, but the United States retained the technological lead. With this capability for each side to destroy the other many times over—along with the rest of the world—a new, chillingly rational theory governed nuclear strategy: Mutual Assured Destruction.

Designed to promote peace through a balance of terror, Mutual Assured Destruction, or MAD as it inevitably became known, lay at the heart of the Strategic Arms Limitation Talks (SALT) that began in Helsinki, Finland, in November 1969. In order to ensure that neither side developed an advan-tage that would destabilize this balance of terror, limits were placed upon the size of certain sections of each nuclear arsenal, along with severe restric-tions on so-called anti-ballistic missile, or ABM, defenses, which could pro-tect territory from incoming missiles. After much formal debate, and a last minute, dramatic intervention by Henry Kissinger, the first SALT agree-ment was signed during a visit by Nixon to Moscow in May 1972. Simulta-neously, and with nuclear war finally recognized as unwinnable (an assumption that had not previously been taken for granted), Nixon or-dered Secretary of Defense James Schlesinger to review the military pos-ture of the United States in light of recent technological developments. The result, known as the Schlesinger Doctrine, was essentially a refinement of the Kennedy administration's strategy of flexible response, in that it was designed to balance Soviet bloc capabilities by threatening retaliation com-mensurate with the threat. The major modification was that it enhanced the role of short-range, relatively small nuclear weapons, as a viable option in a limited nuclear war. Thus, the Schlesinger Doctrine essentially provided the nuclear posture of the United States and the North Atlantic Treaty Orga-nization (NATO) from that time on.

Improving relations with the Soviet Union also led Nixon and Kissinger to embark on one of their most dramatic, imaginative, and successful for-eign policy adventures. The administration clearly desired normalization of relations with China, as indeed did Beijing with Washington. Drawn by common interests, both sides recognized the need to block the expansion-ism of the Soviet Union. Beijing understood, observed Nixon in retrospect, that the United States was the only country with the power to blunt the So-viet thrust for hegemony in Asia; on the other hand, the United States un-derstood that, while China was Communist, it did not directly threaten American interests and could well serve as a counterpoint to Moscow. After a quarter century of U.S.-China animosity, an implicit consensus had been reached all around.[4]

After a vote in the U.N. General Assembly in November 1970 showing a majority of members in favor of finally seating the mainland Chinese government, the White House ordered a review of American policy toward the Communist giant, a process that eventually led to an about face in U.S. policy toward the country. In his second State of the World message to Congress, February 25, 1971, the president broke precedent by referring to the Beijing government by its official title, the "People's Republic of China." Other conciliatory moves from Washington included a further relaxation of the ban on American travel to China, itself reciprocated in an unexpected manner when an American table tennis team, competing in Tokyo, was suddenly invited to visit China in early April. Speculation on the significance of "ping pong diplomacy" was heightened when Prime Minister Zhou Enlai personally greeted the visiting team, observing that a new page in the relations of the Chinese and American people had opened. Determined to take advantage of this historic opportunity and fully prepared to relinquish the fiction that Taiwan was the sole legitimate representative of the mainland Chinese, Nixon stunned the world by his announcement on July 15, 1971, that not only had Kissinger secretly visited China on his recent world tour, but that Nixon had received and accepted an invitation to visit Beijing sometime before May 1972. In the United States, the surprising news got a generally favorable reception, except in strongly conservative circles.[5]

Speculation that the proposed American visit to Beijing augured well for the almost certain admission of Communist China to the United Nations proved accurate, for even while the summit agenda was being fashioned, on October 25, 1971, the General Assembly approved a resolution calling simultaneously for the seating of the People's Republic of China and the expulsion of Taiwan. Accompanied by an army of media personnel, representatives from the State Department, and the ubiquitous Henry Kissinger, Nixon was, for more than one week in February 1972, hosted and toasted by a succession of Chinese dignitaries including Chairman Mao. From a viewing standpoint, it was a television spectacular, replete with the president's walk on the Great Wall of China, which had originally been intended to keep the barbarians at bay.

Atmospherics aside, the actual substance of the talks was contained in the text of the quickly dubbed "Shanghai Communiqué" released at the conclusion of the final meeting between Nixon and Prime Minister Zhou Enlai. After reaffirming the desirability of continued normalization of relations between their countries, the two leaders acknowledged that Taiwan was an "internal" problem for the Chinese people to work out for themselves, though Nixon expected the final solution to be a peaceful one. With this as a goal the President approved the ultimate objective of the withdrawal of American forces and installations from that island, while in the meantime reducing existing forces as tensions in the area diminished.

Finally, the two sides agreed to stay in contact through various channels, including the sending of a senior U.S. representative to Beijing from time to time (later established as a liaison mission), for concrete consultation with a view toward complete normalization of relations, that is, the formal exchange of ambassadors. Looking for an exit from the Vietnam conflict, even at the expense of the South Vietnamese regime, Nixon and Kissinger hoped that China would use its influence on North Vietnam to facilitate an "honorable solution" allowing the United States to withdraw while retaining its prestige. For this, the U.S. was willing to quietly abandon its support for Taiwanese independence and planned to withdraw two-thirds of its forces from the island after the conclusion of the war.[6]

Although Nixon and Kissinger overestimated Mao's influence on the Vietnamese, in its rapprochement with China, the Nixon White House brought American diplomacy closer to a rational view of its strategic interests. The McCarthyism of the 1950s had been predicated on the irrational view that the loss of Jiang Jieshi's China was a disaster for Washington, which could only be explained by treason in high places. Yet, ironically, one of the most expert players of the anti-Communist card, Richard Nixon, proved to be the one politician able to invite "Red China" to take its seat at the world's table.

A CHANGE IN THE WIND

Nixon had come to the presidency with the conviction that the Supreme Court of the 1950s and 1960s under the leadership of Chief Justice Earl Warren had become politically active, attempting to use its interpretation of the law to make American society according to its own ideals. Regarding himself as a legally and politically moderate conservative, Nixon jumped at the opportunity to replace the 78-year-old Warren, who had already indicated his intention to retire. After some consideration, Nixon finally settled upon Judge Warren E. Burger of the District of Columbia Court of Appeals as his choice for the fifteenth chief justice in the nation's history. An exponent of law and order in society and philosophically a moderate conservative, Burger easily won confirmation in the Democratic-controlled Senate in June 1969.

A second opportunity presented itself with the departure, in the same year, of Justice Abe Fortas, who resigned after disclosure of alleged shady financial practices. This time the president ran into rough sledding on his first two choices to the post: two Southerners, Clement Haynsworth, chief judge of the U.S. Court of Appeals in the 4th Circuit; and G. Harrold Carswell, judge of the U.S. Court of Appeals for the 5th Circuit were rejected by the Senate. Civil rights groups opposed Haynsworth as a racist—"laundered segregationalist"—while others opposed him as antilabor; Carswell was opposed both as a racist and as a mediocre mind.

The president's third nomination, Judge Harry A. Blackmun of the federal Circuit Court of Appeals and a Northerner, was, however, unanimously confirmed by the Senate in May 1970. The strict constructionist character of the Burger court was strengthened a year later when the death of Justice Hugo La Fayette Black and the resignation of Justice John Marshall Harlan allowed the administration to place two additional conservatives on the bench: Assistant Attorney General William Rehnquist of Arizona and Lewis Powell, a Virginia attorney and former president of the American Bar Association.[7] Thus, in the space of several years, Richard Nixon had the unique opportunity to change the Supreme Court—although probably not as much as he would have liked.

In the area of civil rights, the administration pursued a policy that was apparently supposed to accommodate as many interest groups as possible. In July 1969, after five months of internal debate, Attorney General John Mitchell and Secretary of Health, Education, and Welfare Robert H. Finch indicated they intended to hold southern school districts—except for those with "bona fide education and administrative problems" such as "serious shortages of necessary physical facilities, financial resources or faculty"—to the September 1969 deadline for desegregation. While far less conciliatory to southern whites than originally expected, the guidelines equally failed to mollify liberal critics, who charged that the policy would open the door to more and more delays in the desegregation of southern schools. Then, in August, the Department of Health, Education, and Welfare (HEW) and the Department of Justice argued in court that HEW-approved desegregation plans should be withdrawn and desegregation delayed. The administration's tactical shift from lawsuits to federal fund cutoffs prompted the resignation of the chief of the Civil Rights Office at HEW, Leon Panetta, a strong advocate of federal intervention.

In March 1970, the president announced that he would request $1.5 billion from Congress to improve educational facilities in so-called racially impacted areas as well as to help resolve problems caused by court-directed desegregation. In emphasizing the distinction between *de jure* segregation grounded in discriminatory legislation and *de facto* segregation reflecting residential patterns—a particularly different problem in northern cities—the chief executive promised that transporting children by bus beyond normal geographical school zones would not be employed to redress racial imbalance. In 1971, as a stop to suburbanites who controlled most legislatures in the urbanized states, the president asserted he would oppose federally forced integration of the suburbs. This assuaged the fears of many such residents as more Americans in metropolitan areas, for the first time in the nation's history, lived outside the city limits rather than within them. Also in 1971, the Voting Rights Act of 1965 was extended to prohibit literacy tests as a qualification for voting in presidential elections and was applied to northern areas where these tests had been required.

Other notable legislation in the first two years of the administration included the National Environment Policy Act of 1969, pledging Washington to a "now or never" fight against pollution; the Water Quality Improvement Act of 1970, which, among other things, authorized the federal government to clean up disastrous oil spills; the Postal Reorganization Act, which replaced the 181-year-old Post Office Department with an independent government agency; the Clean Air Act of 1970, which set a six-year deadline for the automobile industry to develop an engine that would be nearly free of hydrocarbons, carbon monoxide, and nitrogen oxide; the Legislative Reorganization Act, which provided for public recording of roll-call voters in various congressional committees; and a spate of "law and order" acts spearheaded by the Organized Crime Control Act of 1970, which provided for immunity for witnesses giving testimony, special grand juries to investigate organized crime, and limited disclosure of electronic surveillance.

The most controversial legislation in 1971, together with the elimination of funding for the 1,800-mile-per-hour supersonic transport plane, the SST, was the Draft Extension Act. Consuming more than half the Senate's time that year, the act provided for a two-year extension of the president's draft authority to June 30, 1973, an end to student deferments, and no significant limit on the president's conduct of the war in Vietnam or his policy. The increase of total pay and allowances for servicemen of $2.4 billion annually was designed principally to induce enough men to volunteer for the military so that the draft would not be required by the time the new law expired; in its place would stand an all-volunteer force, subsequently achieved.

Nixon also led a legislative response to another growing problem, one that spanned domestic and foreign policy: airplane hijacking. Until 1966–1967, airplane hijackings were relatively rare. Between 1967 and 1972, however, there was a rash of hijackings and bombings as seizing control of airliners became a method of choice for many terrorist organizations for publicity or extortion. As a consequence, hijackings reached epidemic proportions, peaking in an eleven-day period in September 1970 when six hijackings were reported worldwide among the eighty for the year. Most of the hijackings, even those of American planes, involved skyjackers demanding to be flown to Cuba or Middle East terrorists attempting extortion. There were, however, some notable exceptions. One event in particular that captured the public's imagination and spawned several decidedly less successful imitators occurred on November 24, 1971, when a mysterious figure known as "D.B. Cooper" boarded a domestic flight in Portland, Oregon. Once the plane had taken off he threatened to blow up the plane and demanded $200,000 and four parachutes. His demands were met during a stop in Seattle and he then ordered the pilot to take off for Mexico. Once the plane had taken off again, Cooper jumped out of the plane over the forests of Washington state, taking the cash with him. Despite a massive manhunt, he was never found. Most hijackings, however, were not so benign. With the level of violence increasing and death tolls mounting, the government was forced to respond. Through legislation introduced in 1972, new security measures were implemented by the U.S. Federal Aviation Authority, the airlines, and law enforcement agencies. For the first time, mandatory and universal screening of passengers and their carry-on luggage was implemented at all airports across the nation and so-called "sky marshals"—armed undercover security personnel—flew aboard some flights. In January 1973 metal detectors and X-ray devices became mandatory at all airports. The new security measures worked with dramatic effect. After averaging twenty-five hijackings of U.S. planes for the three years from 1970 to 1972, there were just two in 1973 and three the following year. In fact, apart from 1979, 1980, and again in 1983, when there were other bursts of hijacking activity mostly related to the deterioration in the Middle East situation, the number of hijackings of U.S. planes remained in single digits for the remainder of the century, and there were none at all from 1992 to 2000 even though the number of airline passengers had tripled since 1970. The trade-offs for this extra security were longer check-in times and some passenger inconvenience, but these were inconveniences the flying public quickly came to accept.

Nixon found that government intervention in other areas was also necessary. He had come to the presidency with the belief that the American economy operated best with the least governmental interference, but soon found that traditional Republican orthodoxy could do little with the rising cost of living, up by almost 15 percent in the period from his inauguration to the summer of 1971. In fact, the call for fiscal restraint, tight money policy, and high interest rates ran alongside an unprecedented situation in which high unemployment and inflation existed. Added to this, the trade deficit in 1971 placed new and serious strains on the U.S. balance of payments, which reached a deficit of nearly $30 billion, and for the first time in the twentieth century, the nation's balance of trade (exports less imports) ran in the red to the tune of $3 billion. Clearly, something had to be done. On August 15, Nixon imposed a ninety-day freeze on prices, wages, and rents in order to halt inflation. Phase I, the first of such controls in peacetime, was accompanied by the suspension of the convertibility of the dollar into gold, a 10 percent surcharge on imports, and a 10 percent reduction in foreign aid. During the course of the "New Economic Policy," inflation fell from 3.8 percent to 1.9 percent while unemployment fell from 6.1 percent to 5.1 percent by the end of 1972. Other tax changes designed to stimulate the economy, together with an expansionary fiscal policy, became law in December. Gradually phased out by the end of 1974, the Nixon wage and price controls, deemed politically necessary, proved popular in the short term. "But in the long run," reflected Nixon in his memoirs, "I believe it was wrong.

The piper must always be paid, and there was an unquestionably high price for tampering with the orthodox economic mechanism." Few believed the president's conversion to Keynesianism was anything but expedient. His commitment to lowering taxes, freeing agriculture of almost all production controls (realized in 1973), and abolishing controls on international capital movements more clearly mirrored his Republican training than anything else.

TOWARD A NEW CONSERVATIVE MAJORITY

A minority president, with only 43 percent of the total votes, Nixon struggled to create a new majority, including liberals and antiwar factions of both parties, in his first years in office. Despite apparent efforts to talk "consensus politics" and to lower voices, Nixon failed to impress either the liberal press, which did not really believe he was trying hard enough to get out of Vietnam, or liberals in the Senate, who, among other things, rejected his Supreme Court nominations. At this point, and for reasons of its own, the administration changed tack, reverting to partisan and ideological attacks on the president's opponents.

In the name of the "silent majority," peace with honor in Vietnam, and law and order, the president set loose Vice President Spiro Agnew to impugn the programs and honor of the opposition in anticipation of the 1970 congressional election. No stranger to controversy—a year earlier, Agnew had assailed liberal-leaning electronic media coverage as the work of a "small band of network commentators"—the vice president lashed out at "radical liberals" and other "nattering nabobs of negativism." The election results were mixed with the GOP losing nine seats in the House while picking up two in the Senate; the overall effect of Nixon's efforts, according to New York Times writer James Reston, "revived all the old doubts about his [Nixon's] political and personal prejudices, restored all his old battles with the press, and raised the kind of credibility gap that destroyed President Johnson." He even managed to unify the Democrats for a season, never an easy thing.

In his third State of the Union Address, delivered to Congress on January 22, 1971, Nixon introduced the concept of revenue sharing—putting money where the needs were the greatest, putting power to spend it where the people were. As a gesture toward efficiency and a nod to the increasing restiveness of state legislatures, the president asked Congress to set a target of giving state and local governments at least $16 billion annually in order "to close the gap between promise and performance" at all levels of government. The distribution of power was not in question. Under the scheme, approximately one-third of the federal domestic grant program would be placed in a revenue-sharing fund and, from there, dispersed to local and state governments for expenditure under six broad categories: urban development, rural development, education, transportation, manpower training, and law enforcement. This highly touted proposal took shape in October 1972 in the form of a five-year Revenue Sharing Act designed to distribute $30.2 billion of federal tax revenue to state and local governments as supplements to their own revenues, to use generally as they saw fit. The bill, signed into law just two weeks before the presidential election, composed an important part of the "next American revolution" that the administration had promised the nation. Since then, billions of dollars have been disbursed to help pay for a multitude of goods and services, ranging from day care centers to mass transport.

The Democratic National Convention, meeting in Miami in the second week in July, nominated 50-year-old Senator George S. McGovern of South Dakota as candidate for president. A mainstream Democrat, long-time opponent of the Vietnam War, and a major figure in restructuring the party's selection processes and convention procedures, McGovern easily swept aside challenges from Senator Hubert Humphrey of Minnesota and Edmund Muskie of Maine. Defying the polls and the odds, the former historian presided over a convention whose delegate selection process was open to all enrolled party members and whose composition reflected the proportionate representation of minorities, women, and the young. For his running mate McGovern chose Thomas F. Eagleton, a freshman senator from St. Louis, Missouri. An urbane and highly personable lawyer, the 42-year-old Eagleton withdrew from the ticket in late July when it was learned that he had had a history of psychiatric treatment. The Democratic National Committee, at a special meeting held in August, agreed to McGovern's seventh choice for the post, R. Sargent Shriver, former director of the Peace Corps and the late John F. Kennedy's brother-in-law.

The theme of the McGovern campaign was "Come Home America"—home from war in remote places, home from the errant path of wasteful military spending, wasteful unemployment, pandering to special interests, and deception in high places. The latter referred to the break-in of the office of the Democratic National Committee, located in the Watergate, an apartment-hotel complex in Washington, on June 17, 1972, on the eve of the nominating convention. Though this so-called third-rate burglary would have no impact on the campaign, subsequently revealed links between the five men apprehended and White House consultant E. Howard Hunt and counsel to the Committee to Re-elect the President (CREEP) G. Gordon Liddy would open the door to a series of scandals reaching up to the Oval Office.

Assembling in Miami in late August, the Republican National Convention jubilantly nominated Nixon as the GOP's leader for the third time in twelve years. Spiro Agnew easily won reindorsement as vice president. Nixon, in a polished and orchestrated convention, summoned Americans, particularly the young, the old, and disaffected Democrats, to join his "new majority." "I ask everyone listening to me tonight," said the president, drawing a sharp contrast between himself and his liberal challenger, "Democrats, Republicans and independents, to join our new majority, not on the basis of the party label you wear on your lapel but what you believe in your hearts." Nixon pressed the argument that the nation faced the clearest choice of the twentieth century—the 1964 election between Goldwater and Lyndon Johnson apparently having been less so. Furthermore, the choice would not be "between radical change and no change" but between "change that works and change that won't work"—the prudent use of world power or return to isolationism, peace with honor in Vietnam or appeasement, economic growth or stagnation, quality education for all or arbitrary racial balance.

The result of the campaign, which was marked by a minimum of personal appearances by the president and a seeming inability on the part of McGovern to rid himself of his fuzzy image, ended in a landslide for Nixon: 47,740,323 (60.2 percent) to 28,901,598 (37.2 percent). A major factor in the outcome was a massive shift to the GOP of the traditionally Democratic blue-collar workers in northern cities who, according to one Gallup poll analysis, feared McGovern would encourage a permissive society that would accordingly fail to provide safe streets and cities; another factor was the preference given to the administration by the supporters of Governor George C. Wallace, whose own run for the presidency ended in May when a would-be assassin's bullet paralyzed him. In any case, and despite the poor showing in the congressional elections—a net gain of thirteen seats in the House and the loss of two seats in the Senate—the president could well assume that his new conservative majority had finally arrived.

ABUSE OF PRESIDENTIAL POWER

Nevertheless, despite winning a strengthened mandate, Nixon's second term in office was, in the words of Henry Kissinger (who replaced William Rogers as secretary of state in September 1973), "a time of upheaval without precedent in the nation's history." For, commented Kissinger, "a president fresh from the second largest electoral victory in our history was unseated in a revolution that his own actions had triggered and his conduct could not quell.... We had begun ... imagining that we were on the threshold of a creative new era in international affairs.... Within weeks we confronted a nightmarish collapse of authority at home and a desperate struggle to keep foreign adversaries from transforming it into an assault on our nation's security and that of other free peoples."[8] The nightmare Kissinger referred to was the Watergate scandal, which in itself became a symbol of a wide range of illegal actions and misconduct in high places, from the conspiracy to cover up the original Watergate burglary, to presidential impoundment of federal funds, to wiretap and political spying, to perjury and bribery, to illegal campaign contributions, to illegal authorization of bombing targets in Vietnam and Cambodia.

According to secretly made White House tape recordings (a recording system had been installed in early 1971), it is known that as early as June 23, 1972, Nixon and his chief aide, H. R. Haldeman, had conspired to block further FBI investigations into the Watergate case.[9] Other efforts to cover up the burglary included raising money to buy the silence of the defendants who were indicted in September, and perjury before the grand jury by the deputy director of CREEP, Jeb Stuart Magruder. The investigative reporting of *Washington Post* journalists Bob Woodward and Carl Bernstein, which tied ex-Attorney General John Mitchell to a secret fund to finance intelligence operations against the Democrats, was written off by White House press spokesman Ronald Ziegler as "the shoddiest kind of journalism." Yet the story refused to go away. In January 1973, the actual Watergate trial began before Judge John J. Sirica, chief judge of the U.S. District Court for the District of Columbia, who personally interrogated defense witnesses. Though two of the defendants were convicted by a jury, Sirica expressed doubt that the whole story had been determined and called for further investigation.

On February 7, a month before Watergate operative John W. McCord revealed that others had been involved and two months before Haldeman and fellow White House aide John D. Ehrlichman, a former Seattle zoning lawyer, had been abandoned by Nixon, the Senate established a seven-man Select Committee on Presidential Campaign Activities. Senator Sam Ervin of North Carolina was appointed as chairman. Before long, the televised public hearings brought the Watergate affair high public visibility, touching on the origins of a White House "Enemies List" of administration critics, secret funds, a "dirty tricks" unit, and the knowledge, disclosed by Alexander Butterfield, former deputy presidential assistant, that the president had tape recorded all his conversations in the White House and Executive Office Building since February 1971, which the Watergate Special Prosecution Force promptly subpoenaed. When Nixon was finally forced to turn over these tapes as the result of losing a bitter legal struggle, the tapes, which Nixon himself had created, provided irrefutable evidence that the president had abused his presidential power.

In the meantime, Nixon appointed Elliott Richardson as his third attorney general and Professor Archibald Cox of the Harvard Law School as his administration's own special prosecutor. Asserting executive privilege, the president refused to release the tapes either to Cox or the Ervin Committee; Judge Sirica then ordered the chief executive to turn over the tapes to him on August 29, a decision upheld in a higher court in October. After Professor Cox turned down a compromise whereby written summaries of the tapes would be verified by Senator John C. Stennis of Mississippi, Nixon fired Cox, despite the protests and resignation of the attorney general and deputy attorney general. The "Saturday Night Massacre" of October 20 led to general public condemnation of Nixon. Events that followed included the decision of Nixon to obey Judge Sirica's order to hand over some of the tapes, the introduction of sixteen impeachment resolutions in the House of Representatives, and the appointment of Senator William Saxbe of Ohio as the next attorney general and Houston attorney Leon Jaworski as the next special prosecutor. Of the nine tapes requested by Judge Sirica, two were claimed by the White House never to have existed and a third had a sinister gap of eighteen minutes, subsequently determined to be the work of multiple erasures. Disclosures of the tapes revealed more and more shady characters and low thinking in high places.

To make matters worse, Vice President Spiro Agnew resigned on October 9, 1973, after entering a plea of "no contest" in a U.S. District Court in Baltimore to a charge that he had failed to report bribes from Maryland contractors on his 1967 income tax return. Judge Walter E. Hoffman, apparently moved by the tragic sight of the erstwhile vice president of the United States throwing himself on the mercy of his court, placed Agnew on probation for three years and fined him $10,000. In 1982, Maryland's Court of Appeals, the state's highest court, ordered Agnew to pay the state $147,500 for kickbacks he purportedly received from highway contractors from 1967 to 1969, plus $101,235 in interest, the state ultimately upholding the suit of three Maryland taxpayers that Agnew be held accountable for his illegal actions and a payment of nearly $270,000, including interest, was made to the Maryland Treasury in 1983. Under the terms of the Twenty-Fifth Amendment, ratified in 1967 and never used previously, Gerald Ford of Michigan, minority leader of the House of Representatives, was nominated by Nixon two days later to be the fortieth vice president of the United States. Within the next two weeks, Ford was overwhelmingly confirmed by the House and the Senate. For the moment at least, Congress and the president could agree on one thing.

UNDER SIEGE FROM SEVERAL QUARTERS

With the Oval Office under siege from several quarters, two weeks before the "Saturday Night Massacre," on October 6, 1973, the Day of Atonement—the holiest day in the Jewish calendar—the fourth Arab-Israeli War since 1948 broke out. The Arab attack, led by an Egyptian offensive across the Suez Canal and a Syrian offensive on the Golan Heights, took the Israeli government of Prime Minister Golda Meir totally by surprise. On both fronts, the Arabs, fighting with a determination and spirit that fully redeemed the image of the Arab soldier of 1967, met with initial success only to be checked by an Israeli counteroffensive on both the Egyptian and Syrian frontiers. In the former action, Israeli forces achieved a bridgehead on the west bank of the Suez Canal, reaching to within seventy miles of Cairo, managing to encircle the Egyptian Third Army of 20,000 soldiers on the east bank; in the latter situation, the Israelis had managed to reconquer the whole of the Golan Heights and advanced to within twenty miles of Damascus. Washington's response to the conflict was a measured one, consisting mainly of matching Soviet arms to its clients and persuading Moscow to assist in effecting a U.N.-sponsored ceasefire. On October 13, the administration began replenishing Israeli war stocks, while a week later, Congress approved $2.2 billion in aid. The Arab response, lasting until March 1974, was to initiate an oil embargo against the United States.

The first great oil shock of the 1970s exerted a disastrous effect on the American economy, far beyond higher prices of gasoline, home heating, and fuel oil. During the first quarter of 1974, the gross national product of the United States declined 6.4 percent, marking, according to most economic analysts, the end of a post-World War II era of high growth rates and full employment for the industrialized world. Inflation spiked to levels not seen since 1947. After diplomatic skirmishing, the Arabs and Israelis agreed to a U.N. ceasefire on October 24. Meanwhile, Nixon had to exert tremendous pressure on the Soviet Union, principally by placing American troops around the world on alert status, after having considered using nuclear weapons, to dissuade the Kremlin from dispatching an expeditionary force to the Middle East to bring about an observance of the ceasefire. The Soviet leadership grasped the message, and the crisis was dissipated when the U.N. Security Council called for the creation of an emergency force exclusive of the permanent members of the council.

At the conclusion of the fighting, there occurred a spate of diplomatic activities aimed at laying the foundation for a more lasting peace in the Middle East. The most important of these efforts included Secretary of State Kissinger's mission to the area in November, resulting not only in the resumption of U.S. diplomatic relations with Cairo for the first time since 1967, but also in the signing of an Egyptian-Israeli ceasefire instrument on November 11, the first major agreement between Israel and an Arab state since 1949. In January 1974, the secretary achieved a partial Egyptian-Israeli disengagement understanding in the Sinai, completed in September 1975. In May 1974, he also organized a disengagement pact between Syria and Israel in the strategic Golan Heights. These gains for peace were the consequence of Kissinger's so-called shuttle diplomacy, which was estimated at keeping Kissinger away from Washington on the average of approximately one out of every six weeks during 1974 and 1975. Still, a comprehensive peace settlement continued to be elusive.

The Arab oil embargo, with its real threat to the nation's energy needs, made the American winter of 1973–1974 a winter of political discontent. On November 7, 1973, the president announced on television what he called the "stark fact" that the nation was faced with the most acute shortage of energy since World War II. To meet the crisis, he ordered, as a symbolic gesture, heat to be lowered in federal buildings to between 65 and 68 degrees Fahrenheit; asked Congress to give him authority to relax environmental restrictions; asked that the country be returned to daylight savings time; and called for the imposition of a nationwide speed limit of fifty-five miles per hour on federal highway systems. These latter two proposals were quickly made into law. In his January 1974 State of the Union Address, Nixon asserted that "the number one legislative concern must be the energy crisis." Yet, despite the best efforts of conservation, lines of automobiles at gas stations lengthened, supplies invariably ran low, and the price of gasoline soared. All of this, including the gloom-and-doom predictions of instant experts, led to greater inflation and economic recession. As the crisis eased, Americans increasingly looked about for alternative energy sources while continuing to place stock in such legislation as the Trans-Alaska Oil Pipeline projected to supply the United States with an additional two million barrels of oil per day by 1980. In any case and whatever theory of the oil conspiracy one believed—it appeared to some observers that gasoline "shortages" began in the boardrooms of the oil giants at home—life in America, and its love affair with the automobile, would never be quite the same again.

While these crises provided the White House with distraction from the Watergate siege, it did not provide deliverance. The impeachment resolutions of October 1973 were duly handed over to the House Judiciary Committee, headed by Democratic Congressman Peter Rodino of New Jersey. Rodino, granted broad powers of subpoena, began closed hearings in May 1974, two months after a grand jury indicted former Attorney General Mitchell and several of his closest aides, all of whom were subsequently convicted; Nixon was cited as an unindicted co-conspirator in the Watergate cover-up. In response to requests to turn over additional tape recordings, the president gambled by releasing a number of them himself. It was a blunder as the recordings once again depicted the president in the worst kind of light. By late July, 51 percent of the American public had reached the conclusion that there was indeed enough evidence to bring Nixon to trial before the Senate, the final step in impeachment proceedings. So did the House Judiciary Committee, which, between July 25 and July 30, after televised debate, voted three articles of impeachment. Specifically, the committee found that Nixon had "prevented, obstructed, and impeded the administration of justice"; had "repeatedly engaged in conduct violating the constitutional rights of citizens, impairing the due and proper administration of justice in the conduct of lawful inquiries, or contravening the law governing agencies of the executive branch"; and had "failed without lawful cause or excuse to produce papers and things, as directed by duly authorized subpoenas . . . thereby assuming for himself functions and judgments necessary to the exercise of the sole power of impeachment vested by the Constitution in the House of Representatives." For such of-

fences, concluded Rodino's committee, "Richard M. Nixon . . . warrants impeachment and trial, and removal from office."

On August 5, with time running out, Nixon finally yielded the incriminating tapes of June 23, 1972, revealing beyond doubt that he had played a
significant role in the cover-up. With the emergence of the proverbial
"smoking gun," it became apparent that the chief executive had lost the
support of all but his most resolute supporters in the Senate, probably no
more than fifteen members, according to Senator Barry Goldwater. Facing
the inevitable, and with the prospect of a trial, conviction, prison sentence,
and loss of his federal pension before him, the thirty-seventh president of
the United States announced on the evening of August 8 that he was abandoning his fight to remain in office and would resign the next day. At 11:35
A.M. on August 9, the moment Nixon's letter of resignation was turned over
to Secretary of State Kissinger, Vice President Gerald Ford assumed the
power of the presidency as the president and the first lady left the White
House in the presidential helicopter. Then, shortly after noon, President
Ford took the oath of office from Chief Justice Warren Burger in the historic
East Room of the White House. "Our long national nightmare," declared
the new chief executive, "is over."

The Watergate scandal left its mark on the course and quality of American politics and government. It provided a watershed for the American political experience as people subsequently referred to "pre-Watergate" and
"post-Watergate" politics. It led to widespread public disenchantment
with politics in general and constitutional restrictions imposed on the presidency as an institution. The congressional response alone resulted in a
spate of legislation designed to establish new standards of ethics and ac-
countability for holders of the public trust. The new legislation included
campaign financing and budget laws, efforts to curb presidential authority
abroad (which resulted in the War Powers Act), and to institutionalize procedures for the appointment of a special prosecutor to investigate charges
brought against high administration officials. Already disenchanted with
Washington's mishandling of the Vietnam imbroglio, the public's faith in
elected officials reached its lowest point. The nation's media, on the one
hand enjoying a renewed confidence in its own power, on the other hand
found itself distrusted by the public almost as much as the politicians. But
the biggest costs were borne by the presidential office itself. Succeeding
presidents, observed Bob Woodward a quarter of a century later, "were in-
habiting a new world" whether they recognized it or not.[10]

For a long time unrepentant, Nixon finally came to admit that the
break-in by the Watergate "plumbers" was both illegal and, he remarked in
1984, "a very, very stupid thing to do." He also went on to describe the bun-
gled cover-up organized by his administration as "stupidity at the very
highest," and concluded by condemning his own failure to destroy the incriminating Watergate tapes before they were subpoenaed by the investiga-

tion panel. Such an action would probably have saved his presidency though weakened the Republic, perhaps beyond repair. In the end, Nixon's insecure personality, together with an extraordinary set of sycophantic advisers, proved the undoing of the nation's chief executive, who was lucky to have escaped prison. The price of placing one's interests above the interests of the Republic would always be a heavy one for the occupant of the Oval Office. Richard Nixon paid that price.

NOTES

1. Jeffrey Kimball, *Nixon's Vietnam War* (Lawrence: University Press of Kansas, 1998), p. 216; and Charles DeBenedetti, *An American Ordeal: The Antiwar Movement of the Vietnam Era* (Syracuse, NY: Syracuse University Press, 1990), p. 280.

2. Kimball, *Nixon's Vietnam War*, p. 253.

3. Ibid., p. 249.

4. James Mann, *About Face: A History of America's Curious Relationship with China, From Nixon to Clinton* (New York: Vintage, 1998), pp. 13–25.

5. Ibid., pp 26–52.

6. Ibid. See also Qiang Zhai, *China and the Vietnam Wars, 1950–1975* (Chapel Hill: University of North Carolina Press, 2000), pp. 196–97; and Elaine Sciolino, "Records Dispute Kissinger On His '71 Visit to China," *New York Times*, 28 February 2002.

7. On Rehnquist's appointment, see particularly John W. Dean, *The Rehnquist Choice: The Untold Story of the Nixon Appointment that Redefined the Supreme Court* (New York: Free Press, 2001).

8. Henry Kissinger, *Years of Upheaval* (Boston: Little Brown, 1982), p. xix.

9. For a compilation of the transcripts of the incriminating recordings, see Stanley I. Kutler, *Abuse of Power* (New York: Free Press, 1997).

10. Bob Woodward, *Shadow: Five Presidents and the Legacy of Watergate* (New York: Simon and Schuster, 1999), p. xiv.

CHAPTER 11

A Time for Healing

The Vietnam imbroglio and the excesses of Richard Nixon's so-called imperial presidency led to widespread disillusionment with both the White House and Congress. The twin ghosts of Vietnam and Watergate haunted Gerald Ford and Jimmy Carter as they struggled to reclaim the faith of the nation for the presidential office. Ford's task was a difficult one. He came to office when the economy was facing its worst recession since the Great Depression. Carter's pledge to heal America was also undermined by circumstances. Social dissent was becoming increasingly politicized as the feminist movement in particular transformed itself into a potent political force. Internationally, Carter pursued arms control and engaged the Soviet Union on its human rights record, especially in Afghanistan, yet the administration's involvement in the Middle East finally led to its undoing and to severe public backlash. The nation yearned for healing; Ford and Carter both tried to provide it, but neither fully succeeded.

WAKING FROM THE "LONG NATIONAL NIGHTMARE"

Well-liked, hard-working, and conservative as a congressman, Gerald Ford opposed measures such as minimum wage bills, the establishment of the Office of Economic Opportunity, and Medicare; he supported legislation aimed at building the controversial supersonic transport plane (SST), prohibiting the busing of school children, and impeaching controversial Supreme Court Justice William O. Douglas. He ultimately succeeded to the presidency, according to political observer Richard Reeves, because he managed to make himself "the least objectionable alternative."[1] Others depicted him as a model of cornfed common sense, nothing more or less than the basic driven, calculating, not especially distinguished politician. But this much seemed certain: Had it not been for Watergate and Spiro Agnew's choice of resignation over prosecution for taking kickbacks, Ford might only have been recalled as the inarticulate former Big-Ten lineman who once tried—and failed—to impeach Associate Justice Douglas. For himself, Ford was "acutely aware that you have not elected me as your president by your ballots." While he took pride in being "a Ford, not a Lincoln," he also had no doubts that he was "not a Model T." "I have old-fashioned ideas," the new president declared to an enthusiastic joint session of Congress only three days after he took office, "I believe in the basic decency and fairness of America."

President Ford's first order of business was to name Governor Nelson Rockefeller of New York, leader of the liberal wing of the Republican Party and perennial aspirant to the White House, as his vice president. His second order of business was to let his predecessor off the proverbial hook. On September 8, 1974, and despite his own, earlier comment, "I do not think the public would stand for it," Ford granted former President Richard Nixon "a full, free, and absolute pardon" for all crimes he may have committed while president. The nation was stunned as Nixon observed with perhaps no little understatement that "I was wrong in not acting more decisively and more forthrightly in dealing with Watergate." Political reactions to the pardon, which was organized behind the scenes by Nixon's chief of staff, General Alexander Haig, fell mainly, though not entirely, along party lines. Not surprisingly, the congressional mid-term election in November reflected the verdict of the average American when the Democrats were returned to the House (291 to 144) and the Senate (61 to 37) with overwhelming majorities. Ford's honeymoon with Congress had come to an abrupt end.

Unable to command enough congressional support to press his own economic programs, with tight money policy producing high interest rates, and with the impact of the quadrupling of the price of oil hard upon the economy, Ford presided over the worst recession since the Great Depression. Despite the increasing availability of gasoline, by 1975 unemployment had reached the 9 percent mark, with more than one million jobs lost in that year alone; inflation rose to 12 percent, dropping to less than 5 percent in 1976, mainly at the expense of bringing the growth of the economy to a halt.

THE END OF DÉTENTE

The administration and the 94th Congress were at loggerheads from the outset. Opposed to the expansionist monetary policies of the Democrats and unable to push through any legislation of his own, Ford turned to an unprecedented use of the presidential veto. At different times, the former minority leader vetoed a $5.3 billion package designed to fund job-producing projects across the nation on the grounds that "it would exacerbate both budgetary and economic pressures," and a $7.9 billion aid-to-education bill on the grounds it was unsound and would "authorize excessive appropriation levels." All in all, the president resorted to the veto more than sixty times. More positively, Ford signed into law the Energy Policy and Conservation Act of 1975, deregulating the price of oil among other things and the Energy Reorganization Bill of the same year, setting up an Energy Research and Development Administration. In 1976, he issued an executive order restricting the power of the Central Intelligence Agency (CIA) to intrude upon the lives and activities of American citizens.

With Henry Kissinger still in charge of the State Department, Ford generally continued to pursue the foreign policy goals of the Nixon administration. A major breakthrough was reached in the second phase of the Strategic Arms Limitation Talks (SALT) II negotiations at a meeting in Vladivostok in November 1974 between Ford and Soviet General Secretary Leonid Brezhnev. With a view to striking a compromise between the Soviet advantage in numbers of strategic launchers permitted by the temporary five-year accord and America's three-to-one advantage in multiple nuclear warheads, the two sides agreed to an overall limit of strategic nuclear delivery vehicles, a ban on the construction of new land-based inter-continental ballistic missile launchers, and limits on the deployment of new types of strategic offensive areas. On another front, the president traveled to Helsinki in late summer 1975 to sign, along with the heads of the thirty-five nations of Europe, the so-called final act of the Conference on Security and Cooperation in Europe. The high-water mark of détente, the Helsinki Conference declared the current frontiers of Europe "inviolable," thereby endorsing the Soviet Union's post–World War II territorial gains, as well as its hegemony in Eastern Europe. In return, the administration hoped to induce Moscow to open its east European empire to a freer flow of people and ideas, reaffirming the ideal of the dignity of the individual. There was no shortage of critics of détente in the United States—Western Europeans tended to have a more sanguine outlook on the matter—eager to point out that Communist-dominated police states seldom work this way. Détente seemed to such notables as diplomat-emeritus George F. Kennan and Soviet dissident and Nobel prize winner in literature Aleksandar Solzhenitsyn—not to mention the pack of Democrats running for office in 1976—a one-way street.

To make matters worse, evidence on all sides indicated that Moscow had abandoned the conventional rules of the game. Through use of East German and Cuban surrogates, the Soviet Union threw its weight behind the leftist regime in the Angolian civil war, begun in 1975, indicating a new, more belligerent Soviet approach to the Third World. Cribbed and confined by congressional resolutions barring American involvement of any kind in the conflict, the administration could only protest that Moscow's presence in Africa was "harmful" to détente. Perhaps more significant was the public revelation of the CIA's assessment of Soviet defense spending in 1976; according to the study, the percentage of the U.S.S.R.'s gross national product absorbed by defense spending had increased from 6 to 8 percent to 11 to 13 percent. Media reports that the CIA had "doubled" its estimate of Soviet defense expenditures sent shock waves through the national intelligence community. That the figures may have also reflected a heightened American appreciation of how far less efficient Soviet defense industries were than formerly believed—one might suppose "less bang for the ruble"—seemed not to interest the attentive public. Kissinger's strategy of weaving a web of interconnections, whose benefits might seem important enough to the Kremlin to restrain itself, appeared to have lost its rationale and became identified with being "soft" on the Soviet Union.

About the only positive achievement the administration's foreign policy had to show for itself was the retaking of the American ship, the *Mayagüez*, in May 1975, from Cambodian Communists who apparently had not counted on the president to send in the marines. On May 11, 1975, an unarmed American merchant vessel, the *Mayagüez*, was boarded at gunpoint by Cambodian naval personnel many miles off the Cambodian coast and hauled into port with its thirty-nine American crewmen. Ford condemned the seizure as an act of piracy by the new Cambodian government, which had taken control when Communist-led force captured Phnom Penh the previous month. Ford instructed the State Department to demand the immediate release of the ship, adding that "failure to do so would have the most serious consequences." While asking China through Beijing's liaison office in Washington for help in obtaining release of the ship, Ford ordered the aircraft carrier *Coral Sea* and other ships from the Seventh Fleet to sail for the Gulf of Siam. The Cambodians did not have long to wait. On May 14, U.S. forces captured the *Mayagüez* and rescued the crew. The daring rescue, which killed forty-one Americans in the operation, won popular approval until it was revealed that the Cambodians had agreed in principle to release the captured Americans. Secretary of State Kissinger observed at the time that "there were limits beyond which the United States cannot be pushed." He was probably right. The success of the operation was applauded throughout the nation, and it enhanced Ford's stature in the White House.

The Democratic National Convention, meeting in New York for the first time in more than fifty years, nominated outsider and political moderate Governor James (Jimmy) Earl Carter, Jr., of Georgia by an overwhelming margin on the first ballot. Determined, efficient, and luckier than most, Carter began his campaign in 1972, midway through his gubernatorial administration. Born in Plains, Georgia, on October 1, 1924, of modest circumstances, Jimmy Carter appeared a man of a thousand faces, the Lon Chaney of 1976. He was at once, in the words of his campaign autobiography, *Why Not the Best?*, a Southerner—the first major party nominee from the Deep South since Texas-born Lyndon Johnson—an American, a peanut farmer, an engineer, a graduate of the U.S. Naval Academy in 1946, a father and a husband, a born-again Christian, a politician and former governor, a planner, a businessman, a nuclear physicist, a naval officer, a canoeist and, among other things, a lover of Bob Dylan's songs and Dylan Thomas's poetry.

He was above all the consummate technician. Cultivating the simple virtues of honesty, decency, and competency, Carter touched the nation's raw nerve when he told the assembled delegation that "it's now a time for healing. We want to have faith again. We want to be proud again. We just want the truth again." At the convention, Carter chose liberal Senator Walter F. Mondale of Minnesota as his running mate. In the domestic sphere, the party platform rested on means to fight unemployment through public works projects and financial incentives to private enterprise, welfare reform, tax reform, and in extensive and mandatory national health insurance programs; in the foreign affairs and defense spheres, rejection of détente to be replaced by "hard bargaining" with the Soviet Union, a $5.7 billion cut in defense spending, a comprehensive Middle East peace settlement, normalization of relations with Beijing, and "more openness" in foreign policy making.

At the Republican National Convention, held in Kansas City in August, Gerald Ford was nominated in his own right on the first ballot. Ford, who had struggled for seven grueling months to beat off the challenge of Republican conservative Governor Ronald Reagan of California, a popular movie actor-turned politician, selected Senator Robert J. Dole of Kansas as his running mate. A member of the House of Representatives for four terms, a senator since 1969, and one of Nixon's strongest supporters, Dole's appointment could only be explained as appeasement of the growing Reaganite right wing of the Republican Party. The GOP platform opposed national health insurance, preferring instead to expand Medicare payments to hospitals; concentrated on fiscal means to reduce inflation; advocated expansion of Nixon's revenue-sharing program with the states; pledged to keep up U.S. might while still trying to negotiate strategic arms limitations with Moscow (with the use of the word "détente" disappearing from the language); and sought the continuance of Kissinger's "step-by-step" approach toward a Middle East peace solution.

The highlight of the campaign, which was otherwise undistinguished, were the three presidential debates held between the candidates in September and October; these were the first television debates ever between an incumbent and a challenger. They were also decisive. The second debate, held on foreign policy issues, witnessed Ford's unaccountable gaffe regarding the status of nations locked in the Soviet Eastern European empire—they were independent of Moscow—as well as the high tide of his rival's challenge. For his part, Carter found support and votes in claiming to be an anti-Washington, anti-establishment figure, not a lawyer, not a liar. Probably his trump card was his claim that he told the truth and that he would never lie to the American people. "If I ever lie to you, if I ever mislead you, if I ever avoid a controversial issue, don't vote for me," he said. Thus, in the view of one close observer, "Carter cornered the truth market early in a year when the voters sought, above all else, an honest politician"—the kind of candidate the post-Watergate times demanded. He was also fuzzy on the major public issues, in fact almost edgy about them, saying on one occasion, "I don't give a damn about abortion or amnesty or right to work laws. . . . They're impossible political issues."

The formula worked well enough. On polling day, Carter snatched the presidency from his opponent with a popular vote count of 40,825,839 (50 percent) to 39,147,770 (47.9 percent) and an electoral score of 291 to 241. Furthermore, the Democrats held their two-to-one margin in the House of Representatives (292–144) and led in the Senate (61–38, plus the independent Senator Harry Byrd of Virginia). After eight years in the wilderness, the Democrats could look with confidence to working with a chief executive who had reunited the basic elements of Franklin D. Roosevelt's New Deal coalition: organized labor, minorities, urban dwellers, the aged, and committed liberals. Four years after the panel on television's What's My Line could not guess that the mystery guest was governor of Georgia, Jimmy Carter had become president of the United States.

JIMMY CARTER IN THE WHITE HOUSE

"I have no new dream to set forth today," declared the thirty-ninth president of the United States at his inauguration on January 20, 1977, "but rather urge a fresh faith in the old dream. . . . Let us create together a new national spirit of unity and trust." Generally, Carter, a deacon in the Southern Baptist Church with a penchant for quoting Old Testament prophets, committed his administration to enhancing equality of opportunity, to preserving the nation's natural beauty, to fostering respect for human rights at home and abroad, to keeping the nation strong militarily, to eliminating nuclear weapons from the face of the earth and, before all else, to recognizing the nation's limits in being able to solve all problems much less afford to do everything. Then, in a break with tradition and in sharp contrast to the style of Nixon's "imperial presidency," Carter and his family walked the entire mile and a half in subfreezing weather from the Capitol to the White House. The other symbolic action on his first day in office was to pardon, by executive order, all draft evaders of the Vietnam War, which, with Watergate, the former governor was anxious to relegate to the past.

Carter's major cabinet appointments reflected varying degrees of geographical diversity and breadth of experience: Cyrus Vance of New York as secretary of state; Harold Brown of California as secretary of defense; Michael Blumenthal of Michigan as secretary of the treasury; and Zbigniew Brzezinski of New York as national security adviser. To this level, the 52-year-old Democrat added the names of fellow Georgians Bert Lance as director of the Office of Management and Budget; Griffin Bell as attorney general; and Andrew Young as ambassador to the United Nations. The bulk of the White House staff, led by political strategist Hamilton Jordan and press secretary Jody Powell, originated from Georgia as well, a development that brought its own share of criticism. After Nixon and Watergate, many Americans were impressed by Carter's distance from Washington; others were not so certain, equating the distance from Washington with inexperience, and became contemptuous of a White House run by a group of rank amateurs. "With very few exceptions," wrote journalist Ward Just, "he transplanted his campaign staff intact to the White House, and that may be the major difficulty, because successful campaigns do not necessarily make successful bureaucrats."

In nearly twenty-five hundred speeches and hundreds of interviews during a two-year presidential campaign, candidate Carter promised many programs, reforms, and changes, frequently adding the phrase "and you can depend on that." In fact, it required his aides several weeks to compile the president's more than 600 promises in a 110–page book, soon dubbed "Promises, Promises," after a popular Broadway musical. When he entered office, Carter was of the opinion that unemployment (7 percent) rather than inflation (also around 7 percent) was the main domestic issue; by the end of his administration, he was not so sure. Among his campaign promises, the president promised to reduce the military budget, curtail arms sales abroad, balance the budget by 1981, restrain the spread of nuclear weapons, free Americans of their "inordinate fear of communism," bring stability to the Middle East, return the Panama Canal, protect the environment, and establish an effective energy policy. It was not long before public dissatisfaction set in, perhaps from expecting more than he, or anyone else, could have delivered. The cumulative effect of high inflation and high unemployment—despite the appointment of tight-money advocate Paul Volcker to the chairmanship of the Federal Reserve Board—high costs of living, of housing, of borrowing money, and of his overstating the threat of the Afghan crisis (which he described as the most serious confrontation for the United States with the Soviet Union since 1945) took its toll. Carter became within a short time the most unpopular president since Herbert Hoover, widely regarded as incompetent, indecisive, and uninspiring.

Perhaps it was a bad time for the Georgian to be president. Americans increasingly expected more of their leaders; they demanded simple answers and simple solutions. There were none of these. Other matters handicapped President Carter in his efforts to be an effective chief executive. These factors included public mistrust of presidential leadership, diverse special-interest groups and, especially, the growing independence of Congress. Despite the heavy Democratic majorities, the President seemed unable to lead Congress, much less control it; even with the successes he had, there was nearly always more than the usual struggle between the White House and Capitol Hill.

Moreover, there was the intractability of the nation's problems, possibly Carter's greatest handicap. Major problems such as inflation and energy were not of the Georgian's making, and his proposals to deal with them did not bring striking results, though, to be certain, there were some notable achievements. Other political leaders, many of whom had been frustrated in their own recent bid to occupy the Oval Office, failed to come up with better solutions. Finally, but equally troublesome for the president, was the reluctance of Americans everywhere to subordinate local interests to national need. "One cannot fairly assess Jimmy Carter as President," remarked the *New York Times* in June 1979, "without assessing the self-interested people and baffling problems over which he presides." As James Reston pointed out about the Washington outsider who once lost his way to the Oval Office and delighted in throwing frisbees on the White House grounds, "He came to town . . . promising to produce a 'Government as good and generous and unselfish as our people' and on the whole he has kept his promise. Maybe the trouble is that 'the people' are not quite as good and generous and unselfish as he thought."

According to his memoirs, Carter's primary thought on Inauguration Day was about the potential shortage of energy supplies and the need for the American people to stop looking to the federal government as a bottomless cornucopia, a process that had begun with Roosevelt's New Deal. "We desperately need," recalled the president, "a comprehensive program that would encourage conservation, more fuel production in the United States, and the long-range development of alternate forms of energy which could begin to replace oil and natural gas in future years." Furthermore, he continued, "these goals were complicated by the need to protect our environment, to insure quality of economic opportunity among the different regions of our country, and to balance the growing struggle between American consumers and oil producers." In an address to the nation on April 18, 1977, Carter likened the nation's struggle with the energy crisis to the "moral equivalent of war," a phrase coined by psychologist William James many years before and suggested to the former naval officer by Admiral Hyman Rickover, his role model and old boss in the nuclear-powered submarine fleet.

Conscious that the United States stood alone among the developed nations in being without an energy policy, Carter struggled bitterly with Congress during the next three years, attaining most of what he sought.

Essentially, the production of gasoline-inefficient automobiles was deterred by heavy penalties; electric utility companies could no longer encourage waste through their distorted rate structures, having also to join in a common effort to insulate buildings better; higher efficiency of home appliances was required; gasohol production and car pooling were promoted with tax incentives; coal production and use were stimulated together with the use of pollution control devices; and the carefully phased decontrol of natural gas prices had begun. In addition, the president led the drive for the creation of the Department of Energy, coupled the decontrol of crude oil prices with a "windfall" profits tax designed to provide $227 billion in general revenues over ten years, and pushed through a program to develop synthetic fuel as an alternate source of energy. All in all, the administration could take pride in its energy achievements, although no one could guarantee that the mile-long gasoline line had become a thing of the past.

In other areas, the president promoted civil service reform, deregulated such key industries as airlines and trucking, and assisted in the birth of the Department of Education. In the field of environment, Carter rescued the Alaskan wilderness from haphazard development by persuading Congress to set aside 104.3 million acres of that state as environmentally protected lands, regulated strip mining of coal, and created a $1.6 billion fund to finance toxic waste disposal, although this latter initiative proved difficult to implement; years later, no long-term, permanent clean up work had been started at 90 percent of the hazardous waste sites identified by the Environmental Protection Agency as the nation's most dangerous. The administration had little success, however, in placing social security financing on a firmer footing; in instituting national health insurance; or in reforming welfare, affirmative action, or busing programs. Still, more members of racial minority groups were appointed to federal positions than ever before.

THE WOMEN'S MOVEMENT IN THE 1970s

During the decade of the 1970s, the women's liberation movement, the phrase taken from the Viet Cong and Black Liberation Movement, became simply the women's movement, a more benign term to encompass the variety of women's issues and the entire spectrum of women's beliefs. It was also designed to remove the aura of radicalism from the women's movement of the 1960s. The title change, which was never formally declared (by whom?—there was no acknowledged leader), symbolized a new hope that conspicuously absent groups such as African American and Hispanic women would be recruited to the new movement.

The women's movement since congressional passage of the proposed Equal Rights Amendment (ERA), which would have prohibited discrimination based on sex by any law or action of government (federal, state, or local), had not had a single focus. There were just too many political, philosophical, and social differences among movement leaders. The multigenerational feature of the women's movement was preserved in the National Organization for Women (NOW), founded in 1966 by Betty Friedan, but in few of the other single-cause feminist groups. Topics relating to women's sexuality, for example, occupied a great deal of attention within the women's movement: rape, abortion, and battered women all became highly publicized issues. The high incidence of rape in America (and Susan Brownmiller's historical study of the subject[2]) had made rape counseling centers a major priority for many feminists. Similarly, many women lawyers worked with urban police departments to get them to treat women victims of rape respectfully and not to deprive them of their civil rights or their dignity. City councils passed legislation to deal with this issue as well.

The most polarizing issue in the feminist debate—then as now—was abortion. The contraceptive pill, first widely available in the 1960s, had provided women with a powerful tool in making their own choices about reproduction, but many women could not afford the pill or could not take it without endangering their lives. The Supreme Court then entered into the debate; indeed, the Supreme Court of the 1970s played the role of evaluator of much of the civil rights legislation that benefited women in the 1960s. Unfortunately, its decisions were not always clear. In 1973, the Supreme Court ruled, in *Roe v. Wade*, that women had the legal right to an abortion in the first trimester of a pregnancy and in the second trimester under certain medically approved circumstances. The ruling was the first action that the Court had taken in recognizing the woman's right to privacy and control over her own body. But the victory was severely restricted when, four years later, in *Beal v. Ann Doe*, the Court ruled that states were not required to use public funds to perform abortions, thereby making it very difficult for poor women to fund abortions. The ruling meant that although states could still fund welfare women's abortions, they were not compelled to do so, and in difficult economic times, many used this decision to deny women funds for that purpose.

Supreme Court rulings were even more ambiguous in the area of affirmative action programs, which were instituted to aid women and minorities obtain employment in areas where they had traditionally been discriminated against. In 1978, the Supreme Court ruled in *Bakke v. The Regents of the University of California* that Allan Bakke, a white applicant previously rejected by the University of California, be admitted to medical school but also held that "race" may be a factor in affirmative action programs at universities. In 1979, in *Weber v. Kaiser Aluminum*, the court upheld Kaiser's affirmative action program. These challenges endangered special efforts made by federal agencies, education institutions, and private sector companies to recruit women into traditionally all-white, male job categories.

While the Court had been called upon to assess the meaning and consti-tutionality of legislation passed in the 1960s, Congress showed itself less ambitious in the area of women's rights. The most notable accomplish-ments included the 1972 Education Amendments, Title IX (which made it illegal to discriminate on the basis of sex in all public undergraduate insti-tutions and in most private and public graduate and vocational schools re-ceiving federal monies), and the 1977 Equal Employment Opportunity Reorganization Act, which, among other things, amended Title VII (of the Civil Rights Act), broadened the jurisdiction of the Equal Employment Op-portunity Commission to include the Equal Pay Act and the Age Discrimi-nation Act. Otherwise, the Congress of the 1970s, consumed with Watergate and a worsening economy after that, provided little in the way of social legislation generally and women's rights legislation particularly.

The focus of the women's movement became more and more localistic and fragmented. Women's groups tended to work in their own communi-ties to provide counseling for single mothers, battered women, rape vic-tims, and pregnant teenagers. Though most of the groups supported ERA, the organization created to push for its passage found itself floundering af-ter 1975. From 1972 to 1975, thirty-five of the needed thirty-eight states rati-fied the amendment, but then the movement lost its momentum. With Carter's support, Representative Elizabeth Holtzman (Democrat, New York) persuaded Congress to take the unprecedented step of extending the deadline for ratification by two years. Then, on June 30, 1982, the proposed Equal Rights Amendment to the Constitution died, three states shy of the number required for ratification. Foes of ERA, led by Phyllis Schlafly, who contended that women were already protected by the 14th Amendment, of-fering equal protection to "all persons," and that such an amendment would cede states' rights to the federal government, had won the latest, but doubtless not the last, round.

Important gains were made, however, in increasing the education and professional entry of women into traditionally male-dominated fields. So, for the younger women coming of age in the 1970s and beyond, new profes-sions were entered; indeed, more women went to college than before—in 1979, for the first time in American history, there were more women in col-leges and universities than men. Obviously, older generations of women did not share in this good fortune, nor did many younger women of minor-ity groups, most notably African Americans and Hispanics, whose infant mortality rate was about where the white rate was twenty-five years previ-ously. But, all women's share of education was definitely on the increase at a faster pace than men's, and this factor suggested material changes in life-style and the character of the American family that would manifest them-selves in the 1980s. Yet changing such a central aspect of society was a slow and arduous process. One could not avoid the observation that most Amer-ican women still worked in sex-segregated fields: clerks and secretaries in offices and salespersons in shops represented the overwhelming majority of women workers. Though women had increased their share in professional work, they were clustered in education, social work, and librarianship. Administrators in schools, nursing schools, and social work schools were predominantly male. Women in the private sector slowly edged their way toward management positions by increasingly earning MBA degrees at major universities.

Nevertheless, the effects flowed on to the makeup of the "average" family unit. Given choice and career options, women began having fewer children, delaying having the first child until their late twenties or early thirties, utilizing birth control methods, experimenting with different lifestyles, and generally living lives very different from their mothers and grandmothers. The longevity of American women allowed for comparisons never before made: sixty-year-old grandmothers could view their daughters' and granddaughters' lives and find themselves participating in aspects of the new feminism as well. Grandmothers worked part time and continued to be the backbone of volunteer organizations while their daughters returned to school and to careers, and their granddaughters contemplated becoming nuclear physicists.

THE CARTER STYLE

The personnel, style, and emphasis on foreign policy of the Carter administration differed substantially from that of his recent predecessors. The so-called Lone Ranger approach to international affairs, as presumably practiced by Henry Kissinger, was replaced by a more open, team-player concept espoused by Secretary of State Cyrus Vance, a corporate lawyer with strong ties to the liberal eastern establishment. Other major actors included National Security Adviser Zbigniew Brzezinski, a Polish-born Columbia University professor specializing in Soviet affairs and the president's "ideas man," and U.S. Ambassador to the United Nations Andrew Young, former Georgia congressman and black civil rights activist, Carter's deputy to the Third World.

More significantly, Carter's commitment to the expansion of human rights in nations ruled by totalitarian regimes (both on the left and the right), together with his determination to press them at the expense of relations with the U.S.S.R. and Latin American nations, set him apart from the "power politics" or realpolitik orientation of the preceding Nixon and Ford administrations. "As president," recalled Carter, "I hoped and believed that the expansion of human rights might be the wave of the future throughout the world, and I wanted the United States to be on the crest of this movement." Soon cognizant of pursuing such a policy too rigidly, the administration came to define human rights on a number of levels: the right to be free from governmental violation of the integrity of the individual (torture); the right to the fulfillment of such vital needs as food, shelter, health care, and education; and the right to enjoy civil and political liberties. Despite the obvious difficulty of translating general theory into uniform bureaucratic action, and despite charges by Western European allies that the administration was naive and formulated "policy from the pulpit," the president's advocacy of human rights went a long way toward enhancing America's reputation as the leading defender in this area. The administration's reasoning that the defense of basic human rights did not per se constitute interference in the internal affairs of other nations was probably too subtle for the Soviets, whose own influential dissenters drew much inspiration and succor from Washington. In any case, the policy fully distanced the Carter White House from what had gone before.

In other areas, in Panama and China, President Carter built on the firmer foundation of the Nixon and Ford policies. By 1974, the United States and Panama had made much progress in the renegotiation of an entirely new treaty respecting the Panama Canal Zone, agreeing in principle to the abrogation of the original treaty of 1903 and its amendments—elimination of the concept of perpetuity, and the termination of U.S. jurisdiction over Panamanian territory. Carter was determined to complete the task. After prolonged and intense debate throughout 1977, two new treaties ultimately emerged. The first, the Panama Canal Treaty, gave to America the continued primary responsibility for the operation and defense of the canal until the end of 1999[3]; the second, the Treaty Concerning the Permanent Neutrality and Operation of the Panama Canal, pledged Panama to maintain the permanent neutrality of the canal, with the understanding that the United States reserved for itself the right to defend the canal from external aggression as long as it was in operation. Both treaties passed in the Senate in 1978 by identical votes of 68–32, only one more vote than the two-thirds needed for ratification. Unknown to Carter was the order of the Panamanian head of state Brigadier-General Omar Torrijos to the National Guard to attack and blow up the canal if the Senate had rejected the agreement. All in all, the administration managed to retain adequate control of the operation of the vital waterway, re-establish good relations with Panama, and stop dead in their tracks the advance into Central America of those subversive groups who were using the issue of North American colonialism to gain a foothold in the region.

With regard to the thorny issues surrounding the formal recognition of the People's Republic of China (PRC), the president, led by his national security adviser, set out to resolve the problems of how best to effect the resumption of diplomatic relations with Beijing without unduly undermining the stability of the Taiwanese regime. Convinced that Nixon and Kissinger had been overly charmed by Beijing—to the detriment of U.S. interests and allies—Carter was determined to rethink the way the United States did business with China.[4] Then, on the evening of December

15, 1978, a date deliberately chosen as immediately after the November congressional elections, Carter announced on national television that Washington and Beijing had at last agreed to recognize each other and re-establish diplomatic relations. Touted as a long-overdue "normalization" of relations, the surprise move redefined U.S. relations with both China and Taiwan. In return for placing relations with Beijing on an official footing, the administration consented to break diplomatic relations with Taiwan, withdraw its remaining 700 troops from that island, and abrogate its 1954 defense treaty with Taipei. Failure to secure a pledge from Beijing not to use force in the ultimate reabsorption of Taiwan into China provided evidence enough of the Georgian's putative naiveté for the president's growing chorus of mainly conservative critics but also reflected the diplomatic realities of trying to deal with the legacies left by Nixon and Kissinger. Among the most vocal critics of the normalization of relations with China were Ronald Reagan and George Bush, both of whom already had an eye firmly on the 1980 presidential election.[5]

In the Middle East, Carter mounted a major effort to bring about a comprehensive settlement of the problems left there since the Arab-Israeli War of 1973. The administration's three basic elements to the solution to the Middle East question included a firm commitment to complete peace in the area, the establishment of recognized borders, and a resolution of the Palestinian issue. Much to the dismay of the newly elected Israeli government (the right-wing Likud party, headed by Menachem Begin), Carter personally stressed the necessity of resolving the Palestinian question by finding a "homeland" for the Palestinians as opposed to creating a separate Palestinian state carved out of the occupied West Bank and Gaza Strip. Specifically, he believed the Palestinians, numbering roughly four million throughout the Arab world, should be given a chance to shed their status as homeless refugees and partake of a peace settlement, including the possibility of an entity of some kind perhaps in association with Jordan, the recipient of the lion's share of the original Palestine Mandate. It was also hoped to bring all the concerned parties to Geneva where the U.S.S.R., co-chairman of the short-lived Geneva Peace Conference in the Middle East, would preside over "a just and lasting settlement of the Arab-Israeli conflict."

However, little was accomplished until the spectacular diplomatic initiative of Egyptian President Anwar el-Sadat, desperate to preserve the political peace in his country. On November 19, 1977, Sadat electrified the world when he traveled to Israel to put before the Israeli Parliament his own peace proposals; one month later, Begin reciprocated with a similar unprecedented visit to Egypt, bringing his own peace proposals. In reply to Egyptian demands for an unqualified withdrawal from Arab territories occupied during the 1967 Middle East war and the establishment of a Palestinian state carved out of the West Bank of the Jordan River and Gaza Strip, Begin offered the demilitarization of the Sinai, the gradual withdrawal of occupied territory, and limited self-rule for Palestinian Arabs on the West Bank and Gaza. By the end of January 1978, Cairo and Jerusalem had become deadlocked over an agreement of principles that would shape the still-hoped-for Geneva meeting. Then, in an equally dramatic development, Carter met with Sadat and Begin from September 5–17, 1978, at the presidential mountain retreat, Camp David, in order to work out their differences. The outcome, generally considered the most important foreign policy achievement of the administration, resulted in two major agreements: a Framework for Peace in the Middle East, and a Framework for the Conclusion of a Peace Treaty between Egypt and Israel—the latter concluded in Washington on March 26, 1979. While the so-called Camp David accord finally brought peace to Egypt and Israel, the Middle East peace process continued to be bedeviled by problems such as a definition of Palestinian autonomy in the West Bank and the accelerated establishment of Israeli settlements there.[6]

In curbing the arms race, one of Carter's central promises during the campaign, the administration was spectacularly unsuccessful. Despite campaign criticism of Republican preoccupation with the Soviet Union in general and arms controls in particular, the Carter administration found itself devoting equal time and energy to these same matters. Putatively "free of that inordinate fear of communism" that had informed the policies of past administrations, and interested in pushing arms limitation talks into arms reduction talks, Carter approached the Soviets with two arms control proposals. The first was simply to ratify the Vladivostok guidelines worked out in the Ford administration, albeit with overall weapons limits about 10 percent below the previously accepted figures. The second proposal, which was regarded by some as the most revolutionary arms proposal since the beginning of the cold war, required substantial overall reductions in armaments—thereby lessening the vulnerability of either nation to a first strike by the other—imposed stringent limits on qualitative improvements in weapons; and reduced the threat from those missiles of most concern, the large Soviet intercontinental missiles and the proposed American MX (Missile Experimental). The Kremlin replied immediately and negatively to the latter proposal. Further progress was complicated by the administration's decision to develop cruise missiles, cancel the strategic B-1 bomber, and allocate funds for a "neutron" bomb, an enhanced radiation weapon, which had been developed years earlier. When arms limitation talks bore fruit again two years later, SALT II, for the first time, placed equal ceilings on the strategic arsenals of both sides, ending a previous numerical balance in favor of the U.S.S.R. while preserving American options to proceed with forces deemed necessary to maintain the strategic balance. The last-minute details were ironed out in June 1979 when Carter traveled to Vienna to meet with Soviet leader Leonid Brezhnev and to sign the agreement. They also worked out guidelines for what was to have been

SALT III. Brezhnev's admonition that "if we do not succeed, God will not forgive us," struck a particularly responsive chord in the president, who sent the treaty to the Senate for approval on June 22, 1979.

But the times were against ratification. For one thing, the Republicans decided to make a campaign issue of the treaty; for another, the Soviets, perhaps inadvertently, decided to help them. Soviet involvement in the dispute between Somalia and Ethiopia in the Horn of Africa and in the Vietnamese invasion of Cambodia led critics to question the worth of signing a treaty with the Kremlin at that or any other time. The "discovery" of a Soviet brigade in Cuba, consisting of two to three thousand troops—a deployment, incidentally, that had remained in Cuba since the Cuban missile crisis of 1962—which was seen to be contributing to tensions in the Caribbean and Central American regions, reinforced in others a tendency to link Soviet behavior with the passage of SALT II. Whatever chance there was of success for the treaty disappeared altogether after the Soviet invasion of Afghanistan in December 1979, an invasion that gave rise to fears for the security of Pakistan and Iran. In the end, Carter, who viewed invasion as a stepping stone to possible control over much of the world's oil supplies, reacted fiercely to the situation, pledging in his January 1980 State of the Union Address that "an attempt by any outside force to gain control of the Persian Gulf region will be regarded as an assault on the vital interests of the United States of America, and such an assault will be repelled by any means necessary, including military force." In addition to proclaiming the "Carter Doctrine," the President ordered a partial grain embargo of the U.S.S.R., halted exports, and led a worldwide call for a boycott of the summer Olympic Games scheduled to be held in Moscow—a tactic only partially successful, though the United States stayed home. At the same time, Carter announced that because of the Soviet invasion, further Senate consideration of SALT II was to be deferred.

Publicly admitting that he misjudged Soviet intentions, Carter proposed a record-high peacetime military budget of $196.4 billion—a 14.6 percent hike over the previous year—with a "real" increase, after inflation, of 4.6 percent. More than half of the budget was earmarked for personnel and preparedness costs, with the remainder for the new MX land missile, cruise missiles to be launched from bombers, more navy ships, improved army tanks, marine equipment positioned in the Indian Ocean theater as part of the newly created Rapid Deployment Joint Task Force, and research on laser guns for space warfare. The Task Force, renamed Intervention Force, made up of army, marine, navy, and air force units, was designed to project rapid and effective strength to any part of the world where it may be required.

THE SLIPPERY SLOPE

Such a force, however, proved unable to help the administration from its most damaging crisis. The Iranian revolution of January 1979 set in motion a series of crises that would be the virtual undoing of the Carter administration. In late 1977, in a visit to Teheran, Carter lauded the supreme leader of Iran, Shah Mohammed Reza Pahlevi, a "progressive" autocrat and ruler of the Peacock Throne, as one who had managed to maintain an oasis of stability in a region of trouble. The fact of the matter was that the shah had been propped up by strong American support for more than twenty-five years since the CIA-staged coup in 1953 that restored the young monarch to his throne after he had been deposed by Prime Minister Mohammed Mossadegh, who had nationalized Western-owned oil fields. Oil rich and preoccupied with military security, the shah was allowed unlimited access to American arms. Force-marching his people in several decades through changes that in other similar societies had taken centuries brought intense resistance across the broad spectrum of Iranian society, from the Westernized middle class to radical students to right-wing Islamic fundamentalists led by the Shi'a clergy, namely the mullahs and ayatollahs, all of whom were muffled by repressive police action. Under pressure from human rights advocates in the Carter administration, the shah made one concession after another, reining in the dreaded secret police and allowing street demonstrations to take place unopposed. From that point onward the roof fell in on the Peacock Throne as the shah fled from Teheran in January 1979, taking up refuge, consecutively, in Egypt, Morocco, the Bahamas, Mexico, and then Panama.

Meanwhile, the charismatic leader of the Islamic revolution, the Ayatollah Ruhollah Khomeini, who had been in exile in Paris, returned to Iran and soon established himself as the revolutionary leader of Islamic fundamentalists, ruthlessly pushing aside Marxists, liberals, or any other opponents to his regime. Khomeini made it clear, moreover, that he sought the return of the shah "to Iran to stand trial in public, for fifty years of crimes against the Persian people." It thus became a matter of great moment when on October 22, 1979, Carter admitted the shah to the United States ostensibly for cancer treatment; torn between the prospect of rebuilding normal relations with the new Iran and under drumbeat pressure from the shah's closest American friends, including former Secretary of State Henry Kissinger and David Rockefeller, chairman of the Chase Manhattan Bank, host to Iranian assets. Under such pressure, Carter gave in against his better judgment, admittedly based on official Iranian assurances that the American embassy in Teheran would continue to be protected.

This was not the case. On November 4, a group of Iranian militants consisting of Islamic fundamentalists and anti-American factions united mainly in their opposition to what they perceived as the bourgeois, pro-Western government of Iranian Prime Minister Bazargan, seized the American embassy and took sixty-five American hostages, demanding that the United States return the deposed shah. While thirteen hostages were released two weeks later, the plight of the remaining fifty-three hostages dominated the imagination of the national and international public until their release 444 days later. In America it became, without question, the media spectacle of the last half of the twentieth century, with daily reminders from CBS's Walter Cronkite and ABC's Ted Koppel on Nightline of how long the hostages had been held.[7]

At first, Carter moved cautiously, ordering the halt of oil imports from Iran and freezing all Iranian assets in the United States. In retrospect, it is clear that plans for freeing the hostages obsessed the administration, opening the way for bizarre diplomatic contacts of all kinds with Iran. Although supporting their president for many months, Americans gradually were overwhelmed by a sense of collective impotence, stimulated each day by some new affront to a hostage or a new insult to the flag. Even Carter's decision to call off formal campaigning for the 1980 presidential election until the crisis was solved had little effect. The administration itself was torn apart. Secretary of State Cyrus Vance believed that continued diplomatic negotiations would eventually bring the release of the hostages. National Security Adviser Zbigniew Brzezinski was persuaded it would take the use of force, and while the president vacillated between his two top advisers, the administration drifted for several months. As opinion polls turned against Carter, further drift became unacceptable inside the White House. Public impatience now ruled the day.

Finally, with all rational avenues closed—it was difficult to find any one in Iran with whom to deal—the president reached for the military option. On April 24, 1980, Carter ordered into Iran a rescue team of six C-130 transports and eight RH-53D helicopter gunships from the aircraft carrier USS Nimitz, on patrol in the Arabian Sea, to effect the hostages' release. Equipment failure in three of the helicopters had already forced the commander in chief to abort the mission, when two of the remaining aircraft collided on the ground following a refueling operation in a remote desert location in Iran, dubbed "Desert One." Early on the morning of April 25, the president candidly accepted responsibility for the failure of the mission and the loss of Secretary of State Vance, who resigned in protest of Carter's use of force. Vance was replaced by Senator Edward Muskie of Maine.

After much taunting of the administration and the death of the shah in Cairo in July, Khomeini set down in September the conditions for the hostages' release: the return of the Shah's wealth, cancellation of American claims, unfreezing of Iranian assets in American banks, and a promise not to interfere in Iran's affairs. After 444 days in captivity, the hostages were finally freed on January 20, 1981, Inauguration Day, their release coming after weeks of round-the-clock negotiations between the United States and Algeria, selected by Iran to act as intermediary in exchanges concerning the hostages. The relief to the national psyche was overwhelming and no more so than to the Georgian in the White House: "It is impossible for me to put into words how much the hostages had come to mean to me, or how moved

I was that morning to know they were coming home." Carter's greatest wish had been achieved; every single hostage had been released alive and well. But it had come with heavy price for his presidency; Carter lost the 1980 election to an opponent who promised to reverse the perceived slide in American pride and prestige.[8]

NOTES

1. Richard Reeves, *Convention* (New York : Harcourt Brace Jovanovich, 1977).

2. Susan Brownmiller, *Against Our Will: Men, Women, and Rape* (New York: Simon and Schuster, 1975).

3. At the end of 1999, when the treaty expired, U.S. troops withdrew from Panama and control was passed back to the Panamanian government.

4. James Mann, *About Face: A History of America's Curious Relationship with China: From Nixon to Clinton* (New York: Vintage, 1998), pp. 78–79.

5. Ibid., pp. 93–94.

6. Thomas Parker, *The Road to Camp David: U.S. Negotiating Strategy Towards the Arab-Israeli Conflict* (New York: P. Lang, 1989); and William B. Quandt, *Peace Process: American Diplomacy and the Arab-Israeli Conflict since 1967*, rev. ed. (Washington, D.C.: Brookings Institution, 2001).

7. Lawrence Walsh, *Firewall: The Iran-Contra Conspiracy and Cover-Up* (New York: W. W. Norton, 1997); and Warren Christopher, et al., *American Hostages in Iran: The Conduct of a Crisis* (New Haven, CT: Yale University Press, 1985).

8. See Gary Sick, *The October Surprise: America's Hostages in Iran and the Election of Ronald Reagan* (New York: Random House, 1991).

CHAPTER 12

The Conservative Revolution

After the presidencies of Richard Nixon, Gerald Ford, and Jimmy Carter, many Americans perceived their nation to be on a downward slide. Ronald Reagan came to office with the promise of putting America back on track. Hailed by many as a new "golden age," the Reagan era thrived on nostalgia for simpler times. Reacting against big government as practiced by the Democrats and also against the Carter administration's record, American voters in 1980 opted for Republican conservatism, led by an affable and personable former movie star, Ronald Reagan. His formula for pulling America out of the recession was "Reaganomics," an easily explicable policy based on the theory of supply-side economics and cutting taxes to stimulate spending. On the international front, the Soviet threat again became the focus of American foreign policy. Containment was revitalized and backed by massive increases in defense expenditure, which in turn placed increased pressure on Moscow. By the end of the aging Reagan's second term, however, the "golden age" had tarnished, the revolution had faltered, and the administration was struggling under the weight of scandal.

ELECTION OF 1980

While enrolled Republicans accounted for only 27 percent of the American electorate—with Democrats at 42 percent and Independents at 30 percent—the GOP looked forward to the 1980 presidential elections with great expectations. In addition to the growing frustration of the Iranian hostage crisis, the Carter administration faced seemingly intractable economic problems. During the heat of the preconvention primaries, in the spring of 1980, inflation had leaped to 13.3 percent—the highest level since the Great Depression of the 1930s—while unemployment reached 8 percent of the work force. Record high interest rates and a stagnant economy rounded out a fairly dismal picture. Though few had a cure, most believed they knew the cause. By July, according to the Harris poll, 78 percent of Americans disapproved of Jimmy Carter's handling of foreign affairs; an even larger number, 83 percent, disagreed with his treatment of the economy.

It was in this atmosphere of confidence, then, that the Republican National Convention gathered in Detroit in July and nominated Ronald Reagan. The second son of a hapless, alcoholic shoe salesman, Ronald Wilson Reagan was born in 1911 in Tampico, Illinois, but grew up in Dixon, Illinois, ninety-five miles west of Chicago, deep in the American heartland. Reagan's father was Irish-Catholic and his mother was Scottish-Protestant. A product of a Tom Sawyer boyhood (poor but wholesome), Reagan worked his way through Eureka College, a small Christian church college near Peoria, graduated in 1932 with a Bachelor of Arts degree in economics and sociology, and took up sports casting. A job as a radio relay announcer for the Chicago Cubs games in Des Moines, Iowa, led him to California spring training camp, where he won a Warner Brothers screen test and launched his film career.

Beginning in 1937, Reagan was cast in fifty-five motion pictures, ranging from the memorable *Brother Rat* (1938), *Knute Rockne—All American* (1940), and *Kings Row* (1942), to the forgettable *Naughty but Nice* (1939), *John Loves Mary* (1949), and *Bedtime for Bonzo* (1951). Reagan's movie career plummeted in the 1950s, and after his discharge from the Army Air Corps Special Services, he immersed himself in the politics of the Screen Actors Guild, serving six terms as its president. Shifting easily to television, Reagan hosted the popular *General Electric Theater*; as spokesman for the company, he toured plants and lectured workers on the virtues of a free market economy and evils of big government, into the bargain converting from New Deal Democrat liberal to conservative Republican.

Reagan's political career began in earnest in California with a surprise victory over incumbent Governor Pat Brown in 1966, winning re-election in 1970. During his years as governor of California, Reagan developed his own brand of free enterprise conservatism that believed in small government and limited government intervention in economic affairs. In 1968, the erstwhile movie star with the proverbial fire in the belly—a burning lust for high office—made his first bid for the Republican presidential nomination; in 1976 he came within sixty votes of wresting it from Gerald Ford; in 1980, he swept all before him. The only real suspense in Detroit was the Californian's choice of a running mate. After an apparent overture to Gerald Ford, whose price for the proposed "dream ticket" proved too high, Reagan selected George Bush, an easterner and representative of the pragmatic conservative wing of the party, as well as the last challenger in the presidential primaries. Chosen for considerations of geographical balance and experience, Bush had served as a former congressman, chief delegate to the United Nations, and director of the Central Intelligence Agency

"As your nominee," declared the 69-year-old Reagan to the party faithful in his acceptance speech, "I pledge to restore to the federal government the capacity to do the people's work without dominating their lives. I pledge to you a government that will not only work well, but wisely; its ability to act tempered by prudence, and its willingness to do good balanced by the knowledge that government is never more dangerous than when our desire to have it help us blinds us to its great power to harm us." Invoking the spirit if not the works of Franklin Roosevelt—a classic example of divorcing words from their meanings—Reagan proposed to revive the economy by cutting taxes (a 30 percent reduction in income tax over a period of three years), and by cutting federal budgets while vastly increasing defense spending, all of which was supposed to be accomplished by the application of the theory of "supply-side economics."

According to Reagan, who had borrowed the concept from economist Arthur Laffer, who, for his part, had borrowed it from nineteenth-century French economist Jean Baptiste Say, sharp tax cuts would stimulate the economy sufficiently to yield a recovery strong enough to compensate for lost revenue while wiping out the federal deficit. Put another way, supply rather than scarcity would increase demand. A simpler, less painless remedy for the recession could not be imagined. On other specific issues, the GOP party platform opposed the "windfall profits tax" and the peacetime draft; pledged to nominate a woman to the Supreme Court; supported a constitutional ban on court-ordered busing as a "last resort," as well as a similar ban on all abortions except those needed to save a woman's life; supported equal rights for women while at the same time opposing the Equal Rights Amendment; vowed to replace detailed (restrictive) environmental rules with more flexible standards; and proposed giving states and localities greater control over general programs along with federal block grants to pay for benefits.

Embattled, embittered, and more than a little apprehensive of their chances in the fall, delegates to the Democratic National Convention, meeting again in New York in August, renominated President Carter on the first ballot. Throughout the primaries, up to a victory on a key note on rules in the opening session of the convention, Carter managed to contain the challenge of Senator Edward Kennedy of Massachusetts whose own drive for the presidential nomination seemed long on promise but short on performance, with the notable exception of the senator's emotional address to the delegates attacking Ronald Reagan's "voyage into the past." The president's acceptance speech, marking the start of an uphill battle against his

Republican rival, sought to make Ronald Reagan the major issue in the campaign. "The choice—the choice between the two paths to the future—could not be more clear," the Georgian intoned. "If we succumb to a world of fantasy, we will wake up to a nightmare. But if we start with reality and fight to make our dreams a reality, all Americans will have a good life, a life of meaning and purpose as a nation strong and secure."

For others, the choice was more apparent than real. While the popular complaint was that the American people were once again being forced to choose between "the lesser of two evils," veteran columnist James Reston of the *New York Times* complained that the problem was really "the evils of two lessers." Even for some of the president's supporters, it was no more than an "unhappy choice." To journalist Garry Wills, Reagan was "so patently unmalicious as he speaks for war and divisiveness that he may, indeed, kill us with kindness . . . the wholesome hometown sort who can drop the bomb without a second thought, your basic American Harry Truman." As a former governor, generally inexperienced in foreign affairs and an outsider in Washington, Reagan could run only on the promise that he could do the job better than Carter.

Among the more significant aspects of the 1980 presidential election was the alternative candidacy of John B. Anderson, the twenty-year liberal Republican congressman from Illinois, whose ratings in the polls ranged from a high of 20 to 25 percent in the summer to less than 15 percent in September. The chief beneficiary of discontent among the electorate with the direction of the country and the weakness of the party system, Anderson advocated a fifty-cents-a-gallon gasoline tax to enforce conservation, the ratification of SALT II and ERA, and approved enforcement of civil rights laws. With little organization and even fewer funds, Anderson had to content himself with focusing on the major problems on the national agenda while the two principal candidates focused on each other, although the Democrats fretted with the prospect of a vote for Anderson amounting to a vote for Reagan.

The other major feature of an otherwise uneventful campaign was the last-minute television debate between Carter and Reagan in Cleveland in late October, under the auspices of the League of Women Voters. For ninety minutes, Reagan, appearing calm and reasonable, and Carter, appearing unusually stiff and wooden—in any case a far cry from presidential—slogged through a litany of where each stood on the issues and where his rival erred. The debate, watched by a television audience estimated to be between sixty to one hundred million viewers, was perhaps the most important event of the long campaign, while at stake were the opinions of virtually millions of yet undecided voters in key states whose electoral votes would determine the outcome. The debate, though, was inconclusive. According to one analyst, "There was no winner—only survivors. The voters lost." The *New York Times* remarked editorially, "Mr. Reagan is a better salesman but the President, though he keeps dropping the sample case on his own foot, offers better goods." What was astonishing was that Jimmy Carter, saddled with the highest inflation rate since World War II and the Iranian hostage crisis, was still in the race. With just a week to go, the president had managed to wipe out his opponent's seemingly unassailable lead of the summer. In fact, on the eve of the voting, the election appeared "too close to call." What happened next surprised everybody, including the pundits: Reagan won easily, with a margin of about 10 percent in the popular vote 43,642,639 (50.5 percent) to 35,480,948 (41 percent) and a margin of 440 electoral votes (489 to 49). Carter became the first elected incumbent president to be defeated in a bid for re-election since Herbert Hoover in 1932. Significantly, the Republicans wrested control of the Senate for the first time since 1952 (53–46, plus one independent), turning out such well-known liberals as senators George McGovern (Democrat, South Dakota) and Frank Church (Democrat, Idaho). The Reagan-led counter-revolution also substantially reduced the Democratic majority in the House of Representatives (242–192, with one independent). For the first time since World War I, the two houses were controlled by different parties, there having been a Democratic majority in both houses since 1955.

Reagan had survived the election audition and had won the role of a lifetime, and he was determined to make that role count. "Reagan had a singular mission in his administration," recalled long-time White House correspondent Helen Thomas, "to turn the country to the right."[1]

The so-called Reagan Revolution owed much to Ronald Reagan's appeal to traditional Democrats, particularly blue-collar workers, often urban Catholics from the Northeast and Middle West, and southern Protestants, often rural and religious, who had been Democrats since the Civil War. Bringing the traditional party of the country club and the boardroom into the bowling alley and the union hall, while promising to fight crime, end racial disruptions in the schools, cut taxes, shore up the family, and rationalize welfare, required the special talent of the "Great Communicator"—and a lot of money. Electing the president and winning control of the Senate cost the GOP $170 million, five times as much as the Democrats, who spent only $35 million on their own campaigns. Finally, one may attribute the Republican success in 1980 to the widely held view that the average American voter—and only 52.3 percent of the electorate eligible to vote cast their ballots, marking twenty years of a progressive decline in voter turnout—had had enough of Jimmy Carter and the period of national self-questioning with which he was readily identified.[2]

The first certified conservative to enter the White House in more than fifty years, the fortieth president promised, before all else, to "get the Government off the backs of the people." Or, as he put it in his inaugural speech, which was judged a theatrical triumph, "In this present crisis, government is not the solution to our problem; government is the problem." To make his point, only minutes after completing his speech, Reagan ordered a freeze on the hiring of civilian employees by all executive departments and agencies of the federal government—the opening act of a political conservative reformation that aimed at nothing less than the reversal of the liberal New Deal revolution of governmental activism and Democratic party dominance established by Franklin Roosevelt during the Great Depression.

Hoping to unleash the private sector whose instincts, according to Democrats, could not be trusted to produce progress and social justice without the oversight of government, Reagan called upon the creative energy of the American people to "begin an era of national renewal": "Let us renew our determination, our courage and our strength. And let us renew our faith and hope. We have every right to dream heroic dreams. Those who say that we are in a time when there are no heroes—they just don't know where to look." Few could doubt the president had the gift of the gab, so to speak, yet translating the "new beginning" into policy would be something else again.

Reagan filled his administration with, in his words, "people who don't want a job in Government. I want people who are already so successful that they would regard a Government job as a step down, not a step up." Most typical of this kind of thinking was the appointment of Donald T. Regan, chairman of the stock brokerage giant Merrill Lynch, as secretary of the treasury; Caspar V. Weinberger, vice-president and director of the Bechtel Power Corporation, as secretary of defense; and Samuel R. Pierce, Jr., an African American who was then senior partner in one of New York's major law firms, as secretary of housing and urban development. Less typical was the appointment of retired army general and former Supreme Allied Commander in Europe, Alexander M. Haig, Jr., as secretary of state; Richard V. Allen as assistant for national security affairs; and David A. Stockman, a young conservative in a hurry, as director of the Office of Management and Budget. Haig and Allen, for various reasons, were replaced, respectively, by George P. Shultz, an academic and economist also from the Bechtel Corporation, and William Clark from California, Reagan's political crony whose lack of knowledge about world leaders became the stuff of comedy. Prominent women in the cabinet included Jeanne J. Kirkpatrick, a conservative Democrat and political scientist who became U.S. ambassador to the United Nations; Elizabeth Dole (wife of Senator Robert Dole) who became secretary of health and human services; and Margaret M. Heckler, a former congresswoman from Massachusetts who became secretary of transportation.

Without doubt, the most controversial of the appointments was that of Denver attorney James G. Watt, an ultra-conservative and a born-again Christian, to head the Department of the Interior. In the face of strident opposition from environmentalists and conservationists, who had fought for years to keep undeveloped regions in something akin to their natural state,

Watt led the most sweeping and controversial drive in the nation's history to convert federal lands to commercial use and defied congressional critics in his efforts, largely successful, to open huge stretches of the Atlantic and Pacific coasts to offshore oil and gas drilling. All the while, he barred new additions to the wilderness system. In October 1983, the embattled secretary of the interior was forced from his post for referring to the Coal-Leasing Commission as "a black, a woman, two Jews and a cripple." For Watt's place, the president then proposed National Security Adviser "Bill" Clark who, according to Reagan, was "a God-fearing westerner, a fourth-generation rancher, and a person I trust."

Less controversial was the nomination in July 1981 of the first woman in the nation's history to serve on the Supreme Court, Judge Sandra O'Connor, of the Arizona Court of Appeals. Within a short time she forged a close alliance with the Supreme Court's two leading conservatives, Chief Justice Warren E. Burger and Associate Justice William H. Rehnquist, providing a needed vote on issues ranging from criminal laws to presidential immunity. For middle-level appointments in subcabinet offices, independent agencies, and independent regulatory commissions, the administration turned increasingly to people whose lack of experience in, and hostility to, federal government were deemed, it seemed, sole qualifications for their posts. Not surprisingly, a number of the inexperienced brought more than the usual embarrassment: an assistant secretary of housing and urban development was suspended after allegations that he had used his staff to prepare a personal manuscript for publication; the chief of the Veteran's Administration resigned after it was learned that he had retained his chauffeur for personal use and spent $54,000 to redecorate his office; and several appointees at the Legal Services Corporation were dismissed when it was disclosed they had arranged exorbitant consulting fees while attempting to curb legal aid for the poor.

The very tone of the Reagan presidency differed sharply from that of its predecessor. "This is a fun administration," commented a member of the Presidential Inaugural Committee, referring to the conspicuous spending habits of the more visible members of the Reagan White House. Charles Z. Wick, director of the U.S. Information Agency (who, in addition to belonging to the president's "kitchen cabinet" of California business executives, wrote and produced the film *Snow White and the Three Stooges*), suggested that economically pinched Americans of today would probably enjoy viewing the luxurious Washington way of life of the Reagan administration players, as much as Americans who suffered during the Great Depression enjoyed watching Hollywood stars in the movies. At that time, Americans down on their luck would go to the movies because "they loved those glamorous pictures showing people driving beautiful cars and women in beautiful gowns, showing that people were living the glamorous good life." More than willing to oblige her admiring public, the president's wife

Nancy, a former starlet, arrived in Washington with an inaugural wardrobe estimated at $25,000.

The president's personal philosophy of government generally reflected the views of his closest friends, mainly self-made millionaires, who had followed the American Dream to its logical conclusion and in many ways revived the attitude to government first brought to Washington by Dwight D. Eisenhower. "Running the government is like running General Motors," explained a Reagan confidant, the late, controversial Alfred S. Bloomingdale, former board chairman of the Diner's Club. "It's twice General Motors or three times General Motors—but it's General Motors." However, skeptics of the strictly business approach to the government of the United States remained unconvinced.

TOWARD THE NEW FEDERALISM

In its two years, which ended just before the closing days of 1982, the 97th Congress implemented more tax changes than any other Congress. During the first half of the two-year session, Congress under the lash of Reaganomics approved the largest tax cut in American history, an estimated $750 billion over five years. Skillfully utilizing the wave of sympathy that followed an assassination attempt on his life in late March by John W. Hinckley, an enigmatic, 25-year-old, well-off dropout (subsequently found not guilty due to insanity), the president persuaded lawmakers to pass 90 percent of his economic program, comprising "a new beginning." In addition to slashing nearly $140 billion in funding for federal programs over a three-year period, administration accomplishments included, among other things, a 25 percent cut in individual income tax over three years, with a provision to index taxes to changes in the Consumer Price Index (to begin in 1985); a lowering to 50 percent of the maximum tax on investment income; a raising of the estate exemption and gift exclusion taxes; an increase in the exemption of the windfall-profits tax on oil producers; faster depreciation of investments by businesses; and tax relief for small businesses and corporations. The object of the exercise, reversing a fifty-year tide of increased government spending, was supposed to result in a surge of productivity that would ultimately lead to increased federal revenues and lower interest rates and inflation.

As it turned out, supply-side economics had only a few of the answers. Inflation was cut from 12 percent when Reagan took office to 3.9 percent in 1982, the smallest rate of inflation since 1972 when price controls were in effect; similarly, interest rates declined from 21.5 percent to 11.5 percent at the end of 1982. That was the good news. The bad news was the severe recession that accompanied the dramatic reduction in the underlying rate of inflation. In spite of—some said because of—Reaganomics, the economy witnessed a sharp real decline of 5 percent in Gross National Product, the goods and services produced by the nation and the broadest gauge of economic health, while unemployment reached a forty-two-year high of 10.4 percent, with 11.5 million people officially unemployed; at times during 1982, a record 12 percent of the labor force was unemployed. States such as Michigan, with its heavy concentration of automobile manufacturing, reached well above that mark, while white (20.8 percent) and black (48.1 percent) teenagers were the hardest hit. Somewhere between a quarter and three million people were living in the streets of America, and one in seven Americans—nearly 32 million, or 15 percent of the population—were living below the official poverty line, the highest increase since the days of Lyndon Johnson's war on poverty.[3] Joblessness, according to a Gallup poll taken in 1982, had replaced inflation as the number one concern of Americans.

The problem was generally attributed to a federal budget that remained wildly out of balance, with projections of record deficits exceeding $150 billion a year. Put another way, the budget deficits maintained by heavy borrowing from abroad continually threatened to raise inflationary expectations and interest rates, still considered too high, choking off recovery. The president responded in two ways. First, in August 1982, he proposed further cuts of $30 billion over a three-year period from federal programs, including food stamps, Medicare, Medicaid, and pensions. Second, and swallowing hard, Reagan pushed through the same 97th Congress the largest revenue-raising package in history, suggesting that his support of a tax increase in no way represented "any reversal of policy or philosophy" but rather a mid-course correction. Designed to raise $98.3 billion in three years, the measure sought, among other things, to close off special interest loopholes, enforce stricter compliance of current tax laws, and increase excise taxes on cigarettes, telephone service, and airline tickets. Supported by a collection of strange bedfellows, ranging from liberal Democrats such as Senator Edward Kennedy (Democrat, Massachusetts) to the more conservative Robert Dole (Republican, Kansas), the bill passed by a margin of 226 to 107 in the House and 52 to 47 in the Senate. Advocates of supply-side economics, including New Right Republicans who broke ranks with the White House, were furious. "This is not the same man we elected," lamented the high priest of the theory, Arthur Laffer. "This tax package is obnoxious." In fact, supply-siders (none of whom, incidentally, had been appointed to the White House staff) were able to keep the president on course for only his first year in office; after that time, critics argued, the advisers with the readiest access to Reagan were mainly those who saw tax increases as the means to a stronger economy.

In other notable legislation, the 97th Congress made considerable headway. It passed the Voting Rights Act of 1982, extending basic provisions of the voting laws of 1965, 1970, and 1975; a Veteran's bill providing cost-of-living benefit increases averaging 11.2 percent to 2.3 million service-disabled veterans and their survivors; a five-cent-per-gallon increase in the gasoline tax to finance highway repairs and mass transit; and historic legislation setting a timetable and procedure for creating a permanent burial site for radioactive waste, which had been accumulating since World War II.

On his own, the President formally introduced proceedings to disband the Department of Energy, in line with his election promise, and freed oil companies from regulations limiting the amount of lead in petroleum products. Reagan also announced a government-farmer "crop swap" to curb grain production in an effort to relieve economic distress in the nation's farms whose net income had fallen in 1982 to the lowest point since 1933; under the program, the Department of Agriculture would "pay" farmers from stored grain surpluses to hold down their plantings, the aim being to remove 23 million acres of wheat, corn, rice, and sorghum from production.

In the mid-term elections in November, the administration lost twenty-six seats in the House of Representatives, fully twice as many as it expected to lose. At the very least, the Democrats who had momentarily recaptured the image as the party best able to ensure the nation's prosperity (according to the Gallup poll), threatened the ideological majority Reagan had forged to push through so many of his economic proposals during the first half of his term in the White House. The Republicans, however, managed to retain their eight-seat majority in the Senate, each side having made two gains there. Reagan, the first GOP president since Eisenhower to work with a Senate controlled by members of his own party, could once again look forward to the cooperation of the upper chamber. Republican losses arose largely from popular dissatisfaction with Reaganomics, with its association, deserved or not, of unconcern for the needy. The fact that in 1982 Republicans were most popular with white males earning more than $40,000 a year was not lost even on Republicans concerned with widening the party's grass roots appeal.

The president's earlier political magic faded, however, as the 98th Congress repeatedly defied Reagan on economic and military issues. A proposed overhaul of the immigration laws languished in a House-Senate conference, a major civil rights bill overwhelmingly approved by the House was killed in the Senate, and a banking deregulation bill that the Senate approved died in a House committee. Unlike its predecessor, which gave the president the spending, tax, and military bills he sought, the 98th Congress balked at further cuts on social spending and reduced by more than half the increase he sought for the military. It approved $249 billion for fiscal year 1984, rejecting along the way nerve gas weapons but approving funds for MX missiles, B-1 long-range bombers, and testing of anti-submarine weapons. Congress finally approved the Caribbean Basin initiative providing trade and tax benefits to poorer Caribbean nations. In the case of

Nicaragua, Congress approved $24 million in covert aid to rebels, while in El Salvador, it made additional funds contingent on land reforms and improvements in the criminal justice system.

The 98th Congress worked well in other areas. Through a bipartisan commission appointed by the president, a revision of the social security system was finally approved, requiring new federal employees and employees of nonprofit organizations to join the system, new payroll tax increases, a tax on benefits paid to more affluent retired persons, and a rise in the retirement age by two years (to sixty-seven years old by the year 2027). In the sensitive area of abortion, Congress expanded its ban on using federal funds for abortions by prohibiting such use by federal employees' health plans. Congress also approved the program initiated by the president to give farmers government-owned commodities in return for curtailed production of surplus crops—the swap-crop plan. Another bill for the first time would pay dairy farmers for reducing their milk production. Transcending partisanship, the majority of congressional representatives approved legislation for a federal holiday on the birthday of the Reverend Dr. Martin Luther King, Jr., and Congress also repealed the 10 percent withholding tax on interest and dividends scheduled to have taken effect on July 1.

Reagan held that the single greatest failure of the 98th Congress was its inability to pass a responsible budget to help bring down deficits. "By responsible," he said, "I do not mean a budget that reduces spending to match revenues." Lawmakers, on the other hand, replied that the one major reason for the deficit was the president's adamant insistence on higher military spending and lower taxes. Congress was reluctant to close the gap until the administration took the lead and provided political cover for unpopular decisions that would eventually be required.

During the 1980 presidential campaign, Reagan indicated that he wished to move beyond President Nixon's concept of revenue sharing, which accounted for the distribution of $64.9 billion in federal tax revenue to state and local governments since 1972, to a "new federalism," an idea he explained in his January 1982 State of the Union Address. "Basically," he said, "I want to change the course we've been on in which Washington was seen as the answer to all the problems. I want to restore the balance between the different levels of government that has been so distorted in recent decades." In practice it meant that the federal government would assume full responsibility for medical aid to the poor, and the states, in turn, would assume responsibility for the food stamp program and aid to families with dependent children—the principal programs of cash assistance to the poor. In addition, more than forty education, transportation, and social service programs would be taken over by the states, along with some money to pay for them. The plan's simplicity, argued critics, masked its very radicalism, for it sought nothing less than to reverse the powerful centralizing trend in

American public life that dates from the beginning of the century. Under the administration's proposal, a federal trust fund would help finance the programs taken over by the states from 1984 through 1991; after that, the fund would disappear, and the states could raise or lower taxes as they saw fit.

The states, already financially strapped, entertained serious doubts about the economic viability of the proposal. As opposition mounted, the White House revised the plan, reducing the list of programs transferred while retaining the food stamp program. By the end of 1982, this particular plan was dead, according to one influential state governor, the result of it being less a sorting out of programs among federal and state governments, but rather a shift to states, cities, and counties of problems that were beyond their ability to handle. A much watered-down version of the president's "new federalism" plan, turning over even fewer programs to the states while promising them a stable level of funding for five years, was submitted to Congress with small hope of passage.

For many, Reagan demonstrated a regrettable predisposition to turning back the clock on civil rights. Buttressed by arguments of free-market economists with good White House connections and generally antipathetical to federal activism, Reagan entered office adamantly opposed to busing and affirmative action. As a matter of philosophy, if not necessarily of action, the administration had reversed President Carter's support of mandatory busing as a means of desegregating the nation's school systems, calling it ineffective, and instead promoting voluntary transfers. The president, by all accounts a decent and honest man without an apparent racist bone in his body, adhered to the belief that court-ordered busing could be a "violation of the rights of the community," adding that the people who were supposed to benefit most, the black community, were doing much of the protesting. As objectionable as many liberals found such arguments, Reagan was not alone in making them. Forced busing, as a permanent solution to the problem of how to integrate society, was perceived by some as discriminatory to blacks because it was mainly the minority student who was being asked to quit his neighborhood early each morning often with questionable results. "As a black person and as an American," commented a leading exponent of black conservative views, economist Walter F. William, "I'm for high-quality education. But it is not clear to me that to get (it), black people have to go out and capture a white kid for their children to sit beside." Others, equally representative of the nation's 26.5 million blacks—11.7 percent of a total population of 226.5 million—regarded such attitudes as born of frustration and regretted that the administration had elected to raise an issue that was thought settled by the previous three decades. Experience, according to the Reagan Justice Department, had instead shown court-ordered busing to be a failed experiment.

The White House was no less relenting in the matter of job quotas; Reagan made it clear that he would no longer insist that employers found guilty of sexual or racial discrimination abide by quotas in their future job-hiring promises. Specifically, noted the chief of the Justice Department's civil rights division, the administration would "no longer insist upon or in any respect support the use of quotas or any other numerical or statistical formulas designed to provide non-victims of discrimination preferential treatment based on race, sex, national origin or religion." In the future, remedy would only be available to individual members of minority groups who could demonstrate that they had personally been the victims of discrimination. Race-conscious or sex-conscious preferences had, according to this logic, proved historically divisive, well beyond the remedy that was necessary to redress the injured party. Blacks and their liberal allies, looking through the tangle of interpretations that had been placed between them and the customary statutory redress they had come to count upon, found cold comfort in this Republican administration, affording Reagan little political support which he repaid with only a handful of federal appointments.[4]

THE NEW COLD WAR

Not unlike his Republican predecessor in the Oval Office, Richard Nixon, President Ronald Reagan made the management of the Soviet-American relationship the centerpiece of his administration's foreign policy; unlike Nixon, however, he had no faith in the ability of the Kremlin to behave properly. How does one conduct business, the president reasoned publicly, with leaders who reserve "unto themselves the right to commit any crime, to lie, to cheat," all in the name of world revolution? How does one deal with leaders who "don't subscribe to our idea of morality, who don't believe in an afterlife, who don't believe in God or a religion?"

Perceiving the Soviet Union as dangerous, expansionary, and antagonistic to American interests everywhere, the administration, led by Secretary of Defense Caspar Weinberger and Secretary of State Alexander Haig, argued that the only way to deal with the threat was to maintain a much stronger military establishment, beginning with a restoration of the margin of nuclear superiority or safety purportedly lost by Jimmy Carter. To meet what Haig identified as "the most complete reversal of global power relationships ever seen in a period of relative peace," the administration further urged a broad-based, unilateral defense buildup, a strengthening of allied ties and a return to a policy of containing Soviet power and influence—in short, to revitalizing the policy of containment, though just what this meant was never quite clear. As for pursuing the expansion of human rights, the Reagan White House served notice that it had no intention of preaching American ideals to other friendly countries, especially those in Central and Latin America. The world was judged too dangerous a place to do otherwise.

In 1981, the administration committed a staggering $1.5 trillion over the next five years to the largest peacetime military buildup in the nation's history, paying special attention to the modernization of the strategic nuclear forces in order to be in a position of strength at the negotiating table. Specifically, the White House increased defense spending from 1981 to 1982 by 20 percent, to $211 billion, and from 1982 to 1983 by 14 percent, to $241 billion; the requests for 1984 and 1985 were on the order of $245 billion and $277 billion, respectively.

Reagan swept into office, then, committed to the notion of restoring America's presumed margin of nuclear safety (actually, superiority), in the process closing the nation's "window of vulnerability." The president's supporters remained persuaded beyond a shadow of a doubt that the Soviet Union constituted a direct threat of military action of unprecedented proportions. Reagan proceeded apace with the B-1 bomber, the MX missile, and the neutron bomb, an enhanced radiation weapon that left living matter relatively unscathed—the quintessential anti-personnel weapon. This was all too much for the antinuclear movement, which was growing in stature and confidence. It was only a matter of time before thinking the unthinkable—thinking aloud about waging and winning a limited, controlled nuclear war and nuclear "warning shots"—before even Reagan would have to react. And react he did. In November 1981, Reagan announced that the United States would unilaterally reduce its intermediate-range nuclear arms in Europe and promised deeper cuts if the Soviet Union reciprocated.

Two weeks after denouncing the Soviet Union as the "evil empire" and "the focus of evil in the modern world," on March 23, 1983, Reagan announced his intention to pursue an ambitious space-based anti-missile defense system, known officially as the Strategic Defense Initiative (SDI), but more popularly as "Star Wars" after the blockbuster science-fiction movie. Following largely the ideas of the so-called Father of the H-Bomb, scientist Edward Teller, it was designed to provide an "impenetrable shield" to cope with upwards of 5,000 incoming missiles. By implementing this program, Reagan abandoned traditional deterrence theory based on mutual vulnerability and moved instead toward the notion that nuclear war might, in fact, be winnable. Detractors charged that by reducing vulnerability Reagan was inviting a new arms race of immense proportions, since the very nature of SDI meant that it could only be breached by a deluge of missiles. Countering these criticisms, Reagan maintained that SDI was designed to render nuclear weapons obsolete, not to escalate the arms race. Ironically, with the collapse of the Soviet Union at the beginning of the next decade, many claimed that SDI had been a decisive factor in America's "victory" precisely because it did lead to an escalation of the arms race that the Soviet Union could simply not afford. In short, they claimed American capitalism outspent Soviet communism. Yet from the beginning, the program was hampered by more than philosophical qualms. There was vigorous debate amongst scientists and other defense experts on whether such an idea was even possible. Many argued that the idea was a pipe-dream that would waste enormous amounts of resources and furthermore, that in violating the 1972 ABM Treaty, it would lead to precisely the scenario the ABM Treaty was designed to avoid. Yet the serious doubts voiced by many about the project's feasibility were drowned out, and Reagan committed his government to develop the scheme.

In other crisis areas overseas—Afghanistan, Poland, and Lebanon—the administration responded with considerable restraint. While stressing the desirability of an acceptable political solution to the withdrawal of Soviet occupation forces in Afghanistan, the president, true to his election promise, lifted the partial grain embargo on the U.S.S.R. in April 1981. During the campaign, Reagan had called the embargo ineffective and an unfair burden on the American farmer. For Poland where the independent trade union movement, Solidarity, was crushed by martial law in December 1981, the administration imposed various economic sanctions, including the suspension of special trade status for Warsaw, in retaliation for continued repression by that country's Soviet-backed military regime. The White House, together with the North Atlantic Treaty Organization (NATO) allies, warned the Soviet Union in particular that intervention in Poland would fundamentally alter the entire international situation and effectively destroy prospects of workable East-West relations. Persuaded that the Kremlin was deliberately using the crisis to sow dissension within the West, Reagan, encouraged by Secretary Haig, imposed additional economic sanctions against the Soviet Union, principally by reducing exports of advanced technology, to prompt Moscow to back down on Poland. None of these measures, including a failed, heavy-handed effort to curb European participation on the Siberian gas export pipeline, had much apparent success. Finally, in the Middle East, the administration, with the dogged determination of American Ambassador Philip Habib, ended the hostilities that had culminated in the summer of 1982 when Israelis invaded southern Lebanon and Beirut to eliminate the threat posed by large numbers of Palestinian Liberation Organization (PLO) fighters. Shortly afterward, Habib negotiated the evacuation of the PLO and the Syrians from West Beirut; the Syrians had been deeply involved in the Lebanese civil war since 1976. In August and again in October, following the assassination of the newly elected Lebanese president and the massacre of Palestinian civilians in their refugee camps, Reagan sent American troops to join a multinational force to help the new government there begin efforts to restore its authority throughout the war-torn country. On the successful evacuation from Beirut, the president urged what he called a "fresh start" in Middle East peace negotiations, building on the Camp David accords worked out in the Carter presidency. Specifically, he outlined a policy of self-government by the Palestinians of the West Bank and Gaza in association with the state of Jordan; a settlement freeze by Israel; guarantees of the security of Israel; and an undivided Jerusalem, with its final status to be decided through negotiation. Reagan, together with new Secretary of State George Shultz, who had replaced Haig at the height of the Israeli invasion, received little support for their efforts and found themselves thwarted by ancient animosities. Both Israel and the PLO, each for its own reasons, rejected the proposal. Nevertheless, Reagan regarded the Middle East initiative as "probably the greatest" foreign policy accomplishment of his administration. Yet within a year, American policy in the region collapsed. In October 1983, suicide terrorists from Islamic extremist group Hezbollah (Party of God), driving bomb-laden trucks, blew up a U.S. Marine headquarters building in Beirut, resulting in the deaths of 241 Americans; after four months of domestic pressure and in view of the worsening situation in the Lebanese capital, the White House ordered the redeployment of marines from Beirut to warships offshore. Nevertheless, Hezbollah continued its terrorist activities against the West by periodically taking Americans hostage and demanding the release of Islamic activists from Israeli jails.

From the first days of the administration, Secretary of State Haig was uneasy about Central America, particularly El Salvador, the smallest and most densely populated country in the region. Relentlessly, though with scanty proof, Haig mounted a major campaign around the world to draw attention to what he regarded as a "textbook case" of indirect armed aggression directed by Communist powers through Cuba. In this instance, a leftist armed rebellion of about 7,000 guerillas in El Salvador was being supplied by way of Nicaragua, the largest and most sparsely populated country in Central America, under the control of the Marxist-dominated Sandinistas, who in 1979 overthrew the hated right-wing dynasty established by Anastasio Somoza in 1936. The administration had no doubt that Nicaragua was the main support and command base for the Salvadoran guerillas, as well as leftist extremists in Guatemala, Honduras, and Costa Rica; as Reagan later put it, Moscow had another satellite in Latin America.

The situation in El Salvador, according to Haig, presented a strikingly familiar case of Soviet, Cuban, and other Communist military involvement in a politically troubled Third World country. By providing arms, training, and direction to a local insurgency and by supporting it with a global propaganda campaign, the Communists sought to intensify and widen the conflict, deceiving much of the world about the true nature of the revolution. The Communist objective, the former NATO general continued, was to bring about—at little cost to themselves—the overthrow of the established government and the imposition of a regime in defiance of the will of the Salvadoran people. Time was of the essence. Haig, testifying before the House Foreign Affairs Committee in mid-March 1981, asserted that El Salvador was the latest on "a priority target list—a hit list, if you will—for the ultimate [Soviet] takeover of Central America." The stage having thus been set, Haig advocated exerting maximum political, economic, and military pressure in 1981 to treat the problem at its source—Cuba—in effect "to force the issue early" in El Salvador, even if it brought a Soviet response. Haig's memoirs make it clear that his call for action found no support from the highest counselors in the White House who feared "another Vietnam" that in turn would sap public support for the administration's domestic programs. Characteristically, Haig argued that the potential strategic gain of securing Central America far outweighed the risks of involving the Soviet Union; isolated on this and other issues, the general in the State Department found himself more and more outside the administration's thinking, as the White House opted for modest aid to El Salvador and covert action in the region.

Reagan, moving along the path of least resistance, nonetheless portrayed Soviet proxies on the march in Central America—where only U.S. resolve could hold the apocalyptic line against a row of those proverbial falling dominoes. Or, as the president put it, "If we cannot defend ourselves there, we cannot expect to prevail elsewhere. Our credibility would collapse, our alliances would crumble and the safety of our homeland would be put in jeopardy." The trouble with El Salvador was that the widespread terrorism practiced by extremists of both the left and the right appeared indistinguishable to the majority of Americans, haunted by the Vietnam experience, who feared greater involvement in the region where 50,000 people had already been killed in the conflict. Despite assurances from diplomats such as Deane Hinton, then U.S. ambassador to El Salvador—"This ain't Vietnam, and it sure as hell better not end the way Vietnam ended"—most Americans shied away from a larger commitment than the fifty-five advisers the president had sent there.

Midway through its first term, the administration appeared amenable to pragmatism, while responding to the region's economic crises—really, sheer underdevelopment—with the Caribbean Basin Initiative, a modest program consisting of integrated, mutually reinforcing measures in the fields of trade, investment, and financial assistance. Although the initiative was defeated by the 97th Congress, it was finally passed by the 98th Congress. On the military front, the White House adopted a lower profile in El Salvador, at the same time covertly arming former followers of Somoza (Somocistas) resident in Honduras; from there the Somocistas, or Contras, raided across the border into Nicaragua from bases in Honduras and Costa Rica to put heat on the Sandinista regime and attempt to end its support of the Salvadorean rebels. The net result of Washington's activity in the area ironically increased local support for the Sandinistas, inflamed the Nicaraguan-Honduran war, and produced growing hostility in Congress to administration-sponsored aid programs in the region.

In the course of asking for $600 million for maintaining or stepping up support for countries such as El Salvador, the president warned a special joint session of Congress in April 1983 that time was fast running out. Enunciating the so-called Reagan Doctrine for Central America, the president pledged to support "democracy, reform, and human freedom" by using assistance, persuasion, and legitimate leverage to advance "humane democratic systems" in which elections were "open to all, fair and safe." "What I am asking for," the chief executive emphasized in a manner consciously reminiscent of President Truman's plea to Congress in 1947 for aid to Greece and Turkey, "is prompt Congressional approval for the full reprogramming of funds for key economic and security programs so that the people of Central America can hold the line against externally supported aggression." Some thought the president's remarks were a turning point; others were less certain.

No doubt discouraged by the many difficulties inherent in winning congressional approval for his various economic and diplomatic efforts in Central America and perhaps with the 1984 presidential election in mind, the president moved increasingly—or at last visibly—in the direction of a military solution to what he called "the first real Communist aggression on the American mainland"—he sent in the marines. In a show of military force designed to force the left-wing Sandinistas of Managua to leave their neighbors alone, the commander in chief dispatched three U.S. Navy battle groups to the region, flanking both coasts of Central America; for good measure, as many as four thousand American combat troops were sent to join Honduran forces for the first time in extensive, months–long maneuvers—a "military shield" extending protection to Central American countries friendly to Washington. Reagan also planned to send army engineers and air force transport to Honduras. The plan soon backfired. Congressional opponents of the White House attacked both the scale and nature of the military exercise. President Miguel de la Madrid of Mexico, a member of the so-called Contadora Group of Latin American leaders who combined together in early 1983 to find a political framework for a negotiated peace in Central America, appealed to Reagan.

Simultaneously with his decision to show the flag, Reagan established an executive commission to advise him on Central American policy. The commission was first proposed in the spring of 1983 by members of Congress from both parties. The National Bipartisan Commission on Central America emerged in July under the leadership of the controversial former secretary of state, Henry Kissinger, who was charged with the tasks of fashioning long-term policy and building short-term support. Clearly, the president had to do something to quiet the growing chorus of critics, particularly House Democrats, who in June had threatened to end covert collaboration with the Contras in Nicaragua, the best-known dirty little secret in Washington. In January 1984, Reagan received the commission's report, which recommended more of everything: more economic aid, more military aid, and greater determination to confront the fact of a Marxist regime in Managua and the threat of one in El Salvador. Moreover, the commission continued, "the use of Nicaragua as a base for Soviet and Cuban efforts to penetrate the rest of the Central American isthmus, with El Salvador the target of first opportunity, gives the conflict there a strategic dimension." For, "the direct involvement of aggressive external forces makes it a challenge to the system of hemispheric security, and quite specifically, to the security interests of the United States. This is the challenge to which the United States must respond." Accordingly, the commissioners concluded, "there might be an argument for doing nothing to help the government of El Salvador. There might be an argument for doing a great deal more. There is, however, no logical argument for giving some aid but not enough."

As the 1984 presidential election campaign approached, the administration stepped up its covert war against Nicaragua. The reaction was at once swift and ironic as news of the CIA mining of Nicaraguan ports triggered a heightened public awareness of the degree of direct U.S. involvement in the secret war against Managua. The influential vice chairman of the Senate Intelligence Committee, Senator Daniel Moynihan (Democrat, New York), resigned in protest at the failure of the CIA to inform Congress of its involvement in mining Nicaraguan ports. The powerful chairman of the Intelligence Committee, Arizona conservative Senator Barry Goldwater, having already played the fool on the floor of the Senate when he had authoritatively denied the president had approved any mine laying, protested to CIA director William Casey with simple clarity: "I am pissed off." In the aftermath, the GOP-controlled Senate passed a nonbinding resolution urging that no more U.S. funds be spent to mine Nicaraguan ports—in reality, an act of war. The House of Representatives followed suit, and then Congress adjourned for Easter without voting a dime for the Contras. By July, the issue of additional aid for the Contras—the 15,000 CIA-backed Nicaraguan antileftist rebels—was all but "dead." In the process, Congress had begun the inevitable task of weighing "the lessons of Vietnam" against the prospect of the consequences of "who lost El Salvador?"

Meanwhile, Reagan set out to eliminate a perceived Soviet threat from another part of the Caribbean. On October 25, 1983, two days after the terrorist attack on U.S. Marine headquarters in Beirut, the president ordered 1,900 paratroopers to invade the Caribbean Island of Grenada, the once sleepy tourist haven and the smallest independent nation in the Western hemisphere, barely eighty miles off Venezuela, in order to forestall the installation of a militant pro-Marxist regime with close ties to Havana and Moscow. Triggered by the disintegration of the government of Grenada, following the murder of the prime minister and members of his cabinet, as well as concern to ensure the safety of one thousand Americans (most of them medical students trapped on the island), the invasion marked the first time since the end of the Vietnam War that the United States had committed its troops to a combat attack. By December, all American combat troops had withdrawn, their mission accomplished. "We got there just in time," explained the president to a sympathetic nation, "Grenada, we were told, was a friendly island paradise for tourists. It wasn't. It was a Soviet-Cuban colony, being readied as a major military bastion to export terror and undermine democracy." American casualties totaled 18 killed in action and 116 wounded. Despite the condemnation of the U.N. General Assembly and several Latin American nations who feared further U.S. intervention in the region, Reagan's move against the Communist revolutionaries brought him wide support at home.

REPUBLICAN LANDSLIDE

The 1984 presidential election was played out against the background of a resurgent American economy for which the president and the GOP readily took credit. After the worst recession since the 1930s, the country's GNP rose by nearly 5 percent in 1983 and at an annual rate of 8.6 percent in the first half of 1984. Some 6.5 million jobs had been created between the end of 1982 and November 1984. At 7.4 percent, the unemployment rate was slightly below that inherited by Reagan when he assumed office in 1981, thus depriving the Democrats of the claim that the jobless rate had not been brought down below the level of the Carter administration. Equally significant, economic expansion under the Reagan White House had proved disinflationary: prices rose at an annual rate of only 3.2 percent in 1983, down from 6.1 percent in 1982 and 13.3 percent in 1980. High interest rates at home and a towering budget deficit failed to detract from the generally favorable image the public had of the administration. However one assessed the figures, the identification of the president with the return to "good times" made the incumbent an odds-on favorite to retain the White House.

The Democratic National Convention, meeting in San Francisco in July, nominated former Vice President Walter ("Fritz") Mondale on the first ballot, defeating a late bid by Senator Gary Hart of Colorado. The 56-year-old liberal from Minnesota was the son of a Methodist minister whose Norwegian ancestry dated back to the Vikings. A very private person, the former protégé of Hubert Humphrey had the unenviable task of reuniting the Democratic Party in the wake of one of the most turbulent periods in the history of American politics. He was rejected by 61 percent of the voters in the Democratic primaries while turning back the dual challenge of Senator Hart and black leader Reverend Jesse Jackson of Chicago. Hart, a 44-year-old Denver lawyer, set off a chain reaction that transformed the campaign with an electrifying upset primary victory in New Hampshire, while Jackson, a 42-year-old civil rights activist and protest candidate, drew black voters away from Mondale.

In a dramatic gesture a week before the convention, Mondale named Representative Geraldine Ferraro of New York—the first woman candidate on a presidential ticket—as his running mate. A lawyer, mother, and wife of a millionaire property developer, the three-term Queens congresswoman brought a new dimension to the national ticket, prompting predictions that her selection could well make the presidential contest a very close race. Determined in appearance and smooth in delivery, the Italian-American Ferraro complemented the less telegenic Mondale whose own campaign had been based on traditional Democratic Party ties and machine politics.

Meanwhile, fully convinced that the president could not lose the November election, the Republicans gathered in Dallas in August and nominated Reagan and Bush unopposed. Reagan, who never once mentioned Mondale by name, observed that the choice in November was not just between two parties, but between two visions of the future: "their government of pessimism, fear and limits; ours of hope, confidence and growth." In adopting its most right-wing policy platform in 130 years, the GOP offered the American people a sharp choice.

The Republican platform, approved by acclaim in Dallas, flatly opposed tax increases to reduce the nation's budget deficit (running at about $175 billion), advocating instead further tax cuts by increasing individual deductions and repealing the wind-fall profits tax on oil companies. The Democratic platform, written largely by the people who had engineered Mondale's nomination victory, saw tax increases as an integral part of any deficit solution; specifically, it sought a 15 percent minimum corporate tax, rescission of some of Reagan's 1981 tax cuts, less defense spending, and development of a program to cut health care costs. In the area of arms control and foreign policy, the GOP advocated continued production of all current nuclear weapons and major defense systems, including SDI. For their part, the Democrats sought a mutual, verifiable nuclear weapons freeze with the Kremlin and cancellation of the MX missile and B-1 bomber. In Central America, the Republicans wanted to maintain the status quo while the Democrats favored fewer military exercises in the region, aid to El Salvador contingent upon improvement of human rights there, and termination of funds for the guerillas fighting the Nicaraguan government. Closer to home, the GOP continued to abhor the Equal Rights Amendment while expressing disfavor with abortion; on its side, the Democratic Party urged passage of the ERA and strengthening programs for minorities and the poor. The lines were clearly drawn.

Reagan rarely looked anything but a winner. A television joke about bombing the Soviet Union during a voice-level test raised a murmur but his steamroller only really slowed after the first presidential debate. In his first encounter with Mondale, which was devoted to domestic matters and screened on nationwide television, the president badly faltered and showed signs of his age (at seventy-three years old, he was the oldest man ever to serve in that office). Yet by the second debate, devoted to foreign affairs, the more relaxed and rehearsed incumbent had it all together and was well prepared to fend off his challenger. Furthermore, Mondale could not shake off the stigma of being Carter's vice president, and his task was made all the more difficult when he tried to introduce candor to the campaign. The plan backfired and provided easy fodder for the Republican Party's political machine. A week before voting day, the polls gave Mondale the lead in only six out of fifty states; on the day itself, the roof fell in on the Minnesotan.

In the largest victory in American political history, the president defeated his opponent by a popular vote of 54,166,829 (58.5 percent) to 37,449,813 (40.4 percent) and an electoral count of 525 to 13, sweeping everything except the District of Columbia and Minnesota. Only one president before Reagan—Richard Nixon in 1972—ever carried forty-nine states; only Lyndon Johnson in 1964 won more of the popular vote. Reagan swept not only every region of the country but every age group and nearly every demographic voting bloc, including a sizeable share of union households, Catholics, and southern whites, though he lost out among blacks and Jews. Even Geraldine Ferraro appeared to have hurt Mondale at the polls, with 54 percent of female voters pulling the lever for Reagan, no doubt unimpressed with the congresswoman's explanation of her family's financial affairs borne out by the post-election indictment of her husband. For all this, however, the president was unable to translate his historic victory into significantly increasing his party's margin in the Senate, where the Republicans suffered a net loss of two seats (53–47). The Democrats easily kept control of the House of Representatives (266–167), which they had now held for most of the past fifty years.

Still, none could discount the overwhelming public endorsement of Reagan's genial, patriotic leadership and his policies of peace-through-strength abroad and free enterprise at home. Acknowledging victory, the president observed: "America's best days lie ahead. You ain't seen nothin' yet." While liberals visibly shuddered at the time, within a few years, when the administration seemed stuck on a downward spiral, Reagan's bold prophesy offered reason for irony.

During an inauguration ceremony marred by inclement weather, Reagan placed strong emphasis on economic growth and on restoring America's pride. Having campaigned on the slogan "America is Back," he now called on Americans to consolidate the gains of the previous four years. "Let history say of us," he urged, "'these were the golden years—when the American Revolution was reborn, when freedom gained new life, when America reached for her best.'" Believing his economic program to be vindicated by twenty-five straight months of economic growth, he pledged to further cut taxes and reduce the size of government, so as to "unleash the drive and entrepreneurial genius that are the core of human progress."

Despite the heady rhetoric, the luster of Reagan's presidency was showing signs of dimming as his administration was rocked by ongoing scandals. Although Reagan had deliberately cultivated historical parallels with the presidency of Calvin Coolidge, the perpetual air of scandal led many Americans to draw their own parallels with the considerably less impressive administration of Warren G. Harding. During the campaign, Reagan had made his administration's achievements a major campaign issue, proudly pointing to his record of reduced taxes and increased standard of living. Per capita incomes were increasing and the Gross National Product was multiplying. What he did not see, and what became more obvious during Reagan's second term, was that the national debt was soaring. In the 1980 election, Reagan had attacked Carter for his $74 billion deficit. By 1986, the deficit was $221 billion and the national debt over $2.2 trillion. However, for the most part, Americans reveled in the reduced tax burden in their everyday lives, and the president continued to receive strong public approval for his economic management. In 1986, he introduced the Tax Reform Act, which further lowered personal income taxes while exempting a large number of low-income earners, almost six million in all, from personal income tax altogether. The act also went a long way toward fulfilling one of Reagan's long-term promises of simplifying the taxation system.

THE END OF THE COLD WAR

Unquestionably, one of Reagan's greatest triumphs was his strong working relationship with the new chairman of the Soviet Communist Party, Mikhail Gorbachev. Gorbachev had come to power in March 1985 promising reform and appeared to the West to be potentially a reasonable and imaginative leader, at least in comparison with his aging, hard-line predecessors. Two ideas in particular caught the West's attention. *Glasnost* (openness) was aimed at opening up long-suppressed elements of Soviet society by introducing free speech and limited political freedom. *Perestroika* (economic restructuring) was intended to stimulate the static Soviet economy by adopting selected free-market practices of the capitalist West. Knowing that Gorbachev needed to reduce the disproportionate spending on defense in order to unburden the ailing Soviet economy, Reagan tamed his anti-Communist rhetoric to capitalize on Gorbachev's spirit of reform and policy of *perestroika* to advance the other half of his administration's nuclear policy—namely, arms control. On the one hand, the administration was overseeing a fully-fledged war scare that was manifesting itself in an arms race. By developing SDI and making enormous and very public investments into new defense technology, the United States was contributing in large measure to driving this contest to ever more dangerous intensity. On the other hand, it was also pursuing significant arms control measures. Despite being a staunch critic of SALT during the 1980 campaign—he called the treaty fatally flawed because it left virtually untouched the Soviets' impressive ability to mount an effective first strike on U.S. nuclear forces—Reagan agreed to abide by the treaty so long as Moscow did. However, he soon advanced his own nuclear arms control agenda by issuing a call on May 9, 1982, on the occasion of a commencement address at his alma mater, Eureka College in Illinois, for what he termed Strategic Arms Reduction Talks (START). He proposed in the first phase a one-third cut in strategic warheads, a ceiling of no more than one-half of the remaining strategic warheads to be placed on land-based missiles, and a reduction of the total number of ballistic missiles to an equal level of about one-half the current U.S. level. Thus, by shifting the emphasis from limitation to reduction, Reagan pushed arms control in the direction in which it had been going fitfully for some years. In June 1983, Reagan slightly revised the START offer, making the minimum necessary changes in his negotiating approach to capture a congressional majority for the limited production of the MX missile but not enough to reach a breakthrough with the Soviets in Geneva. In order to make room for a new, small, compromise missile with a single warhead—the Midgetman—Reagan raised the proposed ceiling of long-range ballistic missiles on each side from 850 to 1,200. The Kremlin's counterproposal called for a ceiling of 1,800 missiles and long-range bombers for each side, of which 1,450 would be missiles. The "gap" was thus closed to 250. Now, with someone in the Kremlin with whom Reagan felt he could deal, he pursued arms control with greater enthusiasm. A series of proposals and counter-proposals reached a crescendo in November 1985, when Reagan and Gorbachev agreed in principle on making an ambitious 50 percent reduction in strategic warheads. A treaty at this time remained impossible, however, due to a deadlock over the American SDI program.

SDI soon proved to be an even bigger stumbling block. The Reykjavik Summit, convened on short notice in October 1986, rapidly brought the growing euphoria back to earth. It initially appeared as though there might be a major breakthrough when Reagan proposed that all ballistic missiles be eliminated within ten years, and in so doing winning what appeared to be a fail-safe propaganda victory. However, Gorbachev's response upstaged Reagan by counter-proposing the elimination of all nuclear weapons within ten years. But he attached to this proposal a requirement that the United States abandon its development program for SDI—a condition clearly unacceptable to the hawkish mood of Washington. Not surprisingly, the Soviet offer was rejected, and Reagan returned to Washington to control the propaganda fall-out. Nevertheless, Reagan did not return home empty-handed, since the foundation was laid for the START treaty of meaningful reductions. A subsequent agreement on the reduction of intermediate-range nuclear forces and the Soviet withdrawal of 115,000 troops from Afghanistan provided further evidence of the thawing of the cold war.[5]

In late 1986, the Reagan administration suffered its most debilitating scandal when it was embarrassed by revelations that it had been conducting covert activities in two regions that had long been sensitive to U.S. security: the Middle East and Latin America. Earlier in the year, on April 14, American bombers took off from bases in Britain and dropped their payloads on Libyan dictator Colonel Muammar al-Qaddafi's military headquarters and barracks. The surprise attack against targets in Tripoli was in retaliation for continued Libyan sponsorship of terrorists, including the bombing of a West Berlin night club in which a U.S. serviceman was killed and which intercepted Libyan communications confirmed was ordered by Tripoli. Despite one plane being lost in the attack and the retaliatory murder of one American and two British hostages, the air strike greatly enhanced public support for the president's anti-terrorist activities.

Ongoing events in Lebanon, however, were having the opposite effect. The Hezbollah's terrorist activities, specifically taking American citizens living and working in the region as hostages, not only incensed Americans at home but demonstrated that the U.S. government's efforts to prevent such actions were ineffectual. Thus, in Reagan's simple equation, "as President, as far as I was concerned, I had the duty to bring those Americans home." The lengths to which his administration was prepared to go to secure the release of the hostages formed one-half of the Iran-Contra scandal. The other half was America's sensitivity to events in Latin America, particularly in the struggle for power in Nicaragua. American intervention in the region had repeatedly failed, and Congress had explicitly tried to distance itself from direct involvement.

On the Congressional Election Day, 1986, Reagan received two pieces of bad news. The first was that the Republicans had lost their hold over the Senate with the result that the Democrats now controlled both houses of Congress. Worse, however, were press reports that the administration, in collaboration with the Israelis, had been selling arms to Iran in the hope that Iran, in turn, would use its influence with Hezbollah to secure the release of American hostages in Lebanon. The story had first broken in Lebanese newspapers a few days previously in the wake of the release of one of the hostages and found its way across the Atlantic where it was virulently pursued by the American press. Not only did this violate the administration's often-stated refusal to negotiate with terrorists, as well as contravene congressional will, but it also recalled all the negative images of the 1979 Iranian storming of the American embassy.

Yet the parallels to earlier embarrassments of recent memory did not stop there. In revelations reminiscent of Watergate—indeed the new scandal was popularly referred to as "Irangate"—it came to light that the administration had, in fact, constructed a complex web of covert activity spreading from Nicaragua to Iran. Months later is came out that the president himself had instructed his senior advisers "don't talk specifics" about the arms shipments.[6] The hub of the White House operation was Marine Lieutenant-Colonel Oliver North, a much-decorated Vietnam veteran, who in later years held his own political ambitions, but at this time worked as an anti-terrorism specialist for the National Security Council. From the basement of the White House, and apparently under the auspices of the National Security Council, North had created a complex web of intrigue that involved, among other schemes, the funding of the Nicaraguan Contra rebels with profits generated from selling arms to Iranian moderates to secure the release of American hostages. Amid congressional hearings riddled with inconsistencies, it became apparent that far from operating as a renegade individual, North acted with the full authority of Reagan's national security adviser, Robert McFarlane, and his successor, Admiral John Poindexter, as well as the director of Central Intelligence, William Casey. Secretary of Defense Caspar Weinberger was also implicated in the imbroglio, although it was soon revealed that he, along with Secretary of State Shultz, had emphatically opposed the scheme and repeatedly raised objections.[7]

This, however, was not the end of it, with a congressional investigating committee conducting televised hearings. With stories of White House intrigue, cover-ups, covert operations, and the shredding of key documents, the nation watched transfixed as the story unfolded before their eyes. Polls revealed that most Americans believed that Reagan was lying when he told the Tower Commission, an investigative committee headed by former Republican senator John Tower appointed by Reagan to investigate the scandal, that "I just don't remember—period." Reagan further undermined his credibility when he told the nation soon after, "A few months ago I told the American people I did not trade arms for hostages. My heart and my best intentions still tell me that it is true, but the facts and the evidence tell me it is not." The American people were left wondering whether their president was a liar or whether he was incompetent.

The judicial results of the scandal were relatively subdued; only Poindexter was sentenced to jail for his part in lying to Congress, and North's relatively minor convictions were overturned on appeal. Weinberger, McFarlane, and others involved received presidential pardons. Yet for Reagan there was no escape from the fallout. If he did know about the Iran-Contra schemes then he was contravening congressional will, acting illegally, and, worse, lying about it. If he did not know, then he was dangerously out of touch and had lost control of his own administration, if he ever had it. Thus the Iran-Contra scandal had profound ramifications for Reagan's presidency. It tarnished the Reagan image and pierced the president's mystique. Reagan was now vulnerable. Political enemies who had feared his overwhelming sway over public opinion seized the opportunity to challenge the president. Several of his nominees for government office were challenged and rejected by Congress, and his own policies were subjected to increased press and public scrutiny. Meanwhile, however, the economy continued to be strong. With the U.S. Navy escorting oil tankers through the volatile Persian Gulf, thereby improving supply, oil prices continued to fall, driving Wall Street up and sending inflation down.

TWILIGHT OF THE REAGAN YEARS

The resulting confidence led to increased debt at all levels. On a personal level, credit cards became even more frequently used as Americans exceeded their incomes and spent themselves into debt. On a larger scale, businesses big and small based their expenditures on forecasts of continuing prosperity. In mid-October 1987, however, the bottom fell out of the New York Stock Market. After a few days during which there were signs of instability, on October 19, soon to be dubbed "Black Monday," the Dow-Jones index, the conventional gauge of overall stock market trading, plummeted 508 points in the largest dive in a single day since 1914. The scenario was repeated in markets around the world. It soon became apparent that a combination of artificially high prices, or a "Bull Market," and so-called program trading—where computers, triggered by pre-programmed indices, gave the order to buy or sell according to changes in market prices—were largely to blame, and the New York Stock Exchange took steps to prevent a repeat occurrence. While Reagan assured the nation that the crash was an aberration and that the economy was fundamentally sound, almost 15,000 Wall Street jobs, many occupied by the new social group of materially affluent and upwardly mobile urban professionals popularly known as "yuppies," were lost, and many small investors lost their savings. On a larger scale, what the "Crash of '87," revealed was that the spiraling debt of the United States, on a national level as well as a personal level, did not come without its drawbacks. *Business Week* put it succinctly: "The Message of the Crash is clear: Americans have spent too much, borrowed too much, and imported too much. Now it has to stop." Yet, the predicted recession did not follow, and by April 1988, the market appeared to be stable again.

Nevertheless, the crash added Reagan's economic policies to his list of vulnerabilities, ensuring that making an assessment of Reagan's presidency was problematic, mainly due to the irreconcilable interpretations of Reagan himself. His supporters charged that he was a visionary who saw the "big picture." Having lived through the tumultuous years of the twentieth century, including the Great Depression, the Second World War, and the cold war, he was unlikely to be unduly concerned with small matters and was confident that if headed in the right direction the result would be to move forward. More important, they judged, was his larger vision. To his supporters, Reagan's accomplishments were impressive: he "won" the cold war, revitalized American society, made the world safer by pursuing meaningful arms reduction, and restored America's sense of pride. In sharp contrast to this view, Reagan's critics pointed to his many inconsistencies and the frequent flaws in his public statements where Reagan frequently made factual errors and misused anecdotes. He reportedly dozed through meetings, had his schedule vetted by his wife's astrologer, and had no clear idea of what was happening in his administration. Regarding the "winning" of the cold war, they argued that, in fact, the Soviet Union "lost" the cold war all on its own, and if Reagan's policies had any effect it was to slow this process. In sum, they charge that Reagan was quite simply incompetent—an actor reading a script without understanding the words. Few have adopted the middle ground between these two views.

If Reagan had left office in 1986 his legacy would have been assured. The economic recovery of the early years was perhaps his most impressive achievement and was enough to leave an indelible mark on American society. However, as *Time* magazine put it, "The Reagan administration, the phenomenon that had defined so much of the '80s, that had given the decade its agenda and style, seemed to collapse in a bizarre shambles." Indeed, Reagan's second term was littered with paradoxes. The administration was riddled with scandal, yet public support was never higher. He implemented defense policies that heated up the cold war, yet in retrospect many attributed them to winning the cold war. He reduced the size of government and cut taxes while the national debt rose dramatically. His detractors blatantly accused him of incompetence, while his supporters held that his calm was the sign of wisdom and control. The truth is probably somewhere in between.

Reagan's televised valedictory speech to the American people on January 12, 1989, was as memorable as any in his presidency and accurately summed up the epic achievement of a political career that, had it been written as a novel, would have been rejected by any good publishing house as altogether too absurd. In his thirty-fourth broadcast from the Oval Office, the Great Communicator dwelt on the traditional American values of freedom and openness, drawing a link between the Pilgrims who first came to America from Europe two centuries ago and the Vietnamese boat people, both seeking freedom and opportunity. Reagan then claimed two great triumphs: "One is the economic recovery in which the people of America created and filled 19 million new jobs. The other is the recovery of our morale: America is respected again in the world and looked to for leadership." Speaking of his controversial supply-side tax cuts he added, "Common sense told us that when you put a big tax on something the people will produce less of it. So we cut the people's tax rate, and the people produced more than ever before. The economy bloomed like a plant that had been cut back and could now grow quicker and stronger." It was a valid argument that most people could understand. It was also a rare politician who could tell the truth and tell it simply. Despite the huge budget deficit, Reagan's policies brought about the largest peacetime expansion in the American economy since World War II. Nevertheless, on the negative side of the ledger, not all Americans reaped the benefits as income and tax disparities widened the gap between rich and poor.

On foreign policy, Reagan was overall a success, notwithstanding the death of the marines in Lebanon and the unraveling of the Iran-Contra scandal. When he first won office, it was fashionable among intellectuals to write him off as a trigger-happy cowboy or a shallow Hollywood ham. In point of fact, his understanding of the Soviets and the best way to deal with them, from a position of strength, was superior to that of most of the pundits. In modernizing the nuclear arsenal while pursuing the Strategic Defense Initiative, the Reagan administration brought the Soviets seriously to the negotiating table and produced a new sense of realism in superpower relations. His actions in invading Grenada, bombing Libya, and escorting oil tankers in the Persian Gulf showed the world that American could and would act when its national interests were threatened. The Reagan Doctrine, the name for U.S. support of anti-Communist insurgency movements, was an unqualified success, resulting in the Soviets pulling out of Afghanistan, the Cubans quitting Africa, and contributing to the Vietnamese withdrawal from Kampuchea. In restoring American pride, Reagan pushed aside the so-called Vietnam Syndrome, setting the stage for the application of military force in matters that counted.

More than any other leader in the contemporary democratic world, including Margaret Thatcher in Britain, Reagan embodied the conservative revival of the 1980s. Yet at the same time, he was one of the most popular presidents ever to hold office. The key to his massive political strength was his emotional intelligence, his ability to infuse conservatism with emotional warmth, a quality of caring and decency and familiarity that had eluded more flinty proponents of that political persuasion. In another sense though, Reagan's most enduring legacy was perhaps his 372 appointments to the federal bench, including four to the Supreme Court, including the first woman associate justice, Sandra Day O'Connor, in 1981, and William Rehnquist as chief justice. More immediately, Reagan proved that the presidency still worked. Though the position had lost some of its political authority, it was still possible to succeed in the Oval Office by skillfully exercising its power of symbol, ceremony, and vision. In doing so, Reagan showed that the office remains an institution of such extraordinary adaptability that it can be molded to fit all manner of intellects, temperaments, and governing styles. America was reassured.

What does not happen in politics is as important as what does, and the plain fact was that after eight years of the most conservative presidency since Herbert Hoover, the great body of the welfare state remained deeply enmeshed in the nation's social fabric. All of Reagan's efforts to undo the basic New Deal commitment to assist struggling Americans who try to maintain themselves but cannot had failed. None of the major programs such as social security, unemployment insurance, or Medicare were eliminated or seriously limited. For all his efforts, Reagan simply could not shift the great weight of American tradition since the Great Depression that government can be the solution, the revolution in political expectations that people in need might expect to look to Washington for help. And so it remains.

What was fundamentally changing was America's position in the world. By the end of the Reagan administration, almost nothing survived of its early militant posture toward the Soviet Union, no more boasts that it had forced the Kremlin to retreat from the battlefield in favor of the bargaining table. With the exception of the Star Wars budget, the great military buildup of the first administration had been terminated. Arms control negotiations were advancing rapidly as well as inexorably. Reagan, together with Soviet leader Mikhail Gorbachev, had all but called the cold war off. Within a year of Reagan's departure from Washington, the Berlin Wall had fallen; within three years, the flag of the former Soviet Union was lowered for the last time. It was a new world.

NOTES

1. Helen Thomas, *Front Row at the White House* (New York: Scribner, 1999).

2. Elizabeth Drew, *Portrait of an Election: The 1980 Presidential Campaign* (New York: Simon and Schuster, 1981).

3. Richard J. Carroll, *An Economic Record of Presidential Performance: From Truman to Bush* (Westport, CT: Praeger, 1995), pp. 113–15; and John W. Sloan, *The Reagan Effect: Economics and Presidential Leadership* (Lawrence: University Press of Kansas, 1999), pp. 246–62.

4. Norman C. Amaker, *Civil Rights and the Reagan Administration* (Washington, D.C.: Urban Institute Press, 1988), pp. 157–64.

5. John Lewis Gaddis, *The United States and the End of the Cold War* (New York: Oxford University Press, 1992); Raymond L. Garthoff, *The Great Transition: American-Soviet Relations and the End of the Cold War* (Washington, D.C.: Brookings Institution, 1994); and Don Oberdorfer, *From the Cold War to a New Era: The United States and the Soviet Union, 1983–1991*, updated ed. (Baltimore, MD: Johns Hopkins University Press, 1998).

6. Thomas, *Front Row at the White House*, p. 113.

7. See Oliver North and William Novak, *Under Fire: An American Story* (New York: HarperCollins, 1991); Lawrence E. Walsh, *Firewall: The Iran-Contra Conspiracy and Cover-Up* (New York: W. W. Norton, 1997).

Selected Bibliography

Abrams, Elliott. *Undue Process: A Story of How Political Differences Are Turned into Crimes*. New York: Free Press, 1993.

Agnew, Spiro. *Go Quietly . . . or Else*. New York: Morrow, 1980.

Aitken, Jonathan. *Nixon: A Life*. London: Weidenfeld and Nicolson, 1993.

Alexander, Charles C. *Holding the Line: The Eisenhower Era, 1952–1961*. Bloomington: Indiana University Press, 1975.

Alien, Frederick Lewis. *Since Yesterday; The Nineteen-Thirties in America, September 3, 1929–September 3, 1939*. New York: Harper, 1940.

Allen, Craig. *Eisenhower and the Mass Media: Peace, Prosperity, and Prime-Time TV*. Chapel Hill: University of North Carolina Press, 1993.

Allison, Graham T., and Philip D. Zelikow. *Essence of Decision: Explaining the Cuban Missile Crisis*. 2nd edition. New York: Longman, 1999.

Allswang, John M. *The New Deal and American Politics: A Study in Political Change*. New York: Wiley, 1978.

Amaker, Norman C. *Civil Rights and the Reagan Administration*. Washington, D.C.: Urban Institute Press, 1988.

Ambrose, Stephen E. *Eisenhower: Soldier and President*. New York: Simon and Schuster, 1990.

———. *Nixon*. 3 vols. New York: Simon and Schuster, 1987.

Anderson, David. *Trapped by Success: The Eisenhower Administration and Vietnam, 1953–1961*. New York: Columbia University Press, 1991.

Anderson, Karen. *Wartime Women: Sex Roles, Family Relations, and the Status of Women during World War II*. Westport, CT: Greenwood Press, 1981.

Ashmore, Harry S. *Civil Rights and Wrongs: A Memoir of Race and Politics, 1944–1996*. Columbia: University of South Carolina Press, 1997.

Backer, John H. *The Decision to Divide Germany: American Foreign Policy in Transition.* Durham, NC: Duke University Press, 1978.

Baker, James T. *A Southern Baptist in the White House.* Philadelphia, PA: Westminster Press, 1977.

Barber, William J. *From New Era to New Deal: Herbert Hoover, the Economists, and American Economic Policy, 1921–1933.* New York: Cambridge University Press, 1985.

Barnes, Harry Elmer. *Genesis of the World War: An Introduction to the Problem of War Guilt.* New York: Alfred Knopf, 1926.

Bartlett, Bruce R. *Reaganomics: Supply Side Economics in Action.* Westport, CT: Arlington House, 1981.

Baskir, Lawrence M., and William A. Strauss. *Chance and Circumstance: The Draft, the War and the Vietnam Generation.* New York: Knopf, 1978.

Baughman, U.E. *Secret Service Chief.* New York: Harper & Row, 1961.

Beard, Charles, A. *President Roosevelt and the Coming of War, 1941: A Study in Appearances and Realities.* Hamden, CT: Archon Books, 1948.

Beattie, Keith. *The Scar that Binds: American Culture and the Vietnam War.* New York: New York University Press, 1998.

Beitzell, Robert. *The Uneasy Alliance: America, Britain, and Russia, 1941–1943.* New York: Knopf, 1977.

Bell, Coral. *The Diplomacy of Détente: The Kissinger Era.* New York: St. Martin's Press, 1977.

———. *President Carter and Foreign Policy.* Canberra, Australia: Australian National University, 1980.

Bergman, Andrew. *We're in the Money: Depression America and Its Films.* New York: New York University Press, 1971.

Berman, Larry. *Lyndon Johnson's War: The Road to Stalemate in Vietnam.* New York: W. W. Norton, 1989.

———. *Planning a Tragedy: the Americanization of the War in Vietnam.* New York: W. W. Norton, 1982.

———, ed. *Looking Back on the Reagan Presidency.* Baltimore, MD: Johns Hopkins University Press, 1990.

Berman, Ronald. *America in the Sixties: An Intellectual History.* New York: Free Press, 1968.

Bernstein, Carl, and Robert Woodward. *All the President's Men.* New York: Simon and Schuster, 1974.

Bernstein, Irving. *Guns or Butter: The Presidency of Lyndon Johnson.* New York: Oxford University Press, 1996.

———. *Turbulent Years: A History of the American Worker, 1933–41.* Boston: Houghton Mifflin, 1969.

Bernstein, Michael. *The Great Depression: Delayed Recovery and Economic Change in America, 1929–1939.* New York: Cambridge University Press, 1987.

Beschloss, Michael R. *The Crisis Years: Kennedy and Khrushchev, 1960–1963.* New York: Edward Burlingame Books, 1991.

———. *MAYDAY, The U-2 Affair.* New York: Harper & Row, 1986.

Bissell, Richard M. *Reflections of a Cold Warrior: From Yalta to the Bay of Pigs.* New Haven, CT: Yale University Press, 1996.

Blair, Anne. *Lodge in Vietnam: A Patriot Abroad.* New Haven, CT: Yale University Press, 1995.

Blum, John Morton. *V Was for Victory: Politics and American Culture during World War II.* New York: Harcourt Brace, 1976.

Bohlen, Charles E. *Witness to History, 1929–1969.* New York: W. W. Norton, 1973.

Bordo, Michael D., Claudia Goldin, and Eugene N. White, eds. *The Defining Moment: The Great Depression and the American Economy in the Twentieth Century.* Chicago: University of Chicago Press, 1998.

Borg, Dorothy. *The United States and the Far Eastern Crisis of 1933–1938: From the Manchurian Incident through the Initial Stage of the Undeclared Sino-Japanese War.* Cambridge: Harvard University Press, 1964.

Bornet, Vaughn D. *The Presidency of London B. Johnson.* Lawrence: University Press of Kansas, 1984.

Bourne, Peter G. *Jimmy Carter: A Comprehensive Biography from Plains to Post-Presidency.* New York: Scribner, 1997.

Boyer, Paul. *By the Bomb's Early Light: American Thought and Culture at the Dawn of the Atomic Age.* New York: Pantheon, 1985.

Boyle, Peter, ed. *Churchill-Eisenhower Correspondence, 1953–1955.* Chapel Hill: University of North Carolina Press, 1990.

Branch, Taylor. *Parting the Waters: America in the King Years, 1954–63.* New York: Simon and Schuster, 1988.

———. *Pillar of Fire: America in the King Years, 1963–65.* New York: Simon and Schuster, 1998.

Brands, H. W. *Cold Warriors: Eisenhower's Generation and American Foreign Policy.* New York: Columbia University Press, 1988.

Brauer, Carl M. *John F. Kennedy and the Second Reconstruction.* New York: Columbia University Press, 1977.

Brendon, Piers. *Ike: His Life and Times.* New York: Harper & Row, 1986.

Brinkley, Alan. *The End of Reform: New Deal Liberalism in Recession and War.* New York: Knopf, 1995.

———. *Voices of Protest: Huey Long, Father Coughlin, and the Great Depression.* New York: Knopf, 1982.

Broadwater, Jeff. *Adlai Stevenson: The Odyssey of a Cold War Liberal.* New York: Twayne, 1994.

Brodie, Fawn M. *Richard Nixon: The Shaping of His Character.* New York: W. W. Norton, 1981.

Brown, Thomas. *JFK: History of an Image.* Bloomington: Indiana University Press, 1988.

Brzezinski, Zbigniew. *Power and Principle: Memoirs of the National Security Adviser, 1977–1981.* New York: Farrar, Straus, Giroux, 1983.

Buchanan, A. Russell. *The United States and World War II.* 2 vols. New York: Harper & Row, 1965.

Bullock, Alan. *Hitler and Stalin: Parallel Lives.* New York: Knopf, 1991.

Bundy, William. *A Tangled Web: The Making of Foreign Policy in the Nixon Presidency.* London; New York: I. B. Tauris, 1998.

Burk, Robert F. *Dwight D. Eisenhower: Hero and Politician.* Boston: Twayne, 1986.

———. *The Eisenhower Administration and Black Civil Rights.* Knoxville: University of Tennessee Press, 1984.

Burner, David. *Herbert Hoover: A Public Life*. New York: Knopf, 1979.

———. *John F. Kennedy and a New Generation*. Boston: Little Brown, 1988.

Burns, James MacGregor. *Roosevelt: The Lion and the Fox*. 2 vols. New York: Harcourt Brace, 1956.

Butow, Robert J.C. *Tojo and the Coming of War*. Princeton, NJ: Princeton University Press, 1961.

Califano, Joseph A., Jr. *Governing America: An Insider's Report from the White House and Cabinet*. New York: Simon and Schuster, 1981.

———. *The Triumph and Tragedy of Lyndon Johnson: The White House Years*. New York: Simon and Schuster, 1991.

Calvocoressi, Peter, Guy Winter, and John Pritchard. *Total War*. 2nd ed. New York: Pantheon, 1989.

Cannon, James. *Time and Chance: Gerald Ford's Appointment with History*. New York: HarperCollins, 1994.

Cannon, Lou. *President Reagan: The Role of a Lifetime*. New York: Simon and Schuster, 1991.

———. *Reagan*. New York: Putnam, 1982.

Caro, Robert. *The Years of Lyndon Johnson*. 2 vols. New York: Knopf, 1982–90.

Carroll, Richard J. *An Economic Record of Presidential Performance: From Truman to Bush*. Westport, CT: Praeger, 1995.

Carter, Jimmy. *Keeping Faith: Memoirs of a President*. Toronto, Canada: Bantam, 1982.

———. *Why Not the Best?* Nashville, TN: Broadman Press, 1975.

Chamberlain, John. *Farewell to Reform: Being a History of the Rise, Life and Decay of the Progressive Mind in America*. New York: Liveright, 1932.

Chandler, Alfred D., ed. *The Papers of Dwight D. Eisenhower: The War Years*. Baltimore, MD: Johns Hopkins University Press, 1970.

Chandler, Lester V. *America's Greatest Depression: 1929–1941*. New York: Harper & Row, 1970.

Charmley, John. *Churchill's Grand Alliance: The Anglo-American Special Relationship, 1940–1957*. New York: Harcourt Brace, 1995.

Chen Jian. *Mao's China and the Cold War*. Chapel Hill: University of North Carolina Press, 2001.

Churchill, Winston S. *The Second World War*. 6 vols. London: Cassell, 1948–54.

Clausen, Henry C., and Bruce Lee. *Pearl Harbor: Final Judgment*. New York: Crown, 1992.

Cobbs Hoffman, Elizabeth. *All You Need is Love: The Peace Corps and the Spirit of the 1960s*. Cambridge, MA: Harvard University Press, 1998.

Cohen, Lizabeth. *Making a New Deal*. New York: Cambridge University Press, 1990.

Cohen, Warren I., and Nancy B. Tucker, eds. *Lyndon Johnson Confronts the World: American Foreign Policy, 1963–1968*. New York: Cambridge University Press, 1994.

Cole, Wayne, S. *Determinism and American Foreign Relations during the Franklin D. Roosevelt Era*. Lanham, MD: University Press of America, 1995.

———. *Roosevelt and the Isolationists, 1932–1945*. Lincoln: University of Nebraska Press, 1983.

Conkin, Paul K. *Big Daddy from the Perdinales: Lyndon Baines Johnson.* Boston: Twayne Publishers, 1986.

————. *The New Deal.* New York: Crowell, 1967.

Cook, Blanche Wiesen. *The Declassified Eisenhower: A Divided Legacy.* Garden City, NY: Doubleday, 1981.

Cowley, Monica. *Nixon OFF the Record.* New York: Random House, 1996.

Cox, Archibald. *The Warren Court: Constitutional Decision as an Instrument of Reform.* Cambridge: Harvard University Press, 1968.

Cullather, Nicholas. *Secret History: The CIA's Classified Account of its Operations in Guatemala, 1952–1954.* Stanford: Stanford University Press, 1999.

Dalfuime, Richard M. *Desegregation of the US Armed Forces.* Columbia: University of Missouri Press, 1975.

Dallek, Robert. *Flawed Giant: Lyndon Johnson and His Times, 1961–1973.* New York: Oxford University Press, 1998.

————. *Franklin D. Roosevelt and American Foreign Policy, 1932–1945.* New York: Oxford University Press, 1979.

————. *Hail to the Chief: The Making and Unmaking of American Presidents.* New York: Hyperion, 1996.

————. *Lone Star Rising: Lyndon Johnson and His Times, 1908–1960.* New York: Oxford University Press, 1991.

Daniels, Roger. *The Bonus March: An Episode of the Great Depression.* Westport, CT: Greenwood Press, 1971.

————. *Concentration Camp USA: Japanese Americans and World War II.* New York: Holt, Rinehart and Winston, 1971.

Darilek, Richard E. *A Loyal Opposition in Time of War: The Republican Party and the Politics of Foreign Policy from Pearl Harbor to Yalta.* Westport, CT: Greenwood Press, 1976.

Davis, Kenneth S. *FDR.* 5 vols. New York: Random House, 1985–2000.

Dean, John W. *Blind Ambition: The White House Years.* New York: Simon and Schuster, 1976.

Dear, I.C.B., ed. *The Oxford Companion to the Second World War.* New York: Oxford University Press, 1995.

DeBenedetti, Charles. *An American Ordeal: The Antiwar Movement of the Vietnam Era.* Syracuse, NY: Syracuse University Press, 1990.

Dickson, Paul. *Sputnik: The Shock of the Century.* New York: Walker, 2001.

Diederich, Bernard. *Somoza and the Legacy of US Involvement in Central America.* New York: Dutton, 1981.

Divine, Robert A. *Eisenhower and the Cold War.* New York: Oxford University Press, 1981.

————. *The Illusion of Neutrality.* Chicago: University of Chicago Press, 1962.

————. *A Second Chance: The Triumph of Internationalism in America during World War II.* New York: Atheneum, 1967.

Dobrynin, Anatoly. *In Confidence: Moscow's Ambassador to American's Six Cold War Presidents (1962–1986).* New York: Times Books, Random House, 1995.

Dockrill, Saki. *Eisenhower's New Look Security Policy, 1953–61.* Houndmills, UK: Macmillan Press; New York: St. Martin's Press, 1996.

Dodge, Mark M., ed. *Herbert Hoover and the Historians.* West Branch, IA: Hoover Presidential Library Association, 1989.

Doenecke, Justus D. *In Danger Undaunted: The Anti-Interventionist Movement of 1940–1941 as Revealed in the Papers of the America First Committee.* Stanford, CA: Hoover Institution Press, 1990.

Donaldson, Gary A. *Truman Defeats Dewey.* Lexington: University Press of Kentucky, 1999.

Donovan, Robert J. *Conflict and Crisis: The Presidency of Harry S Truman, 1945–1948.* New York: W.W. Norton, 1977.

Drew, Elizabeth. *Portrait of an Election: The 1980 Presidential Campaign.* New York: Simon and Schuster, 1981.

Dudziak, Mary L. *Cold War Civil Rights: Race and Image of American Diplomacy.* Princeton, NJ: Princeton University Press, 2000.

Dugger, Ronnie. *The Politician: The Life and Times of London Johnson: The Drive for Power, From the Frontier to Master of the Senate.* New York: W. W. Norton, 1982.

Dumbrell, John. *The Carter Presidency: A Re-evaluation.* 2nd ed. Manchester: UK; New York: Manchester University Press, 1995.

Duram, James C. *A Moderate among Extremists: Dwight D. Eisenhower and the School Desegregation Crisis.* Chicago: Nelson-Hall, 1981.

Eisenberg, Carolyn. *Drawing the Line: The American Decision to Divide Germany, 1944–1949.* Cambridge, MA: Cambridge University Press, 1996.

Eisenhower, Dwight D. *Crusade in Europe.* Garden City, NY: Doubleday, 1948.

———. *Mandate for Change.* Garden City, NY: Doubleday, 1963.

———. *Waging Peace: The White House Years.* Garden City, NY: Doubleday, 1965.

Emery, Fred. *Watergate: The Corruption of American Politics and the Fall of Richard Nixon.* New York: Times Books, 1994.

Englebrecht, Helmuth C. *Merchants of Death.* Garden City, NY: Garden City Publishing Company, 1937.

Erickson, John, and David Dilks. *Barbarossa: The Axis and the Allies.* Edinburgh, UK: Edinburgh University Press, 1994.

Evans, Rowland, and Robert Novak. *The Reagan Revolution.* New York: Dutton, 1981.

Farnham, Barbara Reardon. *Roosevelt and the Munich Crisis: A Study of Political Decision-Making.* Princeton, NJ: Princeton University Press, 1997.

Fausold, Martin L., and George T. Mazuzan, eds. *The Hoover Presidency: A Reappraisal.* Albany: State University of New York Press, 1974.

Fearon, Peter. *War, Prosperity and Depression: The United States Economy, 1917–1945.* Lawrence: University Press of Kansas, 1987.

Feis, Herbert. *The Road to Pearl Harbor: The Coming of the War Between the United States and Japan.* Princeton, NJ: Princeton University Press, 1950.

Ferguson, Thomas, and Joel Rogers, eds. *The Hidden Election: Politics and Economics in the 1980 Presidential Campaign.* New York: Pantheon Books, 1981.

Ferrell, Robert H. *American Diplomacy in the Great Depression: Hoover-Stimson Foreign Policy, 1929–1933.* New Haven, CT: Yale University Press, 1957.

———, ed. *The Eisenhower Diaries.* New York: W.W. Norton, 1981.

Flynn, George Q. *American Catholics and the Roosevelt Presidency.* Lexington: University of Kentucky Press, 1968.

Forbes, Jack D. *Native Americans and Nixon: Presidential Politics and Minority Self-Determination, 1969–1970*. Los Angeles: University of California Press, 1981.

Ford, Gerald. *A Time to Heal: The Autobiography of Gerald Ford*. New York: Harper & Row, 1979.

Freedman, Lawrence. *Kennedy's Wars: Berlin, Cuba, Laos, and Vietnam*. New York: Oxford University Press, 2000.

Fried, Richard M. *Nightmare in Red: The McCarthy Era in Perspective*. New York: Oxford University Press, 1990.

Friedel, Frank. *Franklin D. Roosevelt*. 4 vols. Boston: Little Brown, 1952.

Friedman, Milton, and Anna L. Schultz. *A Monetary History of the United States, 1967–1960*. Princeton, NJ: Princeton University Press, 1963.

Fulbright, J. William. *The Arrogance of Power*. New York: Vintage, 1966.

———. *The Crippled Giant: American Foreign Policy and Its Domestic Consequences*. New York: Random House, 1972.

Fursenko, Aleksandr, and Timothy Naftali, *"One Hell of a Gamble": Khrushchev, Castro, and Kennedy, 1958–1964*. New York: W. W. Norton, 1997.

Gaddis, John Lewis. *The United States and the End of the Cold War: Implications, Reconsiderations, Provocations*. New York: Oxford University Press, 1992.

———. *We Now Know: Rethinking Cold War History*. New York: Oxford University Press, 1997.

Galbraith, John Kenneth. *The Great Crash*. Boston: Houghton Mifflin, 1955.

Gardner, Lloyd C. *Pay Any Price: Lyndon Johnson and the Wars for Vietnam*. Chicago: Ivan R. Dee, 1995.

Garment, Leonard. *Crazy Rhythm: My Journey from Brooklyn, Jazz, and Wall Street to Nixon's White House, Watergate, and Beyond*. New York: Times Books, 1997.

Garraty, John A. *The Great Depression*. San Diego: Harcourt Brace Jovanovich,1986.

Garrow, David J. *Bearing the Cross: Martin Luther King, Jr., and the Southern Christian Leadership Conference*. New York: W. Morrow, 1986.

———. *Liberty and Sexuality: The Right to Privacy and the Making of Roe v. Wade*. New York: Lisa Drew, 1994.

Garthoff, Raymond L. *Détente and Confrontation: American-Soviet Relations from Nixon to Reagan*. Washington, D.C.: Brookings Institution, 1994.

———. *The Great Transition: American-Soviet Relations and the End of the Cold War*. Washington, D.C.: Brookings Institution, 1994.

———. *Reflections on the Cuban Missile Crisis*. Rev. ed. Washington, D.C.: Brookings Institution, 1989.

Gates, Robert M. *From the Shadows: The Ultimate Insider's Story of How They Won the Cold War*. New York: Simon and Schuster, 1996.

Geelhoed, E. Bruce. *Charles E. Wilson and Controversy at the Pentagon, 1953–1957*. Detroit, MI: Wayne State University Press, 1979.

Gellman, Irwin. *Secret Affairs: Franklin Roosevelt, Cordell Hull, and Sumner Welles*. Baltimore, MD: Johns Hopkins University Press, 1995.

Giglio, James. *The Presidency of John F. Kennedy*. Lawrence: University Press of Kansas, 1991.

Glad, Betty. *Jimmy Carter in Search of the Great White House*. New York: W. W. Norton, 1980.

Goldwater, Barry M. *The Conscience of a Conservative*. Shepherdsville, KY: Victor, 1960.

Goncharov, Sergei N., John W. Lewis, and Xue Litai. *Uncertain Partners: Stalin, Mao, and the Korean War*. Stanford, CA: Stanford University Press, 1993.

Goodwin, Doris Kearns. *London Johnson and the American Dream*. New York: Harper & Row, 1976.

Gorbachev, Mikhail. *Memoirs*. New York: Doubleday, 1996.

Graebner, Norman, ed. *An Uncertain Tradition: American Secretaries of State in the Twentieth Century*. New York: McGraw-Hill, 1961.

————. *The Cold War: A Conflict of Ideology and Power*. Lexington, MA: Heath, 1976.

————, ed. *The National Security: Its Theory and Practice, 1945–1960*. New York: Oxford University Press, 1986.

Graham, Hugh Davis. *The Civil Rights Era: Origins and Development of National Policy, 1960–1972*. New York: Oxford University Press, 1990.

Green, Harvey. *The Uncertainty of Everyday Life*. New York: HarperCollins, 1992.

Greenfield, Kent R. *American Strategy in World War II: A Reconsideration*. Baltimore, MD: Johns Hopkins University Press, 1982.

Greenhaw, Wayne. *Elephants in the Cottonfields: Ronald Reagan and the New Republican South*. New York: Macmillan, 1982.

Greenstein, Fred I. *The Hidden-Hand Presidency: Eisenhower as Leader*. New York: Basic Books, 1982.

————. *The Presidential Difference: Leadership Style from FDR to Clinton*. New York: Free Press, 2000.

Grose, Peter. *Gentlemen Spy: The Life of Allen Dulles*. Boston: Houghton Mifflin, 1994.

Gullan, Harold U. *The Upset that Wasn't: Harry S Truman and the Crucial Election of 1948*. Chicago: Ivan R. Dee, 1998.

Haas, Garland A. *Jimmy Carter and the Politics of Frustration*. Jefferson, NC: McFarland, 1992.

Haig, Alexander M., Jr. *Caveat: Realism, Reagan and Foreign Policy*. New York: Macmillan, 1984.

Halberstam, David. *The Best and the Brightest*. New York: Ballantine, 1993.

————. *The Fifties*. New York: Villard, 1993.

Haldeman, H. R. *The Haldeman Diaries: Inside the Nixon White House*. New York: G.P. Putnam's, 1994.

Halle, Louis J. *The Cold War as History*. New York: Harper & Row, 1975.

Hargrove, Edwin C. *Jimmy Carter as President*. Baton Rouge: Louisiana State University Press, 1988.

Harrington, Michael. *The Other America: Poverty in the United States*. New York: Macmillan, 1962.

Hartman, Susan M. *The Home Front and Beyond: American Women in the 1940s*. Boston: Twayne, 1982.

Hastings, Max. *The Korean War*. New York: Simon and Schuster, 1987.

Hawley, Ellis. *The New Deal and the Problem of Monopoly: A Study in Economic Ambivalence*. Princeton, NJ: Princeton University Press, 1966.

Hearden, Patrick J. *Roosevelt Confronts Hitler: America's Entry into World War II*. Dekalb, IL: Northern Illinois University Press, 1987.

Heath, Jim F. *Decade of Disillusionment: The Kennedy-Johnson Years*. Bloomington: Indiana University Press, 1975.

———. *John F. Kennedy and the Business Community*. Chicago: University of Chicago Press, 1969.

Heinrichs, Waldo H., Jr. *American Ambassador: Joseph C. Grew and the Development of the United States Diplomatic Tradition*. Boston: Little Brown, 1966.

———. *Threshold of War: Franklin D. Roosevelt and American Entry into World War II*. New York: Oxford University Press, 1988.

Herman, Arthur. *Joseph McCarthy: Reexamining the Life and Legacy of America's Most Hated Senator*. New York: Free Press, 2000.

Herring, George C. *America's Longest War: The United States in Vietnam, 1950–1975*. 3rd ed. New York: McGraw-Hill, 1996.

———. *LBJ and Vietnam: A Different Kind of War*. Austin: University of Texas Press, 1994.

Hersh, Seymour. *The Dark Side of Camelot*. Boston: Little Brown, 1997.

———. *The Price of Power: Kissinger in the Nixon White House*. New York: Summit Books, 1983.

Hillman, William, ed. *Mr. President: Personal Diaries, Private Letters, Papers, and Revealing Interviews of Harry S. Truman*. London: Hutchinson, 1952.

Hilsman, Roger. *To Move a Nation: The Politics and Foreign Policy in the Administration of John F. Kennedy*. Garden City, NY: Doubleday, 1967.

Hixson, Walter, ed. *The Vietnam Antiwar Movement*. New York: Garland, 2000.

Hoff, Joan. *Nixon Reconsidered*. New York: Basic Books, 1995.

Hoff-Wilson, Joan. *Herbert Hoover: Forgotten Progressive*. Boston: Little Brown, 1975.

Hogan, Michael J. *A Cross of Iron: Harry S. Truman and the Origins of the National Security State, 1945–1954*. New York: Cambridge University Press, 1998.

Hollenhoff, Clark R. *The President Who Failed: Carter Out of Control*. New York: Macmillan, 1980.

Hoopes, Townsend. *The Devil and John Foster Dulles*. Boston: Little Brown, 1973.

Hoover, Herbert C. *The Memoirs of Herbert Hoover*. 3 vols. New York: Macmillan, 1951–52.

Hughes, Emmet John. *The Ordeal of Power: A Political Memoir of the Eisenhower Years*. New York: Atheneum, 1963.

Hull, Cordell. *Memoirs*. 2 vols. New York: Macmillan, 1948.

Huntington, Samuel P. *The Common Defense: Strategic Programs in National Politics*. New York: Columbia University Press, 1961.

Iriye, Akira. *The Origins of the Second World War in Asia and the Pacific*. New York: Longman, 1987.

Irons, Peter. *Justice at War*. New York: Oxford University Press, 1983.

Johnson, Haynes Bonner. *Sleepwalking Through History: America in the Reagan Years*. New York: W. W. Norton, 1991.

Johnson, Lyndon B. *The Vantage Point: Perspectives of the Presidency, 1963–1969*. New York: Holt, Rhinehart and Winston, 1971.

Jones, Charles O. *The Trustee Presidency: Jimmy Carter and the United States Congress*. Baton Rouge: Louisiana State University Press, 1988.

Jordan, Hamilton. *Crisis: The Last Year of the Carter Presidency*. New York: Putnam, 1982.

Kaplan, Fred. *The Wizards of Armageddon*. Stanford, CA: Stanford University Press, 1983.

Karabell, Zachary. *The Last Campaign: How Harry Truman Won the 1948 Election*. New York: Knopf, 2000.

Kaufman, Burton I. *The Presidency of James Earl Carter, Jr*. Lawrence: University Press of Kansas, 1993.

Keegan, John. *The Battle for History: Refighting World War Two*. New York: Vintage, 1995.

Kennan, George F. *Memoirs: 1925–1950*. Boston: Little Brown, 1967.

Kennedy, David M. *Freedom from Fear: The American People in Depression and War, 1929–1945*. New York: Oxford University Press, 1999.

Kennedy, John F. *Profiles in Courage*. New York: Harper, 1956.

Kennedy, Robert F. *Thirteen Days: A Memoir of the Cuban Missile Crisis*. New York: W. W. Norton, 1971.

Kern, Montague, Patricia W. Levering, and Ralph B. Levering. *The Kennedy Crises*. Chapel Hill: University of North Carolina Press, 1983.

Keynes, John Maynard. *The General Theory of Employment, Interest, and Money*. New York: Harcourt Brace, 1936.

————. *Treatise on Money*. New York: Harcourt Brace, 1930.

Kimball, Jeffrey P. *Nixon's Vietnam War*. Lawrence: Kansas University Press, 1998.

Kimball, Warren F. *Forged in War: Roosevelt, Churchill, and the Second World War*. New York: W. Morrow, 1997.

————. *The Juggler*. Princeton, NJ: Princeton University Press, 1988.

————. *The Most Unsordid Act: Lend Lease, 1939–1941*. Baltimore, MD: Johns Hopkins Press, 1969.

————, ed. *Churchill and Roosevelt: The Complete Correspondence*. Princeton, NJ: Princeton University Press, 1984.

Kindleberger, Charles P. *The World in Depression*. Rev. ed. Berkeley: University of California Press, 1986.

Kissinger, Henry. *Diplomacy*. New York: Simon and Schuster, 1994.

————. *White House Years*. Boston: Little Brown, 1979.

————. *Years of Renewal*. New York: Simon and Schuster, 1999.

————. *Years of Upheaval*. Boston: Little Brown, 1982.

Klehr, Harvey. *The Heyday of American Communism: The Depression Decade*. New York: Basic Books, 1984.

Kornbluh, Peter, ed. *Bay of Pigs Declassified: The Secret CIA Report on the Invasion of Cuba*. New York: New Press, 1998.

Kraus, S., ed. *The Great Debates: Carter vs. Ford, 1976*. Bloomington: Indiana University Press, 1979.

Kutler, Stanley I. *Abuse of Power*. New York: Free Press, 1997.

Lake, Anthony. *Third World Radical Regimes: U.S. Policy under Carter and Reagan*. New York: Foreign Policy Association, 1985.

Lance, Bert. *The Truth of the Matter: My Life In and Out of Politics*. New York: Summit Books, 1991.

Langer, William L., and S. E. Gleason, *The Challenge to Isolation, 1937–1940*. New York: Harper, 1952.

Latham, Michael E. *Modernization as Ideology: American Social Science and "Nation-Building" in the Kennedy Era*. Chapel Hill: University of North Carolina Press, 2000.

Leckie, Robert. *Delivered from Evil: The Saga of World War II*. New York: Harper & Row, 1987.

Leffler, Melvy P. *A Preponderance of Power: National Security, the Truman Administration, and the Cold War*. Stanford, CA: Stanford University Press, 1992.

Leigh, Michael. *Mobilizing Consent: Public Opinion and American Foreign Policy, 1937–1947*. Westport, CT: Greenwood, 1976.

Lekachman, Robert. *Greed Is Not Enough: Reaganomics*. New York: Pantheon, 1982.

Leonard, John. *Smoke and Mirrors: Violence, Television and Other American Cultures*. New York: New Press, 1997.

Lerner, Gerda, ed. *The Female Experience: An American Documentary*. New York: Oxford University Press, 1992.

Leuchtenburg, William E. *Franklin Roosevelt and the New Deal*. New York: Harper & Row, 1963.

Levitan, Sar A., and Robert Taggart. *The Promise of Greatness*. Cambridge, MA: Harvard University Press, 1976.

Lewis, Anthony. *Portrait of a Decade: The Second American Revolution*. New York: Random House, 1964.

Lisio, Donald J. *Hoover, Blacks, and Lily-Whites: A Study in Southern Strategies*. Chapel Hill: University of North Carolina Press, 1985.

Logevall, Fredrik. *Choosing War: The Lost Chance for Peace and the Escalation of War in Vietnam*. Berkeley: University of California Press, 1999.

Lyon, Peter. *Eisenhower: Portrait of the Hero*. Boston: Little Brown, 1974.

Mailer, Norman. *Oswald's Tale: An American Mystery*. New York: Random House, 1995.

Manchester, William. *The Death of a President*. New York: Galahad, 1996.

Mann, Robert. *A Grand Delusion: America's Descent into Vietnam*. New York: Basic Books, 2001.

———. *The Walls of Jericho: Lyndon Johnson, Hubert Humphrey, Richard Russell and the Struggle for Civil Rights*. New York: Harcourt Brace, 1996.

Marcuse, Herbert. *One Dimensional Man*. Boston: Beacon, 1964.

Marks, Frederick W. *Wind over Sand: The Diplomacy of Franklin Roosevelt*. Athens: University of Georgia Press, 1988.

Martin, John Barlow. *Adlai Stevenson and the World: The Life of Adlai Stevenson*. New York: Doubleday, 1977.

Matthews, Christopher. *Kennedy & Nixon: The Rivalry that Shaped Postwar America*. New York: Simon and Schuster, 1996.

Mazlish, Bruce, and Edwin Diamond. *Jimmy Carter: A Character Portrait*. New York: Simon and Schuster, 1979.

McCarthy, Mary. *The Mask of State: Watergate Portraits*. New York: Harcourt Brace Jovanovich, 1974.

McCraw, Thomas K. *TVA and the Power Fight, 1933–1939*. Philadelphia: Lippincott, 1971.

McDougall, Walter A. *Promised Land, Crusader State*. Boston: Houghton Mifflin, 1997.

McElvaine, Robert S., ed. *Down and Out in the Great Depression*. Chapel Hill: University of North Carolina Press, 1983.

McMaster, H. R. *Dereliction of Duty: Lyndon Johnson, Robert McNamara, the Joint Chiefs of Staff, and the Lies that Led to Vietnam*. New York: HarperCollins, 1997.

McNamara, Robert S. *In Retrospect: The Tragedy and Lessons of Vietnam*. New York: Times Books, 1995.

Means, Gardiner C. and Adolf A. Berle, Jr. *The Modern Corporation and Private Property*. New York: Macmillan, 1933.

Meese, Edwin. *With Reagan: The Inside Story*. Washington, D.C.: Regnery Gateway, 1992.

Melanson, Richard A., ed. *Neither Cold War Nor Détente: Soviet American Relations in the 1980s*. Charlottesville: University Press of Virginia, 1982.

Mills, C. Wright. *The Power Elite*. New York: Oxford University Press, 1956.

Moise, Edwin E. *Tonkin Gulf and the Escalation of the Vietnam War*. Chapel Hill: University of North Carolina Press, 1996.

Mollenhoff, Clark R. *The President Who Failed: Carter Out of Control*. New York: Macmillan, 1980.

Morris, Edmund. *Dutch: A Memoir of Ronald Reagan*. New York: Random House, 1999.

Morris, Roger. *Richard Milhous Nixon: The Rise of an American Politician*. New York: Henry Holt, 1990.

Mowry, George E. *The Urban Nation, 1920–1960*. New York: Hill and Wang, 1965.

Moynihan, Daniel P. *The Politics of a Guaranteed Income*. New York: Vintage, 1973.

Naftali, Timothy, and David G. Coleman, eds. *The Presidential Recordings: John F. Kennedy: Volume 4*. New York: W. W. Norton, forthcoming.

Navasky, V. S. *Kennedy Justice*. New York: Atheneum, 1971.

Neal, Steven. *Harry and Ike: The Partnership that Remade the Postwar World*. New York: Scribner, 2001.

Neff, Donald. *Warriors at Suez: Eisenhower Takes America into the Middle East*. New York: Linden/Simon and Schuster, 1981.

Nessen, Ron. *It Sure Looks Different from the Inside*. New York: Simon and Schuster, 1978.

Neustadt, Richard E. *Presidential Power and the Modern Presidents: The Politics of Leadership from Roosevelt to Reagan*. Rev. ed. New York: Free Press, 1991.

Neustadt, Richard E., and Ernest R. May. *Thinking in Time: The Uses of History for Decision-Makers*. New York: Free Press, 1986.

Newfield, Jack. *A Prophetic Minority*. New York: New American Library, 1966.

Newsom, David D. *The Soviet Brigade in Cuba: A Study in Political Diplomacy*. Bloomington: Indiana University Press, 1987.

Niskanen, William A. *Reaganomics: An Insider's Account of the Policies and the People*. New York: Oxford University Press, 1988.

Nixon, Richard M. *RN: The Memoirs of Richard Nixon*. New York: Simon and Schuster, 1990.

———. *Six Crises*. Garden City, NY: Doubleday, 1962.

North, Oliver L., and William Novak. *Under Fire: An American Story*. New York: HarperCollins, 1991.

Oakley, Ronald, Jr. *God's Country: America in the Fifties*. New York: Dembner, 1986.

Oberdorfer, Don. *From the Cold War to a New Era: The United States and the Soviet Union, 1983–1991*. Updated ed. Baltimore, MD: Johns Hopkins University Press, 1998.

O'Connor, Raymond G. *Diplomacy for Victory: FDR and Unconditional Surrender*. New York: W. W. Norton, 1971.

Olson, James S. *Herbert Hoover and the Reconstruction Finance Corporation, 1931–1933*. Ames: Iowa State University Press, 1977.

Paper, Lewis J. *John F. Kennedy: The Promise and the Performance*. New York: Crown, 1975.

Parmet, Herbert S. *Eisenhower and the American Crusades*. New York: Macmillan, 1972.

———. *Jack: The Struggles of John F. Kennedy*. New York: Dial, 1980.

———. *J.F.K.: The Presidency of John F. Kennedy*. New York: Dial, 1983.

———. *Richard Nixon and His America*. Boston: Little Brown, 1990.

Paterson, Thomas C. *Contesting Castro: The United States and the Triumph of the Cuban Revolution*. New York: Oxford University Press, 1994.

———, ed. *Kennedy's Quest for Victory*. New York: Oxford University Press, 1989.

Pells, Richard. *Radical Visions and American Dreams*. New York: Harper & Row, 1973.

Perkins, Van L. *Crisis in Agriculture: The Agricultural Adjustment Administration and the New Deal, 1933*. Berkeley: University of California Press, 1969.

Phillips, Kevin P. *The Emerging Republican Majority*. New Rochelle, NY: Arlington House, 1969.

Podhoretz, Norman. *Why We Were in Vietnam*. New York: Simon and Schuster, 1982.

Polenberg, Richard. *One Nation Divisible: Class, Race and Ethnicity in the US since 1983*. New York: Viking, 1980.

Porter, Gareth. *A Peace Denied: The United States, Vietnam, and the Paris Agreement*. Bloomington: Indiana University Press, 1975.

Posner, Gerald. *Case Closed: Lee Harvey Oswald and the Assassination of JFK*. New York: Random House, 1993.

Powell, Jody. *The Other Side of the Story*. New York: Morrow, 1984.

Powers, Richard G. *Not Without Honor: The History of American Anticommunism*. New York: Free Press, 1995.

Prange, Gordon W. *At Dawn We Slept: The Untold Story of Pearl Harbor*. New York: McGraw-Hill, 1981.

Pruessen, Ronald W. *John Foster Dulles: The Road to Power*. New York: Free Press, 1982.

Public Papers and Addresses of Franklin D. Roosevelt. 5 vols. New York: Random House, 1938–1941.

———. 4 vols. New York: Harper & Brothers, 1950.

Public Papers of the Presidents of the United States: Dwight D. Eisenhower. 8 vols. Washington, D.C.: U.S. Government Printing Office, 1960–1961.

Public Papers of the Presidents of the United States: Gerald Ford. 6 vols. Washington, D.C.: U.S. Government Printing Office, 1975–1979.

Public Papers of the Presidents of the United States: Harry S. Truman. 8 vols. Washington, D.C.: U.S. Government Printing Office, 1961–1966.

Public Papers of the Presidents of the United States: Jimmy Carter. 8 vols. Washington, D.C.: U.S. Government Printing Office, 1977–1982.

Public Papers of the Presidents of the United States: John F. Kennedy. 3 vols. Washington, D.C.: U.S. Government Printing Office, 1962–1964.

Public Papers of the Presidents of the United States: Lyndon B. Johnson. Washington, D.C.: U.S. Government Printing Office, 1964–1970.

Public Papers of the Presidents of the United States: Richard Nixon. 6 vols. Washington, D.C.: U.S. Government Printing Office, 1971–1975.

Public Papers of the Presidents of the United States: Ronald Reagan. 16 vols. Washington, D.C.: U.S. Government Printing Office, 1982–1991.

Quandt, William B. *Peace Process: American Diplomacy and the Arab-Israeli Conflict since 1967*. Berkeley: University of California Press, 2001.

Queen, Richard, and Patricia Hass. *Inside and Out: Hostage to Iran, Hostage to Myself*. New York: Putnam, 1981.

Quester, George H. *American Foreign Policy: The Lost Consensus*. New York: Praeger, 1982.

Rae, John B. *The Road and the Car in American Life*. Cambridge: Massachusetts Insistute of Technology Press, 1971.

Ranch, Basil. *The History of the New Deal, 1933–1938*. 2nd ed. New York: Octagon, 1949.

Reagan, Ronald. *An American Life*. New York: Simon and Schuster, 1990.

Reagan, Ronald, with Richard G. Hubler. *Where's the Rest of Me?* New York: Duell, Sloan and Pearce, 1965.

Reed, Roy. *Faubus: The Life and Times of an American Prodigal*. Fayetteville: University of Arkansas Press, 1997.

Reeves, Richard. *A Ford, Not a Lincoln*. New York: Harcourt Brace Jovanovich, 1975.

———. *President Kennedy: Profile of Power*. New York: Simon and Schuster, 1993.

Reeves, Thomas C. *A Question of Character: A Life of John F. Kennedy*. New York: Free Press, 1991.

Regan, Donald T. *For the Record: From Wall Street to Washington*. New York: Harcourt Brace Jovanovich, 1988.

Reichard, Gary W. *The Reaffirmation of Republicanism: Eisenhower and the Eighty-third Congress*, Knoxville: University of Tennessee Press, 1975.

Reichley, A. James. *Conservatives in an Age of Change: The Nixon and Ford Administrations*. Washington, D.C.: Brookings Institution, 1981.

Reinhard, David W. *The Republican Right since 1945*. Lexington: University Press of Kentucky, 1983.

Remarque, Erich. *All Quiet on the Western Front*. Translated by A.W. Wheen. Boston: Little Brown, 1929.

Reynolds, David. *The Creation of the Anglo-American Alliance, 1937–1941: A Study in Competitive Co-operation*. Chapel Hill: University of North Carolina Press, 1981.

Rhodes, Benjamin D. *United States Foreign Policy in the Interwar Period, 1918–1941*. Westport, CT: Praeger, 2001.

Rhodes, Richard. *Dark Sun: The Making of the Hydrogen Bomb*. New York: Simon and Schuster, 1995.

———. *The Making of the Atomic Bomb*. New York: Simon and Schuster, 1986.

Rice, Gerard. *The Bold Experiment: JFK's Peace Corps*. Notre Dame, IN: Notre Dame University Press, 1985.

Richardson, James L. *Crisis Diplomacy: The Great Powers since the Mid-Nineteenth Century*. New York: Cambridge University Press, 1994.

Roberts, Paul Craig. *The Supply-Side Revolution: An Insider's Account of Policymaking in Washington*. Cambridge, MA: Harvard University Press, 1984.

Rogers, W. D. *The Twilight Struggle: The Alliance for Progress and the Politics of Development in Latin America*. New York: Random House, 1967.

Romasco, Albert U. *The Poverty of Abundance: Hoover, the Nation, the Depression*. New York: Oxford University Press, 1965.

Roosevelt, Kermit. *Countercoup: The Struggle for the Control of Iran*. New York: McGraw-Hill, 1979.

Rose, Lisle A. *Dubious Victory: The United States and the End of World War II*. Kent, OH: Kent State University Press, 1974.

Rose, Mark H. *Interstate: Express Highway Politics, 1939–1989*. Rev. ed. Knoxville: University of Tennessee Press, 1990.

Rovere, Richard H. *Senator Joseph McCarthy*. Berkeley: University of California Press, 1995.

Rubin, Barry. *Paved with Good Intention: The American Experience and Iran*. New York: Oxford University Press, 1980.

Safire, William. *Before the Fall: An Inside View of the Pre-Watergate White House*. Garden City, NY: Doubleday, 1975.

Salinger, Pierre. *America Held Hostage: The Secret Negotiations*. Garden City, NY: Doubleday, 1981.

——. *With Kennedy*. Garden City, NY: Doubleday, 1966.

Salmond, John A. *The Civilian Conservation Corps, 1933–1942*. Durham, NC: Duke University Press, 1967.

——. *"My Mind Set on Freedom": A History of the Civil Rights Movement, 1954–1968*. Chicago: Ivan R. Dee, 1997.

Sartre, Jean Paul. *No Exit*. A Play in One Act. Adapted from the French by Paul Bowles. New York: Samuel French, 1958.

Scharf, Lois. *To Work and to Wed: Female Employment, Feminism, and the Great Depression*. Westport, CT: Greenwood, 1980.

Scharf, Lois, and Joan M. Jensen, eds. *Decade of Discontent: The Women's Movement, 1920–1940*. Westport, CT: Greenwood, 1983.

Scheer, Robert. *With Enough Shovels: Reagan, Bush and Nuclear War*. New York: Random House, 1982.

Schlesinger, Arthur M., Jr. *The Age of Roosevelt*. 3 vols. Boston: Houghton Mifflin, 1957–1960.

——. *The Crisis of the Old Order: 1919–1933*. Boston: Houghton Mifflin, 1957.

——. *The Imperial Presidency*. Boston: Houghton Mifflin, 1973.

——. *Robert Kennedy and His Times*. Boston: Houghton Mifflin, 1978.

——. *A Thousand Days: John F. Kennedy in the White House*. Boston: Houghton Mifflin, 1965.

Schram, Martin. *Running for President 1976: The Carter Campaign*. New York: Stein and Day, 1977.

Schumann, Fraz. *The Foreign Politics of Richard Nixon: The Grand Design*. Berkeley: Institute of International Studies, University of California, 1987.

Schwarz, Jordan A. *The Interregnum of Despair: Hoover, Congress and the Depression*. Urbana: University of Illinois Press, 1970.

Seaborg, Glenn T. *Kennedy, Khrushchev and the Test Ban*. Berkeley: University of California Press, 1981.

Seldes, George. *Iron, Blood and Profits*. New York: Harper and Brothers, 1934.

Shawcross, William. *Sideshow: Kissinger, Nixon and the Destruction of Cambodia*. New York: Simon and Schuster, 1979.

Shogan, Robert. *Hard Bargain: How FDR Twisted Churchill's Arm, Evaded the Law, and Changed the Role of the Presidency*. New York: Scribner, 1995.

———. *Promises to Keep: Carter's First Hundred Days*. New York: Crowell, 1977.

Shogan, Robert, and Tom Craig. *The Detroit Race Riot: A Study in Violence*. New York: Da Capo, 1976.

Shultz, George P. *Turmoil and Triumph: My Years as Secretary of State*. New York: Scribner, 1993.

Sick, Gary. *The October Surprise: America's Hostages in Iran and the Election of Ronald Reagan*. New York: Times Books, 1991.

Silk, Leonard. *Nixonomics: How the Dismal Science of Free Enterprise Became the Black Art of Controls*. New York: Praeger, 1972.

Siracusa, Joseph M. *The American Diplomatic Revolution: A Documentary History of the Cold War, 1941–1947*. Port Washington, N.Y.: Kennikat, 1977.

———. *Into the Dark House: American Diplomacy and the Ideological Origins of the Cold War*. Claremont, CA: Regina, 1998.

———. *New Left Diplomatic Histories and Historians*. 2nd ed. Claremont, CA: Regina, 1993.

Sitkoff, Harvard. *A New Deal for Blacks: The Emergence of Civil Rights as a National Issue*. New York: Oxford University Press, 1978.

———, ed. *Fifty Years Later: The New Deal Evaluated*. Philadelphia, PA: Temple University Press, 1984.

Skinner, Kiron K., ed. *Reagan in His Own Hand: The Writings of Ronald Reagan that Reveal His Revolutionary Vision for America*. New York: Free Press, 2001.

Skotheim, Robert Allen. *Totalitarianism and American Social Thought*. New York: Holt, Rinehart and Winston, 1971.

Sloan, John W. *The Reagan Effect: Economics and Presidential Leadership*. Lawrence: University Press of Kansas, 1999.

Smith, Gaddis. *American Diplomacy during the Second World War, 1941–1945*. New York: Wiley, 1965.

Smith, Gene. *The Shattered Dream: Herbert Hoover and the Great Depression*. New York: Morrow, 1970.

Smith, Hedrick, et al. *Reagan: The Man, the President*. New York: Macmillan, 1981.

Smith, Richard Norton. *An Uncommon Man: The Triumph of Herbert Hoover*. New York: Simon and Schuster, 1984.

Sochen, June. *Herstory: A Women's View of American History*. 2nd ed. New York: Knopf, 1981.

———. *Movers and Shakers: American Women Thinkers and Activists, 1900–1970*. New York: Quadrangle, 1973.

Sorenson, Theodore C. *Kennedy*. New York: Harper & Row, 1965.

———. *The Kennedy Legacy*. New York: Macmillan, 1969.

Spector, Ronald H. *After Tet: The Bloodiest Year in Vietnam.* New York: Free Press, 1993.

Steffens, Lincoln. *The Autobiography of Lincoln Steffens.* New York: Harcourt Brace, 1931.

Stein, Herbert. *The Fiscal Revolution in America.* Chicago: University of Chicago Press, 1969.

Sternsher, Bernard, ed. *Hitting Home: The Great Depression in Town and Country.* Chicago: Quadrangle, 1970.

Sundquist, James L. *Politics and Policy: The Eisenhower, Kennedy, and Johnson Years.* Washington, D.C.: Brookings Institution, 1968.

Susman, Warren, ed. *Culture and Commitment, 1929–1945.* New York: G. Braziller, 1977.

Szulc, Tad. *The Illusion of Peace: Foreign Policy in the Nixon Years.* New York: Viking, 1978.

Talbott, Strobe. *Deadly Gambits: The Reagan Administration and the Stalemate in Nuclear Arms Control.* New York: Knopf, 1984.

Tansill, Charles C. *America Goes to War.* Boston: Little Brown, 1938.

Taylor, A.J.P. *The Origins of the Second World War.* New York: Atheneum, 1962.

Taylor, Telford. *The Anatomy of the Nuremburg Trials: A Personal Memoir.* New York: Knopf, 1992.

Theoharis, Athan G. *The Yalta Myths: An Issue in U.S. Politics, 1945–1955.* Columbia: University of Missouri Press, 1970.

Thomas, Helen. *Front Row at the White House: My Life and Times.* New York: Lisa Drew, 1999.

Thompson, Kenneth W., ed. *The Carter Presidency: Fourteen Intimate Perspectives.* Lanham, MD: University Press of America, 1990.

———. *Portraits of American Presidents: The Truman Presidency, Intimate Perspectives.* Lanham, MD: University Press of America, 1984.

Toland, John. *Infamy: Pearl Harbor and Its Aftermath.* Garden City, NY: Doubleday, 1982.

Trachtenberg, Marc. *A Constructed Peace: The Making of the European Settlement, 1945–1963.* Princeton, NJ: Princeton University Press, 1999.

———. *History and Strategy.* Princeton, NJ: Princeton University Press, 1991.

Tucker, Robert W. *The Purposes of American Power.* New York: Praeger, 1981.

Turner, Stansfield. *Terror and Democracy.* Boston: Houghton Mifflin, 1991.

Tuttle, William M. *"Daddy's Gone to War": The Second World War in the Lives of America's Children.* New York: Oxford University Press, 1993.

Unger, Irwin. *The Best of Intentions: The Triumphs and Failures of the Great Society Under Kennedy, Johnson, and Nixon.* New York: Doubleday, 1996.

———. *The Movement: A History of the American New Left.* New York: Dodd, Mead, 1974.

Utley, Jonathan G. *Going to War with Japan, 1937–1941.* Knoxville: University of Tennesse Press, 1985.

Vance, Cyrus. *Hard Choices: Critical Years in America's Foreign Policy.* New York: Simon and Schuster, 1983.

VanDeMark, Brian. *Into the Quagmire: Lyndon Johnson and the Escalation of the Vietnam War.* New York: Oxford University Press, 1991.

Vestal, Bud. *Jerry Ford, Up Close: An Investigative Biography.* New York: Coward, McCann, and Geoghegan, 1974.

Walker, J. Samuel. *Prompt and Utter Destruction: Truman and the Use of Atomic Bombs Against Japan*. Chapel Hill: University of North Carolina Press, 1997.

Walsh, Lawrence E. *Firewall: The Iran-Contra Conspiracy and Cover-Up*. New York: W.W. Norton, 1997.

Walton, Richard J. *Cold War and Counter-Revolution: The Foreign Policy of John F. Kennedy*. New York: Viking, 1972.

Ware, Susan. *Beyond Suffrage: Women in the New Deal*. Cambridge, MA: Harvard University Press, 1981.

Wecter, Dixon. *The Age of the Great Depression*. New York: Macmillan, 1948.

Weglyn, Michi. *Years of Infancy: The Untold Story of America's Concentration Camps*. Updated ed. Seattle: University of Washington Press, 1996.

Weigley, Russell F. *The American Way of War: A History of United States Military Strategy and Policy*. New York: Macmillan, 1973.

Weinberg, Gerhard L. *A World at Arms: A Global History of World War II*. Cambridge: Cambridge University Press, 1994.

Weinberger, Casper. *Fighting for Peace: Seven Critical Years in the Pentagon*. New York: Warner, 1990.

Weisbrot, Robert. *Freedom Bound: A History of America's Civil Rights Movement*. New York: W. W. Norton, 1990.

———. *Maximum Danger: Kennedy, the Missiles, and the Crisis of American Confidence*. Chicago: Ivan R. Dee, 2001.

White, Mark J. *The Cuban Missile Crisis*. Basingstoke, UK: Macmillan, 1996.

———, ed. *Kennedy: The New Frontier Revisited*. New York: New York University Press, 1998.

White, Theodore H. *America in Search of Itself: The Making of a President, 1956–1980*. New York: Harper & Row, 1982.

Whyte, William H. *Breach of Faith: The Fall of Richard Nixon*. New York: Atheneim, 1975.

———. *The Making of the President, 1960*. New York: Atheneum, 1961.

———. *The Making of the President, 1972*. New York: Atheneum, 1973.

———. *The Organization Man*. New York: Simon and Schuster, 1956.

Wicker, Tom. *One of Us: Richard Nixon and the American Dream*. New York: Random House, 1991.

Wills, Gary. *The Kennedy Imprisonment: A Meditation in Power*. Boston: Little Brown, 1982.

———. *Nixon Agonistes: The Crisis of the Self-Made Man*. Boston: Houghton Mifflin, 1970.

Winters, Francis X. *The Year of the Hare: America in Vietnam, January 25, 1963–February 15, 1964*. Athens: University of Georgia Press, 1997.

Witcover, Jules. *The Year the Dream Died: Revisiting 1968 in America*. New York: Warner, 1997.

Wohlstetter, Roberta. *Pearl Harbor: Warning and Decision*. Stanford, CA: Stanford University Press, 1962.

Wolters, Raymond. *Right Turn: William Bradford Reynolds, the Reagan Administration, and Black Civil Rights*. New Brunswick: Transaction, 1997.

Woods, Randall Bennett. *J. William Fulbright, Vietnam, and the Search for a Cold War Foreign Policy*. Cambridge, UK: Cambridge University Press, 1998.

Woodward, Bob. *Shadow: Five Presidents and the Legacy of Watergate*. New York: Simon and Schuster, 1999.

Wooten, James. *Dasher: The Roots and Rising of Jimmy Carter*. New York: Summitt, 1978.

Worster, Donald. *Dust Bowl: The Southern Plains in the 1930s*. New York: Oxford University Press, 1979.

Wright, Gordon. *The Ordeal of Total War, 1939–1945*. New York: Harper & Row, 1968.

Wyden, Peter. *Bay of Pigs: The Untold Story*. New York: Simon and Schuster, 1979.

Wyman, David S. *The Abandonment of the Jews: America and the Holocaust, 1941–1945*. New York: Pantheon, 1984.

Wynn, Neil. *The Afro-American and the Second World War*. Rev. ed. New York: Holmes and Meier, 1993.

Yoder, Edwin M., Jr. *Joe Alsop's Cold War: A Study of Journalistic Influence and Intrigue*. Chapel Hill: University of North Carolina Press, 1995.

Young, Andrew. *A Way Out of No Way: The Spiritual Memoirs of Andrew Young*. Nashville: T. Nelson, 1994.

Young, Roland. *Congressional Politics in the Second World War*. New York: Columbia University Press, 1956.

Zelikow, Philip D., and Ernest R. May, eds. *The Kennedy Tapes: Inside the White House during the Cuban Missile Crisis,* concise ed. New York: W.W. Norton, 2002.

Zelikow, Philip D., Ernest R. May, and Timothy Naftali, eds. *The Presidential Recordings: John F. Kennedy: The Great Crises*. 3 vols. New York: W. W. Norton, 2001.

Zhai, Qiang. *China and the Vietnam Wars, 1950–1975*. Chapel Hill: University of North Carolina Press, 2000.

Zinn, Howard. *SNCC: The New Abolitionists*. Westport, CT: Greenwood, 1985.

Index

About the Authors

JOSEPH M. SIRACUSA is a Visiting Research Fellow in the Key Centre for Ethics, Law, Justice and Governance, Griffith University, Brisbane, Australia. Among his books are *A History of United States Foreign Policy*; *America's Australia: Australia's America*; and *Into the Dark House: American Diplomacy and the Idealogical Origins of the Cold War.*

DAVID G. COLEMAN is Assistant Professor at the Miller Center of Public Affairs at the University of Virginia. He is co-editor of *The Presidential Recordings: John F. Kennedy* (forthcoming).